St. Bernard

Newfoundland

# A DOG
## OF YOUR OWN

*Long-haired Chihuahua*

# A DOG
## OF YOUR OWN

### JOAN PALMER

**Consultant**
**BRUCE SESSIONS**

Illustrated by
JOHN FRANCIS AND JOHN GREEN

*English Setter*

*Gordon Setter*

a Salamander book

Published by Salamander Books Limited
LONDON

# A Salamander Book

Published by Salamander Books Ltd.,
Salamander House,
27 Old Gloucester Street,
London WC1N 3AF,
England.

© Salamander Books Ltd 1980

ISBN 0 86101 061 2

# Credits

Editor:     Geoffrey Rogers
Designers: Roger Hyde; Jeff Gurney
Colour reproductions:
            Colourcraftsmen Ltd., Essex, England.
            Bantam Litho Ltd., Essex, England.
Monochrome:
            Tenreck Ltd., London, England.
Filmset:    Modern Text Typesetting Ltd.,
            Essex, England.
Printed in Belgium by
            Henri Proost et Cie, Turnhout.

*Miniature Bull Terrier*

*French Bulldog*

# Principal Author

**JOAN PALMER** has been a committee member of The National Dog Owners' Association of Great Britain for the past 15 years, and is its present Honorary Chairman and Publicity Officer. She contributes to the newspaper *Our Dogs*, and has often broadcast on canine affairs, being particularly interested in the role of the companion dog and in promoting pet owner education.

A busy freelance journalist, she also has a number of books to her credit, on domestic animals and careers. Joan and her husband share their Essex home with Chihuahuas and a Chinese Crested 'hairless' bitch. They also have a Siamese cat, a horse and a donkey.

## The Consultant
**BRUCE SESSIONS,** formerly Senior Editor and Consultant to *International Dog Fancy Magazine,* is a widely respected American authority on dogs. Author of three books on dog care and training, he has hosted an American television series on veterinary care and has trained dogs for the U.S. Navy, for the Las Vegas Police Department and for search and rescue work in the state of Oregon.

## Contributing Authors
**KAY WHITE** gained practical experience of dogs from running a large breeding and boarding kennel. She still breeds an occasional litter of Boxers, the latest one — the tenth generation from her original dogs — consisting of 10 vigorous puppies, seven of which were bottle-fed from birth with great success.

A pioneer in promoting veterinary education for dog breeders, Kay White is now veterinary reporter for the weekly paper *Dog World* and she is also News Editor for a paper circulating to the veterinary profession, thus fulfilling a long ambition to bring dog breeders and veterinarians closer to understanding each other.

**MURIEL SHEARWOOD** has been showing and breeding dogs for 20 years, with a particular interest in Newfoundlands and Chihuahuas. She has judged Newfoundlands for several years and has edited the Newfoundland Club magazine. She is particularly concerned that the modern trend towards over-competitiveness is replacing the sense of fun and sportsmanship that showing once enjoyed.

**J. R. HOLMES** M.R.C.V.S. has trained and used dogs all his life as companions, working terriers and formal shooting dogs. A veterinarian for 25 years, he now practises and farms in Sussex, where his hobbies are shooting, fishing, gardening, broadcasting, working dogs, homeopathic medicine and sharing his enthusiasm for life.

**MICHAEL A. FINDLAY** B.V.M.S., M.R.C.V.S. is a veterinarian in practice in London. He has been particularly involved with dog obedience training and is an honorary veterinarian to several dog clubs and shows in England, notably Crufts. He has written or contributed to several books on pet animal care and, as Press Officer to the British Small Animal Veterinary Association, is frequently quoted in the press and on radio.

*Beagle*

# Contents

Part One
**PROFILE SECTION**
Detailed profiles of 190 international breeds, arranged
in order of size.

*Ibizan Hound*

*Pharaoh Hound*

*Old English Sheepdog*

## Parts of a Dog

This annotated drawing shows the main anatomical parts of a dog and the accepted terms used to describe them. Further information on these and the other technical terms used in the book can be obtained from the Glossary starting on Page 232.

*Below: Throughout the Profile Section a size symbol for each breed is shown in scale against an outline of the Wire Fox Terrier, which is 39cm (15½in) at the withers.*

# Part One

# PROFILE SECTION

*Detailed profiles of 190 international breeds, arranged in order of size.*

## Parts of a Dog

**1** Ear
**2** Skull. The upper, back point of the skull is called the occiput or peak. The top of the skull is called the crown.
**3** Eye
**4** Stop
**5** Foreface. The foreface, nose and jaws make up the muzzle.
**6** Nose
**7** Jaws. The fleshy parts of the lips and jaws make up the jowls.
**8** Lips. Pendulous upper lips are called flews.
**9** Cheek
**10** Neck
**11** Shoulder
**12** Upper arm
**13** Elbow
**14** Forearm
**15** Wrist
**16** Stopper pad
**17** Pastern
**18** Toes
**19** Nails
**20** Forefoot
**21** Sternum (Breastbone)
**22** Chest
**23** Flank
**24** Thigh (Upper thigh)
**25** Stifle (Knee)
**26** Second thigh (Lower thigh)
**27** Hock (Heel)
**28** Rear pastern
**29** Hind foot
**30** Pads
**31** Tail. In different types of dog the tail is known variously as the brush, flag, rudder and stern.
**32** Croup
**33** Loin
**34** Back
**35** Withers (Top of the shoulders)
**36** Crest of neck.

Most dog books present the breeds in groups based on the type of dog or on the role it was bred to perform, such as toys or gundogs. These groups vary in different parts of the world. Throughout most of Europe, for example, the ten groups recognized by the Fédération Cynologique Internationale (FCI) apply. These are:
1 Herding breeds
2 Guard dogs, police dogs and working breeds
3 Terriers
4 Dachshunds
5 Hunting breeds (for large game)
6 Hunting breeds (for small game)
7 Pointing gundogs (excluding British breeds)
8 Pointing gundogs (British breeds)
9 Other British gundogs
10 Toy dogs

The British Kennel Club recognizes six groups. These are:
1 Hounds
2 Gundogs
3 Terriers
4 Utility breeds
5 Working breeds
6 Toys

The American Kennel Club recognizes six groups, but these are slightly different from the British ones. These are:
1 Sporting breeds
2 Hounds
3 Working breeds
4 Terriers
5 Toys
6 Non-sporting breeds

The Scandinavian countries recognize eight groups. These are:
1 Spitz breeds
2 Trailing and hunting breeds
3 Gundogs
4 Guard and working breeds
5 Terriers
6 Sighthounds
7 Non-sporting and companion breeds
8 Toys

In Australia the following six groups are recognized:
1 Toys
2 Terriers
3 Gundogs
4 Hounds
5 Working breeds
6 Non-sporting breeds

Since this book is aimed at the widest possible audience, and particularly at those people buying a dog for the first time, the breeds are therefore presented solely in order of size. The profile section is divided into these parts:

Small dogs (up to 12.7kg/28lb)
Medium dogs (12.7-20.5kg/28-45lb)
Large dogs (over 20.5kg/45lb)

But even this system has its problems: height standards alone exist for certain breeds; some dogs fall between two groups; and a few tall but relatively light breeds are by any standards large dogs.

The Show Summaries quoted at the end of most entries are based on the official Standards of the British Kennel Club and are reproduced with their kind permission. A number of Standards are also included from the FCI and the American KC.

Australian Terrier

Cairn Terrier

Cavalier King Charles Spaniel

# A
# Selection of
# SMALL DOGS

Why do you want a small dog? Because you have always loved them? Because you are a town dweller living in a confined space? Because you think a bigger fellow might be more than you can handle? Because a small dog is cheaper to feed?

Whatever your reason, you will never regret it. Little dogs are incredibly brave (often foolishly so), make good watchdogs (don't let them yap, though), and are devoted to their owners. Often scornfully dismissed as lap dogs, tiny breeds will gladly walk as far as you wish and ask for more. Transport is simpler with a small breed: Chihuahuas and Yorkshire Terriers rarely object to riding in a shopping basket. Smaller breeds are often more acceptable guests in hotels; and if not, boarding kennels charge according to the dog's size. Small dogs are intelligent and easy to train, and there is less to groom!

If the man of the family says he won't be seen out with a toy dog, don't believe it—men often become willing slaves to the most delicate-looking animals.

Very small breeds are not a good choice if there are young children in the family, however, as toddlers may think that they really are toys; a good choice for such a family is a dog of Cavalier or King Charles Spaniel size, or a sporty Miniature Schnauzer.

There is a wide range to choose from, in various colours and sometimes in different types of coat. There are also scaled-down versions of larger breeds, such as the Shetland Sheepdog and the Miniature Poodle. Small dogs usually live longer than their heavier relations. They are not cheaper to buy, though; and they do not have large litters.

If you can't bear to leave a dog alone in the house, you can always find room for two small dogs. This is how a lot of us dog folk began . . . but that's another story!

# CHIHUAHUA

## Good points
- *Handy, portable size*
- *Good traveller*
- *Ideal for town dwellers*
- *Intensely loyal and affectionate*
- *Keenly intelligent*
- *Wonderful guard dog in miniature*
- *Inexpensive to keep*

## Take heed
- *May snap at teasing children*
- *Strong willed*
- *Brave to the point of stupidity – would fight a lion!*
- *Clannish – prefers the company of its own breed and owners*
- *Hates the cold – might grow rheumaticky*

The Chihuahua is keenly intelligent, fiercely protective and cheap to keep. Also, being the world's tiniest dog, it is the least likely to fall foul of the landlord.

The adult Chihuahua usually takes a few weeks to reveal its true personality, keeping its new owner under careful surveillance, perhaps giving the impression that it is shy. Actually, it is weighing up which of them is to be master in the home!

Although the pet Chihuahua has become much commoner, many breeders reproduce the species for their own pleasure in achieving and showing a perfect specimen, and it is not uncommon for a breeder owning 20 or more Chihuahuas to refuse to part with one of them.

## Size
Weight between 0.9-2.7kg/2-6lb (under 1.8kg/4lb preferred for show). There is no desired height in this breed's standard.

## Exercise
Contrary to belief, the Chihuahua is ready, and able, to walk as far as most owners would wish, although it doesn't object to an occasional ride in a shopping basket. The fact that its exercise requirements are moderate makes this breed an ideal choice of pet for the elderly.

## Grooming
The Chihuahua should be groomed with a soft brush. A rub down with the proverbial velvet glove, or pad, will make the coat gleam. Nails must be regularly clipped and the ears kept free of dust.

## Feeding
Eating habits vary: some Chihuahuas have voracious appetites, but others, particularly the tiny specimens, often go for a day without nourishment. The requirement of a very small Chihuahua should be 57-85g (2-3oz) of cooked minced beef or branded dog food, with a handful of puppy biscuits. And, as they have small tummies, these dogs fare best on two or three small meals rather than one large daily feed. Bigger specimens can manage up to ½ can (376g,

13.3oz size) of branded dog food, or the equivalent, and a handful of dog biscuits. Uneaten food should be removed: dogs do not fancy stale food any more than we do.

## Health care
Not as delicate as one might imagine, but they dislike the cold and appreciate a coat to keep them warm when out of doors in winter. These dogs are definitely not designed for kennel living. They prefer to snuggle down beneath your eiderdown!

Watch out for the molera, a small opening on top of the skull. The Chihuahua's molera, unlike that of a human baby, may never fill in, so a blow on the head could prove fatal. This breed is prone to hiccups; a spasm can often be cured by lifting the pet purposefully up and down. They also have a tendency to shiver, a habit that evokes sympathy from onlookers and generally makes the owner seem the villain of the piece, folk wrongly imagining that the Chihuahua is terrifed or frozen.

## Origin and history
Named after the state of Chihuahua in Mexico, the Chihuahua is believed to have been the sacred dog of the Incas. Nevertheless, it seems likely that a few may have been used by the American Indians in their cooking pots. There is also a theory that Chihuahuas were once fierce little dogs living in holes in the ground, which could well account for their inclination to huddle together in every warm nook and cranny.

The famous opera singer Madame Adelina Patti did much to publicize the breed when, in 1890, she was presented by the then President of Mexico with a Chihuahua concealed in an enormous bunch of flowers. And in the 1940s the dance band leader Xavier Cugat, who appeared in numerous films, would often conduct with a Chihuahua tucked under his arm. For many people this was their first sight of the fascinating breed.

## SHOW SUMMARY
**General appearance.** An alert and swift-moving little dog with a saucy expression. Small, dainty and compact with a brisk, forceful action.
**Colour.** Any colour or mixture.
**Head and skull.** A well-rounded 'apple dome' skull, with or without molera; cheeks and jaws lean; nose moderately short, slightly pointed; definite stop.
**Feet.** Small with toes well split up, but not spread; pads cushioned. Fine pasterns (neither 'hare' nor 'cat' foot). A dainty foot with nails moderately long.
**Tail.** Medium length, carried up or over the back. Preferred furry, flattish in appearance, broadening slightly in the centre and tapering to a point.

There is a Long-coated Chihuahua as well as the more usual Smooth-

coated variety. The only difference is in the coat, which should be long, of soft texture (never coarse or harsh to the touch), and either flat or slightly wavy (not tight and curly). There should be feathering on the feet and legs, and pants on the hind legs; a large ruff on the neck is preferred, and the tail should be long and full as a plume.

# YORKSHIRE TERRIER

## Good points
- *Affectionate*
- *Healthy and fearless*
- *Sociable with other pets*
- *Good watchdog*
- *Suits apartment living*

## Take heed
- *Lengthy show preparation*
- *Needs weekly bath*
- *Difficult to determine pup's size and colouring*

The Yorkshire Terrier is one of the most popular dogs of the day. It rivals the Chihuahua for the title of the world's smallest dog. It is unlikely to be over-awed by larger animals, however, and is not the ideal choice for the stand-offish, because it wants to make friends with everybody. It has been described as a big dog inhabiting a small dog's body; in fact it thinks it is enormous!

## Size
Weight up to 3.2kg (7lb).

## Exercise
The Yorkie is well suited to town and apartment living, but will prove a tireless companion on a country walk.

## Grooming
Many Yorkie owners are content for their pet to have a somewhat scruffy 'shaggy dog' look as long as they know that it is clean and healthy. The show aspirant, however, has a busy time ahead, for the Yorkshire Terrier is exhibited on a show box, which displays its immaculate coat to advantage, a condition that can be achieved only through endless grooming, shampooing and oiling. The show Yorkie spends much of its life, away from the ring, wearing curlers!

## Feeding
Similar to that of other toy breeds, with four meals given in puppyhood, reducing to one meal at a year old, comprising ½ can of branded dog food or the bought meat equivalent (approximately 199-227g, 7-8oz), lightly cooked and supplemented by biscuits. Lean meat scraps can be given, and bones are appreciated, but never chicken bones, or any that are likely to splinter.

## Health care
The Yorkie has strong, terrier-type teeth, but it is as well to have them scaled by a veterinarian at regular

intervals. Toy breeds tend to lose their teeth at an early age (sometimes as early as three), but the avoidance of titbits will preserve them for as long as is possible.

## Origin and history
Unlike the Chihuahua, the Yorkie cannot trace its ancestry back to antiquity, for it has been with us for little more than 100 years. It is believed that the breed evolved through the crossing of the Skye Terrier with the old Black and Tan Terrier, although it is rumoured that the Maltese Terrier and the Dandie Dinmont Terrier may also have contributed to producing this game little breed, which is renowned as a ratter.

## SHOW SUMMARY
Consult an expert before rushing to buy the first pedigreed pup you see advertised. A roach or sway-backed Yorkie would be a non-starter in the show ring, as would too large a specimen. A breeder cannot guarantee the size to which a puppy will grow, but look at the sire and dam as a useful guide.

Selecting a potential show pup is never easy, because Yorkshire Terriers are born black and it is not until they are between three and five months old that the tan begins to show on their legs. The black on the back may take a year to turn to the desired steely colour.
**General appearance.** Should be that of a long-coated toy terrier, the coat hanging quite straight and evenly down each side, a parting extending from the nose to the end of the tail. The animal should be very compact and neat, the carriage being very upright and conveying an 'important' air. The general outline should convey the impression of a vigorous and well-proportioned body.
**Colour.** A dark steel blue (not silver blue), extending from the occiput (back of skull) to the root of the tail, and on no account mingled with fawn, bronze or dark hairs. The hair on the chest should be a rich bright tan. All tan hair should be darker at the roots than in the middle, shading to a still lighter tan at the tips.
**Head and skull.** The head should be rather small and flat, not too prominent or round in the skull, nor too long in the muzzle, with a perfect black nose. The fall on the head to be long, of a rich golden tan, deeper in colour at the sides of the head above the ear roots, and on the muzzle, where it should be very long. On no account must the tan on the head extend to the neck, nor must there be any sooty or dark hair intermingled with the tan.
**Ears.** Small, V-shaped and carried erect or semi-erect and not far apart, covered with short hair of a very deep, rich tan.
**Feet.** As round as possible; the toe-nails black.
**Tail.** Cut to medium length, with plenty of hair, darker blue in colour than the rest of the body, especially at the end of the tail, and carried a little higher than the level of the back.

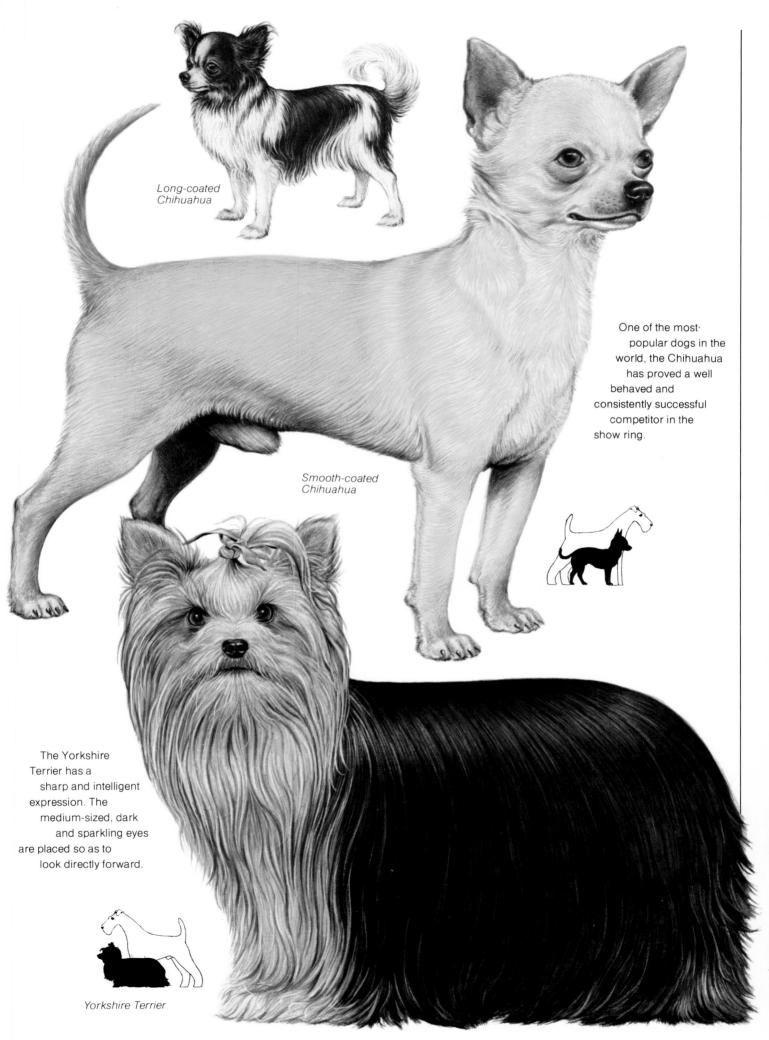

*Long-coated Chihuahua*

One of the most-popular dogs in the world, the Chihuahua has proved a well behaved and consistently successful competitor in the show ring.

*Smooth-coated Chihuahua*

The Yorkshire Terrier has a sharp and intelligent expression. The medium-sized, dark and sparkling eyes are placed so as to look directly forward.

*Yorkshire Terrier*

# PAPILLON
(And Phalene)

## Good points
- Affectionate
- Dainty size
- Good house dog
- Trainable for competitive obedience
- Usually strong and healthy

## Take heed
- Not keen on visitors
- Possessive towards owners

The Papillon is a toy spaniel that takes its name from the French word for 'butterfly'. The breed is often referred to as the 'Butterfly Dog' because of the manner in which its ears are set on the head, fringed like a butterfly's wings. The Phalene is identical except that the ears are dropped, and this variety is known as the 'moth'.

The Papillon is an affectionate, lively little dog. It is resilient, whelps easily, is a good walker, and can adapt to extremes of climate. Its attractive appearance and friendly nature make it the ideal family pet. But, like many toy breeds, it has a tendency to be possessive towards its owners and often resents visitors to the home.

## Size
The ideal height at the withers is 20-28cm (8-11in). The dog will appear to be slightly longer than high when properly furnished with ruff and hind fringes.

## Exercise
Like quite a number of toy breeds, the Papillon will happily walk its owner off his feet, or be content with a walk around the park. One thing is sure: you won't tire it!

## Grooming
Daily grooming is required to keep this breed in good condition.

## Feeding
Recommended would be ⅓-½ can (376g, 13.3oz size) of a branded meaty product, with biscuit added in equal part by volume; or 1-1½ cups of a dry food, complete diet, mixed in the proportion of 1 cup to ½ cup of hot or cold water.

## Origin and history
Believed to be a descendant of the Dwarf Spaniel of the 16th century and to have originated in Spain, the dainty little Papillon has been included in many paintings, including some by Rubens and Van Dyke. The Phalene, or Continental Toy Spaniel, is identical except for its drop ears. In the United States and the United Kingdom they are judged as one breed with almost identical standards except for colour variations, but specimens over 30cm (12in) cannot be shown in America.

The French Fédération Cynologique Internationale (FCI) separates the breeds by both type and weight variations, those over 2.5kg (5½lb) in weight entering a separate class. Papillons have done well in obedience classes.

## SHOW SUMMARY
**General appearance.** This dainty, balanced little toy dog should have an attractive head, an alert bearing and an intelligent and lively expression. Movement should be sound, light and free and not cramped or restricted in any way.
**Colour.** White with patches that may be any colour except liver. A tricolour must be black and white with tan spots over the eyes, and tan inside the ears, under the root of the tail and on the cheeks. The head marking should be symmetrical about a white, narrow, clearly defined blaze.
**Head and skull.** The skull should be slightly rounded between the ears, the muzzle finely pointed and abruptly thinner than the skull, accentuating the stop, which should be well defined. Length from the tip of the nose to the stop is approximately one third of the length of the head. The nose should be black.
**Tail.** Long and well fringed, set on high, arched over the back with the fringes falling to the side to form a plume.
**Feet.** Fine and fairly long, as in the hare. The tufts of hair between the toes should extend far beyond them.

# POMERANIAN

## Good points
- Adaptable
- Devoted to owner
- Handy size
- Happy nature
- Ideal for apartment living

## Take heed
- Will yap if unchecked
- Thinks it is a 'big' dog, so watch out that bigger dogs are not provoked!

The Pomeranian is a happy, active little dog that will adapt cheerfully to life in a one-roomed apartment or a spacious dwelling, revelling in the role of lap dog or enjoying walks with its owner. Alternatively, it will amuse itself adequately in a garden. It makes a faithful and devoted companion.

## Size
Dog 1.8-2kg (4-4½lb); bitch 2-2.5kg (4½-5½lb).

## Exercise
It is wrong to think that toy breeds are of use for little else except sitting decoratively on their owner's knees, and the Pomeranian is no exception. True, they adore being pampered and petted, but they are also lively little dogs, quite able to walk as far as their owner would wish—often further. Alternatively, they will exercise themselves quite happily in a garden.

## Grooming
This is not the breed for those who cannot spare the time for daily grooming. Indeed, the Pomeranian has two coats to care for: a short fluffy under-coat, and a long straight top-coat covering the whole of the body. Daily brushing with a stiff brush is a must. The coat should be damped with cold water, and the moisture rubbed in with the fingertips; finally the dog is rubbed down with a towel.

Working from the head, part the coat and brush it forward from roots to tips. Make a further parting and repeat this procedure until the dog has been covered.

The Pomeranian requires regular trimming; obtain advice from a breeder or breed club as to how this should be carried out.

## Feeding
As for Papillon.

## Origin and history
The Pomeranian takes its name from Pomerania, in Germany, and is generally thought to be of mid-European origin. However, it is a member of the Spitz family, which could mean that its history began in the Arctic Circle.

The known history of the breed dates from the mid-18th century when it was introduced to several European countries. It became very popular until, following the raiding of the Summer Palace in Peking in 1860 and the appearance of the Imperial Pekingese, some of its popularity was usurped by that breed.

The Pomeranian, in those early days, was a very much larger dog, up to 13.6kg (30lb) in weight, and it was bred down until, by 1896, show classes for Pomeranians were divided into those for exhibits over and under 3.6k (8lb). The British Kennel Club withdrew challenge certificates for the over 3.6kg (8lb) variety in 1915.

## SHOW SUMMARY
**General appearance.** The Pomeranian should be a compact, short-coupled, well-knit dog. It should show great intelligence in expression, and activity and buoyancy in deportment.
**Colour.** All whole colours are admissible, but they should be free from black or white shadings. At present the whole-coloured dogs are white, black, brown, light or dark blue (as pale as possible), orange (which should be as self-coloured and bright as possible), or beaver.
**Head and skull.** The head and nose should be foxy in outline, or wedge-shaped, the skull being slightly flat, and large in proportion to the muzzle, which should finish rather fine and be free from lippiness. The hair on the head and face should be smooth and short. The nose should be black in white, orange, and shaded sable dogs; brown in chocolate tipped sable dogs; in other colours it may be self-coloured; but it must never be parti-coloured or white.
**Tail.** The tail is one of the characteristics of the breed, and should be turned over the back and carried flat and straight, being profusely covered with long, harsh, spreading hair.
**Feet.** The feet should be small and compact in shape.

# SMALL GERMAN SPITZ
(Kleinspitz)

## Good points
- Adaptable to town or country
- Beautiful
- Excellent guard
- Loyal companion

## Take heed
- Likes to bark
- Suspicious of strangers

The Small German Spitz is the small variety of the Great German Spitz (Gross-spitz). The only difference between the types is in size; characteristics and conformation are the same.

This is a happy, extremely intelligent little dog. It makes an excellent companion, does not need a great deal of exercise, and adapts well to life in town or country. It usually loves its owners deeply, but does not care much for strangers. Perhaps its only drawback is that it rather likes the sound of its own voice! It is unlikely to chase sheep: guard duty and the protection of its beloved home are far more important.

## Size
Height: 28cm (11in) maximum at withers, weight not more than 3.4kg (7½lb). (The Gross-spitz stands about 40cm [15¾in] high).

## Exercise
Despite its ability to cover immense areas at speed, the Spitz does not require a great deal of exercise; members of this variety can live quite happily in a small town house.

*Above: The Small German Spitz.*

## Grooming
Vigorous daily brushing is necessary if you don't wish to be always vacuuming your carpet!

## Feeding
As for Papillon.

## Origin and history
It is difficult to pinpoint the origin of this variety of Spitz, for the prehistoric remains of such types have been found throughout Asia and the Pacific, and drawings of similar dogs were found among the remains of the ancient Pharaohs. There are a number of Spitz varieties, all of which are very similar in character and type.

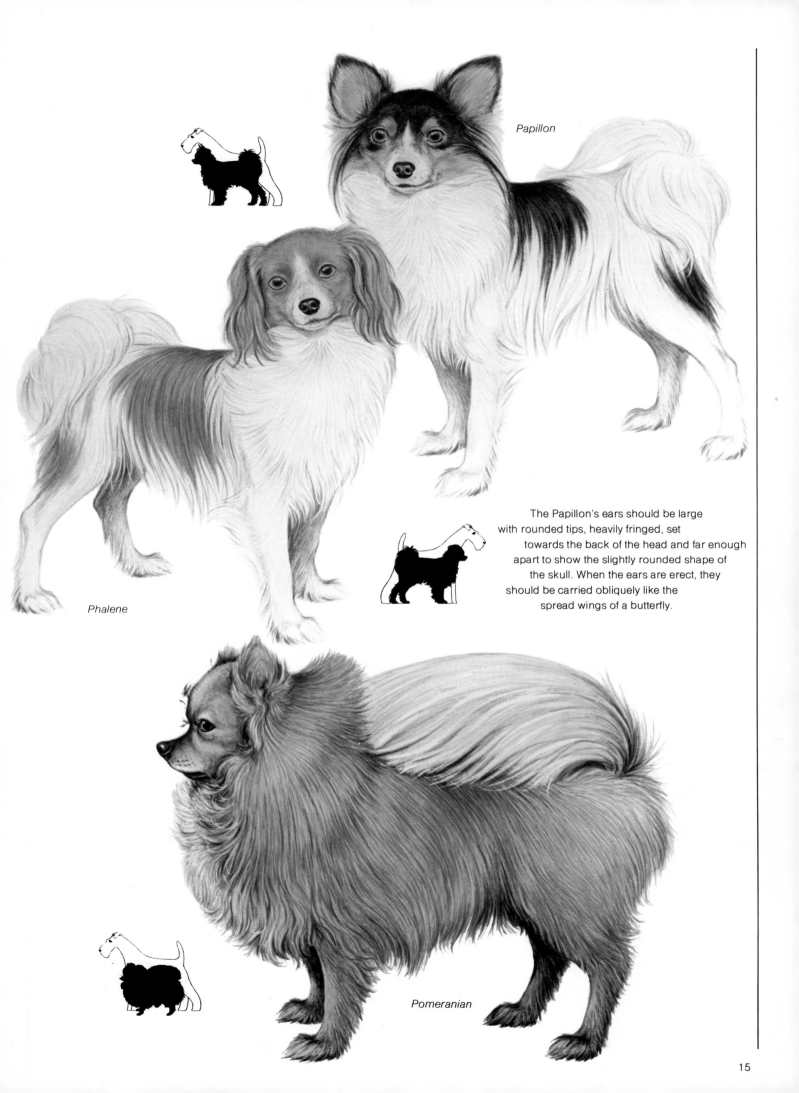

_Papillon_

_Phalene_

The Papillon's ears should be large
with rounded tips, heavily fringed, set
towards the back of the head and far enough
apart to show the slightly rounded shape of
the skull. When the ears are erect, they
should be carried obliquely like the
spread wings of a butterfly.

_Pomeranian_

# MALTESE TERRIER

(Maltese)

## Good points
- *Adaptable about exercise*
- *Extremely good with children*
- *Healthy*
- *Long-lived*
- *Sensitive*
- *Sweet-natured*

## Take heed
- *Needs fastidious daily grooming*

The Maltese Terrier is a good-tempered dog that makes the ideal family pet. It is reliable with children, adaptable about exercise, and usually healthy, and it generally remains playful throughout its long life.

## Size
Not over 25cm (10in) from ground to top of shoulder.

## Exercise
Can manage a long walk or be content with a stroll in the park.

## Grooming
Most important. Use a bristle brush every day from puppyhood and use baby powder on legs and underside to keep the animal clean between baths. Obtain advice from the breeder about show preparation; this breed may not be the ideal choice for new show aspirants.

## Feeding
Recommended would be ⅓ can (376g, 13.3oz size) of a branded meaty product, with biscuit added in equal part by volume; or 1-1½ cups of a dry food, complete diet, mixed in the proportion of 1 cup of feed to ½ cup of hot or cold water. Such a diet is, of course, offered purely as a guide. The owner may occasionally substitute lightly cooked minced beef, mixed with biscuit. Lean meat scraps are appreciated. Water must be available to all breeds at all times.

## Origin and history
The Maltese Terrier is described as the oldest of European toy breeds. However, there is some controversy as to whether it originated in Malta, although the breed has certainly existed there for centuries. The Maltese Terrier also found its way to China and the Philippines, probably due to enterprising Maltese traders.

Like the Papillon, the Maltese has been depicted by many famous artists, including Goya, Rubens, and the famous animal painter Sir Edwin Landseer, who in 1930 produced a portrait entitled *The Lion Dog from Malta – the last of his race,* which shows their rarity on the island at that time. The breed first became established in the United Kingdom during the reign of Henry VIII and was a popular pet among elegant ladies. It had a class of its own for the first time in Birmingham, England, in

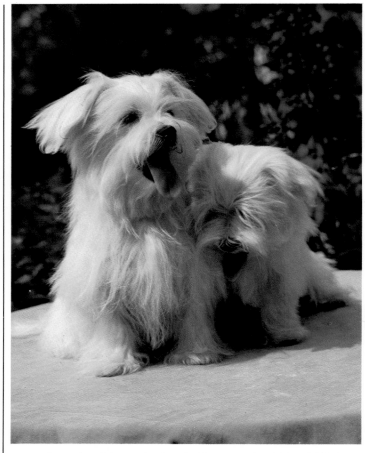

1864, since when it has gained immense popularity in both the United Kingdom and the United States.

*Above: A pair of delightful Maltese puppies enjoy the sunshine. This elegant and good-natured breed has been popular in Europe for centuries, and has been portrayed by several famous artists.*

## SHOW SUMMARY
**General appearance.** Should be smart, lively and alert. The action must be free, without extended weaving.
**Colour.** Pure white, but slight lemon markings should not penalize.
**Head and skull.** From stop to centre of skull (centre between forepart of ears) and stop to tip of nose should be equally balanced. Stop should be defined. Nose should be pure black.
**Tail.** Should be well arched over the back, and feathered.
**Feet.** Should be round, and the pads of the feet should be black.

# GRIFFON

(Griffon Bruxellois, Griffon Brabancon. The Griffon Bruxellois is known in the USA as the Brussels Griffon)

## Good points
- *Happy temperament*
- *Hardy*
- *Intelligent*
- *Long-lived*
- *Obedient*
- *Suitable for town or country living*

## Take heed
- *No drawbacks known*

The Griffon is an attractive, happy little dog that makes a first-class family pet. It has an almost monkey-like face, with a knowing expression, and is hardy, intelligent and terrier-like in temperament. The breed, which is essentially Belgian, was originally used as a guard and catcher of vermin, particularly in stable yards. However, it took the fancy of royalty, thereby becoming a fashionable house pet.

There are two varieties, the Griffon Bruxellois and the Griffon Brabancon. The only difference is in the coat: the Bruxellois is a rough-coat, and the Brabancon a smooth-coat. Rough-coats and smooth-coats can appear in a single litter. The only variation in the breed standard is in the coat: roughs are harsh, wiry and free from curl, preferably with an under-coat; smooths are short and tight.

## Size
Weight: 2.3-5kg (5-11lb), most desirable 2.7-4.5kg (6-10lb).

## Exercise
Like most toy breeds it adapts well to town life and does not need a great deal of exercise, but a romp in the countryside will be greatly appreciated.

## Grooming
The rough-coat needs twice yearly stripping: best to seek advice, or have this done professionally. The smooth-coat should be brushed, towelled, and gently rubbed down with the proverbial velvet glove or a piece of chamois leather. Watch with this and other small breeds that the nails do not grow too long. Purchase the proper nail clippers for the job from a pet store or pharmacy, and be particularly careful to cut down only to the 'quick'.

## Feeding
About ½ can of a branded meaty product (376g, 13.3oz size), with biscuit added in equal part by volume; or 1-1½ cupfuls of a dry food, complete diet, mixed in the proportion of 1 cup of feed to ½ cup of hot or cold water.

## Origin and history
The Griffon was first exhibited at the Brussels Exhibition in 1880 and is a truly Belgian breed. It seems likely that it derives from the Affenpinscher, to which it certainly bears a facial resemblance; the introduction of the Pug may be responsible for the Brabancon, or smooth-coat, which in the early days was not recognized.

An enthusiastic Griffon owner was the late Queen Astrid of the Belgians. Before World War I, the popularity of Griffons in their country of origin was immense, but the breeding programme was severely affected by the war.

Griffons have fortunately now found their way to most countries of the world, but showing differences exist. In its native land the Griffon is shown with cropped ears, a practice that is illegal in the United Kingdom, Scandinavia and Australia, and dependent on individual state law in the USA.

## SHOW SUMMARY
**General appearance.** A well-balanced square little dog, lively and alert, giving the appearance of measuring the same from withers to tail root as from withers to ground. Its action should be free, well-bent hocks giving the correct drive from behind and moving true coming and going. High-stepping front movement should be discouraged.
**Colour.** Clear red, black, or black and rich tan. In the clear red, a darker shade on the mask and ears is desirable. Ideally each hair should be an even red from tip to root. Frosting on the muzzles of mature smooths should not be penalized.
**Head and skull.** The head should be large and rounded but in no way domed, and should be wide between the ears. In the rough variety, hair on the skull should be rather coarse. Nose always black, as short as possible, with large open nostrils, high set, sloping back to the skull with a deep stop between nose and skull. Wide muzzle, neat lips and with good turn-up. Chin prominent and slightly undershot without showing the teeth, and (in the rough variety) furnished with a beard.
**Tail.** Short docked, carried high, emerging at right angles from a level top-line.
**Feet.** Small, thick, cat-like feet with black toe-nails.

The Maltese Terrier's beautiful white coat should hang long, flat and silky over the sides of the body almost, if not quite, to the ground. It should be single, i.e. without an under-coat.

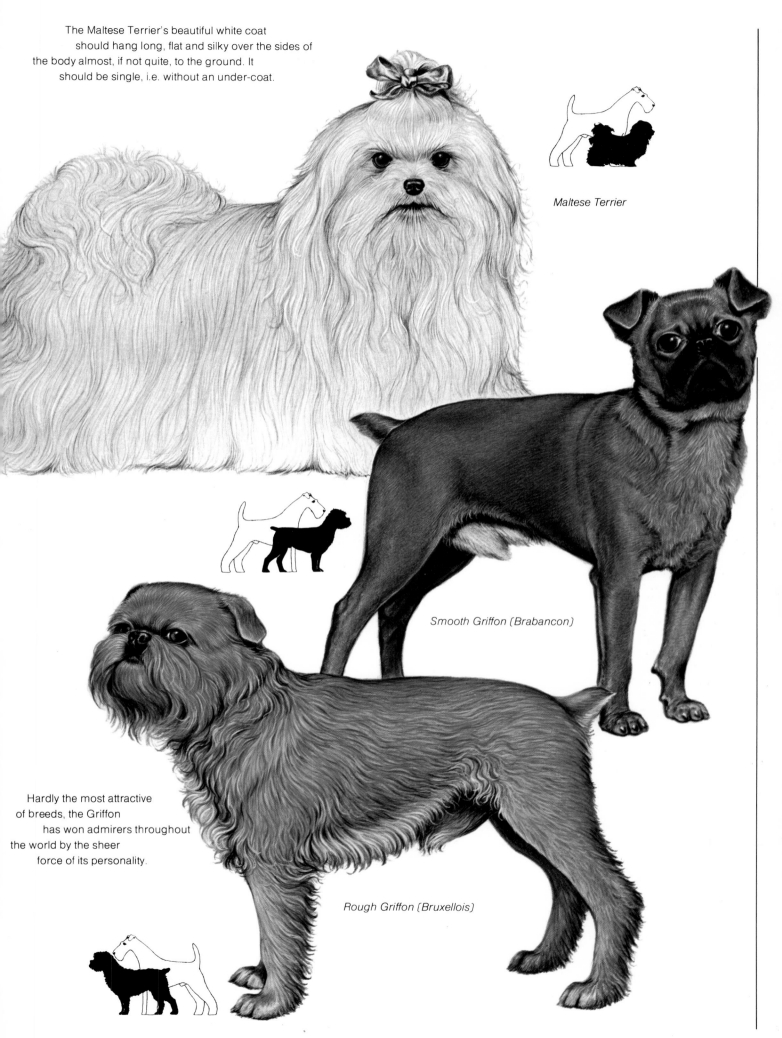

*Maltese Terrier*

*Smooth Griffon (Brabancon)*

Hardly the most attractive of breeds, the Griffon has won admirers throughout the world by the sheer force of its personality.

*Rough Griffon (Bruxellois)*

# ITALIAN GREYHOUND

## Good points
- Affectionate
- Easy to train
- Graceful, diminutive appearance
- Intelligent
- Obedient
- Odourless
- Sensitive
- Rarely moults

## Take heed
- Deeply wounded by harsh words
- Should not be kept in a kennel

The Italian Greyhound is the perfect Greyhound in miniature, a graceful dainty animal that makes an ideal house pet. It does, however, need plenty of exercise and will enjoy a day's rabbiting, should the opportunity arise.

## Size
The most desirable weight is. 2.7-3.6kg (6-8lb), and not exceeding 4.5kg (10lb).

## Exercise
Certainly not the dog to keep shut up indoors all day. It thrives on plenty of exercise, but adapts well to town living provided adequate walks and off-the-lead runs are possible.

## Grooming
The Greyhound needs little more than a rub down with a silk handkerchief. But remember that this breed feels the cold, hates the wind and rain, and needs a coat. Care must be taken of the teeth. Regular scaling by a veterinarian is recommended (this applies to all toy breeds), but cream of tartar — mixed into a paste on a saucer with a little water, and applied with cotton wool — will often remove unsightly stains.

## Feeding
About ½ can of a branded meaty product (376g, 13.3oz size), with biscuit added in equal part by volume; or 1-1½ cupfuls of a dry food, complete diet, mixed in the proportion of 1 cup of feed to ½ cup of hot or cold water.

## Origin and history
This obedient and easy-to-train little dog is thought to originate from the Greyhounds depicted on the tombs of the Pharaohs. But it has existed in its present form for centuries and takes its name from its great popularity in 16th century Italy. It was favoured by Queen Victoria, who did much to popularize so many toy breeds during her long reign. Unfortunately for the breed, some English Toy Terrier blood was introduced in an effort to reduce the size further. This spoiled the breed character, and in an effort to restore it several dogs were imported from America. Alas, this did little to help matters and by the early 1950s only five registrations with the British Kennel Club remained. However, fresh stock was imported from Italy and, thanks to the determined efforts and dedication of breeders, the Italian Greyhound was once more firmly established by the early 1970s.

## SHOW SUMMARY
**General appearance.** A miniature Greyhound, more slender in all proportions, and of ideal elegance and grace in shape, symmetry and action.
**Colour.** Recognized colours, all shades of fawn, white, cream, blue, black and fawn and white pied.
**Head and skull.** Skull long, flat and narrow; muzzle very fine; nose dark in colour.
**Tail.** Rather long, fine, with low carriage.
**Feet.** Long, hare feet.

NB: There are some variations in the US standard.

# MINIATURE PINSCHER

## Good points
- Delightful hackney gait
- Easy to look after
- Fearless
- Good house dog
- Intelligent
- Rarely moults
- Suitable for town or country life

## Take heed
- Do not overfeed

The Miniature Pinscher (or Min Pin), sometimes called the 'King of the Toys', makes an ideal pet for the town dweller who, nonetheless, wants a lively sporting companion, not averse to an occasional day's rabbiting. It will follow a scent and give a good account of itself in obedience competitions. The breed's hackney gait is a delight to watch, as it trots along like a dainty little horse. It has the added advantages of rarely moulting and of requiring the minimum of attention to keep its coat in fine condition.

## Size
The height is 25-30cm (10-12in) at the withers. (There are some slight differences in the US standard as regards acceptable colour and size.)

## Exercise
The Min Pin will exercise itself in a reasonable-sized garden or accompany its owner on a day-long trek. This adaptable dog will be happy living in a flat and being taken for walks around the park, or living a free country life.

## Grooming
A daily brush and rub down with a chamois leather will keep the Min Pin in gleaming condition.

## Feeding
About ½ can of a branded meaty product (376g, 13.3oz size), with biscuit added in equal part by volume; or 1-1½ cupfuls of a dry food, complete diet, mixed in the proportion of 1 cup of feed to ½ cup of hot or cold water.

## Origin and history
The Miniature Pinscher is not a smaller version of the Dobermann Pinscher, but a much older breed descended from the German Smooth-haired Pinscher. It is suggested that the Italian Greyhound and the Dachshund contributed to its make-up. In any event, it achieved pedigree status by the German Pinscher-Schnauzer Klub in 1895.

## SHOW SUMMARY
**General appearance.** The Miniature Pinscher is structurally a well-balanced, sturdy, compact, elegant, short-coupled, smooth-coated toy dog. It is naturally well-groomed, proud, vigorous and alert. The natural characteristic traits that identify it from other toy dogs are the precise hackney gait, fearless animation, complete self-possession and spirited presence.
**Colour.** Black, blue or chocolate, with sharply defined tan markings on cheeks, lips, lower jaw, throat, twin spots above eyes, chest, lower half of forelegs, inside of hindlegs and vent region, lower portion of hocks and feet.
**Head and skull.** Rather more elongated than short and round. Narrow and without conspicuous cheek formation. In correct proportion to the body. The skull should appear flat when viewed from the front. The muzzle must be rather strong and proportionate to the skull. The nose well formed, black only, with the exception of chocolates and blues, which may have a self-coloured nose.
**Tail.** A continuation of the top line, carried a little high and docked short.
**Feet.** Legs straight, medium bone. Feet cat-like; elbows close to body; nails dark.

# ENGLISH TOY TERRIER
(Toy Manchester Terrier)

## Good points
- Affectionate
- Easy to care for
- Good with children
- Intelligent
- Lively
- Good at expelling vermin if need be

## Take heed
- Tends to be a one-person dog that resents outsiders

The English Toy Terrier, which in the USA is called the Toy Manchester Terrier, is a most attractive, affectionate and game little dog, marvellously intuitive and loyal, but tending to attach itself to one person to the exclusion of others. It is usually healthy, easy to keep clean, odourless and an easy whelper if you wish to breed.

## Size
The ideal weight is 2.7-3.6kg (6-8lb), and a height of 25-30cm (10-12in) at the shoulders is most desirable.

## Exercise
Adapts well to town living provided adequate walks and off-the-lead runs are possible.

## Grooming
A daily brushing will suffice. One of the advantages of this short-coated breed is that it does not shed. The coat can be massaged to effect a sheen; or equally beneficial is a weekly teaspoonful of cod liver oil in the food. Dry the coat with a towel after excursions on rainy days. Although the breed is robust it will, in common with most toy breeds, appreciate a warm coat in bitter weather.

## Feeding
Recommended would be ⅓-½ can (376g, 13.3oz size) of a branded meaty product, with biscuit added in equal part by volume; or 1-1½ cups of a dry food, complete diet, mixed in the proportion of 1 cup of feed to ½ cup of hot or cold water. The owner may occasionally substitute lightly cooked minced beef, mixed with biscuit. Lean meat scraps are appreciated. Water must be available to all breeds at all times.

## Origin and history
(See also Manchester Terrier) The English Toy is a smaller version of the Manchester Terrier, once a prodigious ratter and descended from the old Black and Tan Rough-haired Terrier. Their fitness owes something to the Italian Greyhound and the Whippet. The breed began in England under the name Toy Manchester Terrier, and was later known variously as Toy Black and Tan, and Miniature Black and Tan. They were recognized as English Toy Terriers (Black and Tan) by the British Kennel Club in 1962.

## SHOW SUMMARY
**General appearance.** A well-balanced, elegant and compact toy with terrier temperament and characteristics.
**Colour.** Black and tan: the black should be ebony and the tan can be likened to a new chestnut, deeply rich. These colours should not run, or blend into each other, but should meet abruptly, forming clear and well-defined lines of colour division.
**Head and skull.** The head should be long and narrow with a flat skull, wedge-shaped without emphasis of cheek muscles and well filled up under the eyes.
**Tail.** The tail should be thick at the root, tapering to a point, set low and not reaching below the hock. A gay tail carriage is undesirable if displayed to excess.
**Feet.** Dainty, compact, split up between the toes and well arched, with jet black nails; the two middle toes of the front feet are rather longer than the others, and the hind feet are cat-like.

In the late 1800s, the English Toy Terrier was popular as a vermin killer and frequently appeared in the rat pit, a favourite sport among working and upper classes alike. Present day specimens should be sleek and cleanly built, giving an appearance of alertness combined with speed of movement.

*English Toy Terrier*

*Miniature Pinscher*

The Min Pin's tail is docked, and its cropped ears can be pricked or dropped. Indeed, were it not for these characteristics and colour variations, one might be forgiven for mistaking it at first glance for an English Toy Terrier. The broad skull and bulging eyes once prevalent in the breed have been replaced by the wedge-shaped head preferred in the Dobermann.

*Italian Greyhound*

The Italian Greyhound looks more fragile than it really is. It will happily chase small game, and in Scandinavia slightly larger specimens are used for coursing.

# BICHON FRISE
(And Bichon Bolognese)

## Good points
- Good pet
- Happy temperament
- Attractive, lamb-like appearance

## Take heed
- Requires meticulous grooming

The Bichon Frise has been recognized by the British and American Kennel Clubs only over the past 10 years. It is a most appealing and happy little dog, which will surely become more popular when the public becomes acquainted with the breed.

## Size
Height: less than 30cm (12in), smallness being highly desirable.

## Exercise
Will enjoy a romp if you can bear to clean up that muddy coat afterwards! It will fit well into town living and regular walks, but will enjoy the occasional off-the-lead country run and a game in the garden.

## Grooming
This is not the breed for novice exhibitors, or for those who are not prepared to spend time in meticulous grooming, bathing, trimming and scissoring. The effect, when complete, should be of an elegant white 'powder puff', the head and body trimmed to give a rounded effect, but showing the eyes. Hair around the feet should also be trimmed. Ask the breeder for a showing and grooming chart, and for a demonstration.

## Feeding
Recommended would be ⅓-½ can of a branded meaty product (376g, 13.3oz size), with biscuit added in equal part by volume; or 1-1½ cupfuls of a dry food, complete diet, mixed in the proportion

*Below: An alert and appealing Bichon Frise pup. An older dog's coat falls into corkscrew curls.*

of 1 cup of feed to ½ cup of hot or cold water. Always ensure that the dog has ample water.

## Origin and history
The Bichon, like the Caniche, is a descendant of the Barbet (water spaniel), from which the name Barbichon originates; later it was abbreviated to Bichon.

The little dogs are said to have originated in the Mediterranean area and were certainly introduced by sailors to the Canary Islands prior to the 14th century. There were then four varieties: the Bichon Ténériffe, the Bichon Maltaise, the Bichon Bolognese and the Bichon Havanais. The breed later found favour with the French and Spanish nobility and was included in paintings by Francisco Goya (1746-1828).

A period of obscurity followed until, after World War I, soldiers took a few when they left France. A breed standard was written up in France in 1933, when the name 'Bichon à poil frisé' (curly-coated Bichon) was adopted, and the word Ténériffe omitted from its title. Crufts Dog Show in London included a class for the Bichon Frise for the first time in 1980.

The Bolognese is very similar to the Bichon Frise and is registered with the Fédération Cynologique Internationale as an Italian breed.

## SHOW SUMMARY
**General appearance.** This gay, happy little dog has a coat falling in soft, corkscrew curls. The head carriage is proud and high; the eyes are alert and expressive.

**Colour.** Pure white. Under the white coat, dark pigment is preferred: black, blue or beige markings often found on the skin.

**Head and skull.** The skull is longer than the muzzle, but the whole head in balance with the body. The muzzle should not be thick or heavy; nor should it be snipy; the cheeks flat and not very strongly muscled; the stop should be slight and the hollow between the eyebrows just visible. The skull must be flat when touched, although the hair tends to make it look round. The nose should

be round, black, soft and shiny.

**Tail.** Normally carried raised and curled gracefully over the back but never tightly curled. It should not be docked and should not touch the backbone, but the hair should always fall onto the back. Slightly low set.

**Feet.** Small, rounded and well knuckled up. Nails preferably black.

# TOY POODLE

## Good points
- Affectionate
- Dainty and appealing
- Excellent retriever
- Intelligent
- Long-lived
- Good sense of fun
- Useful in obedience competitions

## Take heed
- Noisy if unchecked
- Perhaps not the best choice of child's pet
- Sensitive
- Suggest veterinary examination prior to purchase

The Poodle has a character full of fun. It is intelligent and obedient. In the United Kingdom, it has proved a useful competitor in obedience competitions. It has a fondness for water, if the owner permits, but is much favoured for the show ring where, exhibited in the traditional lion clip, it is a beauty to behold. It is also, debatably, the most difficult breed to prepare for the ring, involving the handler in a day's canine beauty treatment.

## Size
Height at shoulder should be under 28cm (11in). (There is a slight reduction in the height requirement in the United States.)

## Exercise
The Poodle will enjoy a ball game in the garden, practising obedience exercises or trotting beside you in the park. The toy variety is obviously a good choice for the apartment dweller.

## Grooming
Use a wire-pin pneumatic brush and a wire-toothed metal comb for daily grooming. The lion clip is an essential for the show ring, but pet owners generally resort to the more natural lamb clip, with the hair a short uniform length. It is possible to clip your own dog with a pair of hairdressers' scissors. However, if, despite the help which is usually available from the breeder, you find the task tedious, there are numerous pet and poodle parlours to which you should take your dog every six weeks. Regular bathing is also essential.

## Feeding
One third to ½ can (376g, 13.3oz size) of a branded, meaty product, with biscuit added in equal part by volume; or 1-1½ cupfuls of a dry complete food, mixed in the pro-

portion of 1 cup of feed to ½ cup of hot or cold water.

## Health care
Fanciers will confirm that the Standard Poodle is the soundest of the varieties. It is possible to acquire healthy Toy and Miniature stock, but care should be taken to purchase from a breeder who puts quality ahead of daintiness. Watch out for signs of ear trouble, nervousness or joint malformations. Teeth need regular scaling. Nonetheless, a 16-year-old Poodle is not a rarity.

## Origin and history
The Poodle was originally a shaggy guard, a retriever and protector of sheep, with origins similar to the Irish Water Spaniel and, no doubt, a common ancestor in the French Barbet and Hungarian Water Hound.

The Poodle may not be, as many suppose, solely of French origin. It originated in Germany as a water retriever; even the word poodle comes from the German 'pudelnass' or puddle, and from this fairly large sturdy dog, the Standard Poodle, the Miniature and the Toy have evolved.

The breed has been known in England since Prince Rupert of the Rhine, in company with his Poodle, came to the aid of Charles I in battle. The breed was favoured also by Marie Antoinette who, rumour has it, invented the lion clip by devising a style that would match the uniform of her courtiers. It is also popular in the United States.

## SHOW SUMMARY
**General appearance.** A very active, intelligent, well-balanced and elegant-looking dog with good temperament, carrying itself very proudly.

**Colour.** All solid colours. White and cream Poodles to have black nose, lips and eye-rims; black toe-nails desirable. Brown Poodles to have dark amber eyes, dark liver nose, lips, eye-rims and toe-nails. Apricot Poodles to have dark eyes with black points or deep amber eyes with liver points. Black, silver and blue Poodles to have black nose, lips, eye-rims and toe-nails. Cream, apricot, brown, silver and blue Poodles may show varying shades of the same colour up to 18 months. Clear colours preferred.

**Head and skull.** Long and fine with slight peak at the back. The skull not broad and with a moderate stop. Foreface strong and well chiselled, not falling away under the eyes; bones and muscle flat. Lips tight fitting. Chin well defined, but not protruding. The whole head must be in proportion to the size of the dog.

**Tail.** Set on rather high, well carried at a slight angle away from the body; never curled or carried over the back; thick at the root.

**Feet.** Pasterns strong; tight feet proportionately small; oval in shape, turning neither in nor out; toes arched; pads thick; hard and well cushioned.

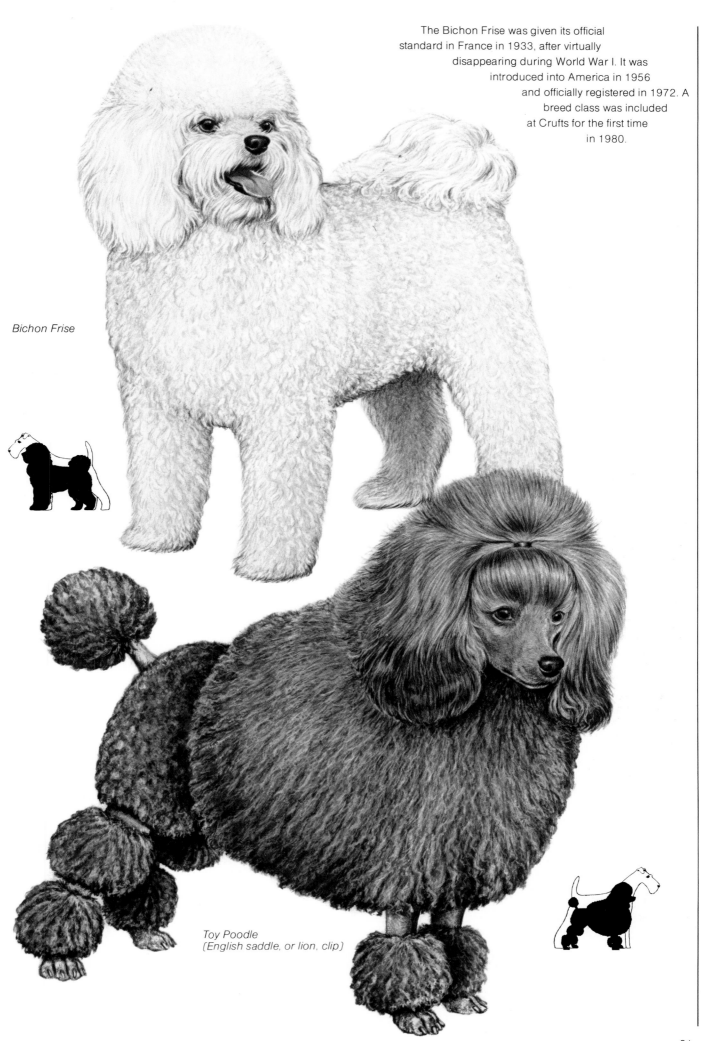

The Bichon Frise was given its official standard in France in 1933, after virtually disappearing during World War I. It was introduced into America in 1956 and officially registered in 1972. A breed class was included at Crufts for the first time in 1980.

*Bichon Frise*

*Toy Poodle
(English saddle, or lion, clip)*

# LOWCHEN

## Good points
- *Affectionate*
- *Happy nature*
- *Intelligent*

## Take heed
- *No drawbacks known, except perhaps the need for skilful clipping*

The Lowchen is a member of the Bichon family, sharing with the imperial Pekingese the title of 'little lion dog', because of the practice of clipping it in the traditional poodle exhibition cut, the lion clip, which, complete with mane and tufted tail, gives it the appearance of a lion in miniature. It is an affectionate, happy, healthy little dog, known in Europe for several centuries.

## Size
Height: 25-33cm (10-13in) at the withers. Weight: 1.8-4.1kg (4-9lb).

## Exercise
This breed adapts well to town or country; although usually presented more suitably for decoration than for sporting activity, it will enjoy regular walks in the park, or a run in the countryside. But many of the exotic breeds are kept in breeding and exhibition kennels where, although extremely well looked after, they never have the chance of a muddy scamper.

## Grooming
Clipping is best left to the expert, at any rate until a pattern has been studied and absorbed. Meanwhile, a daily brushing will keep the Lowchen looking handsome.

## Feeding
Recommended would be ⅓-½ can of a branded meaty product (376g, 13.3oz size), with biscuit added in equal part by volume; or 1-1½ cupfuls of a dry food, complete diet, mixed in the proportion of 1 cup of feed to ½ cup of hot or cold water. Always ensure that the dog has an ample supply of water.

## Origin and history
The Lowchen is thought to be a French dog. It is registered with the FCI as of native origin, under the title 'petit chien lion'. Certainly it was known in both France and Spain from the late 1500s, and is thought to have been favoured by the beautiful Duchess of Alba, for a dog bearing a strong similarity to the Lowchen appears in a portrait of that lady painted by the Spanish artist Francisco Goya (1746-1828). Probably the breed evolved in the Mediterranean area about the same time as the Maltese, the Bichon Frise and the Bichon Bolognese.

The Lowchen is now a frequent contender in the show ring in many countries, but it has yet to become popular as a pet.

## SHOW SUMMARY
**General appearance.** This small, intelligent dog has an affectionate and lively disposition combining all the good qualities of a companion dog. The body is clipped in the traditional lion clip, and the tail, also clipped, is topped with a pompon, giving the dog the appearance of a little lion.
**Colour.** Any colour is permissible, be it self-colour or parti-colour; but the most sought-after colours are white, black and lemon.
**Head.** Short. The skull is wide in proportion.
**Tail.** This is of medium length, clipped, with a tuft of hair left to form a pompon.
**Feet.** These should be small and round.

*Below: Despite its fragile appearance, the Lowchen is a robust dog that will enjoy a country walk.*

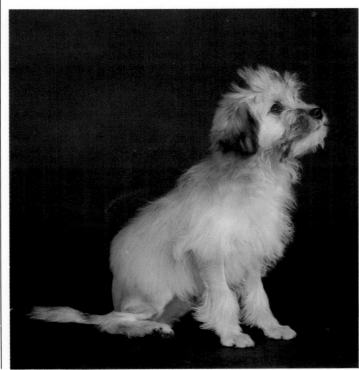

# AFFENPINSCHER

## Good points
- *Affectionate*
- *Cute monkey-like appearance*
- *Excellent ratter despite small frame*
- *Good watchdog*

## Take heed
- *No drawbacks known*

The Affenpinscher is an enchanting little breed, with an almost monkey-like appearance, whence the prefix 'Affen', which is the German word for monkey. In its country of origin it is often called the 'Zwergaffenpinscher' ('Zwerg' means dwarf). The French have dubbed it the 'moustached devil'.

*Above: An adult Affenpinscher, showing the round monkey-like face typical of this lively breed.*

In any event it is an appealing, comical little dog, the smallest of the Schnauzers and Pinschers, alert, gentle and affectionate, but always ready to defend.

## Size
Height: 24-28cm (9½-11in). Weight: 3-4.1kg (6½-9lb).

## Exercise
Like most toy dogs it will be content with a walk around the park, but it will gladly walk you off your feet if that is your pleasure.

## Grooming
Regular brushing will keep the Affenpinscher in good condition.

## Feeding
Recommended would be ⅓-½ can of a branded meaty product (376g, 13.3oz size), with biscuit added in equal part by volume; or 1-1½ cupfuls of a dry food, complete diet, mixed in the proportion of 1 cup of feed to ½ cup of hot or cold water. When giving a dry feed, ensure that the dog has—as always—an ample supply of water.

## Origin and history
Miniature Pinschers and Affenpinschers were, until 1896, classi-

fied as one breed. In that year, at the Berlin show, it was decided that the long-coated variety should thereafter be known as the Affenpinscher.

The Affenpinscher is an ancient German breed that was depicted by Jan van Eyck (1395-1441) and Albrecht Dürer (1471-1528). There is, however, some controversy as to its origin, though its nationality has never been in doubt. Some believe it to be related to the Brussels Griffon; others attribute the Brussels Griffon to the Affenpinscher; a third school of thought is that the Affenpinscher is a toy version of the German coarse-haired terrier, the Zwergschnauzer. In any event, this delightful breed was recognized by the American Kennel

*Above: An Affenpinscher pup, a tiny bundle of fur with a hint of the comic expression of the adult dog.*

Club in 1936, and has now achieved recognition in the United Kingdom, being represented in the 1980 Crufts Dog Show.

## SHOW SUMMARY
**General appearance.** Wire-haired and stout, with an apish expression, the Affenpinscher is small but sturdy in build and not delicate in any way.
**Colour.** This should be black, although dark grey and black with grey, rich tan or brown markings are permissible.
**Head and skull.** The head is fairly small in proportion to the body; a domed forehead, broad brow and marked stop which, however, should not be intended. Muzzle blunt and short but not flattened as far as to cause wrinkling of the skin or difficulty in breathing. The chin should be prominent with a good turn-up. The distance between the dark eyes and black nose should form an equilateral triangle.
**Tail.** The tail should be set high and carried high; it can be left a natural length or docked to the third joint.
**Feet.** These should be small, round and compact, and turn neither in nor out. The pads and nails should be dark.

The Lowchen was first granted
Championship status in the United Kingdom in 1976, but it has yet to be
officially recognized by the American Kennel Club.
After a period of obscurity during the early 1900s,
the breed is enjoying a revival of interest in many
countries of the world

*Lowchen*

The coat is a very
important factor in the
Affenpinscher. It should be short and
dense in certain parts
and shaggy and longer
in others, especially around the
eyes, nose and chin, giving the
breed a monkey-like appearance.

*Affenpinscher*

# AUSTRALIAN SILKY TERRIER

(Silky Terrier/Sydney Silky Terrier; see also Australian Terrier)

## Good points
- *Alert*
- *Affectionate*
- *Dainty nature*
- *Excellent rat catcher*
- *Hardy*
- *Makes a good pet*

## Take heed
- *No known drawbacks*

The Australian Silky Terrier is a dainty little dog, similar to the Yorkshire Terrier in appearance. It is alert and hardy, and has a merry and affectionate nature.

## Size
The most desirable weights are 3.6-4.5kg (8-10lb). Height approximately 23cm (9in) at the withers.

## Exercise
Despite its small stature the Silky has well-developed terrier instincts and is a first-class ratter. It will adapt well to apartment living and town walks, but is in its element chasing across the fields, getting that straight, silky coat into magnificent disarray.

## Grooming
Ideally the Silky should have a well-groomed appearance, which calls for a coat length of 12.5-15cm (5-6in) from behind the ears to the set-on of the tail. Legs from knees and hocks to feet should be free from long hair.

## Feeding
Recommended: 1/3-1/2 can of a branded, meaty product (376g, 13.3oz size), with biscuit added in equal part by volume; or 1-1½ cupfuls of a dry food, complete diet, mixed in the proportion of 1 cup of feed to ½ cup of hot or cold water.

## Origin and history
The Australian (or Sydney) Silky Terrier was derived from crossing Yorkshire Terriers with Skye Terriers, some say by cross-breeding with the Australian Terrier, which has Norwich and Cairn Terrier and probably also Dandie Dinmont in its make-up.

The breed, which in America is shown in toy classes under the name of Silky Terrier, has been recognized in the United States since 1959, but is a relative newcomer to the United Kingdom, where separate standards now exist for the Australian Terrier and the Australian Silky Terrier.

## SHOW SUMMARY
**General appearance.** The dog is compact, moderately low set, of medium length, with a refined structure, but of sufficient substance to suggest the ability to hunt and kill domestic rodents. It should display terrier characteristics, embodying keen alertness, activity and soundness; the parted, straight silky hair should look well groomed.
**Colour.** Blue and tan, or grey-blue and tan – the richer the better. Blue on tail should be very dark. The distribution of the blue and tan as follows: silver-blue or fawn topknot desirable; tan around the base of the ears, the muzzle and on side of cheeks; blue from base of skull to tip of tail, running down the forelegs to near the knees and down the thighs to the hocks; tan line showing down the stifles; and tan from the knees and hocks to the toes and around the vent.
**Head and skull.** Of moderate length, slightly shorter in length from the tip of the nose to between the eyes than from the same position to the top rear of the occiput. It must be strong and of terrier character, being moderately broad between the ears; the skull flat, without fullness between the eyes. Long fall of hair on foreface and cheeks is very objectionable. Fine silky topknot, not falling over the eyes. Nose should be black.
**Tail.** Should be docked and carried erect, but not over-gay.
**Feet.** Small, well padded, cat-like; closely knit toes with black or very dark nails.

Below: The Australian Silky Terrier is an alert and dainty dog. It is also a keen rat catcher and enjoys a good chase over the fields.

# TIBETAN SPANIEL

## Good points
- *Confident*
- *Easy to train*
- *Happy nature*
- *Intelligent*
- *Good household pet*
- *Suitable for town or country*

## Take heed
- *No drawbacks known*

The Tibetan Spaniel is an attractive small dog, with a happy, if independent, nature. It is easily trained and makes an ideal family pet, being reliable with children. In appearance it resembles a rather large Pekingese. It is also an enjoyable dog to show.

## Size
Weight: 4-6.8kg (9-15lb) is ideal. Height about 25cm (10in).

## Exercise
This dog requires average walks and off-the-lead runs.

## Grooming
Needs daily brushing.

## Feeding
Half to 1 can (376g, 13.3oz size) of a branded, meaty product, with biscuit added in equal part by volume; or 1½ cupfuls of a dry complete food, mixed in the proportion of 1 cup of feed to ½ cup of hot or cold water.

## Origin and history
The Tibetan Spaniel was first discovered in the Tibetan monasteries where, to quote a reference in *Champion Dogs of the World* (G. Harrap, 1967), 'Reports indicate that it still turns the prayer-wheel of Tibetans who seek to reap the rewards of a devout life without the inconvenience of physical exertion'. However, this charming practice may have ceased since the Chinese takeover and outlawing of dogs. It is a close relative of the Tibetan Terrier and Lhasa Apso, both of which also originate from Tibet. The Tibetan Spaniel was first seen in England in 1905.

## SHOW SUMMARY
**General appearance.** Should be small, active and alert. The outline should give a well-balanced appearance, slightly longer in body than height at withers.
**Colour.** All colours and mixture of colours allowed.
**Head and skull.** Small in proportion to body and proudly carried giving an impression of quality. Masculine in dogs but free from coarseness. Skull slightly domed, moderate width and length. Stop slight, but defined. Medium length of muzzle, blunt with cushioning, free from wrinkle. The chin should show some depth and width. A black nose is preferred.
**Tail.** Set high, richly plumed and carried in a gay curl over the back when moving. Should not be penalized for dropping tail when standing.
**Feet.** Hare footed, small and neat with feathering between toes often extending beyond the feet. White markings allowed.

Above: First discovered in the monasteries of Tibet, the Tibetan Spaniel makes the perfect pet.

Below: Two delightful Tibetan Spaniel puppies, only a few weeks old. These dogs are easy to train and happily adapt to town life.

The Australian Silky Terrier's attractive coat should be fine and glossy and of a silky texture. It is usually parted on the head and down over the back to the root of the tail. On the top of the head the hair is so profuse as to form a topknot. Groomed carefully for the show ring, the Australian Silky Terrier looks truly magnificent.

*Australian Silky Terrier*

Short-nosed specimens of the Tibetan Spaniel were once likened to the Pekingese, but careful breeding has produced an unmistakable and very popular breed.

*Tibetan Spaniel*

# MEXICAN HAIRLESS
(Xoloitzcuintli)

## Good points
● *Even temperament*
● *Intelligent*
● *Affectionate*
● *No hair on carpet*
● *Pride of ownership—they are almost extinct*

## Take heed
● *This breed must be kept in a warm atmosphere*
● *Cries instead of barking, which could be disturbing*

The Mexican Hairless Dog is one of the oldest breeds in the world, and in danger of becoming extinct. However, rumour has it that these animals are sometimes seen wandering along the waterfront in Hong Kong, and efforts are now being made to protect the breed in its native Mexico.

Unlike the Chinese Crested, this breed is totally hairless except for a tuft of short, coarse, and not very dense hair on the skull, though this should never be of the length or softness of the mane of the Chinese Crested. It is a quiet, rather reserved animal, growling only under provocation, and is similar in build to a Staffordshire Bull Terrier. It is described as gay and intelligent, yet at the same time dignified and unaggressive. Young pups tend to be snub-nosed and short-legged and do not conform to their adult appearance until late in their development.

## Size
Weight 13.6-15.9kg (30-35lb). Height about 48cm (19in).

## Feeding
Its normal diet is fruit and vegetables, but it can adapt to usual canine fare. This was proved when, some 20 years ago, two Mexican Hairless Dogs were quarantined in London Zoo. Recommended would be 1-1½ cans (376g, 13.3oz size) of a branded meaty product, with biscuit added in equal part by volume; or 3 cupfuls of a dry, complete diet mixed in the proportion of 1 cup of feed to ½ cup of hot or cold water.

## Health care
The Mexican Hairless sweats through its skin, unlike other breeds, which sweat through the tongue. They need a warm environment, with a heated kennel, and have a body temperature of 105°F (40.5°C) as against the normal canine temperature of 101.4°F (38.5°C). They have no premolar teeth.

## Origin and history
The Mexican Hairless did not originate in Mexico, but was brought to that country by nomadic tribes of Indians from north-eastern Asia. It may even have come originally from as far away as Turkey, the land of the Turkish Toy Greyhound, another species of naked canine.

The little naked Xoloitzcuintli, as its new owners called it, was considered as a gift from the gods by the Aztecs, because when anyone was sick, the dog could warm the patient with its naked body.

The earliest inhabitants of Mexico, the Toltecs, had kept the blue Chihuahua in their temples for religious purposes. When the Aztecs conquered the Toltecs, dogs of both breeds were kept in luxury inside the temples. However, it is possible that the inevitable inter-breeding of the Mexican Hairless with the Chihuahua may have produced the Chinese Crested breed we know today.

## SHOW SUMMARY
The following desired characteristics are borrowed from the Association Canofila Mexicana (Mexican Kennel Club).
**Colour.** A uniform colour of dark bronze, elephant grey, greyish black or black is preferred. Animals with pink or brown blotches—which are really areas without pigmentation—are acceptable, but this depigmentation on an exaggerated scale is undesirable. The hair on head and tail, if present, should be black in dark animals; in lighter animals it may be of any colour that harmonizes.
**Undesirable points.** A timid character; ears that are not entirely erectile; hair growing elsewhere than as mentioned; exaggerated depigmentation; a skin that is excessively loose, forming folds and creases; and the presence of dew-claws.
**Tail.** Long, tapering to a fine point.
**Feet.** Hare feet with toes retracted. Claws black in dark animals, light in those with unpigmented feet.
**Skin.** Soft and smooth to the touch, particularly in those areas less exposed to the sun. Accidental scars are not penalized, because its skin is sensitive.

# CHINESE CRESTED

## Good points
● *Handy size*
● *No hairs on the carpet!*
● *Intelligent*
● *Devoted companion*
● *Novelty—always the centre of attraction*
● *Good with children, the bitch being particularly gentle*

## Take heed
● *Apt to be greedy*
● *Some folk find the reptilian skin unpleasant*
● *Though no breed should be bought lightheartedly, the Chinese Crested can never be given away—this is a breed that can die of a broken heart if parted from its beloved owner*

The Chinese Crested has much to recommend it, as both pet and show dog. It is a handy size, clean, and odourless, and does not shed. It is dainty, alert, intelligent, courageous and gentle. It seldom requires veterinary aid and is a free whelper. It adjusts to cold or warm climates as its body temperature is 4°F (2.2°C) higher than that of humans; in fact, it has its own central heating system, the body feeling hotter to the touch after the animal has eaten. It has the ability to grip with its paws in a charming, almost human fashion.

A strange fact about the breed is that in almost every litter there are one or two haired pups, known as 'powder puffs'. Although these haired specimens have been excluded from selective breeding over a period of years, they are still apparent. Many people believe that the powder puffs are nature's way of keeping the hairless pups warm. And some think that breeding a hairless dog with a powder puff results in healthier stock, the powder puff being allegedly the stronger. If you intend to breed this species, remember that although a reasonable price may be obtained for a powder puff bitch, because she is quite likely to produce hairless pups, the powder puff dog will command only a very moderate price as a household pet.

## Size
Varies considerably, maximum weight 5.4kg (12lb).

## Exercise
The Chinese Crested is a lively little dog and enjoys a brisk walk. However, it happily works off a lot of surplus energy running after, and playing with, the chews and other toys that it so likes.

## Grooming
The Chinese Crested needs frequent bathing, and the skin should be regularly rubbed with baby oil to prevent cracking and to keep it smooth to the touch. Care must be taken to prevent sunburn and to maintain the skin free of blackheads—to which they are prone in adolescence—and other blemishes. Facial hair and whiskers are usually removed.

## Feeding
Usually a rather greedy dog, this breed should nonetheless be content with ½-¾ can of branded dog food (376g, 13.3oz size) or the fresh meat equivalent, and a cupful of small dog biscuits. It is a good idea to keep a bowl of biscuits accessible, so that the animal may help itself when peckish, but remove them if your pet shows signs of becoming overweight.

## Health care
These dogs lack premolar teeth, and thus it is inadvisable to give them bones. They are also allergic to wool.

## Origin and history
Up until 1966, an elderly lady in the United States owned the only examples of the Chinese Crested in the world. Mrs Ruth Harris introduced four of these to the United Kingdom. Today the Chinese Crested is thriving, and classes for the breed are being included in an increasing number of dog shows. It is recognized by the British Kennel Club, but has yet to achieve Championship Show status.

## SHOW SUMMARY
**General appearance.** A small, active and graceful dog; medium to fine bones; smooth hairless body, with hair on feet, head and tail.
**Crest.** Flat, high or long-flowing; sparse crest acceptable, but full crest preferred.
**Colour.** Any colour, plain or spotted. Skin should be smooth and soft, and warm to the touch.
**Head and skull.** Long skull, slightly rounded; slight stop; moderately long muzzle; lean cheeks.
**Tail.** Up and over the back or looped, never curled. Plume on the lower two thirds of the tail. Sparse plume acceptable, but full plume preferred.
**Feet.** Hare foot, nails moderately long. Hair should not come above the first joint from the floor.

*Below: In almost every litter of Chinese Crested pups there is one with hair, known as a 'powder puff'.*

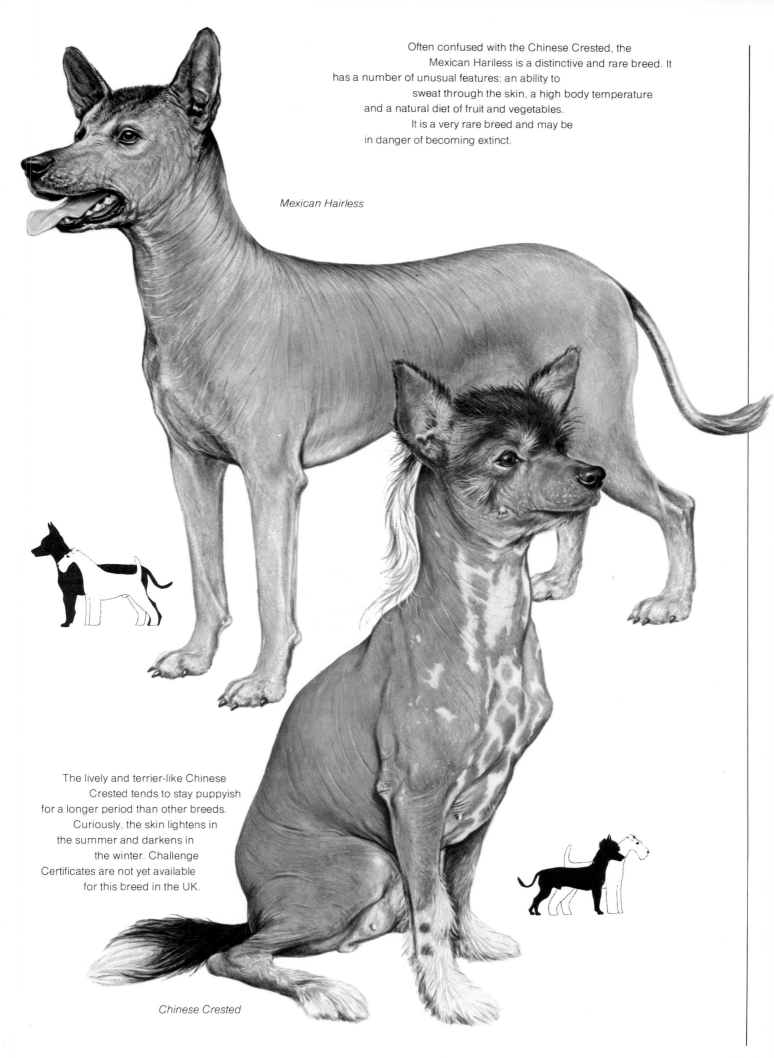

Often confused with the Chinese Crested, the Mexican Hariless is a distinctive and rare breed. It has a number of unusual features; an ability to sweat through the skin, a high body temperature and a natural diet of fruit and vegetables. It is a very rare breed and may be in danger of becoming extinct.

*Mexican Hairless*

The lively and terrier-like Chinese Crested tends to stay puppyish for a longer period than other breeds. Curiously, the skin lightens in the summer and darkens in the winter. Challenge Certificates are not yet available for this breed in the UK.

*Chinese Crested*

# KING CHARLES SPANIEL

## Good points
● *Hardy, despite small stature*
● *Clean*
● *Loves children*
● *Usually gets on with other pets*

## Take heed
● *Needs monthly bath (except in cold weather)*
● *Watch out for canker in ears*
● *Needs daily grooming*
● *A family pet, not suited to outdoor kennels*

The King Charles Spaniel (Black and Tan variety) is known in the USA as the English Toy Spaniel, the varieties of which are Prince Charles (tricolour), Ruby and Blenheim.

In 1903 an attempt was made in the United Kingdom to change the breed name to Toy Spaniel. However, the change was opposed by King Edward VII, a devotee of the breed, and it has retained the name, probably attributed to it because of Van Dyck's 17th-century paintings, which frequently showed King Charles with these pets.

The King Charles is an ideal choice. It is a good mixer, marvellous with children and — despite its small stature — very hardy. It does, however, require daily grooming, regular bathing and, like the Pekingese, to have its eyes wiped every day; care must also be taken lest canker should develop in those well-concealed ears.

## Size
The most desirable weight is 3.6-6.4kg (8-14lb).

## Exercise
The King Charles will look forward to its daily outings, whether accompanying its owner on a shopping trip or going for a scamper in the park. It will be quick to learn how to carry its lead or a newspaper. Don't forget to rub it down with a towel after it has been out in the rain.

## Grooming
Regular brushing with a bristle brush is essential. Examine paws for any trace of interdigital cysts, and ears for canker, often detectable by an unpleasant smell. Wipe eyes with cotton wool dipped in a weak saline solution to keep them clear of unsightly 'tear streaks'.

## Feeding
About ½-1 can (376g, 13.3oz size) of a branded, meaty diet, with biscuit added in equal parts by volume; or, if a dry food, complete diet is used, 1½ cupfuls of feed mixed in the proportion of 1 cup of dry feed to ½ cupful of hot or cold water; or minced beef, lightly cooked, with biscuit added. Meat scraps are acceptable, as are canine chocolate drops as a reward or treat, but don't spoil those teeth by giving your dog cakes or sweet biscuits.

## Origin and history
The King Charles is generally thought of as a British breed, but it can be traced back to Japan in 2000BC. The original breed was much in evidence at the English 16th-century court, when it closely resembled the present-day, longer-nosed Cavalier King Charles. As short-nosed dogs became fashionable, the King Charles Spaniel evolved.

The breed has many royal associations; one was found hidden in the folded gown of Mary, Queen of Scots, after her execution, and Macaulay, in his *History of England,* recalls how King Charles II endeared himself to his people by playing with these spaniels in St James's Park, London, 'before the dew was off the grass'.

*Above: A King Charles pup with black, white and tan markings.*

## SHOW SUMMARY
**General appearance.** Compact and cobby, on refined lines, chest wide and deep, legs short and straight, back short and level. Movement free, active and elegant.
**Colour.** The only recognized colours are: (1) Black and tan — a rich glossy black, with bright, mahogany tan markings on muzzle, legs, chest and linings of ears, under tail, and spots over the eyes. (2) Tricolour — ground pearly white and well-distributed black patches, brilliant tan markings on cheeks and linings of ears, under tail and spots over the eyes; a wide white blaze between the eyes and up the forehead. (3) Blenheim — a ground of pearly white with well-distributed chestnut red patches; a wide clear blaze with the 'spot', a clear chestnut red mark, in the centre of skull. (4) Ruby — whole coloured, a rich chestnut red.
**Head and skull.** Skull massive in comparison to size, well domed, and full over the eyes. Nose black with large wide open nostrils, very short and turned up to meet the skull. The stop between skull and nose should be well defined. Muzzle square, wide and deep, and well turned up; lower jaw wide; lips exactly meeting, giving a nice finish. The cheeks should not fall away under the eyes but be well cushioned up. A protruding tongue is objectionable, but does not disqualify.
**Tail.** Well flagged, and not carried over the level of the back.

# CAVALIER KING CHARLES SPANIEL

## Good points
● *Hardy, despite small stature*
● *Clean*
● *Loves children*
● *Usually gets on with other pets*

## Take heed
● *Needs monthly bath (except in cold weather)*
● *Watch out for canker in ears*
● *Needs daily grooming*
● *A family pet, not suited to outdoor kennels*

Many people find it hard to distinguish between the King Charles and the Cavalier King Charles Spaniel; the Cavalier is larger, and there are marked differences in the head formation — the skull is almost flat between the ears and its stop is much shallower than that of the King Charles. However, it has the same characteristics of courage, hardiness and good nature, which makes it a suitable pet for any age group.

## Size
Weight: 5.4-8.2kg (12-18lb). A small, well-balanced dog within these weights is desirable.

## Exercise
Normal exercise requirements. Will adapt easily to town or country living. It should not, however, be kennelled out of doors.

## Grooming
As for King Charles Spaniel.

## Feeding
As for King Charles Spaniel.

## Origin and history
Reports by Pepys and other British diarists tell us that King Charles II spent more time playing with his 'toy spaniels' during Council meetings that he did dealing with matters of state. He even took his dogs into his bedchamber.

The Cavalier and the King Charles originate from common stock. When it became fashionable to produce a King Charles Spaniel with a short nose, the original type almost disappeared; but in the late 1920s, a group of breeders combined to bring back the old type of King Charles, prefixing its name with the word 'cavalier' to distinguish it from the newer, quite separate variety.

## SHOW SUMMARY
**General appearance.** An active, graceful and well-balanced dog. Absolutely fearless and sporting in character and very gay and free in action.
**Colour.** The only recognized colours are: (1) Black and tan — raven black with tan markings above the eyes, on cheeks, inside ears, on chest and legs and on underside of tail. The tan should be bright. (2) Tricolour — black and white well spaced and broken up, with tan markings over the eyes, on cheeks, inside ears, inside legs and on underside of tail. (3) Blenheim — rich chestnut marking well broken up on a pearly white ground; the markings should be evenly divided on the head, leaving room between the ears for the much-valued lozenge mark or spot (a unique characteristic of the breed). (4) Ruby — whole coloured rich red. Any other colour or combination of colours is undesirable.
**Head and skull.** Head almost flat between the ears, without dome. Stop shallow. Length from base of stop to tip about 4cm (1½in). Nostrils should be well developed and black in colour. Muzzle tapered. Lips well covering but not hound-like. Face should be well filled out underneath the eyes. Any tendency to appear snipy is undesirable.
**Tail.** The docking of tails is optional. No more than one third to be removed. The length of the tail should be in balance with the body.
**Feet.** Compact, cushioned and well-feathered.

*Below: Cavalier pups, showing the Blenheim markings (left) and tricolour markings (right).*

*King Charles Spaniel (Ruby)*

*King Charles Spaniel (Tricolour)*

The Cavalier King
Charles Spaniel is larger
than the King Charles
and it has a longer nose, but
confusion still arises between the two breeds.
In the United States, the King Charles Spaniel is
known as the English Toy Spaniel.

*Cavalier King Charles Spaniel (Blenheim)*

# JAPANESE CHIN
(Japanese Spaniel)

## Good points
● *Affectionate*
● *Loyal family dog*
● *Hardy*
● *Good with children*

## Take heed
● *That silky coat does tend to shed!*
● *Guard against vigorous exertion and overheating in warm weather due to breathing difficulties*

The Japanese Chin (sometimes called Japanese Spaniel) might, at first glance, be mistaken for the Pekingese, and it is possible that the two breeds may have evolved from a common stock. It is, however, a high-stepping, graceful dog that is taller in the leg and has a much lighter body than the Pekingese.

The Japanese Chin, it must be remembered, *is* a 'spaniel' and there are some similarities with the King Charles Spaniel, whose origin can also be traced to Japan. However, it has much more of the perky confidence of the tinier breeds than the slower-moving spaniel, and is a lively but dignified little oriental that likes nothing better than to be the centre of attention and is miserable if its advances are thwarted.

## Size
1.8-3.2kg (4-7lb). (The daintier the better, providing type, quality and soundness are not sacrificed.)

## Exercise
This is a happy little dog that will delight in going for walks and playing games with all the family. It will walk as far as its owners wish, or be happy with a run in the park. The Japanese Chin is quite tough, despite its delicate structure, and will enjoy careful handling by youngsters. But it does like to climb, so be careful it does not fall and injure itself! And don't forget that young pups should not be taken for long walks during the first months of life, when muscles can be strained or over-developed.

*Below: A Japanese Chin puppy with the most widely seen colours.*

## Grooming
Daily grooming with a pure bristle brush will maintain the Chin's luxurious silky coat in good condition. Always give this breed a bath before a show!

## Feeding
170-227g (6-8oz) of cooked minced beef, or ½ can (376g, 13.3oz size) of branded dog food, with a handful of dog biscuits, will keep the Chin in excellent health. Lean meat scraps and the occasional non-splintery bone will be enjoyed and, like most small breeds, the Japanese Chin will find lots of pleasure in doggie chews. Dogs should not be given cakes or sweets but, as a special treat, chocolate drops of the type specially marketed for dogs may be given. These are excellent for use in training as a reward.

## Origin and history
This breed was, for over 1000 years, a favourite of the Japanese emperors, one of whom decreed that all Japanese Chin should be worshipped; some tiny specimens were even kept in hanging cages in the manner of small oriental birds.

The breed is reputed to have found its way to Europe with returning seamen in medieval times. However, the Japanese Chin did not make its appearance in the British show ring until 1862, and is not recorded as being shown in the United States until 20 years later.

Two Japanese Chin were presented to Queen Victoria by Commodore Perry on his return from the Far East in 1853, and this did much to promote the breed. Although they never gained the popularity of the Pekingese, they had a fairly staunch following up until the First World War, when their numbers diminished. Registrations have been on the increase in recent years, and it has become a dependable show dog.

## SHOW SUMMARY
**General appearance.** The Japanese Chin is a lively little dog of dainty appearance, small compact carriage and profuse coat. These dogs should be essentially stylish in movement, lifting the feet high when in motion, and carrying the tail, which is heavily feathered, closely curved or plumed over the back.
**Colour.** Black and white or red and white. Red includes all shades, sable, brindle, lemon or orange. The brighter and clearer the red the better. Colour evenly distributed on the cheeks and ears and as patches on the body. Should be not too heavily marked. White should be clear, not flecked.
**Head and skull.** Large, but in proportion to the size of the dog; broad skull rounded in front, rounded between the ears, but in no way domed.
**Tail.** Set high on a straight back, profusely feathered, closely curved or plumed over the back.
**Feet.** Should be slender and hare-shaped, feathered at tips.

# PEKINGESE

## Good points
● *Beautiful appearance*
● *Loyal and affectionate*
● *Brave guard dog*
● *Healthy and intelligent*

## Take heed
● *Aloof, independent nature*
● *Subject to eye trouble*
● *Needs daily grooming*
● *Best for adults only*
● *Guard against vigorous exertion and overheating in warm weather due to breathing difficulties*

'You have to say please to a Peke.' So said a well-known Pekingese breeder. Tell one off and it will sulk until you feel *you're* in the wrong!

The Pekingese likes to remind its owners of its regal background, and expects to be petted and pampered. It is not, however, a delicate creature; in fact, it is fearless and fun, and loves having toys to play with.

It is good with children, but comes into its own as an adult's sole companion, being the centre of attention and, preferably, having the run of the house. The restricted and neglected Peke is apt to become destructive through boredom. The Peke has a mind of its own and is condescending by nature. But when it decides to offer you its affection, you could not wish for a more loyal and loving companion.

## Size
Dogs: 3.2-5kg (7-11lb). Bitches: 3.6-5.4kg (8-12lb).
There is not, as is often supposed, a miniature Pekingese, but within a litter may be found 'sleeve' specimens weighing no more than 2.7kg (6lb). Sleeve Pekes are so called because they could be concealed in the flowing sleeves of the Chinese mandarins.

## Exercise
The Peke will happily trudge across fields with its owner, or be content with a sedate walk in the park.

## Grooming
The Pekingese needs daily brushing with a brush of soft bristles. The grooming of the underside is usually carried out with the Peke lying on its back, the rest of the job being tackled with the pet standing

*Above: A 'sleeve' Peke, a smaller than usual specimen.*

on a table, or on one's lap. Grooming a dog on a table is good preparation for a possible show career! It isn't necessary to bath a Peke frequently; as an alternative, talcum powder can be applied and brushed through the coat.

## Feeding
The adult Pekingese thrives on about 170-227g (6-8oz) of meat supplemented by biscuits and the occasional non-splintery bone. Like most breeds, they appreciate vitamin tablets, which they will learn to beg for like sweets. An accessible water bowl is, of course, a 'must' for this and all breeds.

## Origin and history
This regal little lion dog came to Europe following the Boxer Rebellion when, in 1860, the British invaded the Summer Palace in Peking and five Imperial Pekingese were looted from the women's apartments. Previous to this, it had been forbidden for anyone other than the Chinese royal family to own a Peke, and their theft was punishable by death.

One of the Pekes taken by the British was presented to Queen Victoria; it was appropriately named 'Looty', lived until 1872, and was the subject of a painting by Landseer.

## SHOW SUMMARY
**General appearance.** A small, well-balanced, thickset dog of great dignity and quality. It should carry itself fearlessly in the ring with an alert, intelligent expression.
**Colour.** All colours and markings are permissible and equally good, except albino or liver. Parti-colours should be evenly broken.
**Head and skull.** Head massive; skull broad, wide and flat between the ears, not domed; wide between the eyes. Nose very short and broad, nostrils large, open, and black; muzzle wide, well wrinkled, with firm under-jaw. Profile should look quite flat with nose well up between the eyes. Deep stop.
**Feet.** Large and flat, not round. The dog should stand well up on its feet, not on its pasterns. The front feet should be turned slightly out. Absolute soundness essential.

The eyes are a distinctive feature of the Japanese Chin. They should be large, dark and set far apart. The white should show in the inner corners, giving the breed a characteristic look of astonishment or even making it look cross-eyed.

*Japanese Chin*

The Pekingese, for many centuries a royal dog in China, was first exhibited in Europe in the late 1800s; the Pekingese Club of America was formed in 1909.

*Pekingese*

# MINIATURE DACHSHUND

(The Dachshund [Miniature]
Long-haired, Smooth-haired and
Wire-haired, Teckel, Dachel,
Dacksel and Badger Hound )

## Good points
- Affectionate nature
- Courageous
- Easy to look after
- Loyal family pet
- Great sense of fun
- Good watchdog

## Take heed
- Prone to disc trouble—don't let it jump, or get overweight
- Self-willed
- Slightly aggressive with strangers, if unchecked

The Dachshund (or Teckel) was bred as a badger hound in its native Germany. Badger hunting required a short-legged hound, with a keen sense of smell, coupled with courage and game-ness; a dog that could burrow—an ability which, if unchecked, today's pet Dachshund will demonstrate in your garden. The Dachsie (Doxie) just loves to dig!

Some Dachshunds are still bred as hunting dogs and will bravely tackle an opponent larger than themselves, such as the badger. They would also defend their owner until death. However, their role nowadays is mainly as a companion. They like children, but can be a little aggressive with strangers if unchecked. They are affectionate, full of fun and, despite their short legs, can cope with as much exercise as you can give them. They have a large bark for their size and are good watchdogs

## Size
Long-haired, Smooth-haired and Wire-haired: ideal weight 4.5kg

*Below: These Smooth-haired Miniature Dachshund pups are full of fun and will make excellent pets.*

(10lb). It is most important that judges should not award a prize to any dog exceeding 5kg (11lb) in weight.

## Exercise
Regular exercise is important as the tendency to put on weight must be discouraged. This doesn't mean you should take your Dachsie on 10-mile treks every day, but short, frequent walks are a must, with plenty of runs in a well-fenced garden.

## Grooming
The Dachshund's coat is easy to keep in condition. The Smooth-haired needs only a few minutes' attention every day with a hound glove and soft cloth. A stiff-bristled brush and comb should be used on the Long-haired and Wire-haired varieties.

## Feeding
About ½ can (376g, 13.3oz size) of a branded, meaty product, with biscuit added in equal part by volume; or 1-1½ cupfuls of a dry complete food, mixed in the proportion of 1 cup of feed to ½ cup of hot or cold water.

## Origin and history
The Dachshund was bred as a badger hound, or hunting dog, and is known to have existed prior to the 16th century and to have been derived from the oldest breeds of German hunting dog, such as the Bibarhund.

When the German Dachshund Club was formed in 1888, there was only one variety—the Smooth-haired Dachshund, whose wrinkled paws, then a characteristic, have been almost bred out. Today there are three varieties, with miniatures of each type: the Smooth-haired, Wire-haired and Long-haired. The Wire-haired Dachshund arose through crossing with the Scottish Dandie Dinmont and other terriers, the Long-haired by crossing the Smooth-haired with the spaniel and an old German gundog, the Stöberhund.

*Above: Long-haired Miniature Dachshunds are well mannered, friendly and good with children.*

Both bandiness, due to a weakness in the tendons, and exaggerated length have now been eradicated.

In his book *The Dachshund* (Popular Dogs), the late Eric Fitch Daglish refers to the severe blow dealt on dog breeding in the United Kingdom and elsewhere, during the 1914-18 war. 'All breeds were affected,' he writes, 'but none, perhaps, so tragically as the Dachshund. Ever since its appearance among us the little Teckel had been recognized as the national dog of the Teutonic Empire, and with the outbreak of hostilities he came in for a share of the scorn heaped on everything made in Germany. This sad state of affairs continued in the United Kingdom and other parts of Europe during the Second World War, when Dachshunds were unfairly discarded, shouted at and even stoned in the streets because of their German ancestry. Happily this is now long past and the sporty, lovable Dachshund has come again to the fore in popularity polls.

The miniatures, like the standards, were also introduced for a purpose. Towards the end of the 19th century, German sportsmen required a hound to go to ground after rabbits. Some were produced by chance, the smaller, weaker members of a litter, but there also appears to have been a miniature type, known as the Kaninchenteckel, which was intentionally produced by mating light-weight Dachshunds to toy terriers or Pinschers. The early miniatures apparently had little of the quality of the show Dachshund about them, but selective breeding produced a far better type—for many years known as the dwarf Teckel—but with the shallow chest, short head and full eye that had characterized its predecessor.

## SHOW SUMMARY
*(all three varieties)*
**General appearance.** In conformation the Miniature Dachshund should be in all respects similar to the Dachshund of standard size. It should be compact, short-legged and long in body, well muscled and strong, with a bold and intelligent expression. The body should be neither so plump as to give an

impression of cobbiness, nor so slender as to impart a weasel-like appearance. Height at shoulder should be half the length of the body measured from the breast bone to the base of the tail, and the girth of the chest double the height at the shoulder. The length from the tip of the nose to the eyes should equal the length from eyes to base of skull.

**Colour.** Any colour. No white is permissible except for a small spot on the breast and even this is undesirable. The nose should be black except in dapples and chocolates, in which it may be flesh-coloured or brown. In all cases the coat colour should be bright and clearly defined. In black and tans, the tan should be rich and sharp. Dapples should be free from large unbroken patches, the dappling being evenly distributed over the whole body.

**Head and skull.** Long and conical when seen from above, sharp in profile and finely modelled. Skull neither too broad nor too narrow, only slightly arched and without prominent stop. Foreface long and narrow, finely modelled. The lips should be tightly drawn but well covering the lower jaw, neither heavy nor too sharply cut away. The corners of the mouth slightly marked.

**Tail.** Set on fairly high, not too long, tapering and without too marked a curve. It should not be carried too high and never curled over the back.

*Above: The Wire-haired Dachshund, most recent of the varieties, has a strong coat for hunting through undergrowth.*

**Feet.** Broad and large in proportion to the size of the dog, straight or turned only slightly outwards. The hind feet smaller than the fore. Toes close together and with each toe well arched. Nails strong. The dog must stand equally on all parts of the foot.

The Smooth-haired Miniature Dachsund has achieved consistently high ratings in the show ring because of its self confidence and gay, lively manner. It is also very popular around the world as a pet dog, especially for people living in small apartments.

*Smooth-haired Miniature Dachshund*

*Long-haired Miniature Dachshund*

The coat of the Wire-haired Miniature Dachsund is evenly short and harsh with a dense soft under-coat to keep out the cold and rain.

*Wire-haired Miniature Dachshund*

# NORFOLK TERRIER

## Good points
- *Adaptable to most life-styles*
- *Equable temperament*
- *Fearless*
- *Good with children*
- *Hardy*
- *Lovable*

## Take heed
- *No known drawbacks*

The Norfolk Terrier co-existed with the Norwich Terrier for more than a century until, in 1932, it gained recognition by the British Kennel Club. There were two types, those with drop ears and those with erect ears. However, in 1964 the British Kennel Club agreed to separate the types, the breed with drop ears becoming the Norfolk Terrier, the prick-eared variety henceforth being known as the Norwich Terrier. The appearance and size of the breed is otherwise the same. They are gay, hardy little dogs with an equable temperament, adapt well to almost any life-style, and are fearless and sporty. (In the United States the Norfolk Terrier was known as the Norwich Terrier (Drop ear) until 1 January 1979, when it was officially recognized as a separate breed.)

## Size
Ideal height 25cm (10in) at the withers.

## Exercise
The Norfolk Terrier will settle for regular walks in a town, but is in its element enjoying off-the-lead runs in the countryside, and is adept at ratting and rabbiting.

## Grooming
Little grooming or trimming is required.

## Feeding
Recommended would be ½-1 can of a branded meaty product (376g, 13.3oz size), with biscuit added in equal part by volume; or 1½ cups of a dry, complete food, mixed in the proportion of 1 cup of feed to ½ cup of hot or cold water. Increase rations if the terrier is in hard exercise.

## Origin and history
These sporty little terriers from the eastern counties of England were once popular with Cambridge students; the dogs were red in colour, rarely weighed more than 4.5kg (10lb), and included both prick-eared and drop-eared varieties. They were shown at dog shows from 1870.

## SHOW SUMMARY
**General appearance.** A small, low, keen dog, compact and strong, with a short back, good substance and bone.
**Colour.** All shades of red, red wheaten, black and tan or grizzle. White marks or patches are undesirable but do not disqualify.

**Head and skull.** Skull wide and slightly rounded with good width between the ears. Muzzle wedge-shaped and strong; length of muzzle slightly less than half the length of the skull. Stop should be well defined.
**Tail.** Medium docked, not excessively gay.
**Feet.** Round, with thick pads.

# NORWICH TERRIER

## Good points
- *Adaptable to most life-styles*
- *Equable temperament*
- *Fearless*
- *Good with children*
- *Hardy*
- *Lovable*

## Take heed
- *No known drawbacks*

Prior to 1964 the Norwich Terrier and the Norfolk Terrier were recognized as one breed by the British Kennel Club. In 1964 the Norwich gained independent status as the prick-eared variety of the two. Its appearance and characteristics are otherwise identical with its Norfolk kin. In the USA both prick-eared and drop-eared varieties were known as the Norwich Terrier until 1 January 1979, when separate breeds were recognized.

## Size
Ideal height 25cm (10in) at the withers; this ideal height must not be attained by excessive length of leg.

## Exercise
The Norwich Terrier will settle for regular walks if living in a town, but is happiest when allowed off-the-

*Below: Norfolk Terriers enjoying a good scamper by the river.*

lead runs in the countryside. It is adept at ratting and rabbiting.

## Grooming
Little grooming or trimming is required.

## Feeding
Recommended would be ½-1 can of a branded meaty product (376g, 13.3oz size), with biscuit added in equal part by volume; or 1½ cups of a dry, complete food, mixed in the proportion of 1 cup of feed to ½ cup of hot or cold water. Increase rations if the terrier is in hard exercise.

## Origin and history
There is some controversy as to whether Colonel Vaughan of Bally-brick, Southern Ireland, or Mr Jodrell Hopkins, a horse dealer from Trumpington, England, deserves credit for founding the Norwich Terrier breed.

Colonel Vaughan hunted in the 1860s with a pack of small red terriers that had evolved from the Irish Terrier. As there were many outcrosses, terriers with drop and prick ears came about, and breeders tended to crop the ears of the drop-eared animals until the practice became illegal. When it did, the Norwich Terrier Club protested loudly about the admittance of the drop-eared variety; when the breed was recognized by the Kennel Club, the Norwich Terrier Club requested that the standard should call for only those with prick ears.

Mr Jodrell Hopkins owned a bitch, a number of whose pups came into the hands of his employee, Frank Jones. Mr Jones crossed them with other terriers, including the Irish and the Glen of Imaal Terrier, using only small examples of these breeds; the progeny were known as 'Jones' or 'Trumpington' Terriers. There is a breeder who claims a direct line from Mr Jones' dogs to the Norwich of today.

The Norwich is a breed that has not been spoilt; for, perhaps surprisingly, it has — in common with the Norfolk — never gained immense popularity.

## SHOW SUMMARY
**General appearance.** A small, low, keen dog, compact and strong, with good substance and bone. Excessive trimming is not

*Above: The Norwich Terrier can prick up its ears when aroused.*

desirable. Honourable scars from fair wear and tear should not be penalized unduly.
**Colour.** All shades of red, wheaten, black and tan and grizzle. White marks or patches are undesirable.
**Head and skull.** Muzzle 'foxy' and strong, length about one third less than the measurement from the occiput to the bottom of the stop, which should be well defined. Skull wide (good width between the ears) and slightly rounded.
**Tail.** Medium docked, set on high to complete a perfectly level back, and carried erect.
**Feet.** Round, with thick pads.

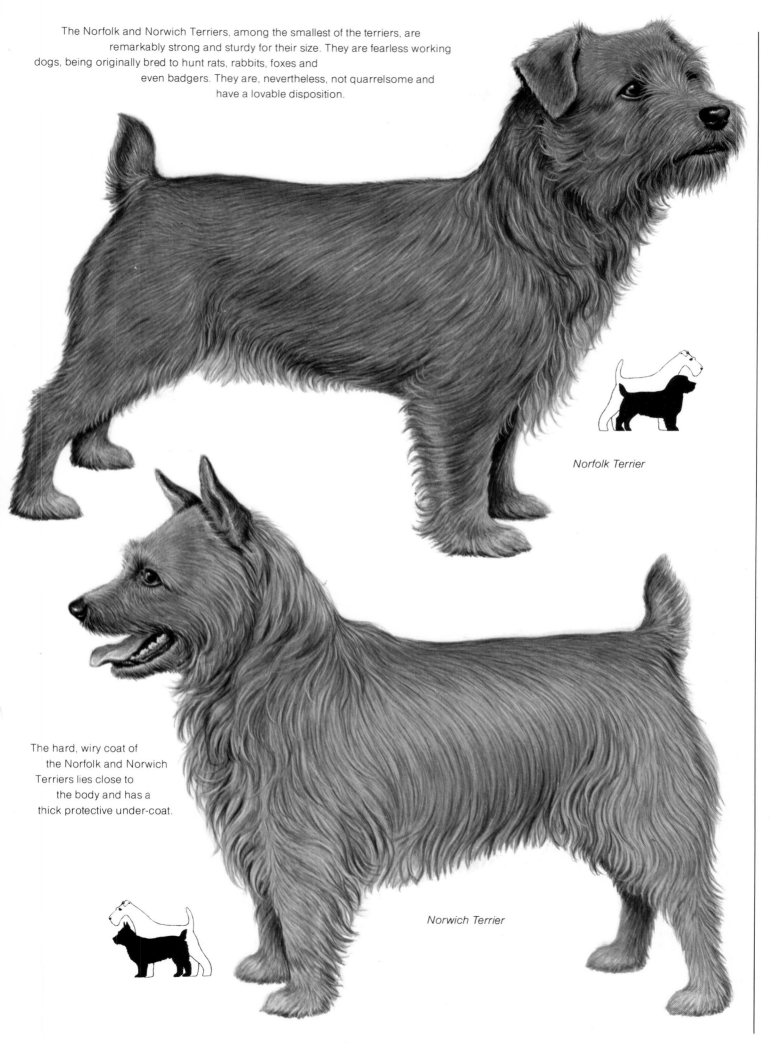

The Norfolk and Norwich Terriers, among the smallest of the terriers, are remarkably strong and sturdy for their size. They are fearless working dogs, being originally bred to hunt rats, rabbits, foxes and even badgers. They are, nevertheless, not quarrelsome and have a lovable disposition.

*Norfolk Terrier*

The hard, wiry coat of the Norfolk and Norwich Terriers lies close to the body and has a thick protective under-coat.

*Norwich Terrier*

# SHIH TZU
(Chrysanthemum Dog)

**Good points**
- Adores human company
- Affectionate
- Arrogant
- Hardy
- Intelligent
- Loves children and other animals
- Suitable for town or country

**Take heed**
- Best to tie back the topknot with a bow, or your pet could develop eye trouble

The Shih Tzu is a happy and attractive little house-pet which adores human company and hates to be neglected. It is extremely intelligent, arrogant, and looks forward to the long, daily grooming sessions for which time must be allocated if you decide to buy this delightful breed.

**Size**
Weight 4.5-8.2kg (10-18lb); ideally 4.5-7.3kg (10-16lb). Height at the withers not more than 26.5cm (10½in).

**Exercise**
Short, regular walks, and off-the-lead runs.

**Grooming**
Daily brushing with a pure bristle brush. Do not neglect this task or combing out tangles will be painful. Keep the topknot from getting into the eyes and take care that the ears are free of matted hair or other objects.

**Feeding**
Half to 1 can (376g, 13.3oz size) of a branded, meaty product, with biscuit added in equal part by volume; or 1½ cupfuls of a dry, complete food mixed in the proportion of 1 cup of feed to ½ cup of hot or cold water.

**Origin and history**
The Lhasa Apso was highly prized by the Dalai Lama of Tibet who would habitually give prized specimens to emperors of China. It is likely that the Chinese may have crossed the Apso with the Pekingese to develop the Shih Tzu. As with the Imperial Pekingese, export of the Shih Tzu from China was forbidden, and it was not until the death of Empress Tzu-hsi in 1908 that the little shaggy dogs were smuggled out to Europe.

**SHOW SUMMARY**
**General appearance.** Very active, lively and alert, with a distinctly arrogant carriage. The Shih Tzu is neither a terrier nor a toy dog.
**Colour.** All colours permissible, but a white blaze on the forehead and a white tip to the tail are highly prized. Dogs with liver markings may have dark liver noses and slightly lighter eyes. Pigmentation on muzzle as unbroken as possible.
**Head and skull.** Head broad and round; wide between the eyes.

*Above: Two beautifully groomed Shih Tzus. These popular show dogs revel in looking good.*

Shock-headed with hair falling well over the eyes. Good beard and whiskers; the hair growing upwards on the nose gives a distinctly chrysanthemum-like effect. Muzzle square and short, but not wrinkled like a Pekingese; flat and hairy. Nose black for preference and about 2.5cm (1in) from tip to stop.
**Tail.** Heavily plumed and curled well over back; carried gaily.
**Feet.** Firm and well-padded. They should look big on account of the wealth of hair.

# LHASA APSO

**Good points**
- Affectionate
- Confident
- Good with children
- Hardy
- Suitable for town or country

**Take heed**
- Needs lots of grooming
- Not keen on strangers

The Lhasa Apso, like the Tibetan Terrier and Tibetan Spaniel, comes from the mountains of Tibet. It is a shaggy little dog, rather like an Old English Sheepdog in miniature, and makes an excellent pet, the only possible drawback being its natural suspicion of strangers.

**Size**
Ideal height: 25cm (10in) at the shoulder for dogs; bitches should be slightly smaller.

**Exercise**
This lively breed needs plenty of walks and off-the-lead runs.

**Grooming**
Brushing and combing daily—and not for a few minutes only.

**Feeding**
Half to 1 can (376g, 13.3oz size) of a branded, meaty product, with biscuit added in equal part by volume; or 1½ cupfuls of a dry, complete food, mixed in the proportion of 1 cup of feed to ½ cup of hot or cold water.

**Origin and history**
This is the dog that the Dalai Lama of Tibet offered to the Chinese emperors. It existed for centuries in the Tibetan mountains until brought to Europe, and elsewhere, by early explorers and missionaries. The words lhasa apso mean 'goat-like' and it was perhaps as guard and protector of the wild goats of Tibet that this glamorous breed of today first found favour.

**SHOW SUMMARY**
**General appearance.** The Apso should give the appearance of a well-balanced, solid dog. Gay and assertive, but chary of strangers.

Free and jaunty in movement.
**Colour.** Golden, sandy, honey, dark grizzle, slate, smoke, particolour, black, white or brown.
**Head and skull.** Heavy head furnishings with good fall over the eyes, good whiskers and beard. Skull moderately narrow, falling away behind the eyes in a marked degree; not quite flat, but not domed or apple-shaped. Straight foreface, with medium stop. Nose black. Muzzle about 4cm (1½in) long, but not square; the length from tip of nose to be roughly one third the total length from nose to back of skull.
**Tail.** High set, carried well over back and not like a pot-hook. There is often a kink at the end. Well feathered.
**Feet.** Round and cat-like, with good pads. Well-feathered.

*Below: A Lhasa Apso with pup. A glamorous show exhibit, this breed also makes an excellent pet.*

The Shih-Tzu was first seen in the United Kingdom in 1931, but it was not until 1940 that the breed was registered separately from the Lhasa Apso. The breed arrived in America in 1938 and was given show classification in the Toy Group on September 1, 1969

*Shih Tzu*

*Lhasa Apso*

The Lhasa Apso is the most recent of the Tibetan dogs to become known in the Western world; it was first exhibited in London in 1929.

# BEDLINGTON TERRIER

## Good points
- *Adores children*
- *Always keeps its figure*
- *Good family pet*
- *Well behaved*

## Take heed
- *Could be dangerous in a pack*
- *Formidable fighter if provoked*

The Bedlington Terrier is an attractive, hardy little dog that resembles a shorn lamb in appearance.

It is a dog whose dainty appearance and love of children belies its first-rate watchdog qualities. It is also a breed that trains easily, and a number have been used successfully in obedience competitions.

## Size
Height should be about 40.5cm (16in) at the shoulder, allowing slight variation below in the case of a bitch and above in the case of a dog. Weight should be 8.2-10.4kg (18-23lb).

## Exercise
The Bedlington, like most terriers, is a lively, inquisitive breed and will enjoy an off-the-lead run or energetic ball game. It will, however, adapt very happily to apartment life as long as it is given regular adequate walks.

## Grooming
This breed's coat does not shed, which makes it a boon for the house-proud, the dead hairs staying in the coat until they are combed out.

The breed should be trimmed regularly (otherwise the coat will become tangly) and given a good brushing every day with a fairly stiff brush. Do not bath the animal too often or this may weaken its coat. Hair should be removed from inside the dog's ears fairly regularly, which can be done quite simply by pulling the hair with finger and thumb or a pair of tweezers.

## Feeding
Recommended would be ¾-1 can of a branded meaty product (376g, 13.3oz size), with biscuit added in equal part by volume; or 1½ cupfuls of a dry food, complete diet, mixed in the proportion of 1 cup of feed to ½ cup of hot or cold water.

## Origin and history
It is possible that the Greyhound or Whippet played some part in the origin of the Bedlington Terrier, and the soft topknot gives strength to the suggestion that it may share common ancestry with the Dandie Dinmont Terrier. Certainly a strain of similar terriers existed with tinkers in Rothbury Forest, Northumberland, in the 18th century, and in 1820 a Mr J. Howe came to Bedlington, Northumberland, with a bitch named Phoebe. This bitch was given to a man called Joseph Ainsley, who mated Phoebe to a dog named Old Piper, producing Young Piper, the first dog with the new name 'Bedlington' Terrier. From that time, 1825, systematic breeding of the Bedlington began. The breed was shown in the ring during the 1860s and the first Bedlington Terrier Club was formed in 1875.

## SHOW SUMMARY
**General appearance.** A graceful, lithe, muscular dog, with no sign of either weakness or coarseness.
**Colour.** Blue, blue and tan, liver or sandy. Darker pigment to be encouraged.
**Head and skull.** Skull narrow, but deep and rounded; covered with a profuse silky topknot that should be nearly white. Jaw long and tapering. There must be no stop.
**Tail.** Of moderate length, thick at the root, tapering to a point and gracefully curved. Should be set on low, and must never be carried over the back.
**Feet.** Long hare feet with thick and well-closed-up pads.

# MINIATURE POODLE

## Good points
- *Affectionate*
- *Dainty and appealing*
- *Excellent retriever*
- *Good sense of fun*
- *Intelligent*
- *Long-lived*
- *Useful in obedience competitions*

## Take heed
- *Noisy if unchecked*
- *Perhaps not the best choice of child's pet*
- *Sensitive*
- *Best to have veterinary examination prior to purchase*

The Poodle has a character full of fun. It is intelligent, obedient and, in the United Kingdom, has proved a useful competitor in obedience competitions. It has a fondness for water, if the owner permits, but is much favoured for the show ring where, exhibited in the traditional lion clip, it is a beauty to behold.

## Size
Height at shoulder should be under 38cm (15in) but not under 28cm (11in).

## Exercise
The Poodle will enjoy a ball game in the garden, practising obedience exercises or trotting beside you in the park. The miniature variety is a good choice for the apartment dweller.

## Grooming
Use a wire-pin pneumatic brush and a wire-toothed metal comb for daily grooming. The lion clip is an essential for the show ring, but pet owners generally resort to the more natural lamb clip, with the hair a short uniform length. It is possible to clip your own dog with a pair of hairdressers' scissors. However, if, despite the help which usually is available from the breeder, you find the task tedious, there are numerous pet and poodle parlours to which you should take your dog every six weeks. Bath regularly.

## Feeding
As for Bedlington Terrier.

## Health care
Fanciers will confirm that the Standard Poodle is the soundest of the varieties. It is possible to acquire healthy Toy and Miniature stock, but care should be taken to purchase from a breeder who puts quality ahead of daintiness. Watch out for signs of ear trouble, nervousness or joint malformations. Teeth need regular scaling. Nonetheless, a 16-year-old Poodle is not a rarity.

## Origin and history
The Poodle was originally a shaggy guard, a retriever and protector of sheep, with origins similar to the Irish Water Spaniel and, no doubt, a common ancestor in the French Barbet and Hungarian Water Hound.

The Poodle may not be, as many suppose, solely of French origin. It originated in Germany as a water retriever; even the word poodle comes from the German 'pudelnass' or puddle, and from this fairly large sturdy dog, the Standard Poodle, the Miniature, and the Toy have evolved.

The breed has been known in England since Prince Rupert of the Rhine, in company with his Poodle, came to the aid of Charles I in battle. The breed was favoured also by Marie Antoinette who, rumour has it, invented the lion clip by devising a style that would match the uniform of her courtiers.

## SHOW SUMMARY
As for Toy Poodle.

# PUG

## Good points
- *Manageable size*
- *Happy disposition*
- *Good with children*
- *Affectionate*
- *Intelligent*

## Take heed
- *Over-feeding will result in a gross, short-lived dog, rather than an elegant, healthy companion*
- *The Pug's breathing apparatus isn't all it might be, so owners must guard against vigorous exertion, bad ventilation and over-heating in warm weather*

The Pug is a gay little dog, which looks extremely elegant if not allowed to indulge its inherent greed. It makes a charming family pet, provided care is taken that it does not develop respiratory trouble through over-heating or vigorous exercise, for with its flat, squashed-looking face it can encounter similar breathing difficulties to the Bulldog.

## Size
The weight should be 6.4-8.2kg (14-18lb), BUT if allowed to over-indulge it will eat itself out of the Toy Dog category.

## Exercise
An energetic dog, the Pug will relish more exercise than many breeds of similar size. But remember that gluttony and a tendency to over-weight go hand in hand, as will fatness and lethargy if the animal's greed is indulged. The Pug will do best walking on the lead, and should not indulge in vigorous exercise for fear of respiratory trouble.

## Grooming
A good daily brushing should be sufficient.

## Feeding
About ½-¾ can of branded dog food (376g, 13.3oz size) or approximately 227g (8oz) of fresh meat daily, supplemented by dog biscuits. Some fanciers prefer to feed meat raw and this must be a matter of choice and, indeed, of the dog's preference.

## Origin and history
The Pug found its way to France with the Turkish Fleet in 1553. They also found favour in Holland, where the tinge of their coat was likened to the colour of the House of Orange. When William and Mary of Orange journeyed to Britain to ascend the throne in 1689, a number of Pugs accompanied them. For 300 years the breed enjoyed a popularity similar to that of the Poodle today.

They gradually declined in numbers until in 1864 even Queen Victoria had difficulty in locating one to add to her kennels. However, some 20 years later the Pug Dog Club was formed and efforts were made to improve and standardize the breed, resulting in the elegant and solid little Pug we know today.

## SHOW SUMMARY
**General appearance.** A decidedly square and cobby dog characterized by compactness of form, well-knit proportions, and hardness of developed muscle.
**Colour.** Silver, apricot, fawn or black. Each should be clearly decided, to make the contrast complete between the colour, the trace and the mask.
**Head and skull.** Head large, massive, round—not apple-headed, with no indentation of the skull. Muzzle short, blunt, square, but not upfaced. Wrinkles large and deep.
**Tail (Twist).** Curled as tightly as possible over the hip. The double curl is perfection.
**Feet.** Neither so long as the foot of a hare, nor so round as that of a cat; well-split-up toes; the nails should be black.

The Bedlington Terrier is a more robust and lively dog than its elegance suggests.
When roused, the eyes should sparkle and the dog look full of temper and
courage. Bedlingtons are capable of galloping at great
speed and should have the appearance of being able to do so.
This action is very distinctive; rather mincing, light and
springy in the slower paces, and could have a slight
roll when in full stride. When galloping, the animal
should use the whole of its body.

*Bedlington Terrier*

*Miniature Poodle
(Lamb clip)*

The Pug shares the foolhardiness of the
Chihuahua and certain other Toy breeds, in
believing that attack is the best form of defence.
Like the Bulldog, the Pug also has
a tendency to snore and to
experience breathing difficulties
in warm weather or during
vigorous exercise.

*Pug*

# BORDER TERRIER

## Good points
- *Good-natured*
- *Handy size*
- *Hardy*
- *Reliable*
- *Sporty working dog*
- *Unspoilt breed*

## Take heed
- *Needs space for exercise*

The Border Terrier is the smallest of the working terriers. It is a natural breed that evolved in the Border counties of England and Scotland, where its task was to worry foxes from their lair.
It is a hardy, unspoilt dog with an equable temperament, and usually gets on well with other animals.

## Size
Weight: dog 5.9-7kg (13-15½lb); bitch 5.2-6.4kg (11½-14lb).

## Exercise
The Border Terrier has immense vitality and is able to keep pace with a horse. It is unfair to keep one unless you can give it adequate exercise.

## Grooming
The coat needs a little trimming to tidy up for the show ring, but otherwise requires the minimum of grooming.

## Feeding
Recommended would be ½-1 can of a branded meaty product (376g, 13.3oz size), with biscuit added in equal part by volume; or 1½ cups of a dry food, complete diet, mixed in the proportion of 1 cup of feed to ½ cup of hot or cold water. Increase rations if the terrier is in hard exercise.

## Origin and history
The Border Terrier was derived in the Border counties of England and Scotland in the middle of the 19th century, when it was the practice to produce a terrier tailor-made for the task it would perform. Sportsmen wanted a hardy dog able to run with hounds and bolt the fox from its lair.
The Border Terrier, with its otter-like head, still works with hounds, and has been less changed to meet the dictates of the show ring than almost any other breed. It was recognized by the English Kennel Club in 1920.

## SHOW SUMMARY
**Colour.** Red, wheaten, grizzle and tan or blue and tan.
**Head and skull.** Head like that of an otter; moderately broad skull, with a short strong muzzle. A black nose is preferable but a liver or flesh-coloured one is not a serious fault.
**Tail.** Moderately short and fairly thick at the base, then tapering; set high and carried gaily, but not curled over the back.
**Feet.** Small, with thick pads.

# AUSTRALIAN TERRIER

## Good points
- *Courageous*
- *Devoted to children*
- *No human enemies*
- *Hardy*
- *Keen, alert watchdog*

## Take heed
- *Has aggression of a natural ratter — watch out for the neighbour's cat!*

The Australian Terrier is a loyal and devoted dog, game, hardy, and utterly reliable with toddlers. It has no human enemies, but will give a good account of itself when called to do battle with other dogs. It is an exceptionally alert watch-dog but, having given the alarm, is more likely to kill intruders with kindness. It makes an excellent companion, and its alertness and speed combine to make it an excellent ratter. The Aussie's coat is weather-resistant, so it can be kept either in the home or in an outdoor kennel.

## Size
Average weight about 4.5-5kg (10-11lb) — in Australia, approximately 6.4kg (14lb). In both the United Kingdom and Australia, the desired height is approximately 25cm (10in) at the withers. (The desired UK weight seems to be changing in line with that of the Australian Kennel Club.)

## Exercise
This is an active and keen scenting dog with the skill and courage to hunt and attack food for itself. Nowadays it is rarely asked to use these abilities, but it should have the opportunity to unleash its energy with regular walks and off-the-lead scampers. Nonetheless, it will adapt to apartment living.

## Grooming
Regular grooming with a bristle brush will stimulate the skin and encourage a good coat growth.
If you are planning to show your Aussie, bath it at least a fortnight before the show; but during spring and summer, when show dates may be close together, don't bath on each occasion, as frequent washing will soften the coat.

## Feeding
About ½-¾ can of a branded meaty product (376g, 13.3oz size), with biscuit added in equal part by volume; or 1½ cupfuls of a complete, dry food, mixed in the proportion of 1 cup of feed to ½ cup of hot or cold water.

## Origin and history
The Australian Terrier was known by various names until 1889, the year in which a club was formed in Melbourne to foster the breed, which had been evolved from several varieties of British terriers brought to Australia by settlers.
It is believed that the development of the purebred Australian Terrier derived from the progeny of a Yorkshire Terrier bitch smuggled in aboard a sailing ship in a lady's muff and mated to a dog resembling a Cairn Terrier.

## SHOW SUMMARY
**General appearance.** A rather low-set dog, compact and active.
**Colour.** First choice, blue or silver grey body, tan colour on legs and face (the richer the tan the better), with a topknot of blue or silver. Second choice, clear sandy or red, with a soft topknot.
**Head and skull.** Head should be long, skull flat and full between the eyes, with a soft hair topknot; long powerful jaw, nose black.
**Tail.** Docked.
**Feet.** Clean, small and well padded with no tendency to spread. Black toe-nails.

# CAIRN TERRIER

## Good points
- *Intelligent*
- *Adaptable*
- *Hardy*
- *Gay disposition*
- *Can live indoors or out*
- *Family companion*

## Take heed
- *A bundle of energy; needs the opportunity to release it occasionally*

The game little Cairn Terrier comes from Inverness in Scotland and, although a popular show dog elsewhere, and drawing large entries in terrier classes, it is still in Scotland that the Cairn really comes into its own as a family pet. Indeed, when I lived in a Scottish village during World War II, it seemed as if every villager was the proud possessor of a perky Cairn Terrier.
The Gaelic word 'cairn' means a heap of stones, and is therefore a most suitable name for a terrier that goes to ground. It is an affectionate, sporty little dog with an almost rain-resistant coat, very active, and rarely stubborn, and it makes an ideal family companion.

## Size
Weight 6.4kg (14lb).

## Exercise
The Cairn is an energetic dog and also an expert killer of rodents. It is in its element trotting with its owner across the fields, or playing a lively ball game with children. It will adapt to controlled walks on the lead and sedate town living, as long as it has a good-sized garden to romp in.

## Grooming
The Cairn is an easy dog to groom or, indeed, to prepare for the show ring, as it is presented in a 'natural' condition. It should be brushed and combed, and have any excess feathering removed from behind the front legs and the tail. Any long hairs about the ears and on the underside should also be removed for tidiness.

## Feeding
Small terriers do well on ¾ can of branded dog food (376g, 13.3oz size) or the fresh meat equivalent, supplemented with a handful of dog biscuits.
The Cairn is not a greedy dog and may prefer to have two small meals each day, rather than receiving its rations all in one go. It also enjoys the occasional large dog biscuit to chew.
A daily teaspoon of cod liver oil will keep the Cairn in good health.

## Origin and history
It is on record that James VI of Scotland (James I of England) ordered from Edinburgh half a dozen 'earth dogs or terrieres' to be sent as a present to France and these, it is believed, were fore-runners of the present-day Cairn, suggesting that more than 300 years ago a working terrier of this type was used for killing vermin in Scotland. Indeed, Mr J.W.H. Beynon in his work, *The Popular Cairn Terrier,* says that every High-land chieftain, in ancient days, had his pack of hounds and terriers, the latter being used to bolt the foxes, badgers and smaller fur-bearing vermin. He also writes that, as far as he could learn, the oldest known strain of Cairns is that founded by the late Captain MacLeod of Drynoch, Isle of Skye, which goes back well over 150 years.
Mr John MacDonald, who for over 40 years was gamekeeper to the Macleod of Macleod, Den-vegan Castle, kept this strain alive for many years, the Cairn then being known as a Short-haired Skye Terrier. Incidentally, inter-breeding of the Cairn with the West Highland, or 'Westie', was permitted until 1924.
The Cairn Terrier became very popular during the 1930s when it was much favoured by members of the British royal family.

## SHOW SUMMARY
**General appearance.** Active, game, hardy and 'shaggy' in appearance; strong, and compactly built. Should stand well forward on its forepaws. Strong quarters, deep in ribs. Very free in movement. Coat hard enough to resist rain. Head small, but in proportion to body. A foxy appearance is the chief characteristic of this working terrier.
**Colour.** Red, sandy, grey, brindled or nearly black. Dark points such as ears and muzzle are very typical.
**Head and skull.** Skull broad in proportion; strong, but not too long or heavy a jaw. A decided indentation between the eyes; hair should be full on the forehead. Muzzle powerful but not heavy. Very strong jaw, which should be neither undershot nor overshot.
**Tail.** Short, well furnished with hair, but not feathery; carried gaily but should not turn down towards back.
**Feet.** Forefeet, larger than hind, may be slightly turned out. Pads should be thick and strong. Thin, ferrety feet are objectionable.

The Border Terrier is essentially a working terrier. It should be able to follow a horse and should combine activity with gameness. The coat is harsh and dense, with a close under-coat that will keep out the cold and wet when the dog is running down a fox in thick undergrowth. The breed also makes a fine pet, being particularly good with children.

*Border Terrier*

The Australian Terrier is supposed to have a hard-bitten appearance; exhibitors should not brush the hair on the muzzle forwards as this gives the dog a Yorkshire Terrier appearance, quite wrong for this breed.

*Australian Terrier*

*Cairn Terrier*

The Cairn Terrier is traditionally a hardy and game working dog. Cairn Terrier Clubs throughout the world have made it their aim to preserve the essential nature of the breed and to resist passing fashions in the show ring that may begin to erode its unique qualities as a sporting terrier.

# IRISH TERRIER

## Good points
- *Alert and loyal protector*
- *Courageous*
- *Excellent ratter*
- *Good with children*
- *Not as snappy as most terriers*

## Take heed
- *Can be a prodigious fighter*

To describe the Irish Terrier as a dog that looks like a small Airedale with a self-coloured yellow coat would far from satisfy the many lovers of this ancient and most attractive breed. We have today in the Irish a fine watchdog, a loyal protector and a most excellent family pet, the only drawback being its somewhat exaggerated reputation for fighting other dogs. True to its terrier blood it is tremendously courageous, and stories of faithfulness to its master are legion.

## Size
The most desirable weight in show condition is: dog 12.3kg (27lb); bitch 11.3kg (25lb). Height at the shoulders should be approximately 46cm (18in).

## Exercise
The Irish Terrier is a sporty little dog, which has been trained successfully to the gun and is first-class at destroying vermin. It has also been a creditable performer in obedience competitions. It will, however, adapt happily to life as a household pet provided it has a garden to romp in and is taken for regular walks and given plentiful off-the-lead runs.

Strangely enough, this breed rarely suffers from car sickness, so if you live in a built-up area you need not worry about your pet's reaction when being driven to a suitable location for a run in open country. But watch out for the farmer's sheep!

## Grooming
Like the Airedale, the Irish Terrier will need hand stripping several times a year and it is best to have this done professionally — at least until you have learned the knack. An inexperienced attempt at stripping could prove a painful experience for the dog and even do irreparable harm to its temperament. Some owners resort to clipping and this is excusable with an elderly animal but causes loss of colour and condition. Normally, a good daily brush will suffice and keep this healthy, hardy dog in smart condition. No doubt you will allow it to keep its thick coat after the show season has finished until the end of the winter months.

## Feeding
Recommended would be 1-1½ cans of a branded meaty product (376g, 13.3oz size), with biscuit added in equal part by volume; or 3 cupfuls of a dry, complete food mixed in the proportion of 1 cup of feed to ½ cup of hot or cold water. This breed will appreciate a big bonemeal type biscuit as an additional treat.

## Origin and history
Irish sources say that the Irish Terrier was established in the country even before the arrival of their patron saint, St Patrick, some going so far as to say that the Irish Terrier is a smaller version of another of their national dogs, the Irish Wolfhound; but the relationship seems somewhat remote. It is more likely that the Irish Terrier is a descendant of the Black and Tan Wire-haired Terriers whose purpose was to hunt fox and destroy vermin in Britain some 200 years ago. Study of the Welsh and Lakeland Terriers will show the similarity between the breeds and it would certainly seem that all have the old Black and Tan Terrier as a common ancestor. It is said that in the area around County Cork in Ireland a large Wheaten Terrier existed that could have been the forerunner of the Irish Terrier and also have contributed to the evolution of the Welsh and Lakeland Terriers.

The standard breeding of the Irish Terrier did not take place until 1879 before which there was considerable variation of type, size and colour; it is said that the Irish Terrier in Antrim was black, brown and white, whereas those in Whitley were of a reddish colour and those in Kerry were black or black/brown. In 1879 a specialist Breed Club was formed, and in the following years the Irish Terrier in its present form and colour became tremendously popular.

It is perhaps worth mentioning that many enthusiasts insist that a terrier similar to the Irish was included in Noah's famous ark.

These dogs were used as messengers in the First World War, and there is a tale about Ordinary Seaman Foc's'le, a nautical terrier on a Canadian destroyer in Atlantic waters during World War II, who raised the alarm when an enemy submarine was not picked up by the ship's instruments, and kept the crew going during the engagement with barks of encouragement.

The Irish Terrier Club was the first body in the United Kingdom to bring about banishment of the practice of cropping dogs' ears.

## SHOW SUMMARY
**General appearance.** The dog must present an active, lively, lithe and wiry appearance, with lots of substance, but at the same time free of clumsiness, as speed and endurance, as well as power, are essential. They must be neither cloddy nor cobby, but should be framed on the lines of speed, showing a graceful racing outline.
**Colour.** Should be self-coloured, the most preferable colours being a bright red, red wheaten or yellow red. White sometimes appears on the chest and feet and is more objectionable on the latter than on the former, as a speck of white on the chest is frequently to be seen in all self-coloured breeds.
**Head and skull.** Head long; skull flat, and rather narrow between the ears, getting slightly narrower towards the eye; free from wrinkles; stop hardly visible except in profile. The jaw must be strong and muscular, but not too full in the cheek, and of a good punishing length. The nose must be black.
**Tail.** Generally docked to about three quarters; should be free of fringe or feather; but well covered with rough hair, set on pretty high, carried gaily, but not over the back or curled.
**Feet.** Should be strong, tolerably round, and moderately small, toes arched, and turned neither out nor in; black toe nails are desirable. Pads must be sound and free from cracks or horny excrescences.

# SHETLAND SHEEPDOG

## Good points
- *Beautiful*
- *Intelligent*
- *Faithful*
- *Ideal for competitive obedience*
- *Intuitive*

## Take heed
- *Best kept in the home (not in a kennel)*
- *May be wary of strangers*

The Shetland Sheepdog is the perfect Rough Collie in miniature, a handy size for the owner who feels, perhaps, that the Rough Collie is too large for his home.

The Sheltie is a good family dog, but a little wary of strangers. It does not take kindly to being petted by those it does not know. It is faithful, supremely intelligent, and generally gives a good account of itself at training classes and in obedience competitions. It is good with horses, and a few are still used as sheepdogs.

## Size
Ideal height measured at the withers 35.5cm (14in) for a bitch, 37cm (14½in) for a dog; anything more than 2.5cm (1in) above these heights is considered a serious fault. A rather larger dog is preferred in America.

## Exercise
Provided the Sheltie has a largish garden in which to expend its energy, and receives regular daily walks, it will be happy.

## Grooming
Not so difficult to keep spick and span as might be believed. Brush regularly with a stiff-bristled brush and use a comb to avoid tangles, particularly behind the ears. Frequent bathing is unnecessary, but is advisable when the bitch loses her winter coat. The Sheltie is meticulous about its appearance and you will often find this breed cleaning itself.

## Feeding
One to 1½ cans (376g, 13.3oz size) of a branded meaty product, with biscuit added in equal part by volume; or 3 cupfuls of a dry food, complete, diet, mixed in the proportion of 1 cup of feed to ½ cup of hot or cold water.

## Origin and history
The Sheltie originated in the Shetland Islands off the north coast of Scotland, an area also famous for its tiny Shetland ponies, which, like the Shetland Sheepdog, have been bred with thick coats to protect them against the harsh climate.

The breed has bred true for some 125 years, but controversy at one time existed as to aims and requirements, the ideals of the club formed at Lerwick in 1908 conflicting with the desires of the Shetland Collie Club, whose desire was simply to produce a Collie in miniature. Both groups were similarly named. Luckily, agreement was reached in 1914 when the English Shetland Sheepdog Club was formed, and the Sheltie received separate classification by the Kennel Club. Today the breed's popularity is universal.

## SHOW SUMMARY
**General appearance.** The Shetland Sheepdog should instantly appeal as a dog of great beauty, intelligence and alertness. Action is lithe and graceful with speed and jumping power great for its size. The outline should be symmetrical so that no part appears out of proportion to the whole. An abundance of coat, mane and frill, with shapeliness of head and sweetness of expression, all combine to present the ideal Shetland Sheepdog.
**Colour.** Tricolours should be an intense black on the body with no signs of ticking, rich tan markings on a tricolour to be preferred. Sables may be clear or shaded, any colour from gold to deep mahogany but in its shade the colour should be rich in tones. Wolf sable and grey colours are undesirable. In blue merles, a clear silvery blue is desired, splashed and marbled with black. Rich tan markings are preferred, but their absence is not to be counted as a fault. Heavy black markings and a slate-coloured or rusty tinge in either top-coat or under-coat are highly undesirable. The general effect should be blue. White markings may be shown in the blaze, collar, chest frill, legs, stifle and tip of tail. All or some tan markings may be shown on eyebrows, cheeks, legs, stifles and under tail. The nose must be black whatever the colour of the dog.
**Head and skull.** The head should be refined, and its shape when viewed from the top or side is a long blunt wedge tapering from ear to nose. The width of skull necessarily depends upon the combined length of skull and muzzle, and the whole must be considered in connection with the size of the dog.
**Tail.** Set on low, tapering bone must reach at least to the hock joint, with abundant hair and slight upward sweep.
**Feet.** Oval; soles well padded; toes arched and close together.

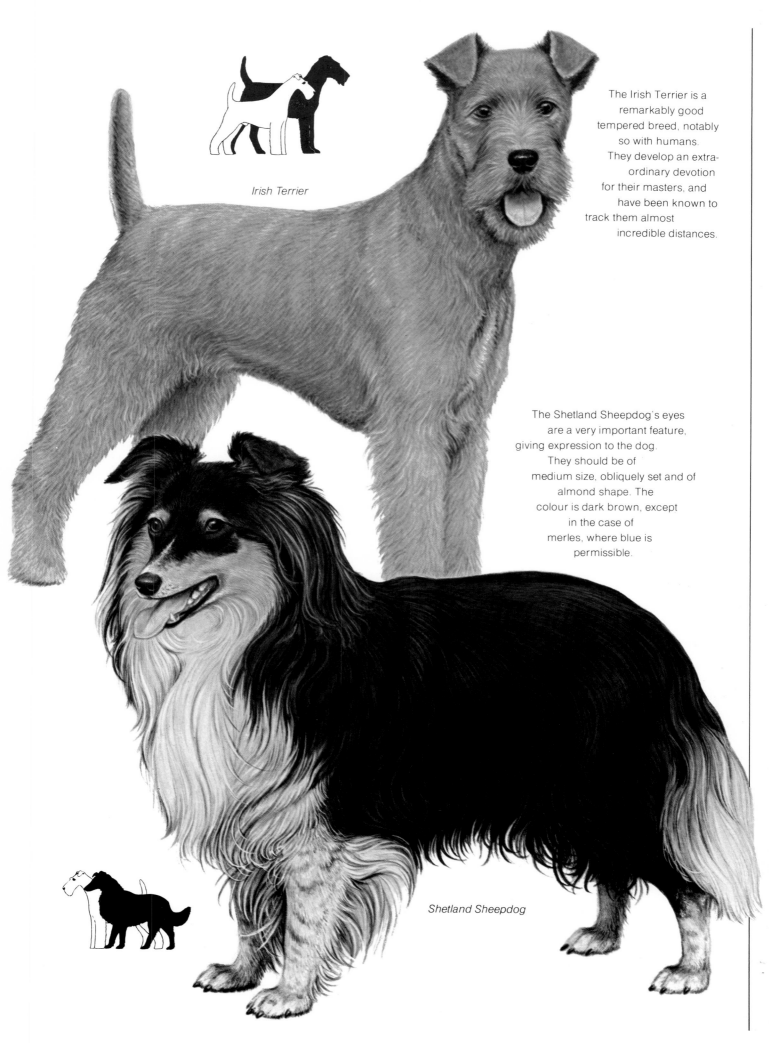

*Irish Terrier*

The Irish Terrier is a
remarkably good
tempered breed, notably
so with humans.
They develop an extra-
ordinary devotion
for their masters, and
have been known to
track them almost
incredible distances.

The Shetland Sheepdog's eyes
are a very important feature,
giving expression to the dog.
They should be of
medium size, obliquely set and of
almond shape. The
colour is dark brown, except
in the case of
merles, where blue is
permissible.

*Shetland Sheepdog*

# GERMAN HUNT TERRIER
(Deutscher Jagdterrier)

### Good points
- *First-class hunter, retriever and gundog*
- *Good traveller*
- *Robust*

### Take heed
- *Needs a lot of exercise*
- *Somewhat aggressive*

The German Hunt Terrier is a popular breed in its country of origin. It is also well established in Austria and other German-speaking regions. It has yet, however, to be recognized by the English or American Kennel Clubs. It can be kept as a household pet, but is essentially a worker, needing plenty of exercise, and has a somewhat aggressive temperament.

### Size
Weight: dog 8.8-10kg (19½-22lb); bitch 7.3-8.2kg (16-18lb). Height at the withers not more than 40.5cm (16in).

### Exercise
Needs plenty of exercise. The German Hunt Terrier is a good car traveller and rarely suffers from sickness.

### Grooming
Daily brushing is required.

### Feeding
Half to 1 can (376g, 13.3oz size) of a branded, meaty product, with biscuit added in equal part by volume; or 1½ cupfuls of a dry, complete food, mixed in the proportion of 1 cup of feed to ½ cup of hot or cold water.

### Origin and history
This is an essentially German breed derived from crossing the English Fox Terrier with the Lakeland and others, with a view to creating a hardy, dark-coated terrier. The first results were not encouraging although good working terriers were produced. However, by 1925, a satisfactory German Hunt Terrier had evolved that was able to go to earth and retrieve small game from land or water. It is a courageous dog willing to take on fox and boar as well as rats and small rodents, but has a somewhat aggressive terrier temperament.

The Association of the German Hunt Terrier has a list of work tests designed specifically for the breed. It accepts for breeding only Hunt Terriers that have achieved high pass marks.

*Right: The compact and sturdy Lakeland Terrier makes a lively pet, for it needs plenty of vigorous exercise to stay in top condition. Originally bred for hunting, the Lakeland Terrier has become a firm favourite in the show ring.*

# LAKELAND TERRIER

### Good points
- *Excellent with children*
- *Fine guard with strong warning bark*
- *Good family dog*
- *Handy medium size*
- *Sporty, but adapts well to home life*

### Take heed
- *Might be too lively for the elderly*

The Lakeland Terrier is similar in appearance to the Welsh and Airedale Terriers. It makes a first-class family pet, being of sound temperament and convenient size, and is also a fine guard. It has been used in the past for both fox and badger hunting, but nowadays is kept mainly as a pet and has, in recent years, been a very successful contender in the show ring.

### Size
The average weight of a dog is 7.7kg (17lb), bitch 6.8kg (15lb). The height should not exceed 37cm (14½in) at the shoulder.

### Exercise
Unless they choose a toy breed, like the Yorkshire Terrier, nobody should choose a terrier unless they want a pet with plenty of zip. The Lakeland Terrier, true to its breed, is gay and fearless, always ready for a walk or a game. It is suitable for apartment living as long as its owner can provide regular exercise and, hopefully, those much loved days out in the country for off-the-lead runs.

### Grooming
Trimming the Lakeland for the show ring requires some skill. Daily brushing will help keep the coat tidy but, even for a pet, professional stripping in spring, summer and autumn is recommended.

### Feeding
Recommended would be ½-1 can of a branded, meaty product (376g, 13.3oz size), with biscuit added in equal part by volume; or 1½ cupfuls of a dry, complete food, mixed in the proportion of 1 cup of feed to ½ cup of cold or hot water.

### Origin and history
The Lakeland Terrier originated in the Lake District of England, hence its name, but was originally known as the Patterdale Terrier where it went to ground working with the local hunts. Although known as a working dog long before, the Lakeland did not make an appearance in the show ring until a Breed Club was formed in 1932.

### SHOW SUMMARY
**General appearance.** Smart and workman-like, with gay fearless demeanour.
**Colour.** Black and tan, blue and tan, red, wheaten, red grizzle, liver, blue or black. Small tips of white on feet and chest do not debar. Mahogany or deep tan is not typical.
**Head and skull.** Well balanced. Skull flat and refined. The jaws are powerful and the muzzle should be broad but not too long. The length of the head from the stop to the nose should not exceed that from the occiput to the stop. Nose should be black.
**Tail.** Well set on, carried gaily but not to curl over the back.
**Feet.** Small, compact, round and well padded.

# WELSH TERRIER

### Good points
- *Affectionate*
- *Bold*
- *Good temperament*
- *Great fun*
- *Handy size*
- *Obedient*

### Take heed
- *No drawbacks known*

The Welsh Terrier has much in common with the Airedale, Irish and Lakeland Terriers and resembles a small Airedale in appearance. It makes a good household pet, generally has a good temperament, and is affectionate, obedient and great fun.

### Size
The height at shoulder should not exceed 39.5cm (15½in). In working condition, 9-9.5kg (20-21lb) is a fair average weight.

### Exercise
Regular daily walks and a romp in the garden will suffice, but like most terriers it will appreciate a run in wide open spaces. They were, after all, originally bred to run with a pack of hounds.

### Grooming
The Welsh Terrier's coat needs stripping twice yearly and regular brushing to maintain it in show condition, but many pet owners resort to clipping their terriers. The coat is usually left on in winter to provide extra warmth.

### Feeding
One to 1½ cans (376g, 13.3oz size) of a branded meaty product, with biscuit added in equal part by volume; or 3 cupfuls of a dry food, complete diet, mixed in the proportion of 1 cup of feed to ½ cup of hot or cold water.

### Origin and history
The Welsh Terrier—like its close relation, the Irish Terrier—is of Celtic origin. In fact, two strains once existed side by side: that evolved by the Welsh from a purpose-bred Coarse-haired Black and Tan Terrier, and an English variety achieved through crossing the Airedale and the Fox Terrier. These two types caused much argument while recognition for the breed was being sought. However, the English variety appears to have died out, and the true Celtic strain was presented in 1885, the Welsh Terrier Club being founded a year later. The following year the Welsh Terrier was awarded championship status by the British Kennel Club. The first Welsh Terriers were taken to America in 1888, but not in any numbers until after 1901.

### SHOW SUMMARY
**Colour.** The colour should be black and tan for preference, or black-grizzle and tan, free from black pencilling on the toes. Black below the hocks is a fault.
**Head and skull.** The skull should be flat and rather wider between the ears than the Wire-haired Fox Terrier. The jaw should be powerful, clean cut, rather deeper and more punishing (giving the head a more masculine appearance) than that usually seen on a Fox Terrier. Stop not too defined; fair length from stop to end of nose, the latter being black.
**Tail.** The tail should be well set on, but not too gaily carried.
**Feet.** The feet should be small, round and cat-like.

The German Hunt Terrier was bred in Germany during the early 1900s for a wide variety of hunting purposes, including retrieval from water. The breed may be kept as a household pet, but it can be fierce and distrustful of strangers.

*German Hunt Terrier*

*Lakeland Terrier*

*Welsh Terrier*

Welsh Terriers are normally hardy and robust, and need no pampering, whilst as working terriers they are second to none, being easily trained to all sorts of game and vermin and to work with gun or ferrets. They also make good water dogs.

# STANDARD DACHSHUND

(Variously known as Teckel, Dachel, Dacksel, Badger Hound)

## Good points
- Affectionate
- Brave
- Easy to look after
- Loyal family pet
- Sense of fun
- Watchdog with loud bark

## Take heed
- Prone to disc trouble
- Self-willed
- Slightly aggressive with strangers, if unchecked

The Dachshund (or Teckel) was bred as a badger hound in its native Germany. What was needed was a short-legged hound, with a keen sense of smell, coupled with courage and gameness; and a dog that could burrow — an ability that, if unchecked, today's Dachshund will demonstrate in your garden.

Some Dachshunds are still bred as hunting dogs and will bravely tackle an opponent larger than themselves, such as the badger. They would also defend their master until death. However, their role nowadays is mainly as a companion. They may be a little aggressive with strangers, if unchecked, but are affectionate and full of fun. Despite their short legs they can cope with as much exercise as you can give them. They have a loud bark for their size, and are first-class watchdogs.

## Size
Long-haired: middle weight up to 8.2kg (18lb) for dogs and 7.7kg (17lb) for bitches.
Smooth-haired: dogs should not exceed 11.3kg (25lb); bitches should not exceed 10.4kg (23lb).
Wire-haired: Dogs should weigh 9-10kg (20-22lb) and bitches 8.2-9kg (18-20lb).

## Exercise
Regular exercise is important, as the tendency to put on weight must be discouraged. This does not mean you must take your pet on 10-mile treks, but short, frequent walks are advisable, with plenty of runs in a well-fenced garden.

## Grooming
The Dachshund's coat is easy to keep in condition. The smooth-coat needs only a few minutes' attention every day with a hound glove and soft cloth. A stiff-bristled brush and comb should be used on the long-hair and the wire-hair.

## Health care
Disc trouble can befall the Dachshund because of its long back and stubby little legs. Anyone who has seen a young dog paralysed, while otherwise in good health, will recognize the need to keep their pet's weight within the breed standard and to prevent it from leaping on and off furniture. Treatment varies from injections of cortisone to an operation; some owners swear by an osteopath!

The Dachshund's teeth are prone to tartar. Regular scaling is recommended, but stains can be removed with a paste of water and cream of tartar, applied with a bit of cotton wool.

## Feeding
Suggested would be ¾ can (376g, 13.3oz size) of a branded meaty product, with biscuit added in equal part by volume; or 1½ cupfuls of a dry food, complete diet, mixed in the proportion of 1 cup of feed to ½ cup of hot or cold water. A satisfactory menu for an adult may be based on 21g (¾oz) of food for each 454g (16oz) the dog weighs, from half to three quarters of this amount being given as meat.

Above: The Long-haired Dachshund's coat is easy to look after.

## Origin and history
The Dachshund was bred as a badger hound, or hunting dog, and is known to have existed before the 16th century and to have been derived from the oldest breeds of German hunting dog, such as the Bibarhund.

When the German Dachshund Club was formed in 1888, there was only one variety, the Smooth-haired Dachshund, whose wrinkled paws, then a characteristic, have now been almost bred out. Today there are three varieties, with miniatures of each type: the Smooth-hair, Wire-hair and Long-hair. The Wire-hair was introduced through crossing with the Scottish Dandie Dinmont and other terriers, the Long-hair by crossing the Smooth-hair with the spaniel and an old German gundog, the Stöberhund. The bandiness in the breed, due to a weakness in the tendons, has now been eradicated, as has exaggerated length.

In Europe during both World Wars, the Dachshund, recognized as the national dog of the Teutonic Empire, was often discarded, shouted at, or even stoned in the streets because of its German ancestry. Happily this sorry state of affairs has long since passed and the sporty, lovable Dachshund is again popular.

## SHOW SUMMARY
### Long-haired
**General appearance.** Form, colour, size and character are similar in all respects to those of the smooth Dachshund, except for the long, soft hair. The form is compact, short-legged and long, but sinewy and well muscled, with bold head carriage and an intelligent expression. In spite of the shortness of the legs the body should be neither too plump nor so slender as to have a weasel-like appearance. Height at shoulder should be half the length of the body measured from the breast bone to the set-on of the tail, and the girth of the chest double the height at the shoulder. The length from the tip of the nose to the eyes should be equal to the length from the eyes to the base of the skull. The tail should not touch the ground when at rest, neither should the leather (i.e. the ears) extend beyond the nose when pulled to the front.

**Colour.** Black and tan, dark brown with lighter shadings, dark red, light red, dappled, tiger-marked or brindle. In black and tan, red and dappled dogs the nose and nails should be black; in chocolate ones they are often brown.

**Head and skull.** Long and conical when seen from above, and in profile, sharp and finely modelled. Skull neither too broad nor too narrow, only slightly arched, without prominent stop. Foreface long and narrow, finely modelled. Lips should be tightly drawn, well covering the lower jaw, neither too heavy nor too sharply cut away, the corners of the mouth slightly marked.

**Tail.** Set on fairly high, not too long, tapering and without too marked a curve; not carried too high; fully feathered.

**Feet.** Broad and large, straight or turned slightly outwards; the hind feet smaller and narrower than the fore feet. Toes close together and with a distinct arch to each toe; nails strong. The dog must stand equally on all parts of the foot.

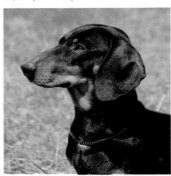

Above: A Smooth-haired Dachshund, carrying its head boldly.

### Smooth-haired
**General appearance.** Long and low, but with a compact and well-muscled body, not crippled, cloddy, or clumsy, with bold carriage of the head and an intelligent expression.

**Colour.** Any colour other than white (except a white spot on the breast). Nose and nails should be black. In red dogs a red nose is permissible but not desirable. In chocolate dogs and dapples the nose may be brown or flesh-coloured. In dapples large spots of colour are undesirable, and the dog should be evenly dappled all over.

**Head and skull.** Long and appearing conical when seen from above; from a side view, tapering to the point of the muzzle.

**Tail.** Set on fairly high, strong and tapering, but not too long and not too curved or carried too high.

**Feet.** The front feet should be full, broad and close-knit, and straight or very slightly turned outwards, the hind feet smaller and narrower.

### Wire-haired
**General appearance.** Low to ground, short-legged, the body long but compact and well muscled. The head should be carried boldly and the expression be very intelligent. Despite its short legs, compared with the length

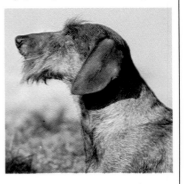

Above: The Wire-haired Dachshund has a distinctive beard.

of its body, it must not be awkward, cramped, crippled or lacking in substance.

**Colour.** All colours are allowed, but a white patch on the chest, though not a fault, is not desirable. The nose should be black, except in the case of chocolates, when it may be brown or flesh-coloured.

**Head and skull.** Looked at from above or from the side, the head should taper uniformly to the tip of the nose and be clean cut. The skull is only slightly arched, being neither too broad nor too narrow, and slopes gradually, without marked stop, to a finely formed, slightly arched muzzle, the nasal bones and cartilage (septum) being long and narrow. The ridges of the frontal bones are well developed, giving prominence to the nerve bosses over the eyes. The jaw has extremely strong bones, is very long and opens very wide; it should not be too square.

**Tail.** Continues line of the spine; slightly curved; must not be carried too gaily or reach the ground when at rest.

**Feet.** The front feet are full, broad in front, straight or turned just a trifle outwards. The four toes forming the foot are compact and well arched and have tough pads; the fifth toe (dew-claw) is usually left on. The nails are strong and short. The dog must stand true and equally on all parts of the foot. The hind feet are smaller and narrower than the forefeet and placed straight, with no dew-claw.
NB: The American Kennel Club standard allows a larger dog.

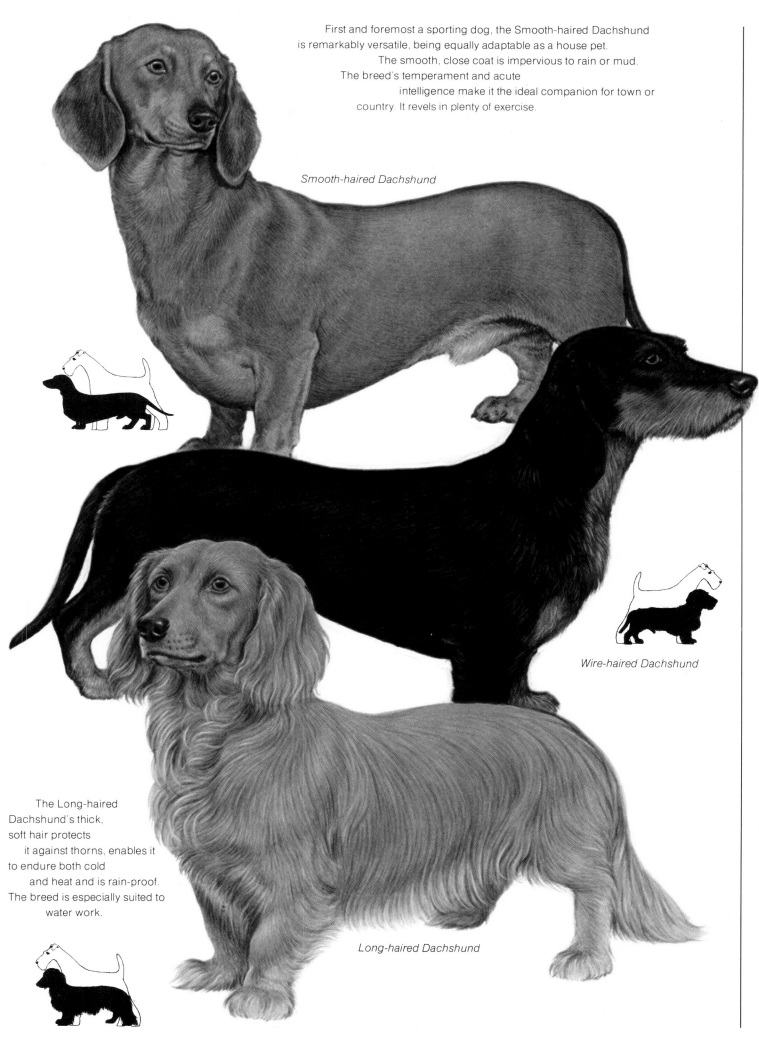

First and foremost a sporting dog, the Smooth-haired Dachshund is remarkably versatile, being equally adaptable as a house pet. The smooth, close coat is impervious to rain or mud. The breed's temperament and acute intelligence make it the ideal companion for town or country. It revels in plenty of exercise.

*Smooth-haired Dachshund*

*Wire-haired Dachshund*

The Long-haired Dachshund's thick, soft hair protects it against thorns, enables it to endure both cold and heat and is rain-proof. The breed is especially suited to water work.

*Long-haired Dachshund*

# WIRE FOX TERRIER

## Good points
- *First-rate companion*
- *Good with children*
- *Intelligent*
- *Smart appearance*
- *Splendid ratter*
- *Trainable*

## Take heed
- *Needs plenty of exercise*
- *Defends itself if provoked*

The Wire-haired Fox Terrier is, when well turned out, a delightful sight to see. It is intelligent, cheerful, and easily trained; a first-rate children's companion, with the typical terrier's 'get up and go'. Nowadays it is seen more frequently than the Smooth-coated variety.

## Size
A full-size well-balanced dog should not exceed 39cm (15½in) at the withers—the bitch being slightly lower—nor should the length of back from withers to root of tail exceed 30cm (12in). Weight 8.2kg (18lb) in show condition, a bitch about 0.9kg (2lb) less, with a margin of 0.45g (1lb) either way.

## Exercise
The Wire-haired Fox Terrier will enjoy nothing more than going rabbiting with its master. It adores sniffing out vermin and is not afraid of a fight, despite its usual good nature. It adapts well to life as a household pet, but really deserves a country home rather than apartment life.

## Grooming
Hand stripping is required in spring, summer and autumn—more frequently if it is the intention to show. Normally a daily brushing will suffice, but watch the coat carefully as terriers are susceptible to eczema. Chalking is usual for a show.

## Feeding
Recommended would be ½ to 1 can of a branded, meaty product (376g, 13.3oz size), with biscuit added in equal part by volume; or 1½ cupfuls of a dry, complete food, mixed in the proportion of 1 cup of feed to ½ cup of cold or hot water.

## Origin and history
The Wire-haired Fox Terrier is a separate breed from the Smooth-coat, although in conformation the breeds are the same. It undoubtedly derived from the wire-haired terriers around the British coalmining areas of Durham, Wales and Derbyshire, where it had existed for some time before gaining the attention of fanciers. It did not appear in the ring until 1872. For a number of years its popularity lagged far behind the Smooth-coat, but now the position has been reversed.

## SHOW SUMMARY
**General appearance.** The dog should be balanced: this may be defined as the correct proportions of a certain point or points, when considered in relation to another point or points. The chief points for consideration are the relative proportions of skull and foreface; head and back; the height at the withers; and the length of the body from shoulder-point to buttock. The ideal of proportion is reached when the last two measurements are the same.

**Colour.** White should predominate. Brindle, red, liver, or slaty blue are objectionable. Otherwise, colour is of no importance.

**Head and skull.** The top line of the skull should be almost flat, sloping slightly and gradually decreasing in width towards the eyes. In a well-balanced head there should be little apparent difference in length between skull and foreface. If, however, the foreface is noticeably shorter, it amounts to a fault, the head looking weak and 'unfinished.' The nose should be black.

**Tail.** Should be set on rather high and carried gaily but not curled. It should be of good strength and substance and of fair length—a three quarters dock is about right—because it affords the only safe grip when handling a working terrier. A very short tail is suitable neither for work nor for show.

**Feet.** Should be round, compact, and not large. The pads should be tough and well-cushioned, and the toes moderately arched and turned neither in nor out.

A terrier with good-shaped forelegs and feet will wear its nails down short by contact with the road surface, the weight of the body being evenly distributed between the toe-pads and the heels.

# SMOOTH FOX TERRIER

## Good points
- *Alert and intelligent family pet*
- *Second to none as a rat-catcher*
- *Smart appearance*
- *Useful medium size*

## Take heed
- *Needs plenty of exercise*

The word terrier comes from the Latin word 'terra' meaning 'earth', the job of the terrier being to kill vermin and to worry or 'boot' the fox from its lair.

The Smooth Fox Terrier is arguably the smartest terrier bred for this purpose. It enjoyed almost unrivalled popularity just before and after the Second World War, and is always a popular contender in the show ring, though it has been said that the elegance of this terrier has been attained at the expense of its former hunting ability. It makes an ideal family pet.

## Size
About 7.3-8.2kg (16-18lb) for a dog and 6.8-7.7kg (15-17lb) for a bitch in show condition are appropriate weights.

## Exercise
The terrier once called 'the little athlete of the dog world' deserves a chance to live up to that title. It will adjust to a regular trot around the park—on a lead, of course—but deserves the opportunity for frequent off-the-lead runs, preferably in the country.

## Grooming
Daily brushing with a stiff brush. Trimming is required a few weeks before a show, paying particular attention to the inside and outside of ears, jaw, and muzzle. Usually a chalk block is used to ensure that the coat is snowy white.

## Feeding
As for Wire Fox Terrier.

## Origin and history
The Smooth-coated Fox Terrier has been around in its present form for at least 100 years. Before then, almost all terriers that went to earth were known simply as fox terriers.

It was in 1862 at the Birmingham, England, National Dog Show that the breed first made its debut in the show ring. Its ancestry probably came about through the terriers in the English counties of Cheshire and Shropshire, and also a hound variety, the Beagle.

## SHOW SUMMARY
**General appearance.** The dog must present a generally gay, lively and active appearance; bone and strength in a small compass are essentials, but this must not be taken to mean that a Fox Terrier should be cloddy, or in any way coarse. Speed and endurance must be looked to as well as power, and the symmetry of the Foxhound taken as a model. The Terrier, like the Hound, must on no account be leggy, nor must it be too short in the leg. It should stand like a cleverly made hunter, covering a lot of ground, yet with a short back.

**Colour.** White should predominate; and brindle, red or liver markings are objectionable. Otherwise this point is of no importance.

**Head and skull.** The skull should be flat and moderately narrow, gradually decreasing in width to the eyes. Not much 'stop' should be apparent, but there should be more dip in the profile between the forehead and the top jaw than in the Greyhound. The nose, towards which the muzzle must gradually taper, should be black.

**Tail.** Should be set on rather high and carried gaily, but not over the back or curled; it should be of good strength.

**Feet.** Should be round, compact and not large; the soles hard and tough; the toes moderately arched, and turned neither in nor out.
*NB* In the United States, the Smooth-haired and the Wire-haired Fox Terriers are not considered separate breeds, but are merely two varieties of the breed known as the Fox Terrier. With the exception of the difference in type of coat, the two are identical in conformation.

# JACK RUSSELL TERRIER

## Good points
- *Affectionate*
- *Handy size*
- *Sporty companion*

## Take heed
- *Excitable in a pack*
- *Not yet a pedigree breed*

The Jack Russell Terrier has become immensely popular in recent years. New owners often become incensed on finding that the breed they have sought and acquired cannot be registered with the British Kennel Club, for it is not as yet a pedigreed dog. The British Kennel Club is aware of efforts to standardize the breed, but unable to accept it while there is so much variation in colour, size and form.

## Size
The Jack Russell Terrier Club of the United Kingdom has drawn up a provisional breed standard aiming to produce a uniform type of Jack Russell Terrier allowing for two different heights: 28-38cm (11-15in) at the shoulder, and under 28cm (11in) at the shoulder.

## Exercise
The Jack Russell Terrier will adapt well to life as a household pet provided regular walks are given. However, it is really in its element in the countryside, ferreting, facing badgers or after foxes.

## Grooming
A daily brushing with a stiff brush.

## Feeding
As for Wire Fox Terrier. Increase the amount if the terrier is working.

## Origin and history
Reverend Jack Russell, a sporting parson in Devonshire, England, who died almost 100 years ago, built up a strain of wire-haired fox terriers that would hunt with his hounds, go to ground and bolt the fox. The dogs were, in fact, hunt terriers. Jack Russell not only bred his unique hunt terriers but also judged terriers at West Country shows and was one of the earliest members of the Kennel Club. It could be that when the breed is established and proper records of pedigree are kept, we may yet see the Jack Russell listed with pedigreed dogs.

## SHOW SUMMARY
(Drawn up by the Jack Russell Terrier Club)
The head should be strong-boned, with powerful jaws, level bite and good strong cheek muscles. Eyes should be almond shaped, and the small V-shaped, dropped ears carried close to the head. The back to be straight with a high-set tail. Hindquarters strong with good angulation. The coat is smooth but woolly; the colour is basically white with black, tan or traditional hound markings.

Wire Fox Terrier

Smooth Fox Terrier

Jack Russell Terrier

The Jack Russell Terrier is a dog
with great spirit and persistence
as far as chasing is concerned.
Although not officially recognized
by a Kennel Club, the breed
is gaining popularity as an affectionate
and sporty companion.

# DANDIE DINMONT TERRIER

## Good points
- Courageous
- Intelligent
- Keen sense of humour
- Excellent watchdog

## Take heed
- Tends to be a one-person dog, whose friendship and respect must be earned

Although once popular as a badger and fox hunter, the Dandie Dinmont is now kept mainly as a household pet: indeed, they fare better indoors as a single pet than living with their fellows in kennels. They do, however, tend to be a little suspicious of strangers, giving all their devotion to their owner. They are excellent guard dogs with a bark that should deter any burglar.

## Size
The height should be 20-28cm (8-11in) at the top of the shoulder. Length from top of shoulder to root of tail should be not more than twice the dog's height, but preferably 2.5-5cm (1-2in) less. The ideal weight for a dog in good working condition is as near 8.2kg (18lb) as possible.

## Exercise
The Dandie Dinmont is an adaptable dog and will be happy whether put to work killing foxes or enjoying the role of an old lady's pet. It would, however, be unfair to keep this active, inquisitive breed in a home without a garden.

## Grooming
Grooming is not a difficult task, the only equipment needed being a stiff brush and comb. Old hairs should be removed with finger and thumb, allowing the under-coat to come through. Incidentally, don't use a trimming knife, because this will ruin the coat. Brush daily and it should always look immaculate.

## Feeding
Recommended would be ½-1 can of a branded meaty product (376g, 13.3oz size), with biscuit added in equal part by volume; or 1½ cupfuls of a dry, complete food mixed in the proportion of 1 cup to ½ cup of hot or cold water.

## Origin and history
Most Dandies can be traced back to the late 1700s, to an individual named Piper Allan, something of a character of his day, who had two Dandie Dinmonts, called Charlie and Peachem. Also well known is James Davidson, who was renowned for his 'pepper and mustard' terriers, so called because of their colour: it was from Davidson that Sir Walter Scott acquired his dogs, and indeed it was from a character in his novel 'Guy Mannering' that the breed received its name.

## SHOW SUMMARY
**Colour.** The colours are pepper or mustard. The peppers range from a dark bluish black to a light silvery grey, the intermediate shades being preferred; the body colour comes well down the shoulder and hips, gradually merging into the leg colour. The mustards vary from reddish brown to pale fawn, the head being creamy white, the legs and feet of a shade darker than the head. The claws are dark, as in other colours. Nearly all Dandie Dinmont Terriers have some white on the chest, and some have white claws. White feet are objectionable.

**Head and skull.** The head should be strongly made and large, but not out of proportion to the dog's size; the muscles show extraordinary development, especially the maxillary. Skull broad between the ears, getting gradually less towards the eye, and measuring about the same from the inner corner of the eye to the back of the skull as it does from ear to ear. The forehead should be well domed. The head is covered with very soft silky hair, which should not be confined to a mere topknot; the lighter in colour and silkier it is the better. The nose is black.

**Tail.** Rather short, say 20-25cm (8-10in), and covered on the upper side with wiry hair of a darker colour than that of the body, the hair on the under side being lighter in colour, and not so wiry, with a nice feather about 5cm (2in) long, getting shorter as it nears the tip.

**Feet.** Flat feet are objectionable. The whole claws should be dark, but the claws of all vary in shade according to the colour of the dog's body. The feet of a pepper dog should be tan, varying according to the body colour from a rich tan to a pale fawn; those of a mustard dog are a darker shade than its head. Hind feet should be much smaller than forefeet.

# SKYE TERRIER

## Good points
- Beautiful in appearance
- Pleasant disposition
- Patient

## Take heed
- Needs plenty of grooming
- Does not take kindly to strangers

The Skye Terrier originated on the Isle of Skye in the Hebrides and is, despite its beautiful appearance, a relentless fighter if aroused. It is not a vicious dog, but tends to give total trust and devotion to its owner and has little time for strangers. Considerable care has to be given to the grooming of this breed. If given the chance they are valiant hunters, having been bred to hunt fox, otter and badger.

## Size
Height 25cm (10in), total length 105cm (41½in), weight 11.3kg (25lb); bitch slightly smaller.

## Exercise
It would be unfair to buy this gay little breed purely as a fashionable accessory, for they are tireless and enjoy nothing better than a long country walk and romp in fresh air.

## Grooming
The Skye should be brushed daily and combed once a week with a wide-toothed comb. Incidentally, the coat does not reach its full beauty until the third year.

## Feeding
Recommended would be 1-1½ cans of a branded meaty product (376g, 13.3oz size), with biscuit added in equal part by volume; or 3 cupfuls of a dry, complete food, mixed in the proportion of 1 cup of feed to ½ cup of hot or cold water.

## Origin and history
The Skye Terrier is a legend – not only in Scotland, but throughout the world – because of the tale of Greyfriars Bobby, whose statue stands near Greyfriars churchyard, Edinburgh. Following his master's death, Bobby would each day, for the next 14 years, visit the café that he had frequented with his master, where he would be given a bun, before retracing his steps to his master's grave, where he spent his days until his own death from old age, when the statue was erected in his memory.

The Skye evolved from the small earth dogs kept in Scotland to hunt foxes, badgers and other vermin. Although the Cairn and other breeds existed in the Highlands it would seem that the Skye owes its appearance to no-one, although the Highland terriers in early days were not separate breeds.

## SHOW SUMMARY
**Colour.** Dark or light grey, fawn, cream or black, with black points. In fact, any self colour allowing shading of the same colour and lighter under-coat, so long as the nose and ears are black. A small white spot on the chest allowed.

**Head and skull.** Head long, with powerful jaws. Nose black.

**Tail.** When hanging, upper part pendulous and lower half thrown back in a curve. When raised, a prolongation of the incline of the back, not rising or curling up.

**Feet.** Large and pointing forward.

# GLEN OF IMAAL TERRIER

## Good points
- Affectionate
- Courageous
- Excellent with children
- Good working dog
- Loyal
- Playful

## Take heed
- Rarely seen in show ring, so not a good choice for that purpose

The Glen of Imaal Terrier originates from a valley of that name in the county of Wicklow in Ireland, where it was – and is – used as a working terrier to dispel fox and badger. It is still mainly to be found in Ireland, combining life as a working terrier with the role of pet and children's protector.

## Size
Height not more than 35.5cm (14in); weight up to 15.9kg (35lb), less for bitches.

## Exercise
Happiest when able to run in open spaces, but an adaptable little dog that will take to normal household life provided it has a garden to play in and is given regular walks.

## Grooming
A good daily brushing.

## Feeding
As for Skye Terrier.

## Origin and history
The Glen of Imaal Terrier is an Irish-bred working terrier and still popular in its area of origin. But although its fame has long spread outside its native Ireland, where it received official breed recognition in 1933, it is not often seen in the show ring. It is also recognized by the British Kennel Club but not by the AKC.

**SHOW SUMMARY** (Taken from FCI Standard, Belgium, 1975)
**General appearance.** Medium long-coated dog of great strength for its size, active and agile, low to the ground. Movement should be free, not hackneyed in action but covering the ground effortlessly.
**Colour.** Blue brindle or wheaten but not toning to black.
**Head and skull.** The head should be of good width and fair length, with a foreface of power bearing to the nose but showing no sign of the bottle head often seen in other breeds. There should be a pronounced stop.
**Tail.** The tail must be strong at the insertion, well set on, and carried gaily.
**Feet.** Compact, with strong, rounded pads.

# CESKY TERRIER

The Cesky Terrier, sometimes known as the Bohemian Terrier, comes from Czechoslovakia and is not widely known. It is a useful short-legged terrier, hardy, healthy and extremely adaptable, being ideally suited as a house pet.

## Size
Dog: 28-35.5cm (11-14in) high, bitch slightly smaller.

## Feeding
As for Dandie Dinmont Terrier.

## Colour
The Cesky comes in two colours, blue grey and light coffee brown.

The coat of the Dandie Dinmont Terrier should be a mixture of hardish and soft hair, which gives a sort of crisp feel to the hand. The hair on the under part of the body is lighter in colour and softer in texture.

*Cesky Terrier*

*Dandie Dinmont Terrier*

Glen of Imaal Terriers that meet the high standard of 'gameness' set by the Breed Club receive an award known as 'Teastors Misneac'.

*Glen of Imaal Terrier*

*Skye Terrier*

# FRENCH BULLDOG

### Good points
- *Affectionate and devoted pet*
- *Loves human company*

### Take heed
- *Lubricate facial creases with petroleum jelly to prevent soreness*

The French Bulldog is a devoted animal and makes the ideal family pet. It has a keen, clownish sense of humour, is intelligent, and adapts well to town or country living. It is perhaps the healthiest of the Bulldogs and does not suffer from the over-developments or nasal difficulties of the Boston Terrier and the English Bulldog.

### Size
The ideal weight is 12.7kg (28lb) for dogs and 10.9kg (24lb) for bitches, but soundness must not be sacrificed to smallness.

### Exercise
Short, regular walks, and off-the-lead scampers.

### Grooming
Normal daily brushing.

### Feeding
One to 1½ cans (376g, 13.3oz size) of a branded meaty product, with biscuit added in equal part by volume; or 3 cupfuls of a dry food, complete diet, mixed in the proportion of 1 cup of feed to ½ cup of hot or cold water.

### Origin and history
Credit must go to the French for the development of this breed. It is, however, uncertain whether it derives from small English Bulldogs taken to France by Nottingham laceworkers in the 19th century, or from crossings with dogs imported to France from Spain. In any event, this delightful animal is obviously the descendant of small Bulldogs, and by the beginning of this century it had found favour in both Britain and the United States.

### SHOW SUMMARY
**General appearance.** A French Bulldog should be sound, active and intelligent, of compact build, medium or small, with good bone, a short smooth coat and the various points so evenly balanced that the dog does not look ill-proportioned.
**Colour.** The colours allowed are brindle, pied and fawn.
1. The brindle is a mixture of black and coloured hairs. This variety may contain white on condition that brindle predominates.
2. The pied is a dog in which the white predominates over the brindle. White dogs are classified with the pieds, but their eyelashes and eye-rims should be black.
3. The fawn dog may contain brindle hairs but must have black eye-rims and eyelashes.

*Above: French Bulldogs love people and have a sense of fun.*

**Head and skull.** Head massive, square and broad. Skull nearly flat between the ears, with a domed forehead, the loose skin forming symmetrical wrinkles. Muzzle broad, deep and laid back with the muscles of the cheek well developed; nose and lips black. Stop well defined. Lower jaw should be deep, square, broad, slightly undershot and well turned up. Nose extremely short, black and wide, with open nostrils and the line between well defined. Lips thick, the lower meeting the upper in the middle, completely hiding the teeth. The upper lip should cover the lower on each side with plenty of cushion, but not so exaggerated as to hang much below the level of the lower jaw.
**Tail.** Very short, set low, thick at the root, and tapering quickly towards the tip, either straight or kinked, but never curling over the back. A good tail is placed so that it cannot be carried gaily.
**Feet.** Should be small, compact and placed in continuation of the line of the leg, with absolutely sound pasterns. The hind feet are rather longer than the fore/feet. Toes compact; knuckles high; nails short, thick and black.

# MINIATURE BULL TERRIER

The Miniature Bull Terrier is a replica of its big brother the Bull Terrier in all respects except size. It is thus the gladiator of the dog world in miniature, perhaps more suited to apartment dwelling than its bigger counterpart. Miniatures are not easy to breed, and are therefore rare and hard to obtain.

Headings relating to the Bull Terrier are identical for the miniature except for:

### Size
Height should be not more than 35.5cm (14in). Weight should be not more than 9kg (20lb).

### Feeding
Recommended would be ½-1 can of a branded meaty product (376g, 13.3oz size), with biscuit added in equal part by volume; or 1½ cups of a dry, complete food diet, mixed in the proportion of 1 cup of feed to ½ cup of hot or cold water. Increase rations if the terrier is in hard exercise.

# BOSTON TERRIER

(Formerly American Bull Terrier)

### Good points
- *Affectionate*
- *Easy to look after*
- *Excellent guard*
- *Good family pet*
- *Odourless*
- *Good with children*
- *Obedient*
- *Playful nature*
- *Rarely sheds coat*
- *Handy size*

### Take heed
- *Avoid draughts*
- *Not the breed for outside kennelling*
- *Not the easiest type to breed and/or produce for showing*
- *Watch out for eye trouble*

The Boston Terrier is a lively and attractive American breed. It is intelligent and trainable, and makes a delightful companion, always ready for a walk or a game. However, achieving the desired markings can be a show aspirant's nightmare, and bitches frequently require caesarean section in whelping.

### Size
Weight: not more than 11.3kg (25lb).

### Exercise
This breed will happily settle for an on-the-lead walk, if you do not have a garden to offer it more freedom of movement. It is essentially a pet dog and should not be confined in an outside kennel.

### Grooming
Daily brushing is needed. In the United States ears are cropped in some states according to state law. This practice is illegal in the United Kingdom. The coat rarely sheds.

### Feeding
Half to 1 can (376g, 13.3oz size) of a branded, meaty product, with biscuit added in equal part by volume; or 1½ cupfuls of a dry, complete food mixed in the proportion of 1 cup of feed to ½ cup of hot or cold water.

### Health care
The Boston is robust but, as in the

*Below: Boston Terrier pups should live indoors, free from draughts.*

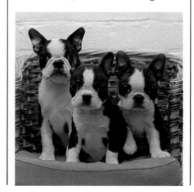

case of the Pekingese and other round-eyed breeds, watch that dust and foreign bodies do not penetrate the eyes.

### Origin and history
The Boston Terrier, sometimes called the 'American gentleman', can trace its ancestry from the mating of a crossbred Bulldog/terrier called Judge, imported to the United States from the United Kingdom in 1865. To later progeny were added a dash of English and Staffordshire Bull Terrier, until the dog we know today evolved. At first it was known as the American Bull Terrier, but as a result of objections from other Bull Terrier clubs it was renamed the Boston Terrier after the city responsible for its development.

### SHOW SUMMARY
**General appearance.** The Boston Terrier should be a lively, highly intelligent, smooth-coated, short-headed, compactly built, short-tailed, well-balanced dog of medium size, of brindle colour and evenly marked with white. The head should indicate a high degree of intelligence and should be in proportion to the size of the dog; the body rather short and well knit; the limbs strong and neatly turned; tail short; and no feature to be so prominent that the dog appears badly proportioned. The dog should convey an impression of determination, strength and activity, with style of a high order; carriage easy and graceful. The gait of the Boston Terrier is that of a sure-footed, straight-gaited dog, forelegs and hind legs moving straight ahead in time with perfect rhythm, each step indicating grace and power.
**Colour.** Brindle with white markings; brindle must show throughout the body distinctly; black and white markings are permissible, but brindles with white markings are preferred. (Ideal colour shall be one in which the brindle colouring is evenly distributed throughout the body) Ideal markings: white muzzle, even white blaze over head, collar, breast, part or whole of forelegs, and hind legs below hocks.
**Head and skull.** Skull square, flat on top, free from wrinkles; cheeks flat; brow abrupt, stop well defined. Muzzle short, square, wide and deep, and in proportion to the skull; free from wrinkles; shorter in length than in width and depth, not exceeding in length approximately one third of length of skull; width and depth carried out well to end; the muzzle from stop to end of nose on a line parallel to the top of the skull; nose black and wide with well-defined line between nostrils. The jaws broad and square. The chops of good depth but not pendulous, completely covering the teeth when mouth is closed.
**Tail.** Set-on low; short, fine and tapering; straight or screw; devoid of fringes or coarse hair, and not carried above horizontal.
**Feet.** Round, small and compact, and turned neither in nor out; toes well arched.

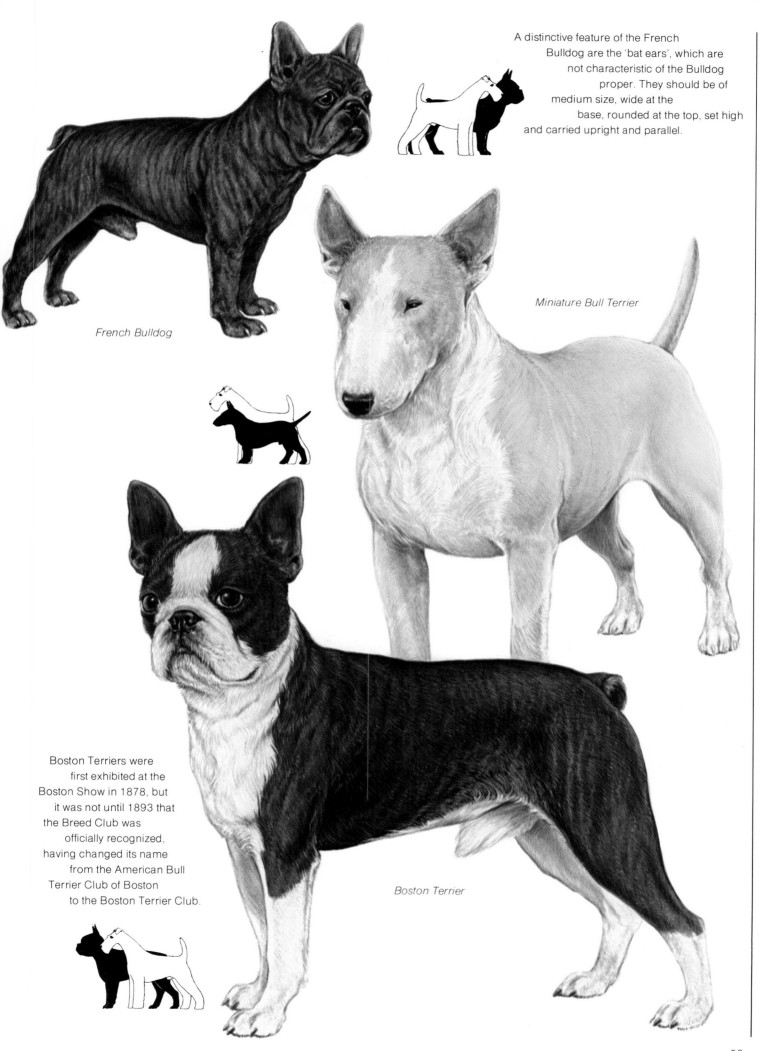

A distinctive feature of the French Bulldog are the 'bat ears', which are not characteristic of the Bulldog proper. They should be of medium size, wide at the base, rounded at the top, set high and carried upright and parallel.

*French Bulldog*

*Miniature Bull Terrier*

Boston Terriers were first exhibited at the Boston Show in 1878, but it was not until 1893 that the Breed Club was officially recognized, having changed its name from the American Bull Terrier Club of Boston to the Boston Terrier Club.

*Boston Terrier*

53

# MANCHESTER TERRIER

## Good points
● *Clean, no trouble*
● *Good family dog*
● *Great sporting companion*
● *Long-lived*
● *Suitable for town or country*

## Take heed
● *Tends to be a one-person dog*

The Manchester Terrier is an ideal choice for those seeking a small, hardy dog that causes no trouble and makes a great sporting companion. It will fit well into family life, but does tend to attach itself to one person.

It is long lived and seldom ill. It can live indoors or outside in a heated kennel, but will be happiest if given a place by the fireside.

## Size
Desired height: dog 40.5cm (16in); bitch 38cm (15in).

## Exercise
The Manchester is in its element running free in the countryside. Town dwellers need not rule out this breed, however, if they can offer regular walks, off-the-lead runs and a garden.

## Grooming
Manchesters do not like rain, despite its proverbial frequency in their place of origin, and should be rubbed with a towel if they get wet. Otherwise, a daily brushing will keep this essentially clean animal looking smart. Its coat condition is always an indication of health.

## Feeding
Half to 1 can (376g, 13.3oz size) of a branded meaty product, with biscuit added in equal part by volume; or 1½ cupfuls of a complete, dry food, mixed in the proportion of 1 cup of feed to ½ cup of hot or cold water.

## Origin and history
The Manchester Terrier can trace its lineage back to the old hunting 'Black and Tan' Terrier, which, in the north of England, had the reputation of rat killer supreme.

The Manchester Terrier — once closely related to a white English terrier that seems to have disappeared, probably because of its tendency to deafness — has evolved as a reliable household pet, retaining its sporting instincts while fitting happily into a home that requires an alert, lively pet. It is usually good with children.

At one time the Manchester Terrier and the English Toy Terrier were shown as Black and Tan Terriers with a weight division. The English Toy Terrier is now separately classified in England, but in the USA, where the Manchester Terrier is popular, breeding of toys and standards is permitted.

A number of Manchesters were exported from the United Kingdom to the United States, Canada and (later) Germany in the 1800s,

and it is thought (see Dobermann Pinscher) that the Manchester aided the make-up of the Dobermann, certainly as far as its short, shiny black and tan coat was concerned. Earlier Manchesters had cropped ears, a practice that became illegal in the United Kingdom in 1895.

## SHOW SUMMARY
**General appearance.** The dog shall be compact in appearance, with good bone, and free from any resemblance to the Whippet.
**Colour.** Jet black and rich mahogany tan distributed as follows: on the head, the muzzle to be tanned to the nose, the nose and nasal bone to be jet black. There shall be a small tan spot on each cheek and above each eye, the under-jaw and throat to be tanned with a distinct tan 'V'. In all cases the black should not run into the tan or vice versa, but the division between the colours should be clearly defined.
**Head and skull.** Long, flat in skull and narrow, level and wedge-shaped.
**Tail.** Short and set on where the arch of the back ends.
**Feet.** Small, semi-harefooted, and strong, with well-arched toes.

# TIBETAN TERRIER

## Good points
● *Charming 'shaggy' appearance*
● *Happy disposition*

## Take heed
● *No drawbacks known*

The Tibetan Terrier is one of three small Tibetan breeds, the others being the Tibetan Spaniel and the Lhasa Apso, both of which are dealt with elsewhere. There is also a Tibetan Mastiff, which is a much larger breed.

The Tibetan Terrier, which in appearance resembles a small Old English Sheepdog, is in truth not a terrier at all, having no history of going to earth.

## Size
Height at shoulders: dog should be 35.5-40.5cm (14-16in); bitches should be slightly smaller.

## Exercise
The Tibetan Terrier enjoys an off-the-lead scamper and the freedom of a garden; otherwise normal, regular walks will suffice.

## Grooming
Needs thorough brushing daily.

## Feeding
As for Manchester Terrier.

## Origin and history
Bred in the monasteries of Tibet, with a history of all-purpose farm work, the Tibetan breeds first reached Europe at the beginning of this century, when both the Lhasa Apso and the Tibetan Terrier were referred to as Lhasa

Terriers. The situation became somewhat confused, and in 1934 the British Kennel Club formed the Tibetan Breeds Association.

The Tibetan Terrier standard is included in the British Kennel Club's Utility group, and over the past 10 years the breed has attracted quite a number of enthusiasts. At the time of writing, however, the Tibetan Terrier has still to be recognized by the American Kennel Club.

## SHOW SUMMARY
**General appearance.** A well-muscled medium-sized dog, in general appearance not unlike a miniature Old English Sheepdog.
**Colour.** White, golden, cream, grey or smoke, black, parti-colour, and tricolour — in fact, any colour except chocolate or liver.
**Head and skull.** Skull of medium length, not broad or coarse, narrowing slightly from ear to eye, not domed but not absolutely flat between the ears. Nose, black.
**Tail.** Medium length, set on fairly high and carried in a gay curl over the back. Very well feathered. There is often a kink near the tip.
**Feet.** The feet should be large, round, heavily furnished with hair between the toes and pads.

# BASENJI
(Variously known as Zande Dog, Belgian Congo Dog, Congo Bush Dog, Bongo Terrier, Congo Terrier, Nyam-Nyam Terrier)

## Good points
● *Adaptable to most climates*
● *Has no bark*
● *Clean*
● *Gentle with children*
● *Intelligent*
● *No 'doggie' smell*

## Take heed
● *Does not like rain*
● *Bitches may come into season only once a year*
● *Mischievous*

The Basenji (the name is the translation of a native word meaning 'bush thing') is an interesting and attractive breed, its main claim to fame being that it has no bark. But only the bark is absent; the Basenji will growl and whine like other breeds, and can express itself feelingly with a distinctive chortle or yodel. The breed's vocal cords are present and it is believed that training, over thousands of years, to hunt game silently may account for their characteristic quietness.

The breed is well known for its gentle disposition and love of children, though it can be aloof with strangers. It has great curiosity and mischievousness.

Appealing features are its curling tail, high set and lying over to one side of the back, its habit of washing with its paw like a cat, and its forehead full of 'worried' wrinkles.

## Size
Ideal height: dog 43cm (17in) at the shoulder; bitch 40.5cm (16in);

but an inch either way should not penalize an otherwise well-balanced specimen. Ideal weight: dog 10.9kg (24lb); bitch 9.5kg (21lb).

## Exercise
The Basenji is a great hunter and if not exercised has a tendency to put on weight. It is fleet-footed, tireless, and enjoys a daily walk and off-the-lead run. It is, incidentally, a breed that is particularly good with horses.

This is a breed that should not be kept in an outside kennel. It is essentially a house dog, which loves to stretch out in front of the fire, or to indulge in its strange habit of reclining in places off the ground. It is suitable for apartment living as long as it is given sufficient exercise.

## Grooming
Regular use of a hound glove is recommended.

## Feeding
About 1½-2 cans of branded dog food (376g, 13.3oz size), with an equal volume of biscuit, or 3 cupfuls of dry food, complete diet, mixed in the proportion of 1 cup of feed to ½ cup of hot or cold water; or ¼ kg (½lb) of fresh meat, with biscuit. Green vegetables should be added to Basenji fare. They are also inveterate grass eaters and should have ample access to fresh grass.

## Origin and history
Dogs of the Basenji type are depicted in many of the carvings in the tombs of the Pharaohs, and it is believed that these dogs were brought as precious gifts by travellers from the lower reaches of the Nile.

The Basenji almost disappeared from public view from Ancient Egyptian times until the mid-19th century, when it was discovered by explorers in the Congo and Southern Sudan.

The foundation stock recognized today derived from the Belgian Congo, with further imports from Sudan and Liberia. It is said that similar dogs are to be found in the Malayan jungle and north of Katmandu, but these do not appear to have been extracted from their homeland.

## SHOW SUMMARY
**General appearance.** The Basenji should be a lightly built, finely boned, aristocratic-looking animal, high on the leg compared with its length, always poised, alert and intelligent.
**Colour.** Pure bright red, or pure black, or black and tan, all with white feet, chest and tail tip.
**Head and skull.** The skull should be flat, well-chiselled and of medium width, tapering towards the nose, with only a slight stop. A black nose is greatly desired.
**Tail.** The tail should be high set with the posterior curve of the buttock extending beyond the root of the tail.
**Feet.** Small, narrow and compact, with deep pads; well-arched toes.

Tibetan Terrier

Manchester Terrier

Basenji

The first successful introduction of the Basenji to Europe was in 1937, the breed appearing at Crufts in that year as the Congo Terrier or Bush Dog. Successful breeding from imported specimens began in America in 1941.

# WEST HIGHLAND WHITE TERRIER

**Good points**
- Easy to train
- Gets on well with other dogs
- Good with children
- Handy size
- Suitable for town or country

**Take heed**
- No drawbacks known

The West Highland White Terrier is a game, hardy little dog that originated in Argyle, Scotland. In recent years it has gained tremendous popularity because of its attractive appearance, sporting instincts and handy size. It gets on well with children and other dogs and makes the ideal family dog.

### Size
About 28cm (11in) at the withers. There is no weight standard for this dog in the United Kingdom or the United States.

### Exercise
The Westie will adapt to town or country, and will live either indoors or in a kennel. However, it will be happiest as a family pet allowed to share the comfort of the fireside, but given adequate free runs in the countryside. Remember that it was originally used as a working terrier, and its job was to hunt fox and badger. It is also, of course, a good ratter. This breed will enjoy an energetic ball game.

### Grooming
Although the Westie may be the ideal choice for someone who wants a healthy and active dog, it is perhaps not so ideal for the show aspirant who does not want to spend much time on grooming. The Westie's coat must be brushed and combed every day, and have surplus stripped twice a year. The neckline is particularly important, and straggly hairs should be removed from ears and tail. Ideally, the Westie's coat should be approximately 5cm (2in) in length, with the neck and throat hair shorter. It is probably wise to ask the breeder to demonstrate what is required before you make your purchase, and to let you have a grooming chart with full instructions. If you feel you cannot handle the task yourself, you can entrust it to a dog grooming parlour.

### Feeding
One to 1½ cans (376g, 13.3oz size) of a branded meaty product with biscuit added in equal part by volume; or 3 cupfuls of a dry, complete food mixed in the proportion of 1 cup of feed to ½ cup of hot or cold water. The Westie loves burrowing in the earth, often retrieving a long-discarded, much-loved bone; so do let it have the occasional marrow or chop bone to get its teeth into—but no splintery bones, please.

### Origin and history
The first West Highland White Terrier clubs were formed in 1905, when breeds such as the Cairn Terrier and Skye Terrier, which in the past had all been classified as Small Highland Working Terriers, attained individual status.

It does appear that in the late 1800s there existed a white Scottish Terrier, or Scottie, a strain of which was bred by Colonel Malcolm of Poltalloch, from which the name Poltalloch Terrier was derived; they were also known as Roseneath Terriers.

### SHOW SUMMARY
**General appearance.** The general appearance of the West Highland White Terrier is that of a small, game, hardy-looking terrier, possessed of no small amount of self-esteem; with a varminty appearance; strongly built, deep in chest and back ribs; level back and powerful quarters on muscular legs, and exhibiting in a marked degree a great combination of strength and activity.
**Colour.** Pure white.
**Head and skull.** The skull should be slightly domed and, when gripped across the forehead, should present a smooth contour. There should be only a very slight tapering from the skull at the level of the ears to the eyes. The distance from the occiput to the eyes should be slightly greater than the length of the foreface. The jaws should be strong and level. The nose must be black and should be fairly large, forming a smooth contour with the muzzle.
**Tail.** About 12.5-15cm (5-6in) long, covered with hard hair, no feather, as straight as possible, carried jauntily, not gay or carried over the back. A long tail is objectionable, and on no account should tails be docked.
**Feet.** The fore/feet are larger than the hind ones, round, proportionate in size, strong, thickly padded and covered with short hard hair. The hind feet are smaller and thickly padded. The undersurface of the pads of the feet and all nails should be black.

# SCOTTISH TERRIER

**Good points**
- Straightforward and honest
- Reliable temperament
- Fine guard
- Utterly loyal
- Home-loving

**Take heed**
- Has little time for strangers; best for a childless couple or unattached owner

The Scottish Terrier or Scottie has been aptly described as a gentleman. It is an honest dog, that will not look for trouble but on finding it will always fight fairly. It is a devoted companion to its owner, but has little time for strangers and is not the most suitable of dogs for a family with children or a couple intending to add to their family. It will fight fox or badger, but enjoys itself just as much in an energetic ball game, and likes nothing better than carrying a stick or a ball in its mouth. Altogether an attractive and sporty little animal.

### Size
Weight: 8.6-10.4kg (19-23lb).
Height: 25-28cm (10-11in).

### Exercise
The Scottie loves nothing more than being out of doors and it would be wrong to deprive it of romps in the garden or regular walks several times a day. It can live happily either indoors or in an outside kennel, heated in winter.

### Grooming
The Scottie needs daily brushing and combing, particularly its fine beard, and should be trimmed in spring and autumn.

### Feeding
Recommended would be 1-1½ cans of a branded meaty product (376g, 13.3oz size), with biscuit added in equal part by volume; or 3 cupfuls of a dry, complete food, mixed in the proportion of 1 cup to ½ cup of hot or cold water.

### Origin and history
The Scottish Terrier, once known as the Aberdeen Terrier, and generally known as the Scottie, has existed in various forms for many centuries, but it was not until after 1800 that line breeding began. The first Scottish Terrier Club was formed in Scotland in 1892, when a standard was laid down for the breed that has changed little up to the present.

### SHOW SUMMARY
**General appearance.** A Scottish Terrier is a sturdy, thickset, short-legged dog of a suitable size to go to ground, alert in carriage, and suggestive of great power and activity in a small compass.
**Colour.** Black, wheaten or brindle of any colour.
**Head and skull.** Without being out of proportion to the size of the dog, the head should be long, the length of skull enabling it to be fairly wide and yet retain a narrow appearance.
**Tail.** Of moderate length to give a general balance to the dog, thick at the root and tapering towards the tip, set on with an upright carriage or with a slight bend.
**Feet.** Of good size, well padded, toes well arched and close-knit.

# SEALYHAM TERRIER

**Good points**
- Beautiful appearance
- Devoted
- Good with children
- Sporting

**Take heed**
- Enjoys a scrap
- Needs lots of grooming
- Obstinate

The Sealyham was bred as a rat and badger hunter but has evolved into an elegant pet and show dog for those with time to devote to its coiffure.

The Sealyham is a game, lovable little terrier that becomes devoted to its owners and is reliable with children. However, it can be obstinate and snappy if not firmly, but kindly, disciplined when young.

### Size
Weight: dog should not exceed 9kg (20lb); bitch should not exceed 8.2kg (18lb). Height should not exceed 30cm (12in) at the shoulder.

### Exercise
This dog will adapt happily to regular walks around the park and off-the-lead runs. But give a Sealyham the chance and it will enjoy getting gloriously dirty scampering in the wet, muddy countryside.

### Grooming
The Sealyham needs hand stripping at least twice a year, and daily combing with a wire comb to remove surplus hair. As mentioned elsewhere, stripping by the inexperienced can prove a disastrous experience for both owner and dog, so do have the job done professionally, or ask an expert to show you how. Clipping is excusable for the older dog, but will ruin the coat for showing.

### Feeding
One can (376g, 13.3oz size) of a branded meaty product, with biscuit added in equal part by volume; or 1½ cupfuls of a dry food, complete diet, mixed in the proportion of 1 cup of feed to ½ cup of hot or cold water. And it will just love bones!

### Origin and history
The Sealyham takes its name from Sealyham in Haverfordwest, Wales, UK, where the breed was created in the mid-1800s, using other terriers with proven ability as hunters of fox, badger and vermin. (Some say that the Sealyham owes its existence to a terrier imported into Wales from Belgium in the 15th century.) Haverfordwest formed the first Sealyham Terrier Club in 1908, and Fred Lewis, founder of the Sealyham Terrier Club, is said to have done much to improve the strain. The breed was recognized by the British Kennel Club three years later. The American Kennel Club also recognized the breed in 1911.

### SHOW SUMMARY
**General appearance.** Should be that of a freely moving and active dog.
**Colour.** Mostly all white, or white with lemon, brown, or badger pied markings on head and ears.
**Head and skull.** The skull should be slightly domed and wide between the ears. Head powerful and long, with a punishing and square jaw. Nose black.
**Tail.** Carried erect.
**Feet.** Round and cat-like, with thick pads.

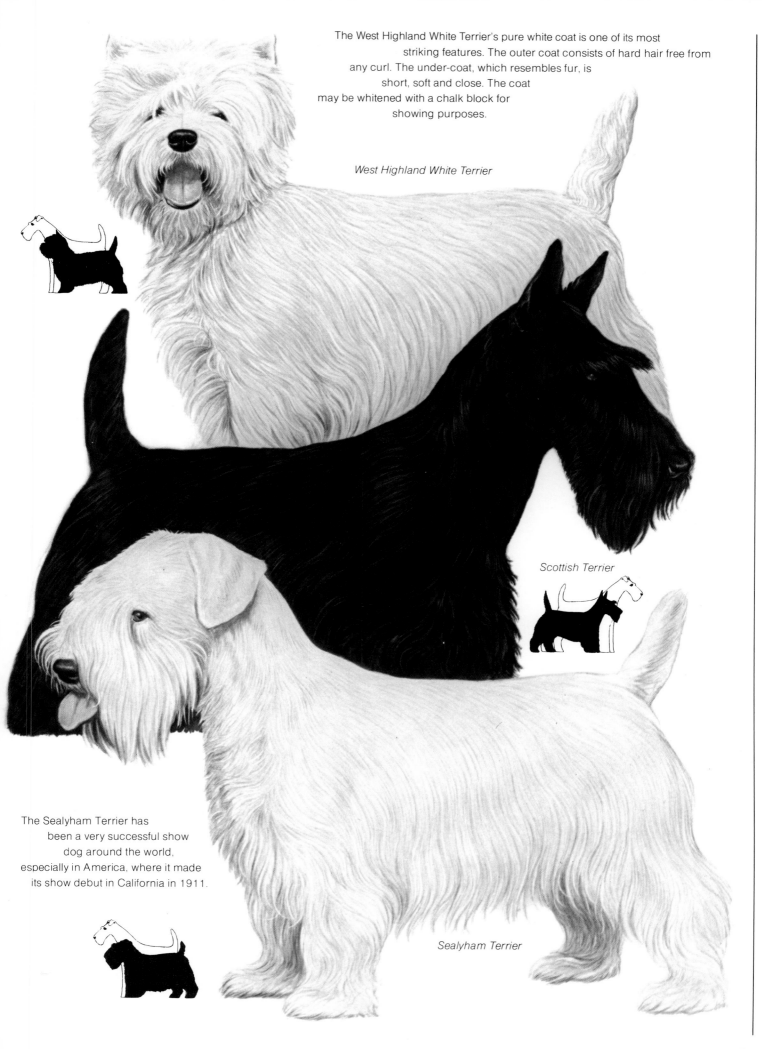

The West Highland White Terrier's pure white coat is one of its most
striking features. The outer coat consists of hard hair free from
any curl. The under-coat, which resembles fur, is
short, soft and close. The coat
may be whitened with a chalk block for
showing purposes.

*West Highland White Terrier*

*Scottish Terrier*

The Sealyham Terrier has
been a very successful show
dog around the world,
especially in America, where it made
its show debut in California in 1911.

*Sealyham Terrier*

# MINIATURE SCHNAUZER

## Good points
● *Intelligent*
● *Obedient*
● *Long-lived*
● *Good with children*

## Take heed
● *Happiest living indoors*

The Miniature Schnauzer is the perfect Schnauzer in miniature, an attractive little dog, with appealing bushy eyebrows. It is good-natured, adores children, and is happiest living with the family indoors, rather than being relegated to an outside kennel. It is long-lived and easy to train, and often does well in obedience competitions.

## Size
The ideal height for bitches shall be 33cm (13in) and for dogs 35.5cm (14in).

## Exercise
The Miniature Schnauzer can be kept in town or country, and does not require a great deal of space, although it does enjoy a garden to romp in and looks forward to good walks and off-the-lead runs.

## Grooming
This breed needs to be hand stripped in spring and summer — more often if a show career is envisaged. Have this professionally done, or get instructions from the breeder — the breed club is sure to have an instruction leaflet — as clumsy, inexperienced hands can ruin a good temperament. A good weekly brushing is essential, and the removal of any dead hair in the under-coat.

## Feeding
Recommended would be ½-1 can (376g, 13.3oz size) of a branded meaty product, with biscuit added in equal part by volume; or 1½ cupfuls of a dry food, complete diet, mixed in the proportion of 1 cup to ½ cup of hot or cold water.

## Origin and history
The Miniature Schnauzer is a replica in miniature of its bigger brother, the Standard Schnauzer, there being some 10cm (4in) difference in height between them. There is strong support for the suggestion that the Miniature Schnauzer evolved through crossing the Standard Schnauzer with the little monkey-faced Affenpinscher, although a Pomeranian or even a Fox Terrier may have been used.

This miniature variety was bred in Germany for at least a century before finding its way to the United Kingdom in 1928, when a black bitch was imported, followed in 1930 by two pepper-and-salt champions. About this time it also began to gain popularity in the United States, where the breed is extremely popular nowadays. Its spread among British fanciers has

*Above: A Miniature Schnauzer, an appealing, good-natured breed.*

been somewhat slower, but the breed has been awarded Challenge Certificates since 1935.

## SHOW SUMMARY
**General appearance.** The Miniature Schnauzer is a powerfully built, robust, sinewy, nearly square dog (length of body is equal to height at shoulder). Its temperament combines high spirits, reliability, strength, endurance and vigour. Expression keen and attitude alert. Correct conformation is of more importance than colour or other purely aesthetic points.
**Colour.** All pepper-and-salt colours in even proportions, or pure black.
**Head and skull.** Head strong and elongated, gradually narrowing from the ears to the eyes and thence toward the tip of the nose. Upper part of the head (occiput to base of forehead) moderately broad between the ears, with flat, creaseless forehead, and well-muscled but not too strongly developed cheeks. Medium stop to accentuate prominent eyebrows. The powerful muzzle formed by the upper and lower jaws (base of forehead to tip of nose) should end in a moderately blunt line, with bristly, stubby moustache and chin whiskers. Ridge of nose straight and running almost parallel to the extension of the forehead. The nose is black and full. Lips should be tight and not overlapping.
**Tail.** Set on and carried high; cut down to three joints.
**Feet.** Short, round and extremely compact, with close-arched toes (cat's paws); deep or thickly padded, pointing forward. Dark nails and hard soles.

# LUNDEHUND
(Puffin Dog; Puffin Hound)

## Good points
● *Alert*
● *Active*
● *Excellent hunter*
● *Faithful companion*

## Take heed
● *No drawbacks known*

The Lundehund has existed for centuries on two islands off the coast of northern Norway, but is little known outside Scandinavia. For many years it was impossible to export a breed member and this may still be the case. The breed is derived from the Miniature Elkhound.

## Size
Weight approximately 5.9-6.4kg (13-14lb). Height: dog 31.5-35.5cm (12½-14in); bitch 30-34cm (12-13½in).

## Exercise
This little dog is a hunter skilful at scaling rocks and precipices. Kept as a pet it is happiest if exercised freely.

## Grooming
Daily brushing with a stiff-bristled brush should be sufficient.

## Feeding
Half to 1 can (376g, 13.3oz size) of a branded, meaty product, with biscuit added in equal part by volume; or 1½ cupfuls of a dry, complete food, mixed in the proportion of 1 cup of feed to ½ cup of hot or cold water.

## Origin and history
The Lundehund, or Puffin Dog, is a Spitz variety that received recognition in Scandinavia in 1943. Its job in life is to locate puffins' nests in rocks and crevices, and to retrieve the eggs and birds, the puffin being a welcome addition to the islanders' meal table. Puffin-hunting is an art that has existed in Scandinavia for at least 400 years.

This dog has five functional toes on each foot (normally there are four); and in the upper part of the ears, the cartilage ends meet and can shut when the ears are partly raised. It is thought that this may prevent water penetrating and damaging the ear.

## SHOW SUMMARY
This breed is not recognized in the United Kingdom or the United States. It is a small variety of Spitz. Colours: black, grey and various shades of brown with white. The coat is rather rough, dense and close to the body, and the tail, which is set on rather high, has a short dense coat, but no flag.

# SCHIPPERKE

## Good points
● *Affectionate*
● *Excellent guard*
● *Good with children*
● *Handy size*
● *Hardy*

## Take heed
● *Not suitable for kennel life*
● *Needs affection and individual attention*

The Schipperke is a delightful breed that originated in Belgium, where its job was to guard canal barges when they had been tied up for the night. The name Schipperke is, in fact, Flemish for 'little captain'.

Apart from being an excellent guard dog, the Schipperke is a most affectionate animal, and particularly good with children. It is also hardy and long lived. However, it needs individual attention and likes to be treated as a member of the family; it also takes a while to accept strangers.

## Size
The weight should be about 5.4-7.3kg (12-16lb).

## Exercise
A Schipperke can walk up to 6 miles or more without any sign of fatigue; but it can manage with a great deal less exercise if its owner lives in a town.

## Grooming
The Schipperke has a dense hard coat that needs very little regular grooming.

## Feeding
Feeding is no problem: a Schipperke will eat anything that is offered to it, and one good meal a day, perhaps with biscuit at night, will suffice. Recommended for its size would be ½-1 can of a branded meaty product (376g, 13.3oz size), with biscuit added in equal part by volume; or 1½ cupfuls of a dry, complete food mixed in the proportion of 1 cup of feed to ½ cup of hot or cold water.

## Origin and history
The Schipperke originated in Belgium, but is often thought to be a Dutch dog, probably because Belgium and the Netherlands have been one country in the past. The breed is well over 100 years old; some claim it to be nearer 200 years old, but there are no records to support this theory.

How the breed evolved is subject to conjecture. Some classify it as a member of the Spitz family, others as the result of a terrier/Pomeranian cross. However, it seems likely that the Schipperke and the Groenendael have a common ancestor, the Schipperke closely resembling a smaller example of that other fine Belgian breed.

## SHOW SUMMARY
**General appearance.** A small, cobby animal, with a sharp expression, and intensely lively, presenting the appearance of being always on the alert.
**Colour.** Should be black, but other whole colours are permissible.
**Head and skull.** Head foxy in type, skull not round, but fairly broad, flat and with little stop. The muzzle should be moderate in length, fine but not weak, and well filled out under the eyes. Nose black and small.
**Hindquarters.** Fine compared to the foreparts; muscular and well-developed thighs; tail-less rump, well rounded. Legs strong and muscular, hocks well let down.
**Feet.** Should be small, cat-like and standing well on the toes.

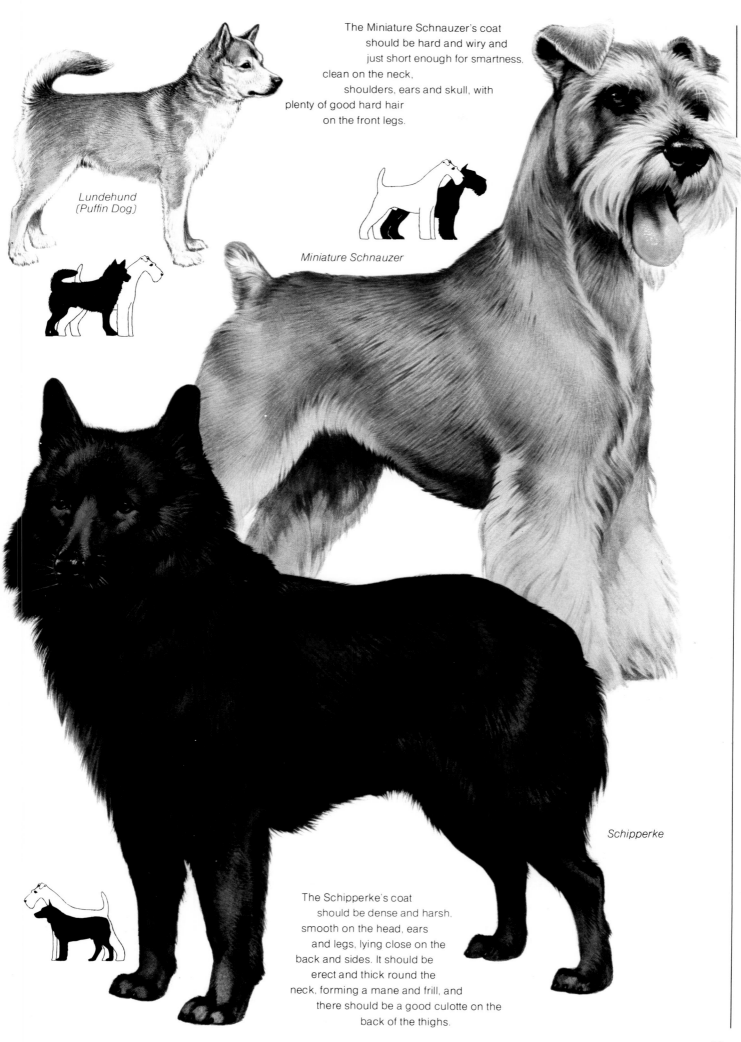

Lundehund
(Puffin Dog)

The Miniature Schnauzer's coat
should be hard and wiry and
just short enough for smartness,
clean on the neck,
shoulders, ears and skull, with
plenty of good hard hair
on the front legs.

Miniature Schnauzer

Schipperke

The Schipperke's coat
should be dense and harsh,
smooth on the head, ears
and legs, lying close on the
back and sides. It should be
erect and thick round the
neck, forming a mane and frill, and
there should be a good culotte on the
back of the thighs.

# AMERICAN COCKER SPANIEL

## Good points
● Adaptable to town or country living
● Beautiful
● Excellent family pet
● Intelligent
● Obedient

## Take heed
● Needs lots of grooming

The American Cocker Spaniel is an excellent hunter, and excels in flushing out and retrieving birds. It is also extremely popular as a household pet, and is an attractive, affectionate, adaptable animal and an excellent companion.

## Size
The ideal height at the withers for an adult dog is 38cm (15in), and for an adult bitch 35.5cm (14in). Height may vary 13mm (½in) above or below this ideal. A dog whose height exceeds 39.5cm (15½in), or a bitch whose height exceeds 37cm (14½in), or an adult bitch whose height is less than 34cm (13½in) should be penalized.

## Exercise
It must be remembered that the Cocker Spaniel was originally bred for hunting and, although it adapts happily to the role of companion and family pet, it will obviously fit in best with families who are prepared to give it two good walks a day and have a garden for it to romp in.

## Grooming
The American Cocker, with its luxuriant coat, needs daily brushing and combing, and a bath and trim every 8-10 weeks. It is best to ask the breeder for advice, or to visit a professional dog groomer, because the skull and muzzle hair must be trimmed to precise accepted lengths with electric clippers, the neck and shoulders carefully scissored, and feathering left on the legs, ears and belly. Feet must also be trimmed. Obviously you may wish to attend to this ritual yourself, but it is advisable to be shown the procedure by an expert first.

## Feeding
Recommended would be 1-1½ cans of a branded meaty product (376g, 13.3oz size) with biscuit added in equal part by volume; or 3 cupfuls of a dry food, complete diet, mixed in the proportion of 1 cup of feed to ½ cup of hot or cold water.

## Origin and history
The American Cocker is smaller than the English Cocker, has a much thicker coat and, although originating from England, has been bred along different lines in the United States. Its elegant trousers and length of coat are the simplest means of clear identification.

An American Cocker was first shown in America at Manchester, New Hampshire, in September 1883, and when permission was given by the American Kennel Club for the two varieties to be shown, there was great enthusiasm for the American Cocker.

## SHOW SUMMARY
**General appearance.** A very serviceable-looking dog with a refined head; standing on straight legs and well up at the shoulders; of compact body and wide, muscular quarters. The American Cocker Spaniel's sturdy body, powerful quarters and strong, well-boned legs show it to be a dog capable of considerable speed combined with great endurance. Above all it must be free and merry, sound, well balanced throughout, keen to work, equable in temperament and with no suggestion of timidity.

**Colour.** Blacks should be jet black; shadings of brown or liver in the sheen of the coat are not desirable. Black and tan (classified under solid colours) should have definite tan markings on a jet black body. The tan markings should be distinct and plainly visible, and the colour of the tan may be from the lightest cream to the darkest red colour. The amount of tan markings should be restricted to 10 percent or less of the colour of the animal; tan markings in excess of 10 percent should be penalized. Tan markings not readily visible in the ring, or the absence of tan markings in any of the specified locations, should be penalized.

In all the above solid colours, a small amount of white on chest and throat, though not desirable, is allowed; but white in any other location should be penalized. Parti-colours: Two or more definite colours appearing in clearly defined markings are essential. Primary colour that is 90 percent or more should be penalized; secondary colour or colours that are limited to one location should also be penalized. Roans are classified as parti-colours and may be of any of the usual roaning patterns. Tricolours are any of the above colours combined with tan markings. It is preferable that the tan markings be located in the same pattern as for black and tan.

**Head and skull.** There should be a good square muzzle with a distinct stop midway between the tip of the nose and the occiput. The skull should be well developed, cleanly chiselled, neither too fine nor too coarse. The cheek bones should not be prominent. The nose should be sufficiently wide to allow for the acute scenting power of this breed.

**Tail.** This should be set on slightly lower than the line of the back; it must be carried in line with the back and never cocked up. The tail should not be docked too long nor too short to interfere with its action.

**Feet.** Feet should be firm, thickly padded and cat-like.

# ENGLISH COCKER SPANIEL

## Good points
● Affectionate, gentle nature
● Excellent gundog
● Good with children
● Long lived
● Merry temperament

## Take heed
● Overfeeding will cause weight problems
● Keep ears out of feed bowl

The 'merry' Cocker, as it is called, makes an ideal family pet – a dog for Dad to take out shooting, or for the children to romp with in the garden. It is manageable, intelligent, and a good all-purpose gundog, second to none at flushing out game.

## Size
The weight should be about 12.7-14.5kg (28-32lb). The height at the withers should be: dog 39.5-40.5cm (15½-16in); bitch 38-39.5cm (15-15½in).

Above: The English Cocker Spaniel, here with pup, makes a gentle pet.

## Exercise
This is an active dog that needs regular exercise. It adores the country and is likely to return from a walk with tail wagging and covered with mud, so it is not perhaps the ideal choice for smart town dwellers; but it does enjoy home comforts, such as a place beside a warm fire.

## Grooming
The Cocker requires daily brushing and combing, care being taken that its coat does not become matted. Particular care must be taken that the ears do not become tangled; and watch out that they do not flop into the feed bowl!

You might consider taping them back while the dog is eating.

## Origin and history
The Cocker Spaniel is particularly popular in Britain, and in the United States it is known as the English Cocker. It is also sometimes referred to as the 'merry' Cocker because of its happy, lively temperament and constantly wagging tail. Other titles bestowed upon it have been the Cocking Spaniel or Cocker, because of its one-time prowess at flushing out woodcock.

The Cocker Spaniel did however originate in Spain – whence the name 'spaniel' – and its ancestry can be traced back to the 14th century. It is believed to have been used in various countries in falconry. Today, however, it is in its element rabbit hunting, flushing out game for its master, then remaining motionless until a shot has been fired. It is also well able to retrieve and is an ideal choice for both working trials and dog training competitions.

## Feeding
Recommended would be 1-1½ cans of a branded meaty product (376g, 13.3oz size), with biscuit added in equal part by volume; or 3 cupfuls of a dry food, complete diet, mixed in the proportion of 1 cup of feed to ½ cup of hot or cold water. Obviously rations will need to be stepped up if the dog is taking vigorous exercise. This is a breed that will plead endearingly for titbits, which should be denied if the owner is to avoid an overweight or smelly pet.

With correct diet and exercise the Cocker Spaniel proves to be one of the healthiest and most long-lived of dogs. Its beautiful, appealing eyes make it difficult to refuse it anything, and there are few breeds in the world to challenge its beauty as a pup.

## SHOW SUMMARY
**General appearance.** A merry, sturdy sporting dog. The Cocker Spaniel should be well balanced and compact and should measure about the same from the withers to the ground as from the withers to the root of the tail.

**Colour.** Various; in self-colours no white is allowed except on the chest.

**Head and skull.** There should be a good square muzzle with a distinct stop, which should be midway between the tip of the nose and the occiput. The skull should be well developed, cleanly chiselled, neither too fine nor too coarse. The cheek bones should not be prominent. The nose should be sufficiently wide to allow for the acute scenting power of this breed.

**Tail.** The tail should be set on slightly lower than the line of the back; it must be carried in line with the back and never cocked up. The tail should not be docked too long nor too short to interfere with its action.

**Feet.** These should be firm, thickly padded and cat-like.

The most noticeable difference between the American and
English Cocker Spaniels is one of size; bred to flush and retrieve
smaller game in America, the American Cocker
Spaniel is a correspondingly smaller breed. Both
breeds have achieved great success in the
show ring, the American being generally
shown with a more profuse coat
than the English breed.

*American Cocker Spaniel*

*English Cocker Spaniel*

# BEAGLE

### Good points
- *Adores children*
- *Good with other pets*
- *Intelligent*
- *Merry and affectionate*

### Take heed
- *Will wander if gate is left ajar*
- *Will soon grow fat if given titbits*

The Beagle is a merry, affectionate little fellow, loving humans and other pets alike. The Beagle adores children and is a wonderful companion, equally ready for a romp or to lie by your feet on the hearthrug. This breed is equally at home in a small house or a mansion, and will guard its home and owner faithfully. It is not a barker, being mostly heard at the chase, in full cry. But, like most other hounds, it has the wanderlust, so care must be taken never to leave the garden gate ajar.

### Size
It is desirable that height from ground to withers should neither exceed 40.5cm (16in) nor fall below 33cm (13in). In the United States the height limit is 38cm (15in) at the shoulder.

### Exercise
Exercise is no problem, because Beagles keep themselves fit as easily in a small garden as on a farm. But, like most dogs, they should be taken for a walk every day. They are notoriously healthy and robust, so you rarely need the services of a veterinarian.

### Grooming
The Short coat of the Beagle is tough and weatherproof, and needs no grooming. It is recom-

*Below: These adorable Beagle pups, playing with their master's slipper, may one day be heard in full cry on the scent of a hare.*

mended that after a muddy walk the Beagle is left in its box for an hour to clean itself up.

### Feeding
One meal a day is sufficient for a full-grown Beagle, with no titbits afterwards, as this is a breed that is inclined to put on weight. One to 1½ cans (376g, 13.3oz size) of a complete meaty diet, to which biscuit should be added in equal part by volume, is adequate; or 3 cupfuls of a dry food, complete diet, mixed in the proportion of 1 cup of feed to ½ cup of hot or cold water.

### Origin and history
The Beagle is one of the smallest of the hounds, embodying all their virtues in the least compass. An ancient breed, it has proved a joy to sportsmen for hundreds of years; Beagles were first mentioned by name in writings published in 1475. Followed on foot and on horseback, they have been hunted in packs after hare from time immemorial, and were first imported into the United States for this purpose.

Beagles are esteemed all over the world and have hunted many different quarries in varying climates, including jackal in the Sudan and Palestine, wild pig in Ceylon and deer in Scandinavia. In the USA and Canada they are used as gundogs to seek out and retrieve game, and to hunt by scent in competitive Field Trials.

### SHOW SUMMARY
**General appearance.** A sturdy and compactly built hound, it should convey the impression of quality without coarseness.
**Colour.** Any recognized hound colour other than liver. Tip of stern should be white.
**Head and skull.** Head fair length, powerful in the dog without being coarse, but finer in the bitch; free from frown and excessive wrinkle. Skull slightly domed, moderately wide, with indication of peak. Stop

*Above: The Beagle enjoys daily walks and a chance to wander.*

well defined and dividing length between occiput and tip of nose as equally as possible. Muzzle not snipy, lips reasonably well flewed. Nose broad and nostrils well expanded; preferably black, but less pigmentation is permissible in the lighter coloured hounds.
**Tail.** Sturdy and of moderate length. Set on high and carried gaily but not curled over the back or inclined forward from the root. Well covered with hair, especially on the underside.
**Feet.** Tight and firm. Well knuckled up and strongly padded. Not hare-footed. Nails short.

# DREVER

### Good points
- *Equable temperament*
- *Excellent nose*
- *Steady but slow worker*

### Take heed
- *No drawbacks known*

The Drever is little known outside Scandinavia. It is, however, one of Sweden's most popular dogs.

It is a steady, though slow worker, and has a good nose for trekking fox, wild boar and roe deer, and will also drive them towards the gun. It has found favour in Scandinavia as a house pet. A similar dog, the Strellufsstövare, is bred in Denmark.

### Size
Height: dog 31.5-38cm (12½-15in); bitch 29-35.5cm (11½-14in).

### Exercise
Needs plenty of exercise. Happiest when hunting.

### Grooming
Normal daily brushing.

### Feeding
One to 1½ cans (376g, 13.3oz size) of a branded, meaty product, with biscuit added in equal part by volume; or 3 cupfuls of a dry, complete food, mixed in the proportion of 1 cup of feed to ½ cup of hot or cold water.

### Origin and history
The Drever is one of the most popular dogs in Sweden, a national breed said to have been derived from the mating of other Swedish hunting dogs with Dachshunds — there is something of the Dachshund and the Beagle in their appearance. At the beginning of the century, the breed was known by the German name of Dachsbracke. However, as it began to alter to meet Swedish requirements, the name was changed and recognition sought with the Swedish Kennel Club under the new name of Drever. This was achieved in 1949 and recognition by the FCI followed in 1953. This breed is not recognized by the British or American Kennel Clubs. It is a strong, muscular dog, bearing some resemblance to the Dachshund. Colours are red and white, yellow and white, or tricolour. White must not predominate but must be apparent from all angles.

# DACHSBRACKE
(See Drever)

### Good points
- *Brave*
- *Dedicated hunter*
- *Equable temperament*

### Take heed
- *No drawbacks known*

The Dachsbracke is little known outside Germany. The breed is a close relative of the Swedish Drever and many authorities refer to the Dachsbracke and Drever as one. There are three varieties, the Westphalian, the Erz Mountains and the Alpine; the former, the smallest of the three, is almost extinct.

The breed stands between 34 and 42cm (13½-16½in), has a short, dense coat and bears a passing resemblance to the Dachshund. A litter was bred in Britain in 1949. However, the Dachsbracke is not recognized by the British or American Kennel Clubs. It gained recognition in Germany in 1896.

The Beagle is renowned for its hunting qualities throughout the world. In America, where Beagles are used for hunting hares, two size varieties are recognized: those not exceeding 33cm (13in) at the shoulder, and those over 33cm but not exceeding 38cm (15in).

The patches of white on the Drever's coat help to make the dog more visible when it is being used to track down deer in the thick forests of its Swedish homeland.

*Beagle*

*Drever*

*Dachsbracke*

In its native Germany, the Dachsbracke excels at tracking prey by scent in rugged country, where slow but steady progress is the best method of hunting animals such as deer.

# SWEDISH VALLHUND
(Västgötaspets)

### Good points
- Active
- Excellent drover/cattle dog
- Loyal

### Take heed
- No known drawbacks

The Vallhund or Västgötaspets is a Swedish breed, similar in appearance to the Welsh Corgi. It is an active, intelligent worker and is rapidly gaining popularity in many parts of the world.

### Size
Height: dog 33cm (13in), bitch 31.2cm (12.3in).

### Exercise
Fares best if given plenty of exercise.

### Grooming
Normal daily brushing.

### Feeding
One to 1½ cans (376g, 13.3oz size) of a branded meaty product, with biscuit added in equal part by volume; or 3 cupfuls of a dry food, complete diet, mixed in the proportion of 1 cup of feed to ½ cup of hot or cold water.

### Origin and history
The Västgötaspets, to give it its Swedish name, looks something like a Cardigan/Pembroke Corgi cross. There is certainly a connection between the Corgi and this attractive breed, but it is impossible to determine whether it evolved as the result of Vikings taking Corgis to Sweden, or if Swedish dogs brought to Britain developed the Corgi. The Swedes certainly claim credit for this fine little cattle dog, which owes its present development and recognition to a Swedish breeder, Björn von Rosen.

*Below: The Vallhund closely resembles the Welsh Corgi in appearance. It was developed in Sweden as a fine cattle dog.*

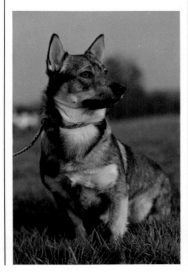

# PEMBROKE WELSH CORGI

### Good points
- Devoted companion
- Excellent guard
- Fond of children
- Hardy
- Tireless

### Take heed
- Needs training when young – the inherent tendency to nip must be discouraged

The Welsh Corgi (Pembroke) has, like the Cardigan, been worked in South Wales for many centuries, but has evolved as a popular and affectionate pet, particularly because it is a breed much favoured by the British royal family, whose pets have been known to take the occasional, much publicized nip!

### Size
Weight: dog 9-10.9kg (20-24lb); bitch 8.2-10kg (18-22lb). Height: 25-30cm (10-12in) at the shoulder.

### Exercise
Although traditionally a worker, the Pembroke adapts well to life as a domestic pet, with daily walks of average length. But beware: if you do not give sufficient exercise this breed will soon lose its figure!

### Grooming
Daily brushing needed. The breed has a water-resistant coat.

### Feeding
Give ½-1 can (376g, 13.3oz size) of a branded meaty product, with biscuit added in equal part by volume; or 1½ cupfuls of a dry food, complete diet, mixed in the proportion of 1 cup of feed to ½ cup of hot or cold water.

### Origin and history
The Welsh Corgi (Pembroke) has worked in South Wales since the Domesday Book survey was instigated by William the Conqueror in the 11th century. Its traditional task was to control the movement of cattle by nipping at their ankles, and then getting quickly out of range. It has, however, a bolder temperament than the Cardigan.

Some say that the Pembroke derives from stock brought to Wales by Flemish weavers who settled in the locality and crossed their dogs with Welsh native stock; others point out the similarity that exists between the Welsh Corgi (Pembroke) and the Swedish Västgötaspets, suggesting that trading between the Welsh and the Swedes introduced the breed to Wales.

In any event, the Welsh Corgi (Pembroke) has been exhibited in Britain since 1925, receiving separate classification from the Welsh Corgi (Cardigan) in 1934. It is, perhaps, one of the best-known breeds in Britain, because of its association with Her Majesty Queen Elizabeth II.

*Above: Pembroke Welsh Corgis make most affectionate pets.*

### SHOW SUMMARY
**General appearance.** Low-set, strong, sturdily built, alert and active, giving an impression of substance and stamina in a small space; outlook bold, expression intelligent and workman-like. The movement should be free and active, elbows fitting closely to the sides, neither loose nor tied. Forelegs should move well forward, without too much lift, in unison with the thrusting action of the hind legs.

**Colour.** Self-colours in red, sable, fawn, black and tan, or with white markings on legs, chest and neck. Some white on head and foreface is permissible.

**Head and skull.** Head foxy in shape and appearance, with alert and intelligent expression; skull fairly wide, and flat between the ears; moderate amount of stop. Length of foreface in proportion to the skull as 3:5. Muzzle slightly tapering. Nose black.

**Tail.** Short, preferably natural.

**Feet.** Oval, the two centre toes slightly in advance of the two outer ones; pads strong and well arched; nails short.

# CARDIGAN WELSH CORGI

### Good points
- Devoted companion
- Excellent guard
- Fond of children
- Hardy
- Quieter temperament than the Pembroke
- Tireless

### Take heed
- This breed had eye defects in the past, so seek a veterinarian's advice if your choice gives you cause for concern

The Welsh Corgi (Cardigan) has been known and worked in South Wales for centuries. It is hardy, fond of children, and tireless, and, despite its original task of nipping the heels of cattle to bring them into line, has a more equable temperament than the Pembroke, and is less likely to nip the heels of unsuspecting visitors.

### Size
Height as near as possible to 30cm (12in) at the shoulder. Weight: dog 10-11.8 kg (22-26lb); bitch 9-10.9kg (20-24lb).

### Exercise
Although traditionally a worker, the Cardigan adapts well to life as a domestic pet, with daily walks of average length. But beware: if you do not give sufficient exercise this breed will soon lose its figure!

### Grooming
Daily brushing needed. The breed has a water-resistant coat.

### Feeding
Give ½-1 can (376g, 13.3oz size) of a branded meaty product, with biscuit added in equal part by volume; or 1½ cupfuls of a dry food, complete diet, mixed in the proportion of 1 cup of food to ½ cup of hot or cold water.

### Health care
Avoid letting your pet jump from heights, especially if overweight; this could lead to painful spine trouble. See also the remarks above on eye defects (progressive retinal atrophy); fortunately, these have now been almost eradicated from the breed.

### Origin and history
The Welsh Corgi (Cardigan) has worked in South Wales since the Domesday Book survey was instigated by William the Conqueror in the 11th century. Its traditional task was to control the movement of cattle by nipping at their ankles, and then getting quickly out of range.

The breed first made its appearance in the British show ring in 1925, classified as one breed with the Welsh Corgi (Pembroke); it received separate classification in 1934. Welsh folklore contains many references to this dependable, ancient breed, which has perhaps missed out on popularity due to the British royal family's particular fondness for its Pembrokeshire cousin.

### SHOW SUMMARY
**General appearance.** Expression as foxy as possible; alertness essential; the body to measure about 91.5cm (36in) from point of nose to tip of tail.

**Colour.** Any colour except pure white.

**Head and skull.** Head foxy in shape and appearance. Skull fairly wide and flat between the ears, tapering towards the eyes, above which it is slightly domed. Muzzle should measure about 7.5cm (3in) in length (or in proportion to the skull as 3:5) and taper towards the snout. Nose black (except in blue merles), slightly projecting and in no sense blunt, with nostrils of moderate size. Under-jaw should be clean cut and strong but without prominence.

**Tail.** Moderately long and set in line with the body (not curled over the back) and resembling that of a fox.

**Feet.** Round and well padded. All dew-claws removed. Rather large.

An ancient breed, the Swedish Vallhund has been part of the agricultural scene in the south and midlands of Sweden since time immemorial, but taken so much for granted that at the beginning of this century it had almost disappeared as a pure breed. Although it resembles the Pembroke Corgi in appearance, in contrast to the bright colours associated with that breed, this little dog has a grey, brownish-yellow or brindle coat.

Swedish Vallhund

Pembroke Welsh Corgi

Cardigan Welsh Corgi

Lapphund

Iceland Dog

Border Collie

# A
# Selection of
# MEDIUM DOGS

Medium-sized dogs are the most popular. The medium-sized dog is not, perhaps, so ostentatious as the animal of diminutive or gargantuan proportions, and so tends to be accepted most readily as part and parcel of the average domestic scene. The couple with a medium-sized house and a medium-sized garden naturally choose a dog that conforms with their life style. In the eyes of its owners, the dog is neither so small as to make them look ridiculous nor so large as to frighten away their visitors. It does not cause them worry about providing exercise and space, or anxiety over the cost of feeding. The medium-sized dog is big enough to play tirelessly with the children, once it is fully grown, and will be a companion for Dad and a faithful protector for the woman of the family. The middle course is often the best.

Medium-sized dogs are usually easiest to find and to cater for. Because their puppies are much sought after, breeders are rarely in short supply. Similarly, baskets, cots and other accessories are usually made with the average pet in mind.

There is a medium-sized breed to suit everyone. The man or woman with a wish to enter their pet in obedience competitions could not make a better choice than a Border Collie; a Whippet should satisfy the buyer who wants an elegant animal that can also share his sporting interests; and there is a spaniel variety suitable for any huntsman. The traditional Bulldog could not be better for a man who is getting on in years, and wants a dog that will not walk him off his feet. And the Beagle or the Basset Hound is ideal for any couple who want an amusing and affectionate pet, but accept that, hound-like, it will give them the slip if it can, and wander off, nose to the ground on the trail of some scent-filled adventure.

# BRITTANY SPANIEL

## Good points
- *Affectionate*
- *Excellent pointer*
- *Good nose*
- *Tireless*
- *Loyal*

## Take heed
- *A devoted, sensitive dog that needs kind handling*

The Brittany Spaniel combines well the roles of hunter and companion. It has a natural talent for pointing and has been described as more like a setter than a spaniel. It has an excellent nose, and can cope with difficult terrain. It is, however, a sensitive animal that expects, and deserves, every consideration from its master. It is easily distinguishable by its short, stumpy tail. This breed is relatively unknown in the United Kingdom, but has been successful in Field Trials in the USA.

## Size
Height: maximum 52cm (20½in), minimum 46.5cm (18¼in); ideal for dog 49-51cm (19¼-20in), for bitch 47.5-50cm (18¾-19¾in).

## Exercise
Relishes plenty of exercise.

## Grooming
Daily brushing. Take care that foreign bodies do not lodge in ears, eyes or paws.

## Feeding
One to 1½ cans (376g, 13.3oz size) of a branded meaty product, with biscuit added in equal part by volume; or 3 cupfuls of a dry food, complete diet, mixed in the proportion of 1 cup of feed to ½ cup of hot or cold water.

## Origin and history
The Brittany probably originated either in Spain or in the Argoat Forests of Brittany. There is also a story that one of the red and white English Setters of a Breton count mated with a Breton bitch, thus starting the development of the Brittany Spaniel.

## SHOW SUMMARY
**General appearance.** A small dog, elegant but vigorous, compact and stocky. The movement is energetic, the expression intelligent, and it has the general look of a fine spaniel.
**Colour.** Orange and white, maroon and white, black and white, tricolour or marked with one or the other of these colours.
**Head and skull.** Skull average length, rounded; hollow stop obvious although lightly falling in or sloping. Forehead shorter than the larger axis of the skull; straight or slightly curved, in the proportion of 3:2 to the skull. Nose a deep shade, according to the colour of the dog. Nostrils well open; nose a little angular. Lips thin and receding; upper lip slightly overlapping the lower.
**Tail.** Straight or drooping, if the animal is not in action; always short, about 10cm (4in); often a trifle crooked and ending in a tuft.
**Feet.** Closed toes, with a little hair between them.

# WELSH SPRINGER SPANIEL

- *Loyal*
- *Willing*
- *Fine gundog*
- *Excellent nose*
- *Good water dog*
- *Makes good pet*

## Take heed
- *Needs training or could become a destructive hunter*

The Welsh Springer Spaniel is a lively dog with plenty of enthusiasm and endurance. It is somewhere between the little Cocker Spaniel and the English Springer in stature. It is a tireless breed, and, in common with most spaniels, provided it is given plenty of exercise and correct feeding it will live to a ripe old age.

## Size
Dog up to 48cm (19in) in height at shoulder, and bitch 46cm (18in) approximately.

## Exercise
Like most spaniels the Welsh Springer is essentially a working animal and is not ideally suited for apartment life or for those with insufficient time to take it for lengthy walks.

## Grooming
Similar care to other spaniels, with regular brushing and combing.

## Feeding
Recommended would be 1-1½ cans (376g, 13.3oz size) of a branded meaty product, with biscuit added in equal part by volume; or 3 cupfuls of a dry, complete diet mixed in the proportion of 1 cup of feed to ½ cup of hot or cold water.

## Origin and history
A dog that would seem to be a forerunner of the Welsh Springer Spaniel is mentioned in the earliest records of the Laws of Wales, circa AD 1300, and indeed it appears that even before that time a similar white spaniel with red markings had been associated with the region. The Welsh Springer Spaniel is, in fact, very similar to the Brittany Spaniel, and makes a first-class gundog and household pet.

## SHOW SUMMARY
**General appearance.** A symmetrical, compact, strong, merry, very active dog; not stilty (i.e. stiff in appearance); obviously built for endurance and hard work. A quick and active mover displaying plenty of push and drive.
**Colour.** Rich red and white only.
**Head and skull.** Skull proportionate, of moderate length, slightly domed, with a clearly defined stop, and well chiselled below the eyes. Muzzle of medium length, straight, fairly square; the nostrils well developed and flesh-coloured or dark. A short, chubby head is objectionable.
**Tail.** Well set on and low, never carried above the level of the back; lightly feathered and lively in action.
**Feet.** Round, with thick pads. Firm and cat-like, not too large or spreading.

# WETTERHOUN
(Dutch Water Spaniel)

## Good points
- *Excellent watchdog*
- *Fearless*
- *Hardworking*
- *Impervious to weather conditions*
- *Intelligent*

## Take heed
- *Somewhat aggressive – needs firm handling*

The Wetterhoun, or Dutch Water Spaniel, was registered in Holland in 1942. However, it was known for many years before that, although then, as now, almost exclusively in Holland. It is an intelligent and fearless hunter, and is now often kept as a household companion. However, its somewhat aggressive nature, inherited from years of hunting, makes firm early training necessary.

## Size
Height at withers: dog about 54.5cm (21½in); bitch should be slightly smaller.

## Exercise
Needs plenty of exercise.

## Grooming
Regular brushing.

## Feeding
One to 1½ cans (376g, 13.3oz size) of a branded meaty product, with biscuit added in equal part by volume; or 3 cupfuls of a dry food, complete diet, mixed in the proportion of 1 cup of feed to ½ cup of hot or cold water.

## Origin and history
Bred from dogs used for otter hunting, the Wetterhoun has evolved as a strong and fearless hunter, much prized as a guard dog. It has in the past been crossed with the Stabyhoun, but is a larger, sturdier dog.

## SHOW SUMMARY
**General characteristics.** A modest dog that, many years ago, was used as an otter hound. It is of solid build, without being either coarse or heavy. In general appearance it seems stronger and more compact than the Stabyhoun. Its skin fits closely to the body without forming any wrinkles, even at the throat. The lips are not pendulous. Its temperament is much more aggressive than that of the Stabyhoun: it is courageous on the attack, and highly prized as a fine guard dog.
**Colour.** Black, brown-white, blue-white.
**Head and skull.** Lean and strong, size in proportion to body. Skull and muzzle of equal length. The skull is slightly rounded and gives the impression of being wider than it is long; it merges well with the cheeks, the muscles of which are of normal development. The nose is large, with open nostrils; black in black or black-and-white dogs, brown in brown dogs; not cleft. The muzzle is strong and narrows gradually towards the nose without being pointed; rather blunt. The nasal bridge is straight, and thus, seen in profile, neither arched nor hollowed; it is broad as seen from above. The lips are close fitting, not pendulous. The teeth are strong and meet in a scissor bite. The stop is not accentuated; the passage from skull to muzzle is gradual.
**Tail.** Set on at moderate height; curled in a spiral, over the croup. The spiral is the chief ornament, and typical of the breed.
**Feet.** Well rounded, with well-developed pads.

*Below: The Wetterhoun is a popular guard and farm dog in its native Holland. Its dense curly coat is impervious to bad weather.*

Although the Brittany Spaniel was not officially recognized in France until 1907, from reports of hunting in the mid-1800s, it appears that its progenitors were popular with poachers because of their excellent pointing and retrieving ability. First introduced into the United States in 1931, it is the only pointing Spaniel to be recognized by the American Kennel Club.

*Brittany Spaniel*

*Welsh Springer Spaniel*

The Welsh Springer Spaniel, or 'starter' as it is known in Wales, is an active, hard-working dog with a hardy constitution. Able to withstand a rigorous climate, and having a long, water-resistant coat, it makes an excellent hunter at all seasons.

# FIELD SPANIEL

**Good points**
- *Sensible*
- *Intelligent*
- *Excellent in the field*
- *Affectionate*
- *Docile temperament*

**Take heed**
- *No known drawbacks*

The Field Spaniel is of similar origin to the Cocker, and it was not until 1892 that they were categorized as separate breeds, after which the Cocker Spaniel improved dramatically and the Field Spaniel did not, becoming, in fact, extremely long bodied and short legged. However, the Field Spaniel Society was reformed in the United Kingdom in 1948 and —thanks to tremendous work and enthusiasm—a standard type has evolved that is breeding true; but it is little known, although recognized, in the United States. The passing of the Field Spaniel would be a tragedy, as it is an extremely docile animal, excellent in the field and a fine house pet. It is intelligent and also has a very steady temperament.

**Size**
Weight: about 15.9-22.7kg (35-50lb). Height: about 46cm (18in) to the shoulder.

**Exercise**
It would be a great pity to keep a Field Spaniel in an apartment or a city environment where it would not get the lengthy walks and runs that it needs and deserves.

**Grooming**
A daily brushing and comb will suffice, taking care that the coat does not become tangled or matted and that nothing becomes lodged between the toes.

**Feeding**
Recommended would be 1-1½ cans (376g, 13.3oz size) of a branded meaty product, with biscuit added in equal part by volume; or 3 cupfuls of a dry, complete diet mixed in the proportion of 1 cup of feed to ½ cup of hot or cold water.

**Origin and history**
The history of the Field Spaniel runs parallel with that of the Cocker, and until the breeds were separated in 1892 they were shown as Field Spaniels under and over 11.3kg (25lb). The breed is recognized in the United States, but there are few registrations.

**SHOW SUMMARY**
**General appearance.** A well-balanced, noble sporting dog; built for activity and endurance; a combination of beauty and utility; unusually docile.
**Colour.** The Field Spaniel should be a self-coloured dog in black, liver, golden liver, mahogany red, roan, or any one of these colours with tan over the eyes and on the cheeks, feet and pasterns. Other colours, such as black and white, liver and white, red or orange and white, although they do not debar a dog, are a fault.
**Head and skull.** The head should be as characteristic as that of the Bulldog or the Bloodhound; its very stamp and countenance should at once convey the impression of high breeding, character and nobility. Skull should be well developed, with a distinct occipital protuberance, which gives the character alluded to; not too wide across the muzzle, long and lean, neither snipy nor squarely cut; and in profile curving gradually from nose to throat; lean beneath the eyes, as a thickness here gives coarseness to the whole head. The great length of muzzle gives surface for the free development of the olfactory nerve, and thus secures the highest possible scenting powers. Nose should be well developed, with open nostrils.
**Tail.** Well set on and carried low, if possible below the level of the back, in a straight line or with a slight downward inclination, never elevated above the back, and in action always kept low; nicely fringed with wavy feather of silky texture.
**Feet.** Not too small; round with short, soft hair between the toes; good, strong pads.

*Below: The Field Spaniel is a willing and tireless worker.*

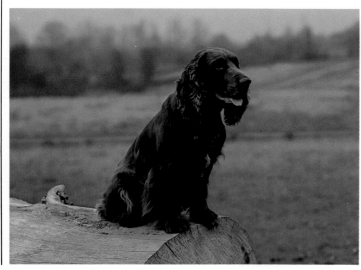

# WACHTELHUND

(German Spaniel; German Quail Dog)

**Good points**
- *Excellent nose*
- *Good in water*
- *Fine retriever/gundog*
- *Hardy*

**Take heed**
- *No known drawbacks*

The Wachtelhund is a hardy breed bearing some resemblance to the English Springer Spaniel. It is little known outside Germany, where it has a sound reputation as a gundog and retriever.

**Size**
Height: 39.5-49.5cm (15½-19½in).

**Exercise**
Needs plenty of exercise.

**Grooming**
Normal daily brushing.

**Feeding**
One to 1½ cans (376g, 13.3oz size) of a branded meaty product, with biscuit added in equal part by volume; or 3 cupfuls of a dry food, complete diet, mixed in the proportion of 1 cup of feed to ½ cup of hot or cold water.

**Origin and history**
The Germans, when they produced the Wachtelhund, wanted to create a breed that could cope with waters and forest and also flush out and retrieve game. The breed was produced by the crossing of a number of small dogs. However, Harrap's *Champion Dogs of the World* credits the old German Stöber with the Wachtelhund's excellent nose, the Stöber having had tracking ability similar to the Bloodhound.

The Wachtelhund, which is not recognized in either the United Kingdom or the USA, is usually dark brown in colour and there can be white marks on chest and toes. It can also be white with brown spots, white and brown, or solid white.

# SUSSEX SPANIEL

**Good points**
- *Loyal*
- *Tireless worker*
- *Intelligent*
- *Alert*

**Take heed**
- *Tends to be a one-person dog*

The Sussex Spaniel has been known in southern England for more than a century; it was very popular with Sussex farmers and thus its name was derived. The breed was first recognized by a Mr Fuller in 1795, when the breed was very much larger than at the present time; later, another strain, called the Harvieston, appeared, which had something of the Clumber and the Bloodhound about it. It is a pity that suddenly the Sussex Spaniel is in danger of extinction, for it is a breed that makes a loyal companion, is active and alert, and has an extremely good nose. This dog has a rich liver-coloured coat, which strangely loses something of its golden hue and darkens if the animal is kept indoors as a pet.

**Size**
Ideal weight: dog 20.5kg (45lb); bitch 18.1kg (40lb). Height: 38-40.5cm (15-16in).

**Exercise**
Like most spaniels the Sussex is essentially a working animal and is not ideally suited for apartment life or for those with insufficient time to take it for long walks.

**Grooming**
A daily brush and comb is necessary, taking care—as with other spaniels—that the ears do not become tangled and that mud does not become caked between the paws or elsewhere in the coat.

**Feeding**
Recommended would be 1-1½ cans (376g, 13.3oz size) of a branded meaty product, with biscuit added in equal part by volume; or 3 cupfuls of a dry, complete diet, mixed in the proportion of 1 cup of feed to ½ cup of hot or cold water.

**Origin and history**
The Sussex is essentially an English breed and has been shown since 1862, when breed members were exhibited at Crystal Palace, London. The breed was kept going between the wars by Mrs Freer of Fourclovers Kennels, who is owed tremendous credit for the survival of the breed. In the mid-1950s fresh blood was introduced by crossing the Sussex with the Clumber, which seems to have resulted in improved bone size and temperament.

**SHOW SUMMARY**
**General appearance.** Massive and strongly built. An active, energetic, strong dog, whose characteristic movement is a decided roll, unlike that of any other spaniel.
**Colour.** Rich golden liver, hair shading to gold at the tips, and the gold predominating. Dark liver or puce is objectionable.
**Head and skull.** The skull should be wide and show a moderate curve from ear to ear, neither flat nor apple-headed, with a centre indentation and a pronounced stop. Brows frowning; occiput decided, but not pointed. Nostrils well developed and liver colour. A well-balanced head.
**Tail.** Set low and not carried above the level of the back. Free action; thickly clothed with hair, but no feather. Docked 12.5-18cm (5-7in).
**Feet.** Circular, well padded, well feathered between toes.

The coat of the Field Spaniel should be flat or slightly waved, silky in texture but sufficiently dense to be weather resistant. It must be glossy, and the chest, underbelly and behind the legs should be well feathered. Any tendency to curl or wiriness is a show fault.

*Field Spaniel*

*Wachtelhund (German Spaniel)*

*Sussex Spaniel*

# PORTUGUESE WARREN HOUND

(Podengo Português)

## Good points
- Attractive
- Choice of size
- First-class hunter

## Take heed
- No drawbacks known

In its native land, the Portuguese Warren Hound is known as the Podengo. It is fairly rare, although by no means unknown, outside Portugal, where it is popular both as a companion and as a hunter of rabbits, hares and even deer. It comes in three sizes, the Podengo Pequeno, which re-sembles a rather large, smooth-coated Chihuahua, a larger (Medio) variety, and the biggest, which more closely resembles the Spanish Ibizan Hound, the Podenco Ibicenco.

## Size
The Podengo Pequeno (small) stands 20-30cm (8-12in) high at the shoulder, the Podengo Medio (medium) stands 51-56cm (20-22in), and the Podengo Grande (large) stands 56-68.5cm (22-27in) high.

## Exercise
Happiest when given plenty of exercise.

## Grooming
Regular brushing is needed. A velvet pad will also improve the appearance of the coat.

## Feeding
For the small Podengo ½-1 can (376g, 13.3oz size) of a branded meaty product with biscuit added in equal part by volume; or 1½ cupfuls of a dry food, complete diet, mixed in the proportion of 1 cup of feed to ½ cup of hot or cold water. For the medium-sized Podengo, 1-1½ cans of a branded meaty product of similar dimensions, with biscuit added in equal part by volume; or 3 cupfuls of a dry food, complete diet, mixed in the proportion of 1 cup of feed to ½ cup of hot or cold water. The large variety should receive 1½-2½ cans of a branded meaty product, of similar dimensions, with biscuit added in equal part by volume; or 5 cupfuls of a dry food, complete diet, mixed in the proportion of 1 cup of feed to ½ cup of hot or cold water.

## Origin and history
The Podengo is well established in its own country, where the small variety, the Pequeno, is used for rabbiting and also for hunting hares; the medium variety also hunts rabbits and hares while the larger dog is used for hunting deer. There is an infusion of blood from a number of gazehounds and although the Pequeno is closely allied to the Chihuahua, the larger variety resembles the Ibizan Hound.

This dog is not currently recog-nized by the AKC, the UK KC or the FCI. However, it is usually fawn in colour and can be rough- or smooth-coated.

# PORTUGUESE WATER DOG

(Cão d'Agua)

## Good points
- Excellent retriever
- First-rate swimmer
- Good watchdog
- Loyal

## Take heed
- Suspicious of strangers

The Portuguese Water Dog is most commonly found in the Algarve area of its native Portugal where it is a true fisherman's dog, acting virtually as a member of the crew and tackling a variety of tasks ranging from guarding the nets to diving and retrieving; it will actually catch an escaping fish in its jaws and swim back with it safely to the boat. It is loyal to its master, but not very trustworthy with strangers.

## Size
Height: dog 51-57cm (20-22½in); bitch 43-52cm (17-20½in). Weight: dog 19-25kg (42-55lb); bitch 15.9-22kg (35-48½lb).

## Exercise
Revels in an active, outdoor life.

## Grooming
The Portuguese Water Dog comes in two coat types, but as this is the only difference there is only one standard for the breed. There is a long-coated variety, which has a lion show trim reminiscent of the Poodle; and a short curly-coated variety, which gives the animal an appealingly scruffy appearance, particularly as it is so often in water. Regular brushing is advised.

## Feeding
One to 1½ cans (376g, 13.3oz size) of a branded meaty product, with biscuit added in equal part by volume; or 3 cupfuls of a dry food, complete diet, mixed in the pro-portion of 1 cup of feed to ½ cup of hot or cold water.

## Origin and history
This unusual dog, which is not only a fine fisherman but can also catch rabbits, has been known for centuries around the Iberian Peninsula, where it was bred for its task of retrieving fish and guarding nets. Formerly used throughout Portugal, it is almost limited today to the region of the Algarve, where fishing traditions continue very much as in the past. It is little known outside its country of origin. This breed should not be confused with the Portuguese Warren Hound (or Podengo), which is mainly found in Northern Portugal, where it is used for rabbiting.

## SHOW SUMMARY
**General charactistics.** A medium-sized dog, very well proportioned, rugged and muscular. Its constant use as a water retriever accounts for the extraordinary muscular development.
**Colour.** Black, white, and various shades of brown; also combina-tions of black or brown with white. A white coat does not indicate albinism provided nose, mouth and eyelids are black.
**Head and skull.** The head is well proportioned and massive. Viewed in profile, the skull is slightly longer than the muzzle. The curve of the skull is rather more accentuated at the back than in front. The occi-put is well defined. Viewed from the front the skull is domed, with a slight concavity in the middle. The forehead is furrowed for two thirds of the length of the parietal bones; the frontal bones are prominent. The muzzle tapers from base to nose. The stop is well defined and lies slightly farther back than the inner corner of the eyes. The nose is wide, with well-open nostrils, which are finely pigmented. Nose colour varies with coat colour. The lips are rather thick, especially in front. The inner mouth is well blacked, the powerful jaws are neither undershot nor overshot. The teeth are not visible when the mouth is closed; the canines are strongly developed.
**Tail.** Not docked; thick at the base, tapering gradually to the tip. It should be set on neither too high nor too low. Extended, it should not reach below the hock. When the dog is on the alert, the tail should be held in a ring, the fore-part of which does not lie beyond the rear limit of the loin. The tail is used actively in both swimming and diving.
**Feet.** The feet are round and rather flat. The toes should not be too long and should not be knuckled up; they are webbed to their tips with a soft membrane well covered with hair. Black nails are preferred but nails of other colours are permitted in confor-mity with colour of coat. Normally the nails are held slightly off the ground. The central pad is very thick, the others normal.

*Below: A long-coated Portuguese Water Dog, an unusual breed little known outside its native country.*

The Portuguese Warren Hound is an elegant, though muscular, dog short and rectangular in build. The fine head is wedge-shaped, flat in the skull with pronounced eyebrow ridges. The tail is medium length and often carried vertically or curled slightly over the back. Although fawn is the most common colour, the coat may be yellow, brown, grey-black or sooty, with or without white patches and spots.

*Portuguese Warren Hound (Medio)*

The Portuguese Water Dog was once common in all the Portuguese and Spanish seaports. Used exclusively as a working dog on fishing boats, it was reputed to be a formidable fighter.

*Portuguese Water Dog*

# BULL TERRIER

## Good points
- *Affectionate*
- *Can cope with most climates*
- *Excellent with children*
- *First-class guard*
- *Healthy*
- *Hardy*

## Take heed
- *Best suited to country life*
- *Needs disciplining when young*
- *Needs plenty of exercise*
- *Powerful dog: you must be strong enough to hold on to the lead!*

The Bull Terrier, despite its somewhat fierce appearance, is a gentle dog and utterly reliable with children, especially the bitch, which will literally let them climb all over her. However, if provoked by another dog, this terrier will happily fight to the death. The Bull Terrier never lets go! It is also a fine guard. It may let an intruder into your house, but one thing is certain: it won't let him out again! No one could call this a beautiful breed, but it has an attraction all of its own.

## Size
The standard has no height or weight limits: the Bull Terrier could be 31.75kg (70lb) in weight, or half that. Maximum substance is required according to the size of the dog.

## Exercise
The Bull Terrier is a powerful dog, with boundless energy, and should not be confined to apartment life, with a run in the back garden. More suitable would be a happily controlled country life with plenty of opportunity to run free.

## Grooming
Normal daily brushing.

## Feeding
If the dog is 9-22.7kg (20-50lb) give it 1-1½ cans (376g, 13.3oz size) of a branded meaty product, with biscuit added in equal part by volume; or 3 cupfuls of a dry food, complete diet, mixed in the proportion of 1 cup of feed to ½ cup of hot or cold water.
If it is 22.7-45.4kg (50-100lb) in weight, give 1½-2½ cans (376g, 13.3oz size) of a branded meaty product, with biscuit added in equal part by volume; or 5 cupfuls of a dry food, complete diet, mixed in the proportion of 1 cup of feed to ½ cup of hot or cold water.

## Health care
The Bull Terrier is a healthy, hardy dog. However, don't buy a white one without checking its hearing: white Bull Terriers are often born deaf!

## Origin and history
This terrier began life as a fighting dog and battled on, seemingly impervious to pain, until bull baiting was outlawed by the British Parliament in 1835. Thereafter a dedicated band of fanciers determined to preserve the breed and refine it while preserving its strength and tenacity. They included James Hinks of Birmingham, England, who, by crossing the White English Terrier with the Bulldog and Dalmatian, produced a new strain of white dogs he called English Bull Terriers. Following the Second World War, coloured Bull Terriers made their appearance. However, the breed as a whole has never regained the tremendous popularity it enjoyed in the 1940s as companion and friend. Perhaps this is all to the good, as there are today few except first-class breeders producing sound, attractive stock, though a criticism has been that some animals are too whippety.

## SHOW SUMMARY
**General appearance.** The Bull Terrier is the gladiator of the canine race and must be strongly built, muscular, symmetrical and active, with a keen, determined and intelligent expression, full of fire and courageous but of even temperament and amenable to discipline. Irrespective of size, dogs should look masculine, and bitches feminine.
**Colour.** For white, a pure white coat; skin pigmentation and markings on the head should not be penalized. For coloured, the colour should predominate. All other things being equal, brindle to be preferred.
**Head.** The head should be long, strong and deep, right to the end of the muzzle, but not coarse. Viewed from the front it should be egg-shaped and completely filled. The nose should be black and bent downwards at the tip. The nostrils should be well developed. The under-jaw should be strong.
**Tail.** Should be short, set on low, and carried horizontally. Thick at the root, it should taper to a fine point.
**Feet.** Round and compact, with well-arched toes.

# AMERICAN STAFFORDSHIRE TERRIER

## Good points
- *Excellent guard*
- *Fearless*
- *Skilful ratter*
- *Good with children*

## Take heed
- *Needs discipline in youth*
- *Stubborn*

The American Staffordshire Terrier is not to be confused with the English Staffordshire Bull Terrier, which is a lighter dog with smaller bones. At one time the American Kennel Club was allowing the American Staffordshire Terrier to be shown with the Staffordshire Bull and, indeed, crossbreeding of the two was allowed. However, although the American Staffordshire's ancestry does originate in England, it has evolved as a quite independent breed.

## Size
Height and weight should be in proportion. A height of about 46-48cm (18-19in) at shoulders for the male and 43-46cm (17-18in) for the female is to be considered preferable.

## Exercise
As for Staffordshire Bull Terrier.

## Grooming
As for Staffordshire Bull Terrier.

## Feeding
As for Staffordshire Bull Terrier.

## Origin and history
The American Staffordshire Terrier is of British origin derived from the traditional English Bulldog and an English terrier. The result was the Staffordshire Terrier, also known as the Pit Bull Terrier and later the Staffordshire Bull Terrier. Once it found its way to the United States, in 1870, it became known variously as a Pit Dog, Yankee Terrier and American Bull Terrier. The breed was recognized by the American Kennel Club in 1935 under the name of Staffordshire Terrier, which was revised on January 1, 1972, to American Staffordshire Terrier.

## SHOW SUMMARY
**General appearance.** The American Staffordshire Terrier should give the impression of great strength for its size, a well put-together dog, muscular, but agile and graceful, keenly alive to its surroundings. It should be stocky, not long-legged or racy in outline. Its courage is proverbial.
**Colour.** Any colour, solid, parti, or patched, is permissible, but all white, more than 80 percent white, black and tan, and liver not to be encouraged.
**Head and skull.** Medium length, deep through, broad skull, very pronounced cheek muscles, distinct stop; and ears are set high. Jaws well defined. Upper teeth to meet tightly outside lower teeth in front. Nose definitely black.
**Tail.** Short in comparison to size, low set, tapering to a fine point; not curled or held over back. Not docked.
**Feet.** Of moderate size, well arched and compact.

# STAFFORDSHIRE BULL TERRIER

## Good points
- *Excellent guard*
- *Fearless*
- *First-class ratter*
- *Good with children*

## Take heed
- *Needs discipline in youth*
- *Stubborn*

The Staffordshire Bull Terrier is a sound breed and excellent family dog derived from the crossing of a Bulldog with a terrier breed sometime in the 1800s. Probably the partner of the Old English Bulldog in this match was the Old English Black and Tan Terrier, which preceded the Manchester Terrier. It is, of course, an English breed, recognized by the British Kennel Club in 1935.

The Staffordshire Bull Terrier, in common with its close relation, the Bull Terrier, is a surprisingly gentle dog beneath a somewhat fearsome exterior. It is a good guard dog but adores its family and is utterly reliable with young children.

## Size
Weight: dog 12.7-17.2kg (28-38lb); bitch 11-15.4kg (24-34lb). Height (at shoulder): 35.5-40.5cm (14-16in).

## Exercise
The Staffordshire Bull Terrier can't resist a fight with another dog if given the chance, so keep this breed on the lead when walking on a public thoroughfare. It is a first-class ratter and a good companion in the field but will adapt to life in a normal-sized house and garden as long as regular walks are given.

## Grooming
This breed requires little attention other than a good daily brushing.

## Feeding
Recommended would be 1-1½ cans per day of a branded meaty product (376g, 13.3oz size), with biscuit added in equal part by volume; or 3 cupfuls of a dry, complete food mixed in the proportion of 1 cup of feed to ½ cup of hot or cold water.

## Origin and history
The Staffordshire Bull Terrier has a bloody history, for it was evolved for the purpose of the once popular sport of bull and bear baiting, and later for dog fighting. Fortunately, however, with the banning of these sports the Staffordshire was developed as a companion dog and in the mid-1930s it was recognized by the Kennel Club as a pure breed, the standard being drawn up and a Breed Club formed in Cradley Heath, South Staffordshire.

## SHOW SUMMARY
**General appearance.** The Staffordshire Bull Terrier is a smooth coated dog. It should be of great strength for its size and, although muscular, should be active and agile.
**Colour.** Red, fawn, white, black or blue, or any of these colours with white. Any shade of brindle or any shade of brindle with white.
**Head and skull.** Short, deep through, broad skull, very pronounced cheek muscles, distinct stop, short foreface, black nose.
**Tail.** The tail should be of medium length, low set, tapering to a point and carried rather low. It should not curl much.
**Feet.** The feet of this breed should be well padded, strong and of medium size.

The ideal Bull Terrier must be well rounded in the body with a short, strong back and a marked spring to the ribs. The shoulders, though powerful, must not be heavy. The legs must be strong boned but not coarse; the forelegs perfectly straight, the hind legs very muscular in the thighs. The overall impression should be one of immense power and strength combined with supple agility.

*Bull Terrier*

*American Staffordshire Terrier*

From its history as a fearless fighter, the modern Staffordshire Bull Terrier draws its characteristics of indomitable courage, high intelligence and tenacity which, coupled with its affectionate and trustworthy nature, make it an excellent all-purpose family pet.

*Staffordshire Bull Terrier*

75

# KERRY BLUE TERRIER

(Irish Blue Terrier)

## Good points
- *First-class guard*
- *Good sporting dog, but mainly kept as a pet*
- *Excellent with children*

## Take heed
- *Loves a scrap, and not averse to starting one*

The Kerry Blue Terrier loves children and makes an ideal house pet. It does, however, have a fine Irish temper when aroused, and needs firm but gentle training when young if you don't want to be plagued with other folks' veterinary expenses.

## Size
Weight: 15-16.8kg (33-37lb); greater tolerance in America.

## Exercise
Bred as a working dog, it needs and deserves plenty of exercise.

## Grooming
Daily brushing with a stiff brush and metal comb. You can easily learn to scissor trim the pet yourself. If you plan to show, however, there is a lot of work involved in show preparation.

## Feeding
One to 1½ cans (376g, 13.3oz size) of a branded meaty product, with biscuit added in equal part by volume; or 3 cupfuls of a dry food, complete diet, mixed in the proportion of 1 cup of feed to ½ cup of hot or cold water.

## Origin and history
The Kerry Blue originates from the county of Kerry in south-western Ireland. The Irish Terrier had a hand in its make-up, to which the Bedlington Terrier and Bull Terrier are also said to have contributed.

The Kerry started life as a hunter of badgers and foxes, and has also done its share of otter hunting, being a keen, strong swimmer. It has guarded livestock and saw Army service during World War II. Now, however, it is predominantly kept as a popular pet and show dog. A Kerry Blue Terrier, Champion Callaghan of Leander, won the Best in Show award at Crufts in 1979.

## SHOW SUMMARY
**General appearance.** The typical Kerry Blue Terrier should be upstanding, compact and well

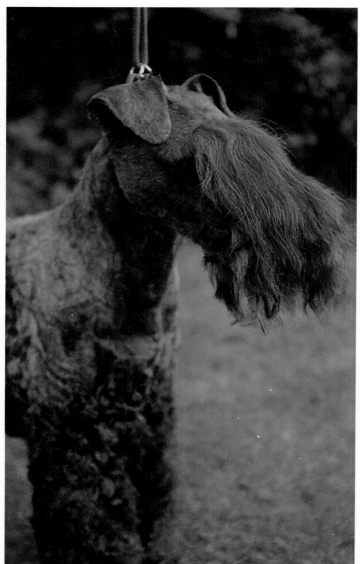

proportioned, showing a developed and muscular body.
**Colour.** Any shade of blue, with or without black points. A shade of tan is permissible in puppies, as is also a dark colour up to the age of 18 months. A small white patch on the chest should not be penalized.
**Head and skull.** Well balanced, long, proportionately lean, with slight stop and flat over the skull. Foreface and jaw very strong, deep and punishing; nose black; nostrils of due proportion.
**Tail.** Set on high to complete a perfectly straight back and carried erect.
**Feet.** Round and small. Toe-nails black.

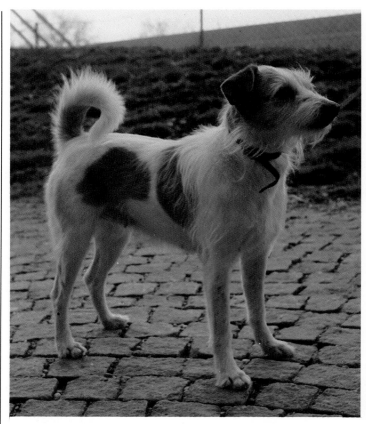

*Above: The Kromfohrländer, which is hardly known outside Germany.*

*Left: The Kerry Blue Terrier — a beautiful, well-proportioned dog kept as a popular pet and a show dog. Its coat, which can be any shade of blue, needs attention.*

# KROMFOHR-LÄNDER

## Good points
- *Excellent temperament*
- *Good companion*
- *Guarding/hunting instincts*
- *Intelligent*

## Take heed
- *No known drawbacks*

This is a faithful and intelligent dog with guarding and hunting instincts. Regrettably it is little known outside Germany.

## Size
Height at the withers 38-46cm (15-18in).

## Exercise
This is a terrier with plenty of energy to unleash.

## Grooming
Normal daily brushing.

## Feeding
One to 1½ cans (376g, 13.3oz size) of a branded meaty product, with biscuit added in equal part by volume; or 3 cupfuls of a dry food, complete diet, mixed in the proportion of 1 cup of feed to ½ cup of hot or cold water.

## Origin and history
The Kromfohrländer has come into being only since the end of World War II when, legend has it, a group of American soldiers, accompanied by a medium-sized dog, passed through the Siegen area of Germany, where the dog was found a new home with a Frau Schleifenbaum, who already owned an English Wire-haired Terrier bitch. The resultant progeny from the first and subsequent litters were so pleasing that it was decided to develop a specific type, eventually known as the Kromfohrländer, which in 1953 received recognition by the German Kennel Club.

## General appearance
There are three varieties of this attractive terrier: the short-haired rough coat, rough coat, and long-haired rough coat. However, the rough coat is by far the most popular. Colours are basically white with markings ranging from light to dark brown on the head, or with a white star on a brown head. Markings should be regular.

An all-purpose dog, the Kerry Blue Terrier makes a first-class pet or working dog. It can be readily trained to the gun and, posessing an excellent nose, will track and retrieve like a gundog. Affectionate and gentle with its friends, but a fearsome adversary, as companion and watchdog it has no equal.

*Kerry Blue Terrier*

*Kromfohrländer*

The Kromfohrländer is a powerful dog with a long, wedge-shaped head, rectangular body and strong, sturdy legs. Developed from a cross between a Griffon and a Terrier, it makes a good dog and a lively, affectionate pet.

# SOFT-COATED WHEATEN TERRIER

### Good points
- *Hardy*
- *Not finicky about food*
- *Intelligent*
- *Excellent guard*
- *Gentle with children*

### Take heed
- *A family dog, not suited to outdoor kennels*

The Soft-coated Wheaten Terrier is an exceptionally intelligent, medium-sized dog, which is defensive without being aggressive. It is an excellent house guard, but gentle with children. The Wheaten has strong sporting instincts, and some have been trained, with success, for the gun.

### Size
Weight: dog approximately 15.9-20.5kg (35-45lb).
Height: dog approximately 46-49.5cm (18-19½in) measured at the withers; bitch slightly less.

### Exercise
The Wheaten will relish plenty of exercise. It has excelled in the past as a hunter of rats, rabbits, otters and badgers, and will work any kind of covert, its soft coat being ample protection against the densest undergrowth.

### Grooming
The Wheaten's coat does not shed. Daily combing should start from puppyhood, as regular grooming will keep the coat clean and tangle-free.

Fuzziness, not natural to the breed, can be aggravated by the use of a wire or plastic brush, and a medium-toothed metal comb should be used instead.

Bathing should be carried out as necessary; if showing, bathing the dog about three days before the event is recommended to avoid a fly-away appearance.

Ears, tail and feet need to be tidied, also any long, straggly hairs underneath the body.

### Feeding
About 1-1½ cans (376g, 13.3oz size) of a branded meaty product with biscuit added in equal part by volume, or 3 cupfuls of a complete dry food, mixed in the proportion of 1 cup of feed to ½ cup of hot or cold water. Meat scraps and non-splintery bones are acceptable.

### Origin and history
The origin of the Soft-coated Wheaten, like that of so many breeds, has been lost in the mists of antiquity. However, from old pictures and records, the breed has been traced back at least 200 years in Ireland, where for many generations there was hardly a farm or smallholding that did not boast an attendant Wheaten that was valued for its sterling qualities.

It is recorded that the Soft-coated Wheaten Terrier is the oldest Irish breed of terrier, said to be the progenitor of the Kerry Blue and Irish Terrier. Legend tells us that a blue dog swam ashore from a ship wrecked in Tralee Bay about 180 years ago. This dog mated the native Wheaten and from this originated the Kerry Blue. Wheaten-coloured pups have appeared in Kerry Blue litters from time to time. There is no record of cross-breeding in the Wheaten and it appears today to be much as it always has been.

### SHOW SUMMARY
**General appearance.** A medium-sized, compact, upstanding terrier well covered with a soft, wheaten-coloured, natural coat that falls in loose curls or waves.
**Colour.** A good clear wheaten, the shade of ripening wheat; a white coat and a red coat are equally objectionable. Dark shading on the ears is not untypical. Dark overall colour and the even darker markings often present in the immature coat clear by about 18 months, if not before.
**Head and skull.** Head moderately long and profusely covered with coat, which should fall forward over the eyes. The skull, while not being coarse, should be narrow. The nose should be black and large for the size of dog. Head in general, powerful without being coarse.
**Tail.** Docked. The tail of the fully grown dog should be about 10-12.5cm (4-5in) long. Set on high, carried gaily, but never over the back. Not curled or too thick.
**Feet.** Strong and compact, turned neither in nor out. Good depth of pad. Toe-nails black.

# BORDER COLLIE

### Good points
- *Intelligent*
- *Loyal*
- *Ideal choice for obedience competitions*
- *Good family and/or working dog*

### Take heed
- *This breed will herd anything, people included, if sheep and cattle are not available*

The Border Collie is a first-class, everyday working dog, famed for herding cattle and rounding up sheep. This is the star of sheepdog trials, the persistent winner of obedience competitions, the breed favoured by those who want a 'working' dog.

The Border Collie (the name refers to the English-Scottish border) was bred for speed, stamina and brains. It makes a first-class companion, is good with children, and is one of the most trainable dogs.

### Size
Dog about 53cm (21in); bitch slightly less.

### Exercise
This is essentially a working dog that enjoys being out of doors, whether trotting at its master's heels on a routine walk, doing exercises at a dog training class, or working on a farm. It will adapt to whatever role you have for it, but is not ideally suited to town life.

### Grooming
Brush regularly with a good pony dandy brush and comb. Inspect the ears for signs of canker, and the ears and feet for foreign matter. Dead fur should be removed when grooming.

### Feeding
As for Soft-coated Wheaten.

### Origin and history
The present-day Border Collie is a modern strain descended from collies of the Lowland and Border counties of England and Scotland. They are working sheepdogs of a distinct, recognizable type, which have been exported to many countries of the world where sheep are farmed, and they are also excellent as guide dogs for the blind.

It was not until July 1976 that a standard for the breed was approved by the British Kennel Club from a combination of several proposed standards submitted to them by interested bodies, including the recognized one from the Australian Kennel Club.

### SHOW SUMMARY
**General appearance.** The Border Collie should be a well-proportioned dog, the smooth outline showing gracefulness and perfect balance, combined with sufficient substance to convey the impression that it is capable of enduring long periods of active duty.
**Colour.** A variety of colours is permissible.
**Head and skull.** Skull should be fairly broad, occiput not pronounced. Cheeks should not be full or rounded. The muzzle, tapering to the nose, should be moderately short and strong; and the skull and foreface should be approximately the same length. Nose black; nostrils well developed. Stop very distinct.
**Tail.** The tail should be moderately long, the bone reaching at least to the hock joint, set on low, well furnished and with an upward swirl towards the end.
**Feet.** Oval in shape; pads deep, strong and sound; toes moderately arched and close together. Nails short and strong.

# STABYHOUN

### Good points
- *Affectionate*
- *Easily trained*
- *Excellent guard dog*
- *Fine all-purpose sporting dog*

### Take heed
- *No drawbacks known*

The Stabyhoun is one of the most popular dogs in its native Holland, but is little known elsewhere in the world.

This is an excellent all-purpose sporting dog, nowadays kept mainly as a companion house dog. It is reliable with children, has an affectionate nature, is easily trained, and has an equable temperament. It is a splendid retriever, with a good nose.

### Size
Dog up to 49.5cm (19½in) at the withers, bitch somewhat smaller.

### Exercise
The Stabyhoun excels at working in the field as a retriever, doing the job for which it was bred. It adapts well to town life as long as it has ample opportunity to run free.

### Grooming
Regular brushing will keep the coat in good condition.

### Feeding
As for Soft-coated Wheaten.

### Origin and history
The Stabyhoun was recognized by the Dutch Kennel Club in 1942, but it has existed in the Netherlands since as long ago as 1800, when it was bred in the Friesland district as an all-purpose gundog, but primarily as a dispeller of vermin. Crossed with the Wetterhoun it made a formidable ratter!

*Above: The affectionate Stabyhoun.*

### SHOW SUMMARY
**General characteristics.** A simple, robust pointer, whose body is longer than it is high; the dog should appear neither too massive nor too fragile.
**Colour.** Dappled black, dappled blue, dappled brown, dappled orange.
**Head.** Lean; in good proportion to the rest of the body; longer than it is broad. Skull and muzzle are of equal length. The skull is slightly rounded, not narrow. The nose is black for brown and orange dogs. It is not divided; the nostrils are well open and large.
**Tail.** Long, reaching to the hocks. It is set on at medium height, and hangs straight, with the last third turned upward. In action, the tail is raised. It is covered all around with long hair, which is neither curled nor wavy and not too thick.
**Feet.** The hind feet are round, with strong pads.

*Soft-coated Wheaten Terrier*

As its name suggests, the coat of the Soft-coated Wheaten Terrier is exceptionally soft and silky, loosely waved or curly, and should be especially abundant on the head and legs. The length and texture of the coat remains the same throughout the year: there is no seasonal variation.

*Border Collie*

Because the Border Collie's background contains a mixture of other sheepdogs, there was considerable individual variation in type, and it is only recently that a standard for the breed has been decided and official recognition granted.

# SHAR-PEI
(Chinese Fighting Dog)

### Good points
- Excellent watchdog
- Loyal to owner
- Amiable unless provoked
- Highly intelligent
- Good with children

### Take heed
- May be more susceptible to disease than other imports, which have built up an immunity

The Chinese Shar-Pei currently has the distinction of being listed in the Guinness Book of Records as the rarest dog in the world, but interest in the breed is steadily rising.

What does it look like? Descriptions vary from a dog that looks as if its skin is several sizes too big for it, to a Bloodhound, but with wrinkles all over.

The Shar-Pei has small, rectangular ears that point towards the eyes, a tail that forms a circle, its tip touching its base, and stiff short hair that stands up. It is likely that its rarity will be short-lived, for at a recent reckoning 14 Shar-Peis were in the kennels of Mr Ernest Albright of California, the man largely responsible for saving the Shar-Pei from extinction. There are also now a handful of Shar-Peis scattered throughout the United States and Canada, the owners of which will doubtless perpetuate the breed, the future of which was put in peril when, in 1947, the tax on dogs in the People's Republic of China rose so steeply that few people could afford to keep them and many were utilized as food. The Shar-Pei may have escaped this fate simply because it was not very tasty!

It is an extremely intelligent dog, an excellent guard, and amiable unless provoked, and it enjoys human companionship; it is also most affectionate, an added advantage being that Shar-Pei pups are said to house-train themselves!

### Size
Weight: 18.1-22.7kg (40-50lb). Height: 46-51cm (18-20in) at the withers.

### Exercise
The Shar-Pei — or, to give it its former name, the Chinese Fighting Dog — was used to hunt wild boar and to herd flocks. It is a breed more suited to those with large gardens, or living near areas where it may unleash its energies, and it needs good daily walks and off-the-lead runs.

It will interest obedience enthusiasts to learn that 'Chin', a Shar-Pei trained by Ernest Albright in the United States, has won three ribbons in obedience trials.

### Feeding
In their land of origin these dogs are undoubtedly fed on rice, a diet that has resulted in instances of rickets and other ailments associated with malnutrition. The Shar-Pei is a hardy dog and, if fed correctly, should have few health problems. The branded canned food requirement for a dog of its size is approximately 1½ cans (376g, 13.3oz size) per day, with the usual biscuit supplement.

### Health care
The breed is susceptible to entropion, an eye disease that can cause blindness if the lashes penetrate the cornea. The disease is curable, and a veterinarian should be consulted at any sign of eye irritation.

A unique feature of this breed is that heat in the female can be at irregular intervals, and with some females the season may not occur until she is 15 months of age or more. Also, when the Shar-Pei is in season, she will not attract the attention of males of other breeds, and only of certain members of her own breed, so planned mating calls for vigilant surveillance.

### Origin and history
Works of art depicting a likeness to the Shar-Pei survive from the Han Dynasty (206 BC to AD 220).

It is possible that the Shar-Pei originated in Tibet or the Northern Province of China about 20 centuries ago, when it was probably a much larger dog than it is now, weighing 38.6-74.8kg (85-165lb). Other sources maintain that the Shar-Pei is a descendant of the Service Dogs that, for thousands of years, lived in the Southern Province near the South China Sea.

Certainly, for hundreds of years it lived up to its name of Chinese Fighting Dog; it was provoked, and then matched against other dogs for the owner's profit, the loose skin of the Shar-Pei making it difficult for its opponent to get a firm grip on its body. It is said that drugs were used to heighten the breed's aggression, for it is basically a loving and gentle animal.

### SHOW SUMMARY
The Shar-Pei Club of America has been formed to discuss and adopt a standard, but it must be realized that there are as yet insufficient breed members to justify the recognition of the American Kennel Club. The following are, therefore, points taken from the tentative standard.

**General appearance.** An active, compact, short-coupled, squarely built dog that stands firmly on the ground with the posture of a warrior.

**Head and skull.** Skull flat, broad and large, with little stop. Occiput not pronounced. Profuse wrinkles on forehead and cheeks. Heavy dewlaps. Muzzle moderately long and broad with no tapering towards the nose.

**Colour.** Self-coloured. May be black, dark fawn, light fawn or cream-coloured. Fawn with dark eyes, blue-grey mask and black nose preferable.

**Tail.** Set very high. Thick and round at base, tapering to a fine point at the tip. Preferably, the tail should be curled tightly in a circle or loosely in a semi-circle, and carried to one side.

**Feet.** Moderate in size; compact and firm; toes well separated; knuckles high.

# BULLDOG

### Good points
- Courageous
- Intelligent
- Good tempered
- Loves children
- Easy to groom

### Take heed
- Best suited to a temperate climate — excessive heat causes heart attacks
- Snores
- Not built for strenuous exercise

The Bulldog, despite its somewhat ferocious appearance, has a docile temperament and generally adores children. It is quick to learn and will enjoy taking part in games. However, its build precludes any fast running, and it must never be allowed to rush about in hot weather, as its nose does not equip it for rapid breathing. It should never be shut in a car or other confined space unless plenty of fresh air is available.

This breed is not renowned for longevity. It can, however, be warmly recommended as a loyal guard and lovable family pet.

### Size
Dog: 25kg (55lb). Bitch: 22.7kg (50lb).

### Exercise
The Bulldog will benefit from a good daily walk on a loose lead. If the owner lives in a safe, rural area, or has a nearby enclosed park, the dog will enjoy being allowed off the lead so that it may amble at its own pace. But please don't drag it, or let it over-exert itself as a pup. Experience will show just how much exercise it enjoys without tiring. But the Bulldog is not the breed for anyone with a penchant for all-day hiking.

### Grooming
A daily brushing with a fairly stiff brush and a rub-down with a hound glove will keep the Bulldog in good condition. Choose a warm summer's day for its annual bath!

### Feeding
The Bulldog needs a full can (376g, 13.3oz) of branded dog food or 454g (1lb) of raw meat daily, with the addition of biscuit meal. A daily teaspoonful of cod liver oil is recommended in winter as a body builder. It is best to feed after exercise so that the meal may digest while the dog sleeps.

### Origin and history
This breed can be traced back to the Molossus, the fighting dog of the ancient Greek tribe at Athens called the Molossi. However, the Mastiff would seem to resemble this powerful breed more faithfully, which suggests that the Mastiff, Bulldog and Boxer may have a common ancestor. Certainly they were all fighting dogs: the Mastiff fought against both gladiators and wild beasts in the arenas of Rome, and the Boxer was known in Germany as 'Bullenbeisser' or bull-baiter.

It is, however, the Bulldog that is generally associated with the unpleasant 'sport' of bull-baiting — seizing the bull by the nose and holding it until it fell. The sport was promoted by a certain Earl Warren of Stamford, Lincolnshire, who, after enjoying the spectacle of two dogs fighting bulls in 1209, sought to bring such a sight to a wider audience.

When bull-baiting became illegal in 1838, the Bulldog was in danger of extinction, for it appeared to have served its purpose. However, a Mr Bill George continued to breed Bulldogs, and to him a debt of gratitude is due in that the breed, despite its fearsome countenance, has developed into a much esteemed, reliable pet. The Bulldog Club, established in 1875, was the first specialist breed club to be set up in Britain. At the beginning of the 20th century, New Yorkers paid very large sums of money for Bulldogs, when the breed became suddenly fashionable there.

### SHOW SUMMARY
**General appearance.** The Bulldog is a smooth-coated, thickset dog, rather low in stature, but broad, powerful and compact. The head is strikingly massive and large in proportion to the dog's size, and the face is extremely short. The muzzle is very broad, blunt and inclined upwards.

**Colour.** The colour should be whole or smut (that is, a whole colour with a black mask or muzzle). The only colours (which should be brilliant and pure of their sort) are whole colours, viz. brindles, reds, fawns, fallows, white and also pied (i.e. a combination of white with any other of the foregoing colours).

**Head and skull.** The skull should be very large — the larger the better — and in circumference should measure (round in front of the ears) at least the height of the dog at the shoulders.

**Tail.** The tail, termed the 'stern', should be set on low, jut out rather straight, then turn downwards. It should be round, smooth and devoid of fringe or coarse hair. It should be moderate in length — rather short than long — and thick at the root, and taper quickly to a fine point.

**Feet.** The hind feet, like the fore-feet, should be round and compact, with the toes well split up and the knuckles prominent. The fore-feet should be straight and turn very slightly outwards, of medium size and moderately round. The toes should be compact and thick, being well split up, making the knuckles prominent and high.

Now perhaps the world's rarest dog, the Shar-Pei originated in the ancient Orient, where it was for centuries bred and trained as a fighting dog. It is believed that drugs were used to provoke the Shar-Pei to aggression, for it is basically an amiable and gentle dog.

*Shar-Pei*

The Bulldog should convey an impression of determination, strength and activity: qualities which have been said to reflect the true character of the British nation, of which the Bulldog has become a popular symbol.

*Bulldog*

# CANAAN DOG

## Good points
- *Excellent guard*
- *Intelligent*

## Take heed
- *Distrusts strangers*

This dog is a native of Israel, where it is used as a guard and protector of livestock. It is alert, intelligent and home-loving. Although distrustful of strangers, it does not look for trouble.

## Size
Weight: 18.1-25kg (40-55lb). Height: 49.5-60cm (19½-23½in).

## Exercise
Regular walks will be sufficient.

## Grooming
Normal daily brushing.

## Feeding
Recommended would be 1½-2½ cans (376g, 13.3oz size) of a branded meaty product, with biscuit added in equal part by volume; or 5 cupfuls of a dry food, complete diet, mixed in the proportion of 1 cup of feed to ½ cup of hot or cold water.

## Origin and history
The Canaan Dog is indigenous to Israel, where it is used as a guard and protector of livestock. During the Israeli wars it was used as a messenger and guard, and created sufficient interest for breed members to be exported to the United States and elsewhere. It is recognized by the FCI and the American Kennel Club but not, as yet, in the United Kingdom.

## SHOW SUMMARY
**General appearance.** There are two types of Canaan Dog, the Collie and the Dingo type, the Dingo appearing to be the heavier variety.
**Colour.** Sandy to red-brown, white or black; large white markings are permissible, even desirable, with all colours. Harlequins are acceptable.
**Tail.** The tail is curled over the back when the dog is alerted; it is set on very high and is very bushy.

# POINTING WIRE-HAIRED GRIFFON

## Good points
- *Easy to train*
- *Equable temperament*
- *Good companion*
- *Intelligent*

## Take heed
- *A reliable and careful, rather than speedy, gundog*

The Pointing Wire-haired Griffon is an intelligent, companionable dog that not only points, but also works well in water. It is an attractive, good-natured animal, which performs its task slowly but surely. It is easily trained.

## Size
Height: dog 54.5-60cm (21½-23½in), bitch 49.5-54.5cm (19½-21½in).

## Exercise
Needs plenty of vigorous exercise.

## Grooming
Regular brushing will keep the coat in good condition.

## Feeding
One to 1½ cans (376g, 13.3oz size) of a branded meaty product, with biscuit added in equal part by volume; or 3 cupfuls of a dry food, complete diet, mixed in the proportion of 1 cup of feed to ½ cup of hot or cold water.

## Origin and history
The Pointing Wire-haired Griffon was developed around 1874 by a Dutch sportsman named Edward Korthals. Korthals was a man of considerable breeding experience, who had managed the kennels of a German prince for many years, and it was his resolve to produce a dog with both courage and hunting ability. He achieved this by experimental crossings with French, Belgian and German gundogs until the Pointing Wire-haired Griffon was established — a pointer that was at home in water and, although not as swift a worker as other gundogs, a reliable and plucky worker. Some say that it is the ideal gundog for the older sportsman. It was first shown in Great Britain in 1888.

## SHOW SUMMARY (FCI)
**Colour.** Preferably steel grey with chestnut markings or uniformly reddish chestnut or roan. White and chestnut and white and orange are also acceptable.
**Head and skull.** Large, long with rough tufted hair, thick but not too long, very pronounced moustache and eyebrows, skull not too wide, muzzle long, strong and square, facial angle not too pronounced, nose invariably brown.
**Tail.** Carried horizontally or with the tip slightly raised; the hair abundant but not plumed. Usually it is docked.
**Feet.** Round and solid, the toes close and webbed.

*Below: These Wire-haired Pointing Griffons are slow but reliable.*

The Canaan Dog has only recently become known outside its
native Israel. Its origin is uncertain: it may have
evolved from the selective breeding of
Middle Eastern Pariah Dogs
(which are themselves domestic
types which have
regressed to a wild state).

*Canaan Dog*

The Pointing Wire-haired
Griffon was first registered with
The American Kennel Club—
as the 'Russian Setter (Griffon)'
—in 1887, but was not
shown in the USA until about
1900. It is now officially
known in the USA as the Wire-haired
Pointing Griffon.

*Pointing Wire-haired Griffon
(Wire-haired Pointing Griffon
in the USA)*

# BEAUCERON
(Beauce Shepherd, Bas-rouge, French Short-haired Shepherd, Berger de la Beauce)

## Good points
● Brave
● Faithful
● Fine guard
● Intelligent

## Take heed
● Ferocious if roused

The Beauceron is a guard and herder of supreme intelligence and loyalty. It resembles the Dobermann in appearance.

## Size
Height at shoulder: dog 63.5-71cm (25-28in); bitch 61-68.5cm (24-27in).

## Exercise
Happiest when working or exercising in the wide open spaces.

## Grooming
Regular brushing will keep the coat in good condition.

## Feeding
Recommended would be 1½-2½ cans (376g, 13.3oz size) of a branded meaty product, with biscuit added in equal part by volume; or 5 cupfuls of a dry food, complete diet, mixed in the proportion of 1 cup of feed to ½ cup of hot or cold water.

## Origin and history
The Beauceron belongs to the four best-known herding breeds of France, all of which derive from different areas, the others being the Briard, Picardy and Pyrenean Mountain Dog. The Beauceron resembles the Dobermann in both colour and appearance. It has come down from an old, less refined shepherd dog, probably used also for hunting, and has been established in its present form only since the end of last century. It is a natural herder, and in recent years its temperament has been greatly improved.

## SHOW SUMMARY
**General characteristics.** A big dog, robust and powerful; muscular but not heavy.
**Colour.** Black, grey, grey with black-and-tan markings (which the French call 'red stockings'), fawn, fawn and black. A white spot on the chest is tolerated but objectionable. For a true working dog, the darker coats are preferred.
**Head.** Long, with a flat or very slightly domed skull. The medial furrow is not prominent; the occipital protuberance is visible. The stop is not pronounced, lying at midpoint between occiput and tip of nose. The bridge is not arched except very slightly toward the extremity. Muzzle long, but neither very narrow nor very pointed. The nose is black. The lower lips are slightly let down, not heavy. The teeth are white and well adapted to their purpose.
**Tail.** Not docked; carried low; should reach at least to the hocks; hanging straight, it may be slightly curved or hooked at the end.
**Feet.** Strong, rounded, with black nails and hard pads. Double dew-claws on the hind legs. Dogs otherwise well qualified as to type but lacking dew-claws can take only a mention.

# PUMI

## Good points
● Good watchdog
● Intelligent
● Pleasant temperament
● Useful farm dog

## Take heed
● Has a somewhat scruffy appearance
● Not keen on strangers

The Pumi is a pleasant companion and guard. However, it prefers its owner's company and will give noisy warning of intruders. It has an unkempt appearance that is unusually appealing. Not often seen outside its native Hungary, where it is mainly a farm dog.

## Size
Weight: 8-13kg (17½-28½lb), height at withers 33-44.5cm (13-17½in).

## Exercise
Happiest running out of doors, but easily trained.

## Grooming
Brushing will help!

## Feeding
One to 1½ cans (376g, 13.3oz size) of a branded meaty product, with biscuit added in equal part by volume; or 3 cupfuls of a dry food, complete diet, mixed in the proportion of 1 cup of feed to ½ cup of hot or cold water.

## Origin and history
The Pumi, like the Komondor, Puli and Kuvasz, is a Hungarian sheepdog. However, in recent years it has been employed mainly as an all-purpose farm dog and herder of cattle in its native country. It also excels at police and guard work. Its history is obscure, but undoubtedly the Puli had a hand in its make-up, perhaps with the Poodle.

## SHOW SUMMARY
**General appearance.** A dog of medium size, vigorous, with many characteristics of the terrier. The head is rather long, with the muzzle even more developed. The ears are semi-erect. The coat is of medium length, and free from matting. The tail is erect. The eyes and muzzle are barely visible because of the long coat, parti-coloured but never brindle.
**Colour.** Many colours occur; dove grey, silver grey and slate grey are common. Black, light grey, white and chestnut are also found. The Pumi must not be mottled or have markings of any kind.
**Head.** The shape of the head is imparted largely by the elongated muzzle. The bridge is straight. The muzzle narrows gradually from the skull to the nose, which is pointed. The tip of the nose is also narrow. The lips fit closely over the gums. The teeth are regular and the jaws meet in a scissor bite. The teeth are well developed and strong. The stop is not pronounced. The occiput is rather narrow but slightly domed. The forehead is slightly rounded and long; development of the supra-orbital ridges is moderate.
**Tail.** Set on high, carried straight out or slightly lowered; should be docked to two thirds of its length.

# HUNGARIAN PULI
(Puli; Hungarian Water Dog)

## Good points
● Easily trained
● Fine guard
● Highly intelligent
● Loyal

## Take heed
● Tends to be a one-person dog

The Hungarian Puli is a loyal, obedient dog, and perhaps the best-known of the Hungarian sheepdogs outside its homeland. It is easily distinguishable by its long, dark, corded coat, which is not so difficult to groom as might be believed.

## Size
Height: dog 40.5-46cm (16-18in); bitch 35.5-40.5cm (14-16in). Weight: dog 13.1-15kg (29-33lb); bitch 10-13.1kg (22-29lb).

## Exercise
Plenty of exercise is preferable, but this adaptable dog will fit in with city life, as long as it is at its owner's side.

## Grooming
The coat hangs in long black cords, which in the adult dog reach to the ground, giving a tousled, unkempt look. The cords have to be separated by hand and regularly brushed and combed. Cleanliness is essential.

## Feeding
One to 1½ cans (376g, 13.3oz size) of a branded meaty product, with biscuit added in equal part by volume; or 3 cupfuls of a dry food, complete diet, mixed in the proportion of 1 cup of feed to ½ cup of hot or cold water.

## Origin and history
The Puli is better known than other Hungarian sheepdogs, such as the Pumi, the Komondor and the Kuvasz, probably because in its native land it directs the flock by jumping on or over the sheep's backs. It is said to have existed for 1000 years, being a descendant of the sheepdogs brought to Hungary by the Magyars. It has proved itself as a fine water retriever, and has done well in obedience and police work. Hungarian shepherds favour their dark colour, which is easily picked out among the flock.

## SHOW SUMMARY
**General appearance.** A lively, agile, intelligent, undemanding dog of medium size. It has a solid physique, lean and muscular throughout. The outline of the body and limbs is square. Examination of the individual parts of the body is difficult, because the Puli is completely covered with a thick, long, wavy coat that tends to mat. The head gives the impression of being round because of the long hair that comes down over the eyes, concealing the true shape. The shaggy tail, long and curled up about to the loins, makes it seem that the hindquarters slope upward. The precise body lines are hard to follow, as a glance will show; even the individual parts are difficult to see clearly because of the Puli's unique coat.
**Colour.** Today breeders are producing Pulis that are black, or black with reddish or white ticking, as well as several varieties of grey.
**Head.** Small and fine. From the front it appears round, whereas in profile it seems elliptical. The nose is relatively large, and is black, like the eye-rims and lips. The bridge is shorter than the skull, its length being 35 percent that of the head. The lips fit closely over the gums. The bridge is straight, the muzzle rounded. The jaws are equally developed, with strong, regular teeth; and the jaws meet in a scissor bite. The lower canines are set slightly forward of the upper; the other teeth meet precisely. The stop is accentuated. The skull is rounded; the supra-orbital ridges are pronounced.
**Tail.** Carried over the loin. Its hair mingles with the rump hair so that the tail is virtually invisible.

Below: This Puli was photographed in Hungary. The cords of its coat are thicker than those of a Puli living outside its native land.

In spite of its name, the Beauceron derives from the Brie region of France rather than that of Beauce: its name was probably given to avoid confusion with the Briard herding breed. Less popular than the Briard, the Beauceron is still a working dog in France and is not often seen outside its native country.

*Beauceron*

*Pumi*

*Hungarian Puli*

# FINNISH SPITZ
(Suomenpystykorva)

### Good points
- *Beautiful*
- *Brave*
- *Excellent guard/housedog*
- *Faithful*
- *Good with children*
- *Hunter*
- *Home-loving*
- *Sociable*

### Take heed
- *No known drawbacks*

The Finnish Spitz is Finland's national dog. It is popular in Scandinavia as both a hunter (mainly of birds) and a show dog. It also has devotees in Great Britain, where it is kept mainly as a pet and show dog. It is a beautiful animal with the habit of cleaning itself like a cat.

### Size
Height: dog 44.5cm (17½in), bitch 39.5cm (15½in).

### Exercise
This is a real outdoor dog, which likes to run free whenever possible. However, it also relishes its place by the fireside, so it should not be kept kennelled.

### Health care
Although a hardy, healthy dog in adulthood, it can prove delicate as a pup, and this Spitz type is not the easiest to breed.

*Below: The Finnish Spitz puppies enjoying the sun can be delicate to raise, but will grow into beautiful pets or show dogs.*

### Grooming
Normal daily brushing.

### Feeding
Recommended would be 1-1½ cans (376g, 13.3oz size) of a branded meaty product, with biscuit added in equal part by volume; or 3 cupfuls of a dry food, complete diet, mixed in the proportion of 1 cup of feed to ½ cup of hot or cold water.

### Origin and history
Known for centuries in its own country prior to official recognition when the Finnish Kennel Club gained acceptance by the FCI. It originates from the Eastern zone of Finland and is mentioned in the country's epic the *Kalevala*.

Called the 'Finkie' by Lady Kitty Ritson, who pioneered the breed in Britain in the 1920s, it is related to the Russian Laika breed, a member of which was to orbit the Earth in an early space flight. It is a descendant of the earliest hunter dogs of Lapland and Scandinavia.

### SHOW SUMMARY
**General appearance.** Body almost square. Bearing bold. The whole appearance, and particularly the eyes, ears and tail, indicates liveliness.
**Colour.** On the back, reddish-brown or yellowish-red, preferably bright. The hairs on the inner sides of the ears, on the cheeks, under the muzzle, on the breast and abdomen, inside the legs, at the back of the thighs, and under the tail are of a lighter shade. White markings on feet and a narrow white stripe on the breast can be permitted, also some black hairs on the lips and sparse separate hairs with black points along the back.
**Head and skull.** Medium sized and clean cut, forehead slightly arched, stop pronounced. Muzzle narrow and clean cut, seen from above; and from the sides, evenly tapering. Nose should be pitch black. Lips tightly closed and thin.
**Tail.** Curves vigorously from its root in an arch, forward, downward and backward, then pressing down against the thigh, with its tip extending to the middle part of the thigh. Extended, the tail vertebrae usually reach to the hock joint.
**Feet.** Preferably roundish.

# NORRBOTTEN SPITZ
(Norrbottenspets)
(See also Finnish Spitz and Norwegian Buhund)

### Good points
- *Excellent guard*
- *Good with children*
- *Happy nature*
- *Lively*
- *Strong herding instinct*

### Take heed
- *No drawbacks known*

The Norrbotten Spitz is named after the northern region of Sweden Norrbotten, from which it originates. It is Sweden's answer to the Finnish Spitz and the Norwegian Buhund, though smaller and lighter. It makes an excellent companion, house dog and farmyard protector.

### Size
Maximum height 40.5cm (16in).

### Exercise
This dog is a natural herder that enjoys its freedom. However it adapts well to the life of a house pet, with regular walks.

### Grooming
Normal daily brushing.

### Feeding
One to 1½ cans (376g, 13.3oz size) of a branded meaty product, with biscuit added in equal part by volume; or 3 cupfuls of a dry food, complete diet, mixed in the proportion of 1 cup of feed to ½ cup of hot or cold water.

### Origin and history
The Norrbotten Spitz is little known outside Sweden, having been declared extinct by the Swedish Kennel Club in 1948. Luckily this proved to be untrue, and there was an upsurge of interest in the 1960s, resulting in sufficient registrations for the breed to become re-established. Its Spitz origin probably derives from Finnish Spitz or Norwegian Buhund ancestry. The Norrbotten Spitz is not yet recognized in either the United Kingdom or the USA.

### SHOW SUMMARY
**General appearance.** This is a small dog, compact, but light in build, of the Spitz type, with good carriage.
**Colour.** All colours are permissible, although preference is given to white as the base colour with russet or yellow markings. Each colour area should be distinct from the others.
**Tail.** Set on high; curved, generally carried on the side, and when down the tip reaches mid-thigh. The tail joints should not reach below the hock. A docked tail is permissible, but not desirable.

# JAPANESE SPITZ

### Good points
- *Courageous*
- *Intelligent*
- *Loyal*
- *Lively*

### Take heed
- *Tends to be a one-person dog*
- *Distrustful of strangers*

The Japanese Spitz is a close relation of the Norrbotten Spitz, but has developed as a separate breed in Japan, to which it was undoubtedly imported long ago. It has only recently come upon the international scene and is still comparatively rare.

### Size
Height: dog, 30-40.5cm (12-16in); bitch, 25-35.5cm (10-14in).

### Exercise
This dog is a natural herder, and enjoys its freedom. However, it adapts well to the life of a house pet, with regular walks.

### Grooming
Normal daily brushing.

### Feeding
One to 1½ cans (376g, 13.3oz size) of a branded meaty product, with biscuit added in equal part by volume; or 3 cupfuls of a dry food, complete diet, mixed in the proportion of 1 cup of feed to ½ cup of hot or cold water.

### SHOW SUMMARY
**General appearance.** Profuse pure white off-standing coat. The dog should have a sharply pointed muzzle and triangular ears standing erect. The bushy tail is carried over the back. The body should be firm, strong and flexible. Fore- and hindquarters should be well proportioned and balanced.
**Head and skull** Head of medium size, without coarseness, moderately broad and slightly rounded. Skull broadest at occiput. Well defined stop. Cheeks rounded, full head not protruding; muzzle sharply pointed, neither too thin nor too long. Lips firm and tightly closed. The nose round, small and black.
**Colour.** Pure white.
**Tail.** Moderate in length; root set high; carried over the back.
**Feet.** Toes should be small, round and cat-like. Well padded, with good pigment; nails should be hard and black or dark.

The Finnish Spitz is characterized by its courage, fidelity and eagerness to hunt. Its coat is short and close-lying on the head and legs (except on the backs of the thighs, where it is long and dense). The outer coat on the shoulders is considerably longer and coarser, particularly in males, and the under-coat short, soft and dense.

*Finnish Spitz*

Originally bred as a hunting dog, the Norrbotten Spitz is now known as an affectionate and lively house dog. It is little known outside Sweden, where it was re-established in 1960.

*Norrbotten Spitz*

It is possible that the Japanese Spitz is a fairly long-coated version of the family popularly known as Japanese Large Size, Middle Size and Small Size Dogs. It is still seldom seen outside Japan.

*Japanese Spitz*

# BASSET HOUND

## Good points
- Equable temperament
- Good with children
- Ideal family pet

## Take heed
- Needs lots of exercise
- Likes to wander

The Basset Hound is an affable dog that gets on with most people and makes the ideal family pet. It does, however, retain strong hound instincts and will wander miles if a gate is left conveniently open. Basset owners are always telling folk about their Basset's roamings, often quite far afield, but it is up to them to see that their properties are adequately fenced. Like the Beagle, the Basset has a mind of its own; it is eminently lovable, but not always obedient — unless it chooses!

## Size
Height: 33-38cm (13-15in).

## Exercise
Most important. If you can't give a Basset Hound plenty of exercise, don't have one.

## Grooming
Daily brushing and combing. Pay attention to ears and toe-nails.

## Feeding
One to 1½ cans (376g, 13.3oz size) of a branded meaty product, with biscuit added in equal part by volume; or 3 cupfuls of a dry food,

*Below: Lovable pets, Basset Hounds can be wilful at times.*

complete diet, mixed in the proportion of 1 cup of feed to ½ cup of hot or cold water. Careful feeding in puppyhood is advocated for this fast-growing breed.

## Health care
Choose the specimen with the straightest limbs, even if those knobbly knees seem attractive.

## Origin and history
The Basset Hound is of French origin, being derived from the French Basset Artésien-Normand, which was imported to England and crossed with the Bloodhound. It is a slow but sure tracker, still used in Britain to hunt hare. Primarily, however, it is kept as a popular household pet. French sources maintain that the first Bassets appeared in a litter of normal long-legged hounds, and that in breeding from these the Basset (which means 'dwarf') Hound appeared.

## SHOW SUMMARY
**General characteristics.** A short-legged hound of considerable substance, well-balanced and full of quality. Action is most important. A smooth free action with forelegs reaching well forward and hind legs showing powerful thrust and the hound moving true both front and rear. Hocks and stifles must not be stiff in movement nor must any toes be dragged.
**Colour.** Generally black, white and tan, or lemon and white; but any recognized hound colour is acceptable.
**Head and skull.** Domed, with some stop and the occipital bone prominent; of medium width at the brow and tapering slightly to the muzzle; the general appearance

of the foreface is lean but not snipy. The top of the muzzle is nearly parallel with the line from stop to occiput, and not much longer than the head from stop to occiput. There may be a moderate amount of wrinkle at the brows and beside the eyes, and the skin of the head should be so loose as to wrinkle noticeably when drawn forward or when the head is lowered. The flews of the upper lip overlap the lower substantially.
**Tail.** Well set-on, rather long, strong at the base and tapering with a moderate amount of coarse hair underneath. When the hound is moving, the stern is carried well up and curves gently sabre-fashion over the back, but is never curling or gay.
**Feet.** Massive, well knuckled-up and padded. The forefeet may point straight ahead or be turned slightly outwards, but in every case the hound must stand perfectly true, the weight being borne equally by toes with pads together so that the feet would leave the imprint of a large hound and no unpadded areas in contact with the ground.

# BASSET GRIFFON VENDEEN

## Good points
- Excellent family pet
- Friendly
- Likes human company
- Voice will deter unwelcome callers

## Take heed
- Needs plenty of exercise
- Not suitable for apartments or tiny gardens

The Basset Griffon Vendéen (Petit) is an ancient French hunting breed. As its name implies, it is a short-legged (basset) rough-coated (griffon) hound, originating in the district of Vendée, and is one of the four breeds of Basset Hounds found in France, the others being the Basset Artésien Normand, the Basset Bleu de Gascogne, and the Basset Fauve de Bretagne.

The Basset Griffon Vendéen (Petit) is a cheerful, active, busy little hound, intelligent and inquisitive. Its friendly nature and liking for human companionship make it an excellent family pet, and its deep resonant voice is a deterrent to unwelcome callers.

## Size
Height: 34-38cm (13½-15in). A tolerance of 1cm (²∕sin) is allowed.

## Exercise
The Basset Griffon Vendéen (Petit) is an active, energetic breed needing plenty of exercise, and is not recommended for life in small apartments or houses with tiny gardens unless great care, time and trouble can be given to its needs and well-being.

## Grooming
Its rough coat needs little attention.

## Feeding
Recommended would be ½-1 can (376g, 13.3oz size) of a branded, meaty product, with biscuit added in equal part by volume; or 1½ cupfuls of a dry food, complete diet, mixed in the proportion of 1 cup of feed to ½ cup of hot or cold water.

## Origin and history
The Griffon Vendéen (Petit) [to quote Monsieur P. Doubigne, an expert on the breed is a miniature Basset reduced in size and proportions, while retaining all the qualities of the breed: the passion for hunting, fearlessness in the densest coverts, activity and vigour. It was bred down from a larger variety, the Basset Griffon Vendéen (Grand), which was originally used for wolf hunting and is now used, in France, for hunting wild boar.

## SHOW SUMMARY
**General appearance.** A small hound, lively and vigorous, with a body of medium length. Tail carried proudly. Coat rough and long without exaggeration. Expressive head. Ears well turned, garnished with long hair, attached below the line of the eye, and not too long.
**Colour.** Unicolour; hare grizzle; grey; fawn, although this colour is not encouraged. Bicolour: orange and white; black and white; grey and white; tan and white. Tricolour: black, white and tan; white, hare and tan; white, grey and tan.
**Head and skull.** Skull slightly convex, and of moderate length; not too wide, and narrow below the eyes. Stop marked. Occipital bone showing.
**Tail.** Set high, strong at base and gradually tapering. Not too long, carried sabre fashion. Lively.
**Feet.** Not too strong; hard and tight-padded. Nails solid.

# BASSET ARTESIEN NORMAND

The Basset Artésien Normand is virtually identical to the Basset Hound and has the same feeding and grooming requirements and general characteristics. It is of ancient French origin, descended from the old French Bloodhound and the St Hubert Hound. Its job was to trail deer and small game.

This breed found favour as a hunting dog in France, but was adopted by the British, who crossed it with the Bloodhound to develop the Basset Hound, now so popular as a pet.

The breed stands 25-33cm (10-13in) high. Colours are white or white and orange. A tricoloured dog must be widely marked, with tan on the head and a mantle of specks of black or badger colour.

The long ears of the Basset Hound should be set on low but not excessively so, and never above the line of the eye. Narrow throughout their length and curling well inwards, they should reach at least to the end of a muzzle of correct length and be supple, fine and velvety in texture.

*Basset Hound*

*Basset Griffon Vendéen*

*Basset Artésien Normand*

# WHIPPET

### Good points
- *Clean*
- *Elegant*
- *Gentle and affectionate*
- *Good with children*

### Take heed
- *Strong hunting instincts*

The Whippet is an excellent choice for those who want a dog that will combine the role of an affectionate and gentle pet with performance on the track and/or in the show ring. It has a peaceful temperament, but can be a little nervous in strange surroundings.

### Size
The ideal height for dogs is 47cm (18½in) and for bitches 44.5cm (17½in). Judges should use their discretion and not unduly penalize an otherwise good specimen.

### Exercise
The Whippet is a racer, capable of 56-64km (35-40 miles) an hour. It will adapt to life away from the excitement of a track, but make sure that you can give it plenty of exercise.

### Grooming
Needs little grooming, but tail usually needs tidying up for show. Teeth should be scaled regularly. Nails will need clipping.

### Health care
Whippets are hardy, despite their delicate appearance, but should sleep indoors and be kept out of draughts.

### Feeding
Recommended would be ½-1 can (376g, 13.3oz size) of a branded meaty product, with biscuit added in equal part by volume; or 1½ cupfuls of a dry food, complete diet, mixed in the proportion of 1 cup of feed to ½ cup of hot or cold water.

### Origin and history
The Greyhound obviously had a hand in the Whippet's make-up, but there is some controversy as to whether the cross was with a terrier, a Pharaoh Hound or some other imported hound. The breed has been popular in Britain since the beginning of the century, and was exhibited at Crufts as early as 1897, being recognized by the British Kennel Club five years later. The Whippet is also popular in America, where the standard allows for a slightly larger dog. It was designed for racing and coursing, in which it excels. Many Whippet owners derive immense pleasure from keeping a dog that not only satisfies their sporting interests, but is also a popular show contender and loving household pet.

### SHOW SUMMARY
**General appearance.** Should convey an impression of beautifully balanced muscular power and strength, combined with great elegance and grace. Symmetry of outline, muscular development and powerful gait are the main considerations; the dog being built for speed and work, all forms of exaggeration should be avoided. It should possess great freedom of action; the forelegs should be thrown forward and low over the ground like a thorough-bred horse, not in a hackney-like action. Hind legs should come well under the body, giving great propelling power. Movement should not be stilted, high stepping or mincing.
**Colour.** Any colour or mixture of colours.
**Head and skull.** Long and lean, flat on top, tapering to the muzzle, rather wide between the eyes; jaws powerful and clean cut. Nose black; in blues a bluish colour is permitted, and in livers a nose of the same colour; and in whites or parti-colours a butterfly nose is permissible.
**Tail.** No feathering. Long and tapering; when in action, carried in a delicate curve upward but not over the back.
**Feet.** Very neat, well split up between the toes; knuckles highly arched; pads thick and strong.

# AUSTRALIAN KELPIE AND CATTLE DOG

### Good points
- *Brave*
- *Excellent working dog*
- *Good companion*
- *Loyal*

### Take heed
- *No known drawbacks*

The Australian Kelpie is a superb sheepdog descended from working imported Scottish stock. It is famed for the way it runs along the backs of sheep to reach the head of the flock. It is extremely fast and has an almost camel-like ability to go without water for lengthy periods. It is an attractive prick-eared dog with great intelligence and loyalty to its master.

The Australian Cattle Dog is an intelligent dog, amenable and first-rate at its job of driving cattle, sometimes covering vast distances. Like the Kelpie, it has an equable temperament and makes a loyal companion. Both these breeds are seen in the show ring in Australia.

### Size
*Kelpie.* Weight: 13.6kg (30lb). Height: 46-51cm (18-20in) at the shoulder.
*Cattle dog.* Weight: 15.9kg (35lb). Height: 51cm (20in) at shoulder.

### Exercise
The Australian Kelpie and the Australian Cattle Dog are accustomed to plenty of exercise in the great outdoors.

### Grooming
These breeds will benefit from regular vigorous brushing.

### Feeding
One to 1½ cans (376g, 13.3oz size) of a branded meaty product, with biscuit added in equal part by volume; or 3 cupfuls of a dry food, complete diet, mixed in the proportion of 1 cup of feed to ½ cup of hot or cold water.

### Origin and history
The Kelpie derives from Collies brought to Australia by early settlers. Its ancestry can be traced to a pup named Caesar, later mated to a bitch named Kelpie, whose offspring included the famous King's Kelpie, winner of the first ever sheepdog trials in Australia in 1872. The Scottish writer Robert Louis Stevenson refers to the 'Water Kelpie' in his famous adventure story *Kidnapped,* giving credence to the suggestion that Kelpies derived from the working Scottish Collie.

The Australian Cattle Dog has emerged from crossings with the Old English Sheepdog (or Bobtail), Scottish Collies, Dingos and Red Bobtails.

# STANDARD SCHNAUZER

### Good points
- *Affectionate*
- *Lively and playful*
- *Good with children*
- *Intelligent*
- *Excellent watchdog*

### Take heed
- *Mistrustful of strangers*

The Schnauzer is a good-natured, lively dog that loves both children and games. However, it does not trust strangers. It is terrier-like — thus a great ratter, intelligent and an excellent guard.

### Size
Ideal height: bitch 46cm (18in); dog 48cm (19in). Any variation of more than 2.5cm (1in) in these heights should be penalized.

### Exercise
Enjoys regular walks and ball games, but will adapt to country or apartment living.

### Grooming
The Schnauzer should be brushed every day, and trimmed in spring and autumn.

### Feeding
Recommended 1-1½ cans of a branded, meaty product (376g, 13.3oz size), with biscuit added in equal part by volume; or 3 cupfuls, of a dry, complete food, mixed in the proportion of 1 cup of feed to ½ cup of hot or cold water.

### Origin and history
As the name implies, the Schnauzer is of German origin, and there is a statue in Stuttgart, dated 1620, depicting a watchman with a dog similar in appearance to the Schnauzer of today. The breed originated in Bavaria and Württemberg where it was esteemed as a ratter and a cattle driver. However, when cattle driving died out, the breed found its way to the city, where it gained popularity, coming to the attention of serious fanciers about 1900.

### SHOW SUMMARY
**General appearance.** The Schnauzer is a powerfully built, robust, sinewy, nearly square dog, the length of its body being equal to its height at the shoulders. Its temperament combines high spirits, reliability, strength, endurance and vigour. Expression is keen and attitude alert.
**Colour.** All pepper and salt colours in even proportions, or pure black.
**Head and skull.** Head strong and elongated, gradually narrowing from the ears to the eyes and forward from there to the tip of the nose. Upper part of the head (occiput to base of the forehead) moderately broad between the ears, with flat, creaseless forehead and well-muscled but not too strongly developed cheeks. Medium stop to accentuate prominent eyebrows.
The powerful muzzle formed by the upper and lower jaws (base of the forehead to tip of the nose) should end in a moderately blunt line, with bristly, stubbly moustache and chin whiskers. Ridge of the nose straight and running almost parallel to the extension of the forehead. The nose is black and full. Lips should be tight.
**Tail.** Set on and carried high; cut down to three joints.
**Feet.** Short, round, extremely compact, with close-arched toes (cat's paws), dark nails and hard soles. The feet also deep or thickly padded, pointing forward.

# MEDIUM PINSCHER

(German Pinscher)

### Good points
- *Alert guard*
- *Elegant appearance*
- *Lively pet*
- *Loyal to owner*

### Take heed
- *Aggressive to strangers*
- *Fiery temperament*

The Medium Pinscher, previously known as the German Pinscher, is a very old breed, yet it is virtually unknown outside its homeland. This, the middle-sized of the Pinschers, bears far more similarity to the Dobermann than to the Miniature Pinscher and, like the Dobermann, has its ears cropped in its native country. The tail is docked and the coat is smooth and glossy. Colour usually black with small tan markings or self red. There is also a most attractive and distinctive harlequin Pinscher.

The Medium Pinscher was bred as a ratter, but nowadays is mainly kept as an alert, lively pet. Height is 40.5-48cm (16-19in).

The coat of the Whippet should be fine, short and as closely-textured as possible. Its chest should be very deep and its back broad, well-muscled and arched over the loin.

Medium Pinscher

Whippet

Australian Kelpie

The Schnauzer breed was first shown in the USA at the beginning of the 20th century, when some confusion was caused because both Schnauzers and Dobermanns were generally called Pinschers.

Standard Schnauzer

# SWISS HUNTING DOGS

(Schweizer Laufhund, Bruno de Jura, Lucernese, Bernese)

## Good points
- *Active*
- *Friendly*
- *First-rate hunting dogs*

## Take heed
- *Not really suitable as household companions*

There are some four varieties of the Swiss Hunting Dog (not to be confused with smaller types), all of which, with the exception of the Jura, have the same standard in their country of origin. They are friendly, active and powerfully built. They predominantly hunt hare and are speedy and excellent trackers with a good nose. Their lively disposition and strong hunting instincts do not equip them for the role of household companion.

## Size
Minimum height: 44.5cm (17½in) all types, but varies considerably.

## Exercise
Need plenty of vigorous exercise for full fitness.

## Grooming
Regular brushing.

## Feeding
One to 1½ cans (376g, 13.3oz size) of a branded meaty product, with biscuit added in equal part by volume; or 3 cupfuls of a dry food, complete diet, mixed in the proportion of 1 cup of feed to ½ cup of hot or cold water. This should be increased when the hound is in hard exercise.

## Origin and history
The Swiss Hound, particularly the Laufhund, is a breed previously little known, but now gaining recognition internationally. To trace the origin of the Swiss Hounds we must go back to the pre-Christian era, when similar hunting dogs were introduced into Egypt by the Phoenicians and the Greeks, eventually finding their way to Switzerland when it was under Roman rule. The antiquity of the breed is verified by illustrations made during the 12th century, which can be seen in Zurich Cathedral. The heaviest of the four is the Jura, which is of the St Hubert type and similar to the French Ardennes Hound. When it gets the scent, it will brief with a drawn-out note that can be heard for many miles around: in fact it is rather like the English Bloodhound. The Bruno type of Jura is about the same size but appears sleeker and faster.

## SHOW SUMMARY
*Schweizer (Swiss), Lucernese and Bernese*
**General appearance.** The general appearance of this Swiss breed

*Above: A powerfully-built Bernese Swiss Hound, with tan markings on its cheek and above the eye.*

should be that of a dog of medium size, fairly long, selected for vigour, resistance, nobility and general overall conformation; they are lively, intelligent, and have great enthusiasm for the hunt. The head is lean and long, with huge, folded ears set on low and back. The forelegs are strong and vertical, the hind legs powerful and well muscled; the back is rather long, straight and muscular; the loins are very muscular and the shoulders long and sloping; the rib cage is deep. All these qualities indicate great powers of resistance. These dogs are excellent hunters, combining a number of fine talents, such as a very keen sense of smell and the utmost self-reliance in the field, with a powerful voice; they are, moreover, very good in the roughest terrain. All Swiss tracking hounds (except those of the Bloodhound type) have the same general characteristics, differing only in colour and coat.
**Colour.** *Schweizer:* White coat, with more or less large markings of orange or yellow-orange. Dogs with red coats are admissible. An occasional small red spot is not to be considered a fault.
*Lucernese:* White background with grey or blue specklings and broad dark or black markings. It also has tan markings or yellow-brown areas of colour on the head, body and feet. Similarly, beneath the white hair, the skin is speckled with more or less dark markings. When the coat is wet the white disappears and the dog seems to be much darker, slate grey or blue.
*Bernese:* The coat is invariably tricolour – white, black and more or less intense tan markings. The background is white, with huge black markings and small black spots here and there. The tan markings are above the eyes, on the cheeks, on the inner part of

*Below: Lively and intelligent, the Schweizer Laufhund is one of four varieties of the Swiss Hunting Dog.*

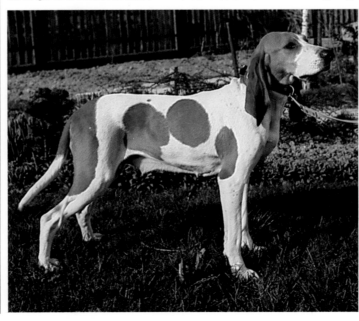

the ears and at the root of the tail.
**Head.** Lean, long, in good proportion to the overall size of the dog. The stop is well defined. The nose is black and fairly large, with broad, well-open nostrils; the bridge is slightly arched. The lips are not heavy. The muzzle is long; the jaws very strong, with well-adapted teeth, and close in either a pincer or a scissor bite.
**Tail.** Not too long; should be carried horizontally or slightly curved; should never be curled. Pointed at the tip, the tail should be well feathered, smooth in smooth-haired dogs and proportionately thicker in the coarse-haired dogs, without being tufted.
**Feet.** Rounded, with hard, wrinkled pads and solid nails.

*Bruno de Jura*
**General appearance.** This is the most massive of the Swiss Hounds. The back is long and broad; the members are strongly boned. The dewlap, the heavy, massive head with its long muzzle, the lips, the wrinkles on the forehead, the eye with its profound and melancholy expression, the ears set on low, long and folded – all these features distinguish this variety and have attracted attention to it.
**Colour.** The coat may be solid brown-yellow or reddish brown; or it may have a huge black saddle on the back; or it may be black, with tan markings above the eyes, on the cheeks and on the underparts of the body. Sometimes there is a white mark on the chest.
**Head.** Powerful and massive. The skull is broad and fully rounded. The forehead is wrinkled in a characteristic manner, and the occipital protuberance is very pronounced.
**Tail.** Of medium length, ending in a pointed tip, strong and well feathered, but never tufted; carried rather high, without appreciable curving; never carried above the back.
**Feet.** Rounded, well closed, with hard wrinkled pads; nails strong and black.

The Bruno de Jura, a keen, clear-voiced hound, has only one variety of coat—short, dense and hard. The Bruno should not be below 44.5cm (17½in) in height, but the lighter Short-Legged Jura Hound, somewhat resembling the Basset Artésien Normand, is below 38cm (15in) at the shoulder.

*Bruno de Jura*

*Lucernese*

The Lucernese is a medium-sized hound of graceful build and somewhat leggy appearance. Its narrow ears, set well back and very low, should be of sufficient length to reach the tip of its muzzle. A smaller variety, the Short-Legged Lucernese, stands 29-38cm (11½-15in) at the shoulder.

*Schweizer Laufhund*

# LAPPHUND
(Lapland Spitz)

## Good points
● *Easy to train*
● *Friendly*
● *Lively*

## Take heed
● *Suspicious of strangers*

The Lapphund was bred to hunt reindeer, but since the need for this type of work has ceased, the breed has been used not only as a cattle dog, but also as a household pet, a role into which it has fitted happily, being both friendly and easy to train.

## Size
Height: dog 44.5-49.5cm (17½-19½in) at the shoulder; bitch 39.5-44.5cm (15½-17½in).

## Exercise
Needs regular walks and off-the-lead runs for full fitness.

## Grooming
Regular brushing will keep the coat in good condition.

## Feeding
One to 1½ cans (376g, 13.3oz size) of a branded meaty product, with biscuit added in equal part by volume; or 3 cupfuls of a dry food, complete diet, mixed in the proportion of 1 cup of feed to ½ cup of hot or cold water.

## Origin and history
The Lapphund was produced as a hunter and herder of reindeer. When the reindeer became a farm animal, the Lapphund was given a new role as a cattle dog, but a larger number found their way to the south of Sweden, where they began to be kept as family pets. The breed is slowly but surely becoming very popular in its country of origin.

## SHOW SUMMARY
**General characteristics.** A medium-sized dog, rather tall, with very strong jaws, prick ears, and either a ring or a docked tail.
**Colour.** Dark brown, black, or brown-white. Solid colours are preferable, although not required. A white spot on the chest is also allowed, as are a white collar, white chest, and markings on the feet and on the nape.
**Head.** The head is roughly conical, with a straight bridge and dark nose that should ideally be jet black. The lips fit well over the gums. The muzzle is rather short and practically a cone, broad at the base and narrowing to a point at the nose. The teeth close in a scissor bite. The stop is well defined. The skull is domed and broad between the ears. The ridge above the eyes is rather prominent.
**Tail.** Well curled up onto the back, resplendent in its thick feathering, and normally short tail or a docked tail is acceptable.
**Feet.** Rather long and powerful, with close toes, well arched, with hair between them.

# LAPPISH VALLHUND
(Laplandic Herder)

## Good points
● *Fine herder/guard*
● *Makes a good pet*

## Take heed
● *No drawbacks known*

The Lappish Vallhund is similar to the Swedish Lapphund. It is, however, a Finnish Spitz, mainly used for herding reindeer. It also makes a good pet and companion.

## Size
Height: dog 48-54.5cm (19-21½in); bitch 43-48cm (17-19in).

## Exercise
Provide liberal amounts of vigorous exercise for good health.

## Grooming
Regular brushing will keep the coat looking healthy.

## Feeding
Recommended would be 1½-2½ cans (376g, 13.3oz size) of a branded meaty product, with biscuit added in equal part by volume; or 5 cupfuls of a dry food, complete diet, mixed in the proportion of 1 cup of feed to ½ cup of hot or cold water.

## Origin and history
Writing in *Dogs of the World*, Bo Bengtson and Ake Wintzell suggest that, when communications between the native peoples of Lapland in northern Scandinavia increased, their dogs interbred with various southern breeds. This resulted in southern breeders preserving the pure strain of the original Lapphund while the Laplanders' own dogs were ruined for their task of reindeer herding through crosses with unsuitable dogs of other breeds. Subsequently they set about breeding out imported, undesirable traits, the result becoming known as the Laplandic Herder.

# ICELAND DOG
(Icelandic Sheepdog)

## Good points
● *Faithful*
● *Intelligent*
● *Trustworthy*

## Take heed
● *No drawbacks known*

The Iceland Dog has been known since the last century and is a reliable sheepdog. It is similar in appearance to the Finnish Spitz and Norwegian Buhund.

## Size
Height about 48cm (19in).

## Exercise
Needs plenty of exercise.

## Grooming
Normal daily brushing.

## Feeding
One to 1½ cans (376g, 13.3oz size) of a branded meaty product, with biscuit added in equal part by volume; or 3 cupfuls of a dry food, complete diet, mixed in the proportion of 1 cup of feed to ½ cup of hot or cold water.

## Origin and history
A standard was introduced for the Iceland Dog in Denmark in 1898. It is also recognized in the United Kingdom but not in the USA; registrations are very low, however, and the breed is rarely exhibited. It would seem that the role of the Iceland Dog, like that of the Buhund, is a reliable, all-purpose farm animal.

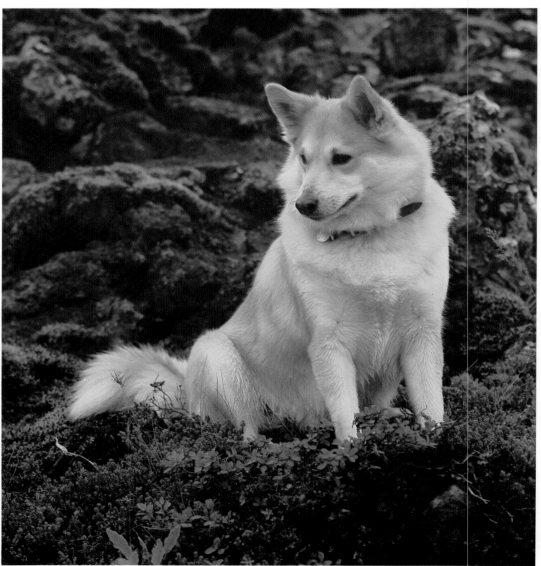

*Below: The faithful Iceland Dog resembles the Finnish Spitz and Norwegian Buhund in appearance.*

Strongly built and of alert, intelligent appearance, the Lappish Vallhund shares many of the features of the Spitz family, but is a little longer in the back. The loosely-curling tail is sometimes carried over the back and sometimes droops over one thigh. The FCI approved this dog as a separate breed in 1946.

*Lappish Vallhund*

*Lapphund*

*Iceland Dog*

Although the Lapphund is no longer used as a herder, it is increasingly popular as a household pet. The Swedish Army has recently begun to breed Lapphunds for employment as guard dogs.

# KEESHOND

**Good points**
● *Equable temperament*
● *Good watchdog*
● *Long-lived*

**Take heed**
● *Needs lots of grooming*
● *One-person dog*

The Keeshond, Holland's national dog, began life as a barge dog, and still has the knack of finding an out-of-the-way corner for itself. It is a loyal dog, of sound temperament, but needs a lot of grooming and tends to favour one member of the family. It is an excellent watchdog and generally has a very long life.

**Size**
Height: dog 46cm (18in), bitch 43cm (17in).

**Exercise**
Average requirements.

**Grooming**
Regular attention with a stiff brush. A choke chain should not be used on this breed or it will spoil the ruff.

**Feeding**
Recommended would be 1-1½ cans (376g, 13.3oz size) of a branded meaty product, with biscuit added in equal part by volume; or 3 cupfuls of a dry food, complete diet, mixed in the proportion of 1 cup of feed to ½ cup of hot or cold water.

*Below: A Keeshond and her pup. Note the ruff on the adult dog; this breed needs regular grooming.*

**Origin and history**
The Keeshond (plural Keeshonden), pronounced Kayshond, has a romantic history. During the period of uncertainty that preceded the French Revolution, the patriots were led by a man named Kees de Gyselaer, a dog lover who owned a little dog of this breed. The dog, named Kees, became the symbol of the patriots, and gave the breed its name.

The Keeshond has never become very popular outside Holland, despite Mrs I. Tucker's Champion Volkrijk of Vorden being Best in Show at Crufts in 1957. It has, however, a staunch band of devotees who breed for soundness and quality. In common with other Spitz varieties, the Keeshond must originally have evolved in the Arctic Circle, and it has the traditional Spitz tail tightly curled over the back.

**SHOW SUMMARY**
**General appearance.** A short, compact body; alert carriage, fox-like head. Small pointed ears, and a well-feathered, curling tail, carried over the back. Hair very thick on the neck, forming a large ruff; head, ears and legs covered with short thick hair. Dogs should move cleanly and briskly (not lope like a German Shepherd Dog) but movement should be straight and sharp. Dogs should show boldly.
**Head and skull.** Head well proportioned to the body, wedge-shaped when seen from above; from the side showing a definite stop. Muzzle should be of medium length, neither coarse nor snipy.
**Colour.** Should be wolf, ash-grey; not all black or all white; markings should be definite.
**Tail.** Tightly curled; a double curl at the end is desirable. Plume should be white on the top where curled, with a black tip.
**Feet.** Round and cat-like, with black nails.

# NORWEGIAN BUHUND
(Norsk Buhund)

**Good points**
● *Friendly*
● *Gentle with children*
● *Good guard*

**Take heed**
● *Natural herder*

The Norwegian Buhund is a lively and alert dog, but a natural herder that will, like the Border Collie, round up anything, be it poultry, cattle or people. It needs lots of exercise and makes the ideal playmate for children.

**Size**
Dog not more than 45cm (17¾ in); bitch somewhat less.

**Exercise**
Needs plenty of exercise to unleash its boundless energy.

**Grooming**
Regular brushing and combing. Easy breed to prepare for showing.

*Above: A young Norwegian Buhund adopts his favourite position, typical of Spitz dogs.*

**Feeding**
One to 1½ cans (376g, 13.3oz size) of a branded meaty product, with biscuit added in equal part by volume; or 3 cupfuls of a dry food, complete diet, mixed in the proportion of 1 cup of feed to ½ cup of hot or cold water.

**Origin and history**
The Buhund is one of Norway's national dogs and was developed as an all-purpose farm dog to control sheep and cattle. It is, however, only since the 1920s that the breed has become known and appreciated outside its homeland, particularly in the United Kingdom, where it is gaining in popularity. The word buhund is Norwegian for 'farm dog', the Norwegian Buhund being a true farm dog, still occasionally used for herding.

**SHOW SUMMARY**
**General appearance.** The Norwegian Buhund is a typical Spitz dog of under middle size, lightly built, with a short compact body, fairly smooth coat, erect pointed ears, tail carried curled over the back, and an energetic character. It is of prime importance that the Buhund should be a well-balanced dog, free from all exaggeration, and capable of arduous work.
**Colour.** Wheaten (biscuit), black, red (if not too dark), wolf-sable. Preferably self-coloured but small symmetrical markings — such as white on chest and legs, blaze on head, narrow ring on neck, black mask and ears and black tip to the tail — are permissible.
**Head and skull.** Head lean, light, rather broad between the ears, wedge-shaped, narrowing towards the point of the nose. Skull and back of head almost flat; marked but not sharp stop; muzzle of medium length, tapering evenly from above and side, with straight bridge; lips tightly closed.
**Tail.** Placed high on; short, thick and hairy, but without long hair; tightly curled.
**Feet.** Rather small, oval in shape, with tightly closed toes.

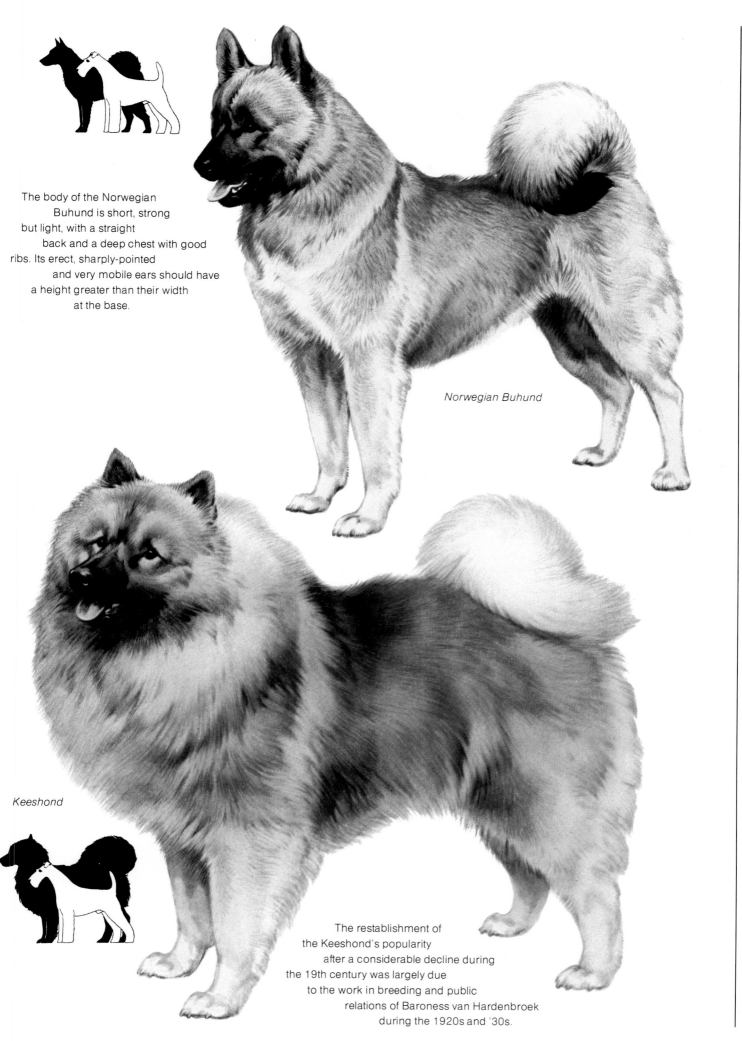

The body of the Norwegian
Buhund is short, strong
but light, with a straight
back and a deep chest with good
ribs. Its erect, sharply-pointed
and very mobile ears should have
a height greater than their width
at the base.

*Norwegian Buhund*

*Keeshond*

The restablishment of
the Keeshond's popularity
after a considerable decline during
the 19th century was largely due
to the work in breeding and public
relations of Baroness van Hardenbroek
during the 1920s and '30s.

# SIBERIAN HUSKY

## Good points
- *Adaptable*
- *Friendly*
- *Good with children*
- *Intelligent*
- *Reliable*

## Take heed
- *Needs lots of exercise*

The Siberian Husky is perhaps the most friendly of all Arctic Spitz breeds, having a long history of friendship with man, combining the roles of household companion with work-mate, hauling the sled or herding. It is faithful and reliable.

## Size
Height at the withers: dog 53-60cm (21-23½in); bitch 51-56cm (20-22in). Weight: dog 20.5-27.2kg (45-60lb); bitch 15.9-22.7kg (35-50lb). Weight should be in proportion to height.

## Exercise
Famed for sled racing, remarkable endurance and great powers of speed, this is not a dog to keep confined in a small back yard.

## Grooming
Regular brushing will keep the coat in good condition.

## Feeding
Recommended would be 1½-2½ cans (376g, 13.3oz size) of a branded meaty product, with biscuit added in equal part by volume; or 5 cupfuls of a dry food, complete diet, mixed in the proportion of 1 cup of feed to ½ cup of hot or cold water.

## Origin and history
The Siberian Husky was bred by the nomadic Chukchi tribes of north-east Asia. Their purpose in breeding the Husky, from other local dogs, was to produce a hardy animal of great endurance that would combine the roles of companion and hunter with that of a speedy sled dog which, at times, would be their only means of transport.

More recently, the Siberian Husky has been recognized as a show dog. It performed creditably as a Search and Rescue dog for the American Air Force in World War II, and has popularized the sport of sled racing in America and elsewhere in the world.

## SHOW SUMMARY
**General appearance.** A medium-sized working sled dog, quick and light on its feet, free and graceful in action, with a moderately compact and well-furred body, erect ears and brush tail. The characteristic gait is smooth and seemingly effortless. Its body proportions and forms reflect a basic balance of power, speed and endurance. It should never appear heavy and coarse, nor light and fragile. The males should be masculine but never coarse; the

*Above: The Siberian Husky is a graceful dog with great powers of speed and endurance. It was bred to hunt and haul sleds in north-east Asia as well as provide intelligent and reliable companionship. It is now famed for sled racing, popular in America.*

bitches should appear feminine but without weakness of structure. Both sexes should be capable of great endurance. In proper condition, with firm and well-developed muscle, the Siberian Husky does not carry excess weight. Any appearance of excessive bone or weight; constricted or clumsy gait; straight or loose shoulders; weak pasterns; weak, sloping or roach back; straight stifles; feet soft and splayed, too large and clumsy, or too small and delicate, is undesirable.

**Colour.** All colours, including white, are allowed, and all markings. A variety of markings on the head is common, including many striking patterns not found in other breeds.

**Head and skull.** The head should be of medium size and in proportion to the body, neither clumsy nor too fine. It should be slightly rounded on top, tapering gradually from the widest point to the eyes. The muzzle should be of medium length and width, neither snipy nor coarse, and taper gradually to the rounded nose. The distance from the tip of the nose to the stop should be equal to the distance from the stop to the occiput. The stop should be clearly defined but not excessive, and the line of the nose straight from the stop to the tip. The nose should be black in grey, tan or black dogs; liver in copper dogs; and may be flesh-coloured in pure white dogs. In winter a pink-streaked 'snow nose' is acceptable.

**Tail.** The well-furred tail of round fox-brush shape should be set on just below the level of the top line, and should usually be carried over the back in a graceful sickle curve when the dog is at attention. When carried up, the tail should not curl

too tightly, nor should it curl to either side of the body or snap flat against the back. The hair on the tail should be of medium length, and approximately the same length all round. A trailing tail is normal for the dog when it is either working or in repose.

# SAMOYED

## Good points
- *Beautiful*
- *Devoted to owner*
- *Obedient*
- *Intelligent*

## Take heed
- *Slightly independent*
- *That white coat sheds*

The Samoyed, or 'Sammy' as it is often called, is a beautiful, somewhat independent breed that should, according to its standard, show 'marked affection for all mankind'. These dogs adore the snow and are happiest in the wide open spaces. But having said that, I know of some living happily in semi-detached houses, and one that has become a TV star.

## Size
Height at the shoulder: dog 51-56cm (20-22in); bitch 46-51cm (18-20in). Weight in proportion to size.

## Exercise
Needs a liberal amount of exercise and, if possible, some obedience work, even if this is only weekly attendance at a dog training club – which, after all, is recommended for all breeds.

## Grooming
Regular brushing and combing, and a towelling after getting wet. The under-coat sheds once a year; at such times it is best to comb out as much surplus hair as one can. Bathing helps, as this tends to loosen the hair.

## Feeding
Recommended would be 1½-2½ cans (376g, 13.3oz size) of a branded meaty product, with biscuit added in equal part by volume; or 5 cupfuls of a dry food, complete diet, mixed in the proportion of 1 cup of feed to ½ cup of hot or cold water.

## Origin and history
The Samoyed is a beautiful Spitz-type that takes its name from the Siberian tribe of the Samoyedes. It is a sled dog in its native country, and is also used as a guard and herder of reindeer. Some Sammies were used by the explorer Nansen on his journey to the North Pole.

The breed came to Britain in 1889, and much of the present-day stock can be traced to the original pair. British stock has done much to popularize the breed in other countries of the world.

## SHOW SUMMARY
**General appearance.** The Samoyed, being essentially a work-

*Above: The Samoyed is a beautiful and devoted dog and is growing increasingly popular. Coming from a cold climate, its heavy and weather-resistant coat needs regular brushing and combing. It also needs plenty of exercise and should attend obedience classes.*

ing dog, should be strong and active and graceful; and as its work lies in cold climates, its coat should be heavy and weather-resistant. It should not be too long in the back, because a weak back would make the dog practically useless for its legitimate work; but at the same time a cobby body, such as a Chow's, would also place it at a great disadvantage as a draught dog. Breeders should aim for a happy medium, viz. a body not long, but muscular, allowing liberty, with a deep chest and well-sprung ribs, a strong neck proudly arched, straight front and exceptionally strong loins. Both dog and bitch should give the appearance of being capable of great endurance, but should be free from coarseness. A full-grown dog should stand about 53cm (21in) at the shoulder. On account of the depth of chest required, the legs should be moderately long; a very short-legged dog is to be deprecated. Hindquarters should be particularly well developed, stifles well angulated, and any suggestion of unsound stifles or cow hocks severely penalized.

**Colour.** Pure white; white and biscuit; cream.

**Head and skull.** Head powerful and wedge-shaped, with a broad, flat skull; muzzle of medium length; a tapering foreface not too sharply defined. Lips black. Hair short and smooth before the ears. Nose black for preference, but may be brown or flesh-coloured. Strong jaws.

**Tail.** Long and profuse, carried over the back when alert; sometimes dropped when at rest.

**Feet.** Long, flattish and slightly spread out. Soles well cushioned with hair.

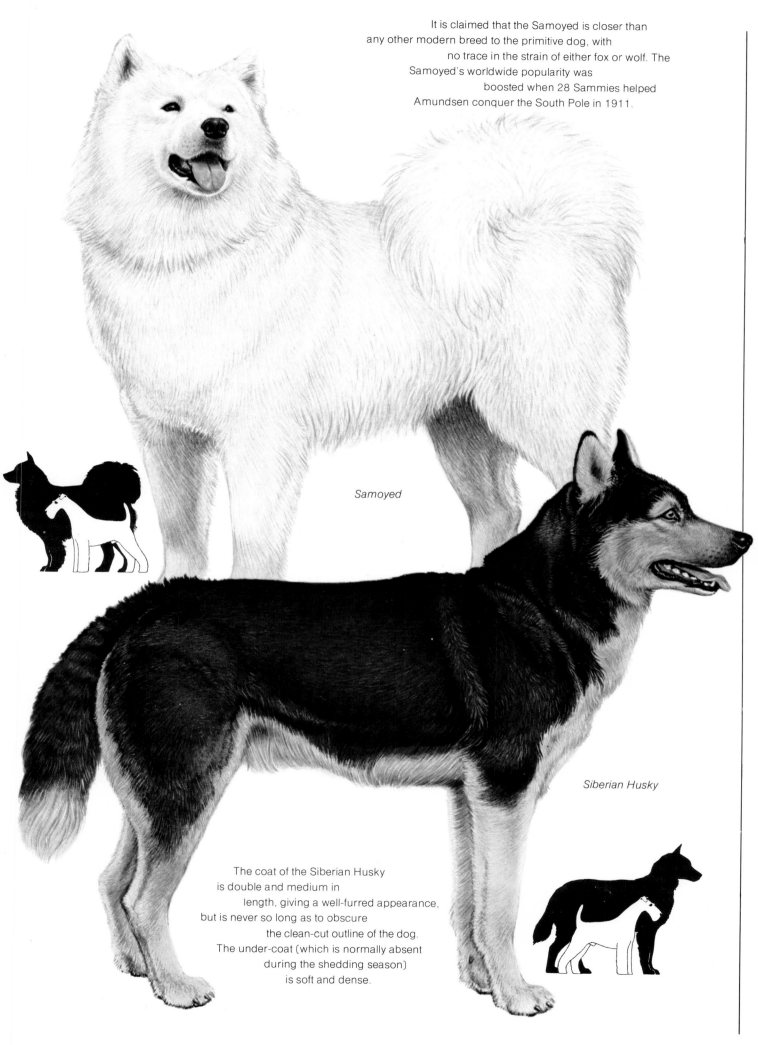

It is claimed that the Samoyed is closer than any other modern breed to the primitive dog, with no trace in the strain of either fox or wolf. The Samoyed's worldwide popularity was boosted when 28 Sammies helped Amundsen conquer the South Pole in 1911.

*Samoyed*

*Siberian Husky*

The coat of the Siberian Husky is double and medium in length, giving a well-furred appearance, but is never so long as to obscure the clean-cut outline of the dog. The under-coat (which is normally absent during the shedding season) is soft and dense.

Bullmastiff

Neapolitan Mastiff

Irish Wolfhound

# A
## Selection of
# LARGE DOGS

Large dogs are magnificent, impressive, and un-doubtedly useful. They also often attract the wrong owners, reminding one of the old adage that there are no bad dogs, only bad owners.

The right reasons for wanting a large dog are basic-ally that you like and admire them, you want to work a specific type at the task for which it was bred, you need a guard, you aim to enter obedience com-petitions, or you wish to have a large, lovable pet for the family. Any of these reasons is acceptable, pro-vided that you select a breed carefully, have adequate space, and are able to give the dog the liberal feeding and exercise it will probably need.

Don't buy a large, ferocious-looking animal because you are a timid type and think that having a German Shepherd Dog on a chain will have the immediate effect of making you feel, and look, 10 feet tall; or, if you've never owned a dog before, buy a GSD thinking it is some kind of super-charged burglar alarm. The German Shepherd Dog is an intelligent animal that likes, and deserves, a job to do. It is loyal and affectionate, but it also has a strong protective and guarding instinct, so don't leave it about the house all day getting bored.

The Rottweiler and Dobermann also make excellent guards, but settle for an Airedale bitch if you want your guard dog as a part-time children's Nanny, or leave the kids with a lovable, reliable St Bernard. Big dogs whelp easier than small ones and generally have large litters. Most are good-natured, but they benefit from firm, but kindly, dis-cipline in puppyhood and attendance at dog training classes, which can develop from chore to hobby and thence to obsession.

Large dogs—with a few noted exceptions—tend to resemble large, aggressive men who become putty in the little woman's hands and revel in companionship and fondling almost as much as in vigorous outdoor activity. A picture that will always remain in my memory is of a small child, fast asleep on a bench at Crufts, cuddled up to the protective, majestic body of an Irish Wolfhound. That massive dog was living up to its breed's reputation of 'gentle when stroked, fierce when provoked'. The little girl could not have been safer.

# STANDARD POODLE

### Good points
- Eye-catching appearance
- Good temperament
- Intelligent
- Recommended household pet
- Good sense of fun
- Splendid retriever
- Has stamina
- Useful in obedience competitions
- Usually good with children and other dogs

### Take heed
- Do not make a clown or fashion model out of a fundamentally outdoor type

The Poodle has a character full of fun. It is intelligent and obedient. In the United Kingdom it has proved a useful competitor in obedience competitions. It has a fondness for water, if the owner permits, but is much favoured for the show ring where, exhibited in the traditional lion clip, it is a beauty to behold. It is also, debatably, the most difficult breed to prepare for the ring, involving the handler in a day's canine beauty treatment.

### Size
Height: 38cm (15in) and over.

### Exercise
This is a robust, healthy dog that loves the outdoors, has plenty of stamina and has lost none of its retrieving sporting instincts. It will enjoy plenty of exercise.

### Grooming
Use a wire-pin pneumatic brush and a wire-toothed metal comb for daily grooming. The lion clip is an essential for the show ring, but pet owners generally resort to the more natural lamb clip with the hair a short uniform length. It is possible to clip your own dog with a pair of hairdressers' scissors. However, if, despite the help which is usually available from the breeder, you find the task tedious, there are numerous pet and poodle parlours to which you should take your dog every six weeks. Bath regularly.

### Feeding
About 1½ cans (376g, 13.3oz size) of a branded, meaty product, with biscuit added in equal part by volume; or 3 cupfuls of a dry, complete food, mixed in the proportion of 1 cup of feed to ½ cup of hot or cold water.

### Origin and history
The Poodle was originally a shaggy guard, a retriever and protector of sheep, with origins similar to the Irish Water Spaniel and, no doubt, a common ancestor in the French Barbet and Hungarian Water Hound.

The Poodle may not be, as many suppose, solely of French origin. It originated in Germany as a water retriever; even the word poodle comes from the German 'pudel-nass' or puddle. From this fairly large sturdy dog, the Standard Poodle, the Miniature and the Toy have evolved.

The breed has been known in England since Prince Rupert of the Rhine, in company with his Poodle, came to the aid of Charles I in battle. The breed was favoured also by Marie Antoinette who, rumour has it, invented the lion clip by devising a style which would match the uniform of her courtiers. It is also popular in the United States.

### SHOW SUMMARY
**General appearance.** A very active, intelligent, well-balanced and elegant-looking dog with good temperament, carrying itself very proudly.

**Colour.** All solid colours. White and cream Poodles to have black nose, lips and eye-rims; black toe-nails desirable. Brown Poodles to have dark amber eyes, dark liver nose, lips, eye-rims and toe-nails. Apricot Poodles to have dark eyes with black points or deep amber eyes with live points. Black, silver and blue Poodles to have black nose, lips, eye-rims and toe-nails. Cream, apricot, brown, silver and blue Poodles may show varying shades of the same colour up to 18 months. Clear colours preferred.

**Head and skull.** Long and fine with slight peak at the back. The skull not broad and with a moderate stop. Foreface strong and well chiselled, not falling away under the eyes; bones and muscle flat. Lips tight fitting. Chin well defined, but not protruding. The whole head must be in proportion to the size of the dog.

**Tail.** Set on rather high, well carried at a slight angle away from the body; never curled or carried over the back; thick at the root.

**Feet.** Pasterns strong; tight feet proportionately small, oval in shape, turning neither in nor out; toes arched; pads thick, hard and well cushioned.

# IRISH WATER SPANIEL

### Good points
- Brave
- Easily trained
- Equable temperament
- Intelligent
- Loving

### Take heed
- No drawbacks known

The Irish Water Spaniel is a most attractive animal, loyal, intelligent and with a deeply affectionate nature. It is an excellent retriever and a strong, fearless swimmer, most useful for wild-fowling.

### Size
Height: dog 53-58.5cm (21-23in); bitch 51-56cm (20-22in).

### Exercise
Needs plenty of exercise.

### Grooming
Daily brushing and weekly combing. Seek advice on stripping of unwanted hair. Take care that mud does not become caked in the toes.

### Feeding
One to 1½ cans (376g, 13.3oz size) of a branded meaty product, with biscuit added in equal part by volume; or 3 cupfuls of a dry food, complete diet, mixed in the proportion of 1 cup of feed to ½ cup of hot or cold water.

### Origin and history
It is not surprising that there is some resemblance between the Standard Poodle and the Irish Water Spaniel, because they are, or were, both water retrievers. This dog was developed in Ireland from several spaniel breeds towards the end of the 19th century. Unfortunately, perhaps, it has never gained immense popularity.

### SHOW SUMMARY
**General appearance.** The Irish Water Spaniel is a gundog bred for work in all types of shooting, and particularly suited for wild-fowling. Its fitness for this purpose should be evident in its appearance; it is a strongly built, compact dog, intelligent, enduring and eager.

**Colour.** A rich dark liver, with the purplish tint or bloom peculiar to the breed and sometimes referred to as puce-liver.

**Head and skull.** The head should be of good size. The skull high in dome, of good length and width sufficient to allow adequate brain capacity. The muzzle long, strong and somewhat square with a gradual stop. The face should be smooth and the skull covered with long curls in the form of a pronounced topknot growing in a well-defined peak to a point between the eyes. Nose large and well-developed, dark liver colour. There should be an impression of fineness.

**Tail.** Peculiar to the breed, should be short and straight, thick at the root and tapering to a fine point. It should be low set, carried straight and below the level of the back; and in length should not reach the hock joint. About 7.5-10cm (3-4in) of the tail at the root should be covered by close curls that stop abruptly; the remainder should be bare or covered by straight fine hairs.

**Feet.** Should be large and somewhat round and spreading; well-covered with hair over and between the toes.

# AMERICAN WATER SPANIEL

### Good points
- Equable temperament
- Excellent working dog
- Hardy

### Take heed
- No drawbacks known

The American Water Spaniel is little known outside its country of origin, where it has found great favour as a working gundog. It is a strong swimmer, an excellent water-fowler and an efficient retriever of most game.

### Size
Height: 38-46cm (15-18in).
Weight: dog 12.7-20.5kg (28-45lb); bitch, 11.3-18.1kg (25-40lb).

### Exercise
Needs plenty of exercise.

### Grooming
Daily brushing and weekly combing. Seek advice on stripping of unwanted hair. Take care that mud does not become caked in the toes.

### Feeding
One to 1½ cans (376g, 13.3oz size) of a branded meaty product, with biscuit added in equal part by volume; or 3 cupfuls of a dry food, complete diet, mixed in the proportion of 1 cup of feed to ½ cup of hot or cold water.

### Origin and history
The American Water Spaniel is believed to have originated through the crossing of an Irish Water Spaniel with a smaller spaniel breed and/or with a Curly-coated Retriever.

In some parts of America it is still known as the Boykin Spaniel, after Whit Boykin, one of the pioneers of the breed in Boykin, South Carolina. It was recognized by the American Kennel Club in 1940, but, at the time of writing, has still to be recognized in the United Kingdom.

### SHOW SUMMARY
**General appearance.** Medium in size, of sturdy typical spaniel character, curly coat, an active muscular dog, with emphasis placed on proper size and conformation, correct head properties, texture of coat and colour. Of amicable disposition; demeanour indicates intelligence, strength and endurance.

**Colour.** Solid liver or dark chocolate, a little white on toes or chest permissible.

**Head and skull.** Moderate in length, skull rather broad and full, stop moderately defined, but not too pronounced. Forehead covered with short smooth hair and without tuft or topknot. Muzzle of medium length, square and with no inclination to snipiness, jaws strong and of good length, and neither undershot nor overshot, teeth straight and well shaped. Nose sufficiently wide and with well-developed nostrils to ensure good scenting power.

**Tail.** Moderate in length, curved in a slightly rocker shape, carried slightly below level of back; tapered and covered with hair to tip; action lively.

**Feet.** Should harmonize with size of dog. Toes closely grouped and well padded.

The Poodle's potential for glamour has sometimes obscured its essentially active and sporting character. Because its intelligence enables it to be trained to perform complex tricks, and because it can be attractively clipped, it was formerly employed as a circus dog.

*Standard Poodle*

*Irish Water Spaniel*

*American Water Spaniel*

# ENGLISH SPRINGER SPANIEL

## Good points
- *Excellent with children*
- *Good worker in the field*
- *Intelligent*
- *Loyal*
- *Good house pet*

## Take heed
- *Could develop skin trouble and/or put on weight, if under-exercised*

The English Springer Spaniel makes an excellent dual-purpose gundog and pet. It gives a good account of itself in obedience competitions and excels as a happy, efficient retriever.

## Size
The approximate height should be 51cm (20in). The approximate weight should be 22.7kg (50lb).

## Exercise
Needs plenty of exercise, or is likely to put on weight. Lack of exercise often leads to skin troubles, too.

## Grooming
Daily brushing. Take care that mud does not become caked in the paws, and make sure that the ears are kept clean and tangle-free to prevent infection.

## Feeding
One to 1½ cans (376g, 13.3oz size) of a branded meaty product, with biscuit added in equal part by volume; or 3 cupfuls of a dry food, complete diet, mixed in the proportion of 1 cup of feed to ½ cup of hot or cold water.

## Origin and history
The English Springer is the oldest of the British spaniels except for the Clumber, but it has never gained the popularity of the smaller Cocker Spaniel, tending to be favoured, in the main, by those with an interest in shooting and/or field trials. Incidentally, the English Springer was appreciated by the Americans as a 'bird' dog before it had even been recognized by the Kennel Club in London. There is some controversy as to whether the dog, originally called a Norfolk Spaniel, came from the county of Norfolk, England, or took its name from the famous Norfolk family. Certainly the name 'springer' is derived from its early task of 'springing' game for the hunter's nets.

## SHOW SUMMARY
**General appearance.** The general appearance of the modern Springer is that of a symmetrical compact, strong, upstanding, merry and active dog, built for endurance and activity. It is the highest on the leg and the raciest in build of all British land spaniels.
**Colour.** Any recognized land spaniel colour is acceptable, but

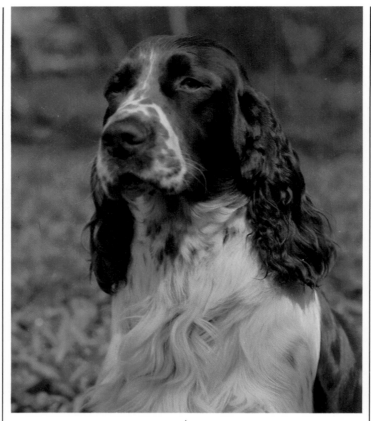

*Above: The English Springer Spaniel needs regular grooming and plenty of long energetic walks.*

liver and white, black and white, or either of these colours with tan markings is preferred.
**Head and skull.** The skull should be of medium length, fairly broad and slightly rounded, rising from the foreface, making a brow or stop, divided by a fluting between the eyes gradually dying away along the forehead towards the occiput bone, which should not be peaked. The cheeks should be flat, i.e. not rounded or full. The foreface should be of proportionate length to the skull, fairly broad and deep without being coarse, well chiselled below the eyes, fairly deep and square in flew, but not exaggerated to such an extent as would interfere with comfort when retrieving. Nostrils should be well developed.
**Tail.** The stern should be low and never carried above the level of the back; well feathered, and with a lively action.
**Feet.** Feet tight, compact, and well rounded, with strong full pads.

# CLUMBER SPANIEL

## Good points
- *Even temperament*
- *Intelligent*
- *Reliable*

## Take heed
- *Slow but sure worker*

The Clumber is the heaviest of the spaniels and is thought to be of French origin, brought about by crossing the Basset Hound with the Alpine Spaniel (which is now extinct).

It is a brave, attractive and reliable dog; a slow but sure worker that excels for rough shooting and is an excellent retriever.

## Size
Dog about 25-32kg (55-70lb); bitch about 20.5-27kg (45-60lb).

## Exercise
This is essentially a working dog, best suited to country life and needs plenty of exercise and off-the-lead runs in open spaces.

*Below: Attractive and massive, Clumbers make reliable workers.*

## Grooming
Routine brushing. Keep coat tangle free and take care that mud does not become lodged between the toes.

## Feeding
Recommended would be 1½-2½ cans of a branded meaty product (376g, 13.3oz size), with biscuit added in equal part by volume; or 5 cupfuls of a dry food, complete diet, mixed in the proportion of 1 cup of feed to ½ cup of hot or cold water. Rations should be stepped up or decreased, according to the amount of work the dog is asked to do.

## Origin and history
The Clumber Spaniel was fostered and promoted by the Duc de Noailles in the years before the French Revolution. The breed became renowned as beaters and retrievers in the field.

With the advent of war, the Duc de Noailles brought his dogs to England and entrusted them to the Duke of Newcastle at Clumber Park, from which the name is derived. The Duc de Noailles was killed in the revolution, but he left the legacy of his spaniels in England.

## SHOW SUMMARY
**General appearance.** A dog with a thoughtful expression, very massive, but active; it moves with a rolling gait characteristic of the breed.
**Colour.** Plain white, with lemon markings, orange permissible; slight head markings and freckled muzzle; white body preferred.
**Head and skull.** Head large, square and massive, of medium length, broad on top, with a decided occiput; heavy brows with a deep top; heavy muzzle, well-developed flew (pendulous upper lip), and level jaw and mouth; nose square and flesh-coloured.
**Tail.** Set low, well feathered, and carried about level with the back.
**Feet.** Large and round, well covered with hair.

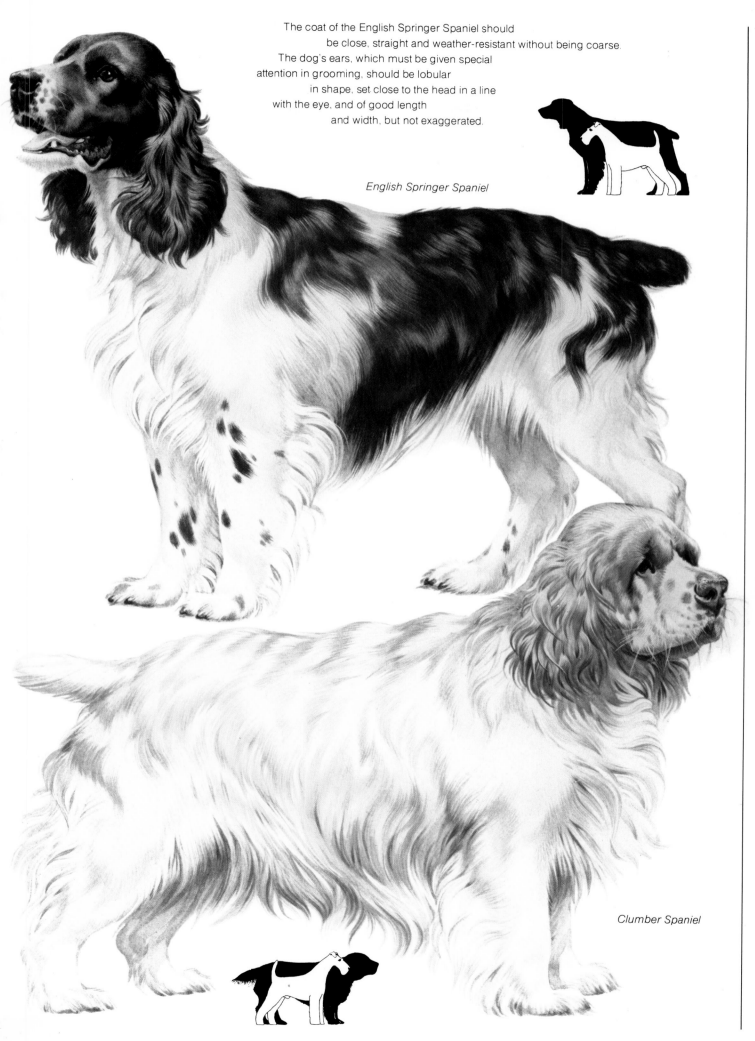

The coat of the English Springer Spaniel should
be close, straight and weather-resistant without being coarse.
The dog's ears, which must be given special
attention in grooming, should be lobular
in shape, set close to the head in a line
with the eye, and of good length
and width, but not exaggerated.

*English Springer Spaniel*

*Clumber Spaniel*

# KARELIAN BEAR DOG

### Good points
- *Brave*
- *Fine hunter*
- *Hardy*
- *Loyal to its owner*

### Take heed
- *Does not get on with other dogs*
- *Unsuitable as a family pet*

The Karelian Bear Dog is a sturdy hunter of bear and elk. It is a brave dog, and loyal to its master. It does not get on with other dogs and can not, ideally, be recommended as a family pet.

### Size
Height at shoulder: 53-61cm (21-24in) for dogs, 48-53cm (19-21in) for bitches.

### Exercise
Needs plenty of exercise to stay healthy.

### Grooming
Daily brushing will keep the coat in good condition.

### Feeding
One to 1½ cans (376g, 13.3oz size) of a branded meaty product, with biscuit added in equal part by volume; or 3 cupfuls of a dry food, complete diet, mixed in the proportion of 1 cup of feed to ½ cup of hot or cold water.

### Origin and history
The Karelian Bear Dog is a Spitz belonging to the Russian breed of Laikas, but this type evolved in Finland. It is known throughout Scandinavia as a fearless hunter of bear and elk. (The Russians decreed, in 1947, that only four distinct types of Spitz should in future be referred to as Laikas, and these are neither known nor exported outside the USSR.)

### SHOW SUMMARY
**General appearance.** The Karelian Bear Dog is medium-sized, of robust build, strong and slightly longer than high; it has a thick coat, cocked ears and an introverted nature, and is brave and persistent. Its senses, particularly that of scent, are keen, and it is admirably adapted to big game hunting.
**Colour.** Black, preferably slightly brownish or dull, mostly with white markings or spots on the head, neck, chest, belly and legs.
**Head.** Shaped like a blunt wedge, fairly broad at the forehead and cheeks. Forehead slightly arched; stop gently sloping; slight protuberance above the eyes. The muzzle is high and its bridge is preferably straight, tapering slightly only toward the nose. Nose black and well developed.
**Tail.** Of medium length, usually arched; a full arch is most desirable.
**Feet.** Hind feet slightly longer and lower than forefeet. Paws thick, high and roundish.

# ELKHOUND
(Norwegian Elkhound)

### Good points
- *Good household pet*
- *Lacks doggy odour*
- *Reliable with children*
- *Sensible guard*

### Take heed
- *Needs firm but gentle discipline in puppyhood*

The Elkhound is a happy breed, loyal and devoted to its master and reliable with children. It has a great love of the outdoors, is energetic, and is not recommended for those unable to provide exercise.

### Size
Height at shoulder: dog 52cm (20½in); bitch 49.5cm (19½in). Weight: dog 22.7kg (50lb); bitch 19.5kg (43lb).

### Exercise
Needs plenty of exercise to stay healthy.

### Grooming
Daily brushing and combing.

### Feeding
One to 1½ cans (376g, 13.3oz size) of a branded meaty product, with biscuit added in equal part by volume; or 3 cupfuls of a dry food, complete diet, mixed in the proportion of 1 cup of feed to ½ cup of hot or cold water.

### Origin and history
The job of the Elkhound was to seek out the elk and hold it at bay until its master moved in for the kill. It has existed in Norway for centuries, but was not considered a show prospect until 1877, the year in which the Norwegian Hunters' Association first held a show.

Today's Elkhound has been tailored to meet the ideal decided upon by various Scandinavian clubs and societies, whereby other Spitz breeds fell by the wayside, a

*Above: The powerful Elkhound has a thick, weather-resistant coat that looks good in the show ring.*

Norwegian breed standard emerging for the dog that has become its national breed.

### SHOW SUMMARY
**General appearance.** It has a compact and proportionately short body, a coat thick and abundant but not bristling, and prick ears; tail tightly curled over back.
**Colour.** Grey of various shades, with black tips to the long outer coat; lighter on the chest, stomach and legs, and the underside of the tail. Any distinctive variation from the grey colour is most undesirable, and too dark or too light a colouring should be avoided. Pronounced markings on legs and feet are also not desirable.
**Head and skull.** Broad between the ears; the forehead and back of the head are slightly arched with a clearly marked but not large stop. Muzzle moderately long, broader at the base and gradually tapering — whether seen from above or from the side — but not pointed; bridge of the nose straight, jaw strong with lips tightly closed.
**Tail.** Set high, tightly curled over the back but not carried on either side; hair thick and close.
**Feet.** Compact, oval in shape and not turned outwards; toes tightly closed; toe-nails firm and strong.

# SWEDISH ELKHOUND
(Jämthund)

### Good points
- *Brave*
- *Equable temperament*
- *Excellent hunter*

### Take heed
- *No drawbacks known, but remember it is essentially a hunter*

The Swedish Elkhound is little known outside its native country, where its popularity surpasses that of the Norwegian Elkhound. It has great stamina and makes a bold and energetic hunter. It is also an excellent guard. It is loyal to its master, of a calm temperament, and extremely agile.

### Size
Height at shoulder: dog 58.5-63.5cm (23-25in), bitch 53-58.5cm (21-23in).

### Exercise
Needs plenty of exercise to stay in tip-top condition.

### Grooming
Daily brushing and combing.

### Feeding
One to 1½ cans (376g, 13.3oz size) of a branded meaty product, with biscuit added in equal part by volume; or 3 cupfuls of a dry food, complete diet, mixed in the proportion of 1 cup of feed to ½ cup of hot or cold water.

### Origin and history
The Swedish Elkhound is similar to the Norwegian Elkhound, but despite continuing popularity in its country of origin it is little known elsewhere — unlike the Norwegian Elkhound, which has had universal success in the show ring.

The breed was evolved by Swedish huntsmen who considered their local Spitz breeds superior to the Norwegian Elkhound for hunting. It is taller than the Norwegian dog and the Swedes are adamant that it is also a better hunter.

### SHOW SUMMARY
**General appearance.** A large Elkhound of the Spitz type, with erect ears, and a well-curled but not tightly curled tail carried high over the back. The breed is robust, compact and lean, without heaviness; it should not look long. Courageous and energetic, this breed is at the same time calm and reflective.
**Colour.** Dark grey or light grey; parts of the muzzle, cheeks and throat are light grey or cream, and these are characteristic of the breed. Varicolour on legs, chest and belly and around the vent is allowed.
**Head.** Long, lean, relatively broad between the eyes. The skull is very slightly rounded. The stop is clearly defined but is not pronounced. The nose is broad, the bridge straight, wide and strong. The lips are close-fitting over the jaws. The muzzle is slightly shorter than the skull, tapering gently and uniformly to the nose. It should not, however, be pointed as seen either from above or in profile. The cheeks are flat. The teeth should meet in a level bite.
**Tail.** Set on high, of medium length and uniform thickness. It is well feathered but without fringe; it is carried curled up over the back, not too much to the side.
**Feet.** Robust, not turned out, slightly elliptical, with closed toes.

*Elkhound*

The Elkhound has a longish and coarse top coat, dark at the tips, with a light-coloured, soft and woolly under-coat. About the neck and the front of the chest, where the coat is longest, it forms a kind of ruff which, allied to the dog's pointed and very mobile ears, expressive eyes and tightly curled tail, gives an alert and energetic appearance.

*Karelian Bear Dog*

The Karelian Bear Dog, named from Karelen province in eastern Finland, was recognized as a pure breed in 1935 and officially recognized by the FCI in 1946. Of striking and attractive appearance, it is widely shown in Finland and is thought likely to increase in popularity elsewhere in the world.

*Swedish Elkhound*

The Swedish Elkhound survived the adoption of the Norwegian Elkhound as the 'official' Scandinavian elk-hunting Spitz, around the turn of the century, and was recognized as a separate breed in 1946.

# ENGLISH FOXHOUND

## Good points
- *First-rate hunter*
- *Lively*

## Take heed
- *Noisy*
- *This breed does not make a suitable pet*

The Foxhound is not suitable as a household pet. It is almost always the property of a foxhunting pack. Hunt supporters often take on the role of puppy walker, in order to accustom a young hound to road hazards and livestock before returning it to its pack. Hounds are attractive, vivacious pups, but far too active and destructive for the average household. It is not possible in the United Kingdom to purchase a Foxhound as a pet. Hounds are always counted by the pack in couples: the huntsman will talk of having 30 couples of hounds.

## Size
Height: dog 58.5cm (23in); bitch just a little less.

## Exercise
Vigorous exercise is necessary. Foxhounds should have the stamina to spend all day running foxes with the hunt.

## Grooming
Use a hound glove.

## Feeding
Foxhounds are not fed as household pets, pack members being trencher-fed with horse flesh and an oatmeal mash called a 'pudding'. The leaner hounds are led to the trough first, so that they may eat their fill, and then the remainder are led in. They are not fed the day before a hunt.

## Origin and history
The Foxhound is descended from the heavier St Hubert Hounds, brought to England by the Norman invaders, and from the now extinct Talbot Hounds. The Ardennes Hounds derived their name of Hubertus Hounds from the Bishop of Liege who later became St Hubert, patron saint of all hunters.

The Foxhound is never exhibited at ordinary dog shows, but has its own events under the auspices, in the United Kingdom, of the Association of Masters of Foxhounds.

## SHOW SUMMARY
**Colour.** The Masters of Foxhounds declare that no hound can be a bad colour.
**Head and skull.** Skull broad.
**Feet.** The toes of the feet should be close together, and not open.
**Tail.** Should be well put on at the end of good quarters, and these quarters should in no way end abruptly and be of the type that hound-men term 'chopped off behind'. A curly stern, although unsightly, will not be detrimental to the hound's hunting qualities.

# AMERICAN FOXHOUND

## Good points
- *First-rate hunter*
- *Lively*

## Take heed
- *Noisy*
- *This breed does not make a suitable pet*

The American Foxhound is a lighter, racier-looking dog than the English Foxhound. It is exhibited in the show ring in the United States.

## Size
Height: dogs should not be under 56cm (22in) nor over 63.5cm (25in); bitches should not be under 53cm (21in) nor over 61cm (24in). Measurements made across the back at the point of the withers, the hound standing in a natural position with its feet well under it.

## Exercise
Needs plenty of vigorous exercise.

## Grooming
Use a hound glove.

## Feeding
Foxhounds are not fed as household pets, pack members being trencher-fed with horse flesh and an oatmeal mash called a 'pudding'. The leaner hounds are led to the trough first, so that they may eat their fill, and then the remainder are led in. They are not fed the day before a hunt.

## Origin and history
The American Foxhound is believed to have been derived from a pack of Foxhounds taken from Britain to America by Robert Brooke in 1650. They are very fast, their quarry—the American red fox—being a speedier prey than its English counterpart. In about 1770, George Washington also imported Foxhounds from Great Britain and received the gift from Lafayette of some excellent French specimens in 1785. The French and English breeds were crossbred, producing the Virginia Hounds, which form today's American Foxhound.

## SHOW SUMMARY
**Colour.** Any colour is acceptable.
**Head and skull.** The skull should be fairly long, slightly domed at occiput, with cranium broad and full. Ears set on moderately low, long, reaching when drawn out nearly, if not quite, to the tip of the nose; fine in texture, fairly broad, with almost entire absence of erectile power—setting close to the head with the forward edge slightly turning to the cheek—round at tip.
**Feet.** Fox-like. Pad full and hard. Well-arched toes. Strong nails.
**Tail.** Set on moderately high and carried gaily, but not turned forward over the back; with slight curve and very slight brush.

# HAMILTON HOUND (Stövare)

## Good points
- *First-rate hunter*
- *Lively*

## Take heed
- *Noisy*
- *This breed does not make a suitable pet*

This medium-sized hound was named after Count Hamilton, who created the breed by crossing the English Foxhound with the best German hounds, including the Holstein Hound and the Hanoverian Haidbracke. It is the most popular hunting hound in Sweden. Count Hamilton was the founder of the Swedish Kennel Club.

## Size
Height: dog 49.5-58.5cm (19½-23in); bitch 46-57cm (18-22½in).

## Exercise
Requires plenty of strenuous exercise.

## Grooming
Use a hound glove.

## Feeding
As for Foxhounds.

## SHOW SUMMARY
**General appearance.** The dog should be well built, giving an impression of strength and ruggedness, and should have a tricolour coat.
**Head and skull.** Long, rectangular and lean. The skull is moderately arched and broad; the occipital protruberance is not prominent. The stop is not pronounced. The nose is always black, fairly large, and with wide nostrils. The bridge is straight and parallel to the line of the skull. The upper lips should be full but not excessively pendulous. The muzzle is robust, rectangular and quite long. The zygomatic arch should not be overly prominent. The teeth are strong and should be without any defect; they should close in a scissors bite.
**Tail.** Set on high, almost as a continuation of the backline; when down it should reach the hocks. Thick at the root, it tapers towards the tip; it should be carried straight out or slightly curved.
**Feet.** They should be strong and directed forward, with elastic and well-closed toes and large pads. Wolf feet are not desirable.

# HARRIER

## Good points
- *First-rate hunter*
- *Lively*

## Take heed
- *Noisy*
- *This breed does not make a suitable pet*

The Harrier bears some similarity to the Beagle but more closely resembles the Foxhound, with which it has been so interbred that few purebred Harriers exist today. It is slower than the Beagle and Foxhound and is generally used to hunt the hare on both foot and horseback, although it is also used for foxhunting.

## Size
Height varies from 46 to 56cm (18-22in).

## Exercise
Needs liberal amounts of exercise.

## Grooming
Use a hound glove.

## Feeding
As for Foxhounds.

## Origin and history
The Harrier is extremely popular in the United States but is, in fact, an ancient British breed, the first pack of which was recorded in the year 1260. This pack, the Penistone, was established by Sir Elias de Midhope and existed for over five centuries. The word 'harrier' is Norman French for 'hunting dog', and at one time all hunting dogs in Britain were known as Harriers. The breed is similar in appearance to the Foxhound. Primarily used for fox and rabbit hunting, it has an additional, unexpected chore in South America and Ceylon, where it is used for leopard hunting. Harriers are exhibited in dog shows in the United States. It is also popular with the American drag hunt.

## SHOW SUMMARY
(American Standard)
The points of the modern Harrier are very similar to those of the English Foxhound. The Harrier, however, is smaller than the English Foxhound and the most popular size is 48-53cm (19-21in). They should be active, well balanced and full of strength and quality, with shoulders sloping into the muscles of the back, clean and not loaded on the withers or point.

The back level and muscular, and not dipping behind the withers or arching over the loin. The elbow's point set well away from the ribs, running parallel with the body and not turning outwards. Deep, well-sprung ribs, running well back, with plenty of heart room, and a deep chest.

Good straight legs with plenty of bone running well down to the toes, but not overburdened, inclined to knuckle over very slightly but not exaggerated in the slightest degree. Round catlike feet, and close toes turning inwards. Hind legs and hocks stand square, with a good sweep and muscular thigh to take the weight off the body.

The head should be of medium size with good bold forehead, and plenty of expression; head must be well set up on a neck of ample length, and not heavy; stern should be set well up, long and well controlled.

The Masters of Foxhounds Association antedates the
Kennel Club and, because of the preservation of stud
books, the ancestry of English Foxhounds can be traced
back beyond that of other breeds. A count in 1880
showed 7,000 Hounds in English packs!

English Foxhound

American Foxhound

As well as being used for mounted
fox-hunting, the American Foxhound
is bred for field trials; for fox-hunting
with a gun; for
drag hunting or
racing; and also
for the show ring.

Harrier

Hamilton
Hound

# HYGEN HOUND
(Hygenhund)

**Good points**
- *Excellent hunting dog*

**Take heed**
- *Not recommended as a household pet*

The Hygen Hound excels in trekking and retrieving. It is a fine hunting dog, dignified and of equable temperament. It is, however, little known outside Scandinavia.

**Size**
About 61cm (24in).

**Grooming**
Used a hound glove daily.

**Feeding**
One to 1½ cans (376g, 13.3oz size) of a branded meaty product, with biscuit added in equal part by volume; or 3 cupfuls of a dry food, complete diet, mixed in the proportion of 1 cup of feed to ½ cup of hot or cold water; or hound diet (see Foxhound).

**Origin and history**
The breed takes its name from a Norwegian named Hygen who, in 1830, bred the now extinct Ringerike Hounds. The Hygen Hound emerged as a separate variety, and was then crossed with the Dunker, and an attempt was made to register the progeny under the name of Norwegian Beagles. This venture failed, and the breeds have gone their separate ways. Similarities in appearance remain but the Hygen Hound is heavier and less poised than the Dunker, and it also retains the colour of the Ringerikes.

**Colour**
Red, yellow or black-brown; white with red or yellow spots.

# SMALANDS HOUND
(Smalandsstövare)

**Good points**
- *Keen hunting instinct*
- *Strong and sturdy*

**Take heed**
- *Not suitable as pet or house dog*

The Smalands Hound is, in company with the Hamilton Hound and Schiller Hound, one of the three oldest hunting varieties in Sweden. It is somewhat smaller than the other hunting varieties, strong, sturdy and able to cope with the dense forest that covers a large area of Smaland in southern Sweden. It is a born hunter of considerable strength and is not recommended as a house pet.

**Size**
About 49.5cm (19½in).

**Grooming**
Use a hound glove daily.

**Feeding**
One to 1½ cans (376g, 13.3oz size) of a branded meaty product, with biscuit added in equal part by volume; or 3 cupfuls of a dry food, complete diet, mixed in the proportion of 1 cup of feed to ½ cup of hot or cold water.

**Origin and history**
This breed, although well known throughout Scandinavia, is little known elsewhere and is not recognized by the British or American Kennel Clubs. There are, however, numerous historical references to the breed in its country of origin, many of which refer to the breed's naturally short tail; it is never docked.

Baron von Essen is credited with perfecting the breed at the beginning of the 20th century through crossing the best of Swedish hounds with the Schiller Hound. The Smalands Hound was recognized by the Swedish Kennel Club in 1921.

**Colour**
Black with tan markings; white marking is allowable on both the chest and feet.

**Tail**
Short, or reaching to the hocks; naturally short seems to be preferred, never docked.

# SCHILLER HOUND
(Schillerstövare)

**Good points**
- *Excellent hunting dog*

**Take heed**
- *Not recommended as a household pet*

The Schiller Hound, like the Hamilton Hound, is one of Sweden's most popular hunting dogs, but is slightly shorter. It was evolved through crossing with hounds from Germany, Austria and Switzerland. The Schiller Hound is possibly the fastest of the Scandinavian hounds. It is also used for tracking.

**Size**
About 49.5-61cm (19½-24in).

**Feeding**
One to 1½ cans of a branded meaty product (376g, 13.3oz size), with biscuit added in equal part by volume; or 3 cupfuls of a dry food, complete diet, mixed in the proportion of 1 cup of feed to ½ cup of hot or cold water.

**Grooming**
Use a hound glove daily.

**Colour**
The Schiller Hound is black, with reddish brown or yellow markings, and with white about the muzzle, neck, chest and legs.

# FINNISH HOUND
(Suomenajokoira)

**Good points**
- *Excellent hunting dog*

**Take heed**
- *Not recommended as a household pet*

The most popular dog in Finland, used in its native land for hunting not only hare and fox, but also moose and lynx. The breed was established in the 19th century by a goldsmith named Tammelin, by careful crossing of English, German, Swiss and Scandinavian hounds. The Finnish Hound is good-natured and friendly but has a strong streak of independence.

**Size**
Height: dog, 54.5-61cm (21½-24in); bitch, 51-57cm (20-22½in).

**Feeding**
One to 1½ cans of a branded meaty product (376g, 13.3oz size), with biscuit added in equal part by volume; or 3 cupfuls of a dry food, complete diet, mixed in the proportion of 1 cup of feed to ½ cup of hot or cold water.

**Grooming**
Use a hound glove daily.

**Colour**
Tricolour combination of tan, black saddle and white marking on throat, breast, lower part of legs and tail.

# HALDEN HOUND
(Haldenstövare)

**Good points**
- *Excellent hunting dog*

**Take heed**
- *Not recommended as a household pet.*

This is a medium-sized hound, of considerable stamina, little known outside Scandinavia. It is a Norwegian breed named after the town of Halden. This gentle and affectionate hound has evolved through the crossing of Norwegian hounds by careful selection with hounds imported from Britain, Germany, France and, it is suggested, Russia.

**Size**
About 63.5cm (25in).

**Feeding**
One to 1½ cans of a branded meaty product (376g, 13.3oz size), with biscuit added in equal part by volume; or 3 cupfuls of a dry food, complete diet, mixed in the proportion of 1 cup of feed to ½ cup of hot or cold water.

**Grooming**
Use a hound glove daily.

**Colour**
White with black patches, and brown shadings on head and legs and surrounding the black. Small black or brown spots are not liked; black must not predominate.

# DUNKER HOUND
(Norwegian Hound)

**Good points**
- *Excellent hunting dog*

**Take heed**
- *Not recommended as a household pet*

The Dunker Hound is a Norwegian variety, has considerable trekking ability and is a good retriever. It is popular in Sweden and throughout Scandinavia but is not recognized by the British or American Kennel Clubs. It has staying power rather than speed and is used to hunt the hare. The Dunker Hound is a strong dog, with a deep chest and long legs. It is both affectionate and trustworthy, but is not, however, recommended as a household pet.

**Size**
Height: 47-56cm (18½-22in).

**Grooming**
Use a hound glove.

**Feeding**
One to 1½ cans (376g, 13.3oz size) of a branded meaty product, with biscuit added in equal part by volume; or 3 cupfuls of a dry food, complete diet, mixed in the proportion of 1 cup of feed to ½ cup of hot or cold water; or hound diet (see Foxhound).

**Origin and history**
The Dunker takes its name from Wilhelm Dunker who, around the middle of the last century, mated his hound, renowned as a trekker and retriever, with the best bitches in order to perpetuate these hunting qualities. It is understood that crossing with the Hygen Hound took place at one time and an effort was made to register the progeny as Norwegian Beagles. However, the suggestion was rejected and the breeds have since gone their separate ways, both retaining considerable tracking ability.

**Colour**
Black or harlequin (blue marbled) with fawn and white markings. Deep chestnut is objectionable, and white with harlequin or liver markings would disqualify the hound in a competition.

*NB.* The Scandinavian hounds are not usually kept in packs. They hunt in forests, in countryside calling for a tallish hound with a good nose and able to give tongue loud and clear for the benefit of the following huntsmen.

Hygen Hound

Smalands Hound

Schiller Hound

Halden Hound

Finnish Hound

Dunker Hound

111

# PHARAOH HOUND

## Good points
● *Affectionate*
● *Excellent hunter*
● *Full of fun*
● *Good with children*

## Take heed
● *Not suitable for town life*
● *Wary of strangers*

The Pharaoh Hound is the oldest domesticated dog in recorded history. Two hounds hunting gazelle are depicted on a circular disc dating back to around 4000 BC, certainly before the First Dynasty.

The dog, and particularly the hunting dog, played an intimate part in the daily life of kings and nobles in Ancient Egypt. It is therefore not surprising to find them frequently depicted in the reliefs carved on the tomb walls of these men.

The Pharaoh Hound is a medium-sized hound, elegant, powerful and swift. It is intelligent, affectionate and full of fun; also very good with children, but a little diffident at first with strangers. Out hunting it is keen and fast. Unlike the Greyhound it hunts by both scent and sight.

## Size
Height: dog ideally 56-63.5cm (22-25in); bitch ideally 53-61cm (21-24in). Overall balance must be maintained.

## Exercise
This is a breed that needs plenty of exercise. It is unsuitable for town or apartment living.

## Grooming
The silky, smooth coat needs little attention for a smart appearance.

*Below: Elegant and alert, a Pharaoh Hound bitch is seen here with her two puppies. This breed is very affectionate and full of fun. It is the oldest in recorded history and has hardly changed in 5000 years.*

## Feeding
This is a hardy and healthy breed, yet on the island of Gozo (near Malta), to which it is believed the Pharaoh Hound was brought by Phoenicians, it was fed almost entirely on a meat-free diet of soup and goat's milk. Nowadays it enjoys a more traditional canine diet, but care must be taken that it does not become over-weight.

Recommended would be 1-1½ cans of a branded, meaty product (376g, 13.3oz size), with biscuit added in equal part by volume; or 3 cupfuls of a complete, dry food, mixed in the proportion of 1 cup of feed to ½ cup of hot or cold water. Increase rations if working.

## Origin and history
It is thought that the Phoenicians took these hounds with them when they settled on Malta and Gozo, and that the preservation of the breed, which has changed little in 5000 years, can be accredited to Malta, where it is known to have existed for over 2000 years. In Malta, Pharaohs are bred for rabbit hunting and are known by the Maltese as 'kelb-tal-fenek' (rabbit dog).

In 1935 the Harvard-Boston expedition, under Dr George Reisner, working in the great cemetery west of the Pyramid of Cheops at Giza, found an inscription recording the burial of a dog named Abuwtiyuw. The burial was carried out with all the ritual ceremonies of a great man of Egypt, by order of the kings of Upper and Lower Egypt.

Like other Egyptian nobles, the dog was in constant attendance, a daily fact in the life of the king; and when it died, the monarch ordered that it be buried ceremonially in a tomb of its own, in order that, like human beings buried in this way, its 'ka' might enter the afterlife as an honoured spirit. Thus, after death, its future existence might be assured to continue attendance on the king.

## SHOW SUMMARY
**General appearance.** The Pharaoh Hound is medium sized, and of noble bearing, with clean-cut lines. It is graceful yet powerful, and very fast, with a free, easy movement and an alert expression.

**Colour.** Tan or rich tan, with white markings allowed as follows: white tip on tail is desirable; white on chest (called the 'star'); white on toes; slim white blaze on centre line of face permissible. Flecking or white other than as above is undesirable.

**Head and skull.** Skull long, lean and well chiselled. Foreface slightly longer than the skull. Only slight stop. Top of skull parallel with the foreface. The whole head represents a blunt wedge when viewed in profile and from above.

**Tail.** Medium set, fairly thick at the base and tapering (whip-like), reaching just below the point of the hock in repose. Carried high and curved when the dog is in action. The tail should not be tucked between the legs. A screw tail is a fault.

**Feet.** Strong, well knuckled and firm, turning neither in nor out. Paws well padded. Dew-claws may be removed.

# IBIZAN HOUND

## Good points
● *Excellent with children*
● *Good gundog*
● *Kind disposition*
● *Seldom fights*
● *Wonderful house pet*

## Take heed
● *Has acute hearing so must not be shouted at*
● *Sensitive and easily hurt*

The Ibizan Hound is a kind dog loved by children, in whom it seems to inspire confidence. It is easily hurt, however, and due to its acute hearing must not be shouted at or its spirit can be crushed. It has great stamina and can, according to the natives of Ibiza, hunt by day or by night, singly or in pairs. But it is not a dog to go off on its own and not return. These dogs seldom fight, and have to be pushed to do so. They willingly retrieve and are often taken hunting on the island without guns. It is said that a pair can catch 1000 rabbits in a day. They are useful as gundogs, and make wonderful house pets.

## Size
Weight 22.2-22.7kg (49-50lb); height 56-71cm (22-28in), for a dog, less for a bitch.

## Exercise
It would be unkind to keep this hound in a confined space, for it is a tireless dog, able to retrieve and to jump great heights. It is an excellent companion for a sportsman. It must not be kennelled; ideally it should be kept as a companion in the home.

## Grooming
The Ibizan needs a good brush every day but is not difficult to maintain in good condition.

## Feeding
Recommended would be 1-1½ cans (376g, 13.3oz size) of a branded meaty product, with biscuit added in equal part by volume; or 3 cupfuls of a dry food, complete diet, mixed in the proportion of 1 cup of feed to ½ cup of hot or cold water. The addition of raw fish and fruit to the diet of the Ibizan is beneficial.

## Origin and history
We known that hounds like the Ibizan were owned by the ancient pharaohs of Egypt, because hunting dogs of this type were drawn on rock, stone and papyrus as early as 3000 BC. Indeed, bones of similar hunting dogs have been found from about 4770 BC. The dogs of the pharaohs probably spread through trade to neighbouring lands. On the invasion of Egypt by the Romans, their neighbours the Carthaginians and the Phoenicians were driven out to the island of Ibiza in the 9th century BC, where they lived for about a century; but the hounds that they brought with them remained on Ibiza for the next 3000 years. Although some fine hounds have recently been taken from Ibiza to Majorca, the purest hounds are still found on Ibiza, retaining all the colours shown in the Egyptian drawings, i.e. spotted red and lion on white, or any of these as a single colour.

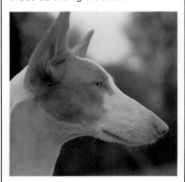

*Above: The noble head of the Ibizan Hound. This ancient breed makes a sensitive and gentle pet.*

## SHOW SUMMARY
**General appearance.** Tall, narrow, finely built, large erect ears.

**Colour.** White, chestnut, or lion solid colour, or any combination of these.

**Head and skull.** Fine, long flat skull with prominent occipital bone. Stop not well defined, slightly convex muzzle, the length of which from the eyes to the tip of the nose should be equal to the length from the eyes to the occiput. Nose flesh coloured, should protrude beyond the teeth, jaw very strong and lean.

**Tail.** Long, thin, low set, reaching well below the hock, when passed between the legs and round the flank should reach the spine; may be carried high when excited.

**Feet.** Well arched toes, thick pads, light coloured claws. Front feet may turn slightly outwards. Dew-claws should not be removed in front. No hind dew-claws.

At the beginning of this century the Ibizan
Hound was common as a hunting dog on
the Spanish mainland. Although
generally used for coursing rabbit and
hare, in some regions it would hunt stag and
bear, and was also used as a gundog. More
recently, it has become popular throughout
southern Europe, and is seen frequently
in large numbers at all the major
shows. Despite its antiquity, the
the modern Ibizan Hound very closely
resembles its ancestors of almost 50 centuries ago.

*Ibizan Hound*

*Pharaoh Hound*

Although reputedly the first breed of dog to be
domesticated, in 1970 the Pharoah
Hound was still virtually unknown outside
Malta. Thanks to the efforts of a few specialist breeders,
by 1975 the breed had been granted
official recognition, and is now creating
a tremendous impression at shows
across Europe.

# SLOUGHI

## Good points
- *Excellent guard*
- *Good companion*
- *Healthy*
- *Intelligent*
- *Odour-free*
- *Reliable with children*

## Take heed
- *Has strong hunting instincts*

The Sloughi is one of the rarest sighthounds (hounds that hunt by sight) known in the West and — like the Saluki, which it closely resembles — is capable of great speed. In the East, it is used for hunting the gazelle.

This is an intelligent, gentle dog, which, although retaining strong hunting instincts, adapts well to life as a domestic companion.

## Size
Height at shoulder 56-76cm (22-30in).

## Exercise
Ownership should not be contemplated by those unable to provide a large garden or suitable exercise area.

## Grooming
Brush daily with a soft brush, and also use a hound glove.

## Feeding
Recommended would be 1½-2½ cans (376g, 13.3oz size) of a branded meaty product, with biscuit added in equal part by volume; or 5 cupfuls of a dry food, complete diet, mixed in the proportion of 1 cup of feed to ½ cup of hot or cold water.

*Below: The sandy-coloured Sloughi is capable of great speed and is used to hunt gazelle.*

## Origin and history
The Sloughi is frequently mistaken for a smooth-coated Saluki but is a heavier dog, often with characteristic black markings around the eyes. It evolved in Morocco and shares with the Saluki the distinction of being the only other dog recognized by the Arabs as purebred. They call it 'el hor', the aristocrat. It is said that its sandy colour assists the Sloughi in hunting gazelle because, in the desert, its quarry is unable to distinguish it until the danger is at hand. This breed is recognized by the FCI.

## Colour
Sandy, all shades of fawn, with or without a black mask or black saddle. Also off-white, brindle, or black with tan and brindle.

# SALUKI
(Gazelle Hound)

## Good points
- *Excellent guard*
- *Good companion*
- *Healthy*
- *Intelligent*
- *Odour-free*
- *Reliable with childen*

## Take heed
- *Strong hunting instincts*

The Saluki and the horse are prized Arab possessions, the Saluki being capable of great speed and able to keep pace with the fleet-footed Arab stallions. It is still used in the Middle East for hunting the gazelle, but in the West it is kept mainly as an elegant companion, pet and show dog. It is intelligent and somewhat aloof, but is a faithful, gentle companion and trustworthy with children. Care must be taken, particularly in country areas, that the Saluki is kept under control; despite its

*Above: A Saluki and her pup. These elegant and intelligent dogs make good and trustworthy pets.*

domestic role, it retains very strong hunting instincts.

## Size
Height of dog should average 58.5-71cm (23-28in), bitch slightly smaller.

## Exercise
Salukis need plenty of exercise, and ownership should not be contemplated by those without a large garden or other exercise area.

## Grooming
Brush daily with a soft brush, and use a hound glove. Combing of ear and tail fringes may be necessary.

## Feeding
One to 1½ cans (376g, 13.3oz) of a branded meaty product, with biscuit added in equal part by volume; or 3 cupfuls of a dry food, complete diet, mixed in the proportion of 1 cup of feed to ½ cup of hot or cold water.

## Origin and history
The Saluki is one of the most ancient breeds of dog and, like the Afghan and Greyhound, is a sight hound that derives from the Middle East. The Saluki is said to take its name from Saluk in the Yemen, but its likeness is portrayed on the tombs of the Egyptian Pharaohs.

The breed did not gain recognition by the American Kennel Club until 1927. In Britain it was known long before, for a litter bred in London Zoo in 1836 was shown as the 'Persian Greyhound'; but it was another 60 years before the Amherstia foundation kennels were started from two imported hounds. The breed was recognized by the British Kennel Club in 1922.

## SHOW SUMMARY
**General appearance.** The whole appearance of this breed should give an impression of grace and symmetry, and of great speed and endurance coupled with strength and activity to enable it to kill

gazelle or other quarry over deep sand or rocky mountain. The expression should be dignified and gentle with deep, faithful, far-seeing eyes.

**Colour.** White, cream, fawn, golden, red, grizzle and tan, tricolour (white, black and tan), and black and tan, or variations of these colours.

**Head and skull.** Head long and narrow; skull moderately wide between ears, not domed, the stop not pronounced, the whole showing great quality. Nose should be black or liver.

**Tail.** Long, set on low and carried naturally in a curve; well feathered on the underside with long silky hair, not bushy.

**Feet.** Of moderate length, toes long and well arched, not splayed out, but at the same time not cat-footed; the whole strong and supple, and well feathered between the toes.

*Below: The Saluki has strong hunting instincts and must be kept under control in country areas.*

The Sloughi is a tall, elegant, short-coated sighthound, similar to a Greyhound in appearance but with a flatter, slightly shorter back. Although the breed was adopted by the Moroccan aristocracy and bred in their kennels, it has been allowed to intermingle with other breeds, and a pure-bred Sloughi is now extremely rare.

*Sloughi*

Although more often regarded in the West as a prize-winning show hound, the Saluki is the traditional hunting dog of the nomadic Bedouin tribes. Perfectly built for speed, lithe and sturdy and tough in constitution, this dog has always been a treasured possession of the tribesmen, often hidden from strangers and fiercely protected as a member of the family.

*Saluki*

# AFGHAN HOUND

## Good points
- *Beautiful in appearance*
- *Loyal and affectionate*
- *Good with children who do not tease*

## Take heed
- *Independent*
- *Needs plenty of exercise*
- *Must have space — not suitable for apartments*
- *Needs daily grooming*
- *Must have firm, loving handling*
- *Can be fiery tempered, particularly in adolescence*

The Afghan is dignified, aloof and fond of comfort. Though it enjoys nothing more than surveying the scene from a cosy armchair, the Afghan is not the ideal choice for apartment dwellers or even those with a small house and garden. For despite its beautiful house manners, the Afghan is basically a hunting dog, warmly affectionate to its owners and usually trustworthy with children, but independent in character and often quite fiery in temper, particularly in adolescence.

It is impossible to show an Afghan too much affection, and it shouldn't be bullied. But it is important to maintain superiority from the first, especially during showing and training sessions, or later you may suffer the indignity, and physical near-impossibility, of publicly wrestling with a powerful creature armed with a mouthful of large teeth.

## Size
Ideal height: dog 68.5-73.5cm (27-29in), bitch approximately 5-7.5cm (2-3in) smaller.

## Exercise
Afghans need free running to keep fit and happy; their original task was to hunt wolves and gazelles in the deserts of Afghanistan, so a stroll in the park or a run up and down a suburban garden will not be enough to subdue their boundless energy. A puppy, from the first, should be allowed unrestricted exercise in its waking hours. This should be in a safe enclosed place. An adult should have a minimum of half an hour's free galloping a day, as well as disciplined walking on the lead.

## Grooming
Daily grooming is vitally important to prevent the dog's thick coat from matting; the well-groomed Afghan is a delight to behold, the neglected specimen an abomination. Indeed, this breed is definitely not for those with little time on their hands for grooming and exercising.

The only type of brush capable of getting through an Afghan's coat is one with an air cushion behind the tufts. The best of all is a Mason Pearson real bristle —

made for humans, and expensive. The nylon version is cheaper but remember to use a coat lubricant with this, otherwise static electricity will build up and cause the hair to become brittle. An air-cushioned brush with steel pins is excellent, and is not expensive.

## Feeding
Recommended would be 1½-2½ cans (376g, 13.3oz size) of a branded meaty product, with biscuit added in equal part by volume; or 5 cupfuls of a dry food, complete diet, mixed in the proportion of 1 cup of feed to ½ cup of hot or cold water.

## Origin and history
The Afghan is an ancient breed reputed to have been among those creatures taken into the Ark by Noah, and, to quote the book *Champion Dogs of the World*, 'even if one rejects this claim it still remains virtually certain that some sort of Afghan existed thousands of years ago in the Middle East'. Present-day experts believe that it was crossed with the Saluki.

A papyrus found in Sinai dated *c.* 3000 BC was, from early translations, thought to refer to a Cynocephalus, or monkey-faced hound; this could have been the forerunner of the Afghan, which because of its facial resemblance is often called a 'monkey dog'. However, later work on the translation confirmed belief that it referred not to a dog but to a hound-faced baboon.

At any rate a Greyhound-like dog was destined to find its way, perhaps through Persia, to Afghanistan, where it grew a long, shaggy coat for protection against the harsh climate and found favour with the royal and aristocratic families of that land.

The first Afghan Hound Breed Club was formed in the United Kingdom in 1926, the same year as the breed was officially recognized by the American Kennel Club.

## SHOW SUMMARY
**General appearance.** The Afghan Hound should be dignified and aloof with a certain keen fierceness. The Eastern or Oriental expression is typical of the breed; the Afghan looks at, and through, one. The gait of the Afghan Hound should be smooth and springy with a style of high order. The whole appearance of the dog should give the impression of strength and dignity combining speed and power. The head must be held proudly.
**Colour.** All colours are acceptable. (You will see the breed in fawns, silvers, grey and tan grizzles, and black and tan.)
**Head and skull.** Skull long, not too narrow, with a prominent occiput. Foreface long, with punishing jaws and slight stop. The skull should be well balanced and surmounted by a long topknot. Nose preferably black, but liver is no fault in light-coloured dogs.

**Tail.** Not too short. Set on low with a ring at the end. Raised when in action. Sparsely feathered.
**Feet.** Forefeet strong and very large in both length and breadth and covered with long thick hair; toes arched. Pasterns long and springy, especially in front, and pads well down on the ground. Hind feet long, but not quite so broad as the forefeet, and covered with long thick hair.

# GREYHOUND

## Good points
- *An aristocrat, built for speed*
- *Adaptable*
- *Affectionate*
- *Good with adults and children — rarely snaps unless teased*
- *Loyal*

## Take heed
- *It is the Greyhound's natural instinct to chase small, fast-moving objects!*
- *Has a tendency to rheumatism and arthritis*

One of the most ancient breeds and, some say, the most misunderstood, for although built for speed and used for racing and coursing, the Greyhound is basically lazy. It adapts well to life as a family pet, and will enjoy nothing better than lazing on a settee or mattress, which is what it will have done for many hours when living in racing kennels. It is a good-natured, friendly and affectionate dog, and is very gentle with children.

Good pet homes are always needed for ex-racing Greyhounds, so those with a love for the breed may consider making enquiries at their local track, or (in the United Kingdom) of the National Greyhound Racing Club's Retired Greyhound Trust, to discover where dogs are available.

The retired Greyhound racer is not an aged animal; it is unlikely to be more than three or four years old, and may be as little as 18 months if it has proved unsuitable for racing. But remember that it will require a period of de-training. There is no overnight magic formula for preventing the Greyhound from chasing cats and other small moving objects, because this is its natural instinct. And out of doors this dog must be kept on a lead at all times.

## Size
Dog 71-76cm (28-30in); bitch 68.5-71cm (27-28in). There is no standard desired weight.

## Exercise
Three or four short walks every day will be sufficient. Although the Greyhound must never be exercised off the lead in a public place, it will enjoy the opportunity to run free in open country, away from sheep and other livestock. It is a highly sensitive creature, and will learn to respond quickly to the tone of voice, which helps greatly in obedience training.

Speed enthusiasts may like to know that the Greyhound has clocked in at 60 kph (37 mph)!

## Grooming
Daily use of a hound glove will keep the coat shining.

## Feeding
A retired Greyhound is like every other dog in that it responds best to a regular routine, especially where feeding and exercise are concerned. During their racing careers they are fed twice daily, in the early morning and in mid-afternoon, and exercised four times a day. There is no need to continue this routine once the Greyhound has settled in a new home, but it is kind to allow it to adapt gradually to its new lifestyle.

The canned food requirement for a Greyhound is between 1½ and 2½ cans of branded dog food (376g, 13.3oz size) per day and this, or 340-454g (12-16oz) of minced or chopped meat, should be mixed with 284-454g (10-16oz) of biscuit meal and moistened with bone stock, for Greyhounds are used to sloppier food than most breeds. They should also be pampered with a thick slice of brown bread crumbled into 0.28l (½pt) of milk at breakfast time, and have a small drink of milk with two large-sized dog biscuits at bedtime.

## Health care
A retired Greyhound may at first be restless in its new surroundings. It must be remembered that the home is a very different environment from a racing track, and it is unlikely that a retired racing Greyhound, when it leaves the track, will have seen home appliances such as television sets.

## Origin and history
The Greyhound is a pure breed: that is, it has not evolved from crossings with other types. Indeed, it seems unlikely that this breed has altered materially since early Egyptian times, as proved by a carving of a Greyhound in an Egyptian tomb in the Nile Valley, circa 4000 BC.

## SHOW SUMMARY
**General appearance.** The general appearance of the typical Greyhound is that of a strongly built, upstanding dog of generous proportions, muscular power and symmetrical formation, with a long head and neck, clean well-laid shoulders, deep chest, capacious body, arched loins, powerful quarters, sound legs and feet, and supple limbs.
**Colour.** Black, white, red, blue, fawn, fallow or brindle, or any of these colours broken with white.
**Head and skull.** Long, and of moderate width; flat skull, slight stop. Jaws powerful and well chiselled.
**Tail.** Long, set on rather low, strong at the root, tapering to tip, carried low, and slightly curved.
**Feet.** Moderate in length, with compact well-knuckled toes and strong pads.

The Greyhound has been used for coursing game for many centuries, probably since Roman times. More recently, its development has proceeded along three distinct lines: the larger and rather narrow show dog; the smaller, agile coursing hound; and the lean and muscular track-racing dog, the finest of which are now bred in Ireland.

*Greyhound*

*Afghan Hound*

The Afghan Hound must surely be the most glamorous dog in the world; the star of any show with its remarkably long, flowing coat and sweeping grace.

# LARGE MUNSTERLANDER

## Good points
● *Affectionate*
● *Easily taught*
● *Good house pet*
● *Loyal*
● *Trustworthy*

## Take heed
● *Needs plenty of space for exercise*

The Large Munsterlander is officially recorded as the youngest pointing retriever gundog breed, but has been known in Germany for as long as all the other German gundog breeds. It resembles a setter in both build and coat, and has a head like that of a spaniel. It is a multi-purpose gundog, ideal for the rough shoot: it has an excellent nose and staying power, and works equally well on land or in water. It also makes an intelligent and likeable family pet.

## Size
Height: dog approximately 61cm (24in); bitch approximately 58.5cm (23in). Weight: dog approximately 25-29.5kg (55-65lb); bitch approximately 25kg (55lb).

## Exercise
This is an energetic dog needing plenty of exercise.

## Grooming
A daily brushing will maintain it in tip-top condition.

## Feeding
One and a half to 2½ cans of branded dog food (376g, 13.3oz size) supplemented by biscuit in equal part by volume; or, if you prefer, 5 cupfuls of a dry food, complete diet, mixed in the proportion of 1 cup of feed to ½ cup of hot or cold water; meat scraps and the occasional bone. Increase the rations if your Munsterlander is doing hard work.

## Origin and history
In bygone days, the best working dogs were mated to the best work-

*Below: The keen expression of the intelligent Small Munsterlander.*

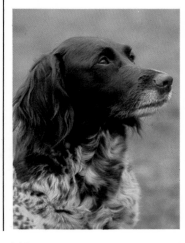

ing bitches, with little regard to colour, breeding or coat texture. Early in the 19th century, however, people became breed- and colour-conscious and records of the best dogs were kept. So it was with the Large Munsterlander, which was then classed as a Long-haired German Pointer.

When the German Kennel Club was founded and the general stud book came into operation, only brown and white Long-haired German Pointers were permitted registration. The litters containing 'odd-coloured' puppies were frequently given away, finding their way into the hands of farmers and gamekeepers, who were delighted to have such well-bred dogs that would work. They were not bothered by the dogs' lack of colour or of registration. This was fortunate, for it resulted in the saving of the breed now known as the Large Munsterlander.

## SHOW SUMMARY
**General appearance.** Alert and energetic, with a strong, muscular body, having good movement with drive.
**Colour.** Head solid black; white blaze, snip or star allowed. Body white with black patches, flecked, ticked, or combination of these.
**Head and skull.** Well proportioned to the body, elongated. Skull sufficiently broad, slightly rounded, with no pronounced occiput. Strong jaw muscles, well-formed black nose, wide soft nostrils, slight rise from the nasal bone to the forehead but no pronounced stop. Lips slightly rounded and well-fitting.

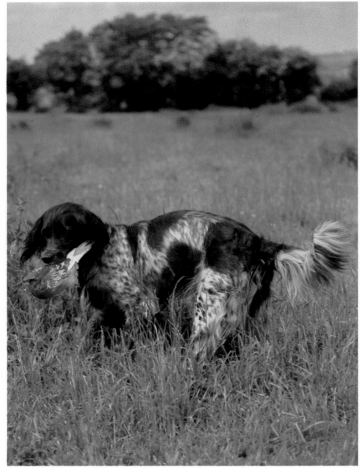

*Above: The Large Munsterlander makes an ideal gundog. It has an excellent nose, plenty of energy and a good, strong jaw.*

**Tail.** Well set on, in line with the back. Base thick, tapering evenly towards the tip, well feathered. It should be carried horizontally or curved slightly upwards. Docking optional, 1-2cm (0.4-0.8in).
**Feet.** Tight, moderately rounded and well-knuckled, with dense hair between the toes; well padded. Nails black and strong.

The Small Munsterlander (or Moorland Spaniel) is a smaller lighter dog, 43-56cm (17-22in) tall. Its coat is brown and white, usually with a brown head.

# DRENTSE PARTRIDGE DOG
*(Drentse Patrijshond, Dutch Partridge Dog)*

## Good points
● *Affectionate*
● *Equable temperament*
● *Excellent gundog*
● *Intelligent*

## Take heed
● *No drawbacks known*

The Drentse Partridge Dog is little known outside Holland. This is a pity, because not only is it an attractive dog — something like the Springer Spaniel in appearance — but it also admirably combines the

role of all-purpose gundog with that of an affectionate family pet. It will point and retrieve, and has been a successful competitor in Field Trials in its homeland.

## Size
Height about 58.5-61cm (23-24in).

## Exercise
Needs plenty of exercise to stay healthy.

## Grooming
Regular brushing will maintain the coat in good condition.

## Feeding
One to 1½ cans (376g, 13.3oz size) of a branded meaty product, with biscuit added in equal part by volume; or 3 cupfuls of a dry food, complete diet, mixed in the proportion of 1 cup of feed to ½ cup of hot or cold water.

## Origin and history
The Drentse Partridge Dog, or Patrijshond, comes from the Drentse district of north-east Holland, where it has existed for some 300 years, no doubt having evolved through early crossings with long-haired German sporting breeds. It is an accomplished wildfowler, and obviously justifies more widespread popularity.

## SHOW SUMMARY
**General appearance.** This well-proportioned breed has a body that is longer than the height at the withers. Although the hair on the body is not long, it gives the impression of being so because of the fringe on the neck, ears, legs and tail.
**Colour.** White background, with brown or orange markings.
**Head.** The skull is rather broad and flat; the stop scarcely defined. The passage from skull to muzzle should be gradual, with no sudden transition whether seen from front or in profile. The occipital protuberance is not accentuated; the masseters (main jaw muscles) are very slightly pronounced; the supra-orbital ridges are well developed. The nose is large and brown, and the nasal bridge is straight, neither arched nor hollowed; a slight arching is allowable, but a pug nose is absolutely unacceptable. The lips are thin and close-fitting; the muzzle is wedge-shaped and cut blunt at the end. The teeth are strong, with an efficient bite.
**Tail.** Natural, not docked; set on rather high. In length it reaches the point of the hock. Carried low or as a sabre tail. When the dog is in action, the tail is carried almost horizontally with the final third turned upward. A characteristic of the Patrijshond is that when it wags its tail, the tail moves in a circle, especially when the dog has caught the scent of game; it is never carried over the back. The fringes, which begin at the set-on of the tail, should be abundant, growing shorter toward the tip.
**Feet.** Round or oval, with well-closed toes and well-developed pads.

A German breed, the Large Munsterlander has been known in its country of origin for many centuries. But as it was bred principally for work, and only the most proficient working dogs were used for breeding, individual variation in type and size was considerable. Selective breeding since the beginning of the century, however, has produced the typical setter-like gundog recognized today.

*Large Munsterlander*

*Drentse Partridge Dog*

Intelligent, easy to train and adaptable, the Drentse Partridge Dog has remained very much the same in appearance for at least the last 300 years. In type the dog resembles a cross between a setter and a spaniel, and it is possible that it represents the ancestor of many of the modern gundogs.

# AIREDALE

### Good points
- *Attractive, sporty appearance*
- *Intelligent*
- *Faithful (if formidable) guard*
- *Loyal to owner*
- *Good with children*
- *Sound temperament*

### Take heed
- *That hard, wiry coat ought to be hand stripped*
- *Can be over-protective*
- *If it gets into a fight, you could end up with the other chap's veterinarian's bill! But it doesn't usually fight unless provoked.*

The Airedale is the king of the terriers and the largest of the terrier group. It is a splendid-looking animal with plenty of stamina, and combines ideally the roles of family pet and guard.

Prior to the First World War, the Airedale worked as a patrol dog with dock and railway police. It served during the war in the Russian Army and the British Army. It also worked for the Red Cross, locating the wounded and carrying messages. Indeed, at that time its abilities as a messenger and guard were considered superior to those of the German Shepherd Dog. The Airedale also took part in the Second World War, but was gradually superseded by the German Shepherd Dog, the Dobermann, the Boxer and others.

### Size
Approximately 25kg (55lb). Height: dogs 61cm (24in) at the shoulder, bitches slightly less.

### Exercise
One of the useful features about this dog is that although large it will adapt easily to living in a reasonably confined space, provided that it has at least two good 20-minute walks and an off-the-lead run every day. Alternatively, it will be in its element running with horses in the country and squelching, with wagging tail, through muddy fields. The Airedale can live indoors, if the owner wishes, or outside in a heated kennel with an adequate run.

### Grooming
The Airedale needs a daily grooming with a stiff brush, and if you plan to enter the dog in the show ring it is essential that its coat is regularly hand stripped. Ask the breeder to show you how this is done and don't be ashamed if you eventually resort to having the job done by a skilled canine beautician. If you do not plan to show, you need have your Airedale stripped only in spring and summer for coolness and neatness, but allow it to keep its thick coat for winter protection.

### Feeding
The Airedale needs at least 1-1½ cans (376g, 13.3oz size) of a branded meaty dog food, or the fresh meat equivalent, every day, plus a generous supply of biscuit meal. It will also appreciate the occasional large dog biscuit.

Watch the Airedale's weight and, if it shows signs of becoming too heavy, reduce the supply of biscuit meal. Its girth will depend on how active a life the dog leads.

Incidentally, the old adage 'give a dog a bone' can be misleading. Almost all dogs will gnaw a bone with relish, but whereas one may show no after-effects, the fatty content may make another very sick. The owner must be guided by experience.

### Origin and history
The Airedale is named after the valley of Aire in Yorkshire from which its ancestors came. It was originally called the Waterside, or working terrier. The forerunner of the present-day Airedale was kept for vermin control by Yorkshire gamekeepers and it was probably crossed with the Otterhound.

In the late 1800s the Fox Terrier enjoyed immense popularity, and much thought and care went into the breeding and development of this bigger terrier as an attractive and, at the same time, useful dog. It was soon adopted as a companion, but—when given the chance—can still prove itself as an expert ratter and ducker. It can also be trained to the gun. I can recall a family Airedale coming to the rescue when we kept a rather fierce Muscovy drake; the dog would round it up, and carrying the bird gently back to the pen in its mouth.

### SHOW SUMMARY
**General appearance.** Keen of expression, quick of movement, on the tip-toe of expectation at any moment. Character is denoted and shown by the expression of the eyes and by the carriage of the ears and tail.
**Colour.** The head and ears, with the exception of dark markings on each side of the skull, should be tan, the ears being of a darker shade than the rest. The legs up to the thighs and elbows also should be tan, the body dark grizzle.
**Head and skull.** The skull should be long and flat, not too broad between the ears, and narrowing slightly to the eyes. The skull should be free from wrinkles, with stop hardly visible and cheeks level. Both the jaws should be deep, powerful, strong and muscular, as strength of foreface is an essential characteristic of the Airedale, but there must be no excess development of the jaws to give a rounded or bulging appearance to the cheeks, as 'cheekiness' is not desired. Lips should be tight, and the nose black.
**Tail.** The tail should be set on high and carried gaily, but not curled over the back. It should be of good strength and substance, and of fair length.
**Feet.** These should be small, round and compact with a good depth of pad, well cushioned and the toes moderately arched, not turned either in or out.

# DOBERMANN
(Dobermann Pinscher; Doberman

### Good points
- *Alert*
- *Brave*
- *Loyal*
- *Ideal guard*
- *Intelligent*

### Take heed
- *Stands aloof from those outside the family circle*
- *Likely to be the victor in any battle*
- *If kennelled outside, heated, draught-proof kennels are essential*

The Dobermann is a strong, alert guard that will enjoy the comforts of its master's fireside and protect him and his family with its life. It is unlikely to have to give its life, however, for the Dobermann generally gets the better of any opponent and is one of the best guard dogs in the world. It is an aloof animal that takes its responsibilities seriously, is skilled at tracking, and makes a fine police dog.

### Size
Ideal height at withers: dog 68.5cm (27in); bitch 65cm (25½in). Considerable deviation from this ideal to be discouraged.

### Exercise
Certainly at least 40 minutes each day, which must include a 10-minute off-the-lead run.

### Grooming
The Dobermann, with its short coat, needs little grooming other than a daily rub down with Turkish towelling to remove loose hairs.

### Feeding
Recommended would be 1½-2½ cans (376g, 13.3oz size) of a branded, meaty product, with biscuit added in equal part by volume; or 5 cupfuls of a dry food, complete diet, mixed in the proportion of 1 cupful of feed to ½ cupful of hot or cold water. Yeast tablets are beneficial at meal-times, especially during winter; also cod liver oil. These dogs fare well on raw meat, which keeps them in excellent condition, but the choice of whether to feed meat, cooked or raw, must be left to the preference of the individual dog and its owner.

### Origin and history
Louis Dobermann of Apolda, in Thuringia, Germany, was a tax collector during the 1880s. Having a penchant for fierce dogs, he decided to breed the ideal animal to accompany him on his rounds. It was a relatively easy task for him, as he was keeper of the local dog pound, with access to numerous strays. He had in mind a medium-to large-sized dog, which must be short-coated (thus easily maintained), with courage, alertness and stamina.

The existing German Pinscher was considered to be both aggressive and alert, so it was around

*Above: A delightful 10-week old Dobermann lazing in the sun.*

this breed that Louis Dobermann founded his stock, introducing the the Rottweiler—a dog with great stamina and tracking ability—and, it is believed, the Manchester Terrier, which at that time was a much larger animal; no doubt it is from the Manchester that the Dobermann obtained its gleaming coat and black and tan markings. Possibly the Pointer was also used.

### SHOW SUMMARY
**General characteristics.** The Dobermann is a dog of good medium size, with a well-set body, muscular and elegant. It has a proud carriage, and a bold, alert temperament. Its form is compact and tough and, owing to its build, capable of great speed. The gait is light and elastic. The eyes show intelligence and firmness of character, and the Dobermann is loyal and obedient. Shyness or viciousness must be heavily penalized by show judges.
**Colour.** Colours allowed are definite black, brown or blue, with rust red markings. Markings must be sharply defined, appearing above each eye and on the muzzle, throat and fore-chest, on all legs and feet, and below the tail. White markings undesirable.
**Head and skull.** Must be proportionate to the body, long, well filled under the eyes and clean cut. Its form, seen from above and from the side, must resemble a blunt wedge. The upper part of the head should be as fat as possible, and free from wrinkle. The top of the skull should be flat with a slight stop, and the muzzle line should extend parallel to the top line of the skull. The cheeks must be flat and the lips tight. The nose should be solid black in black dogs, solid dark brown in brown dogs. and solid dark grey in blue dogs.
**Tail.** Should be docked at the first or second joint, and should appear to be a continuation of the spine, without material drop.
**Feet.** Fore-feet should be well arched, compact and cat-like, turning neither in nor out. All dew-claws to be removed. Long, flat deviating paws and weak pasterns should be penalized. Hindfeet should be well arched, compact and cat-like turning neither in nor out.

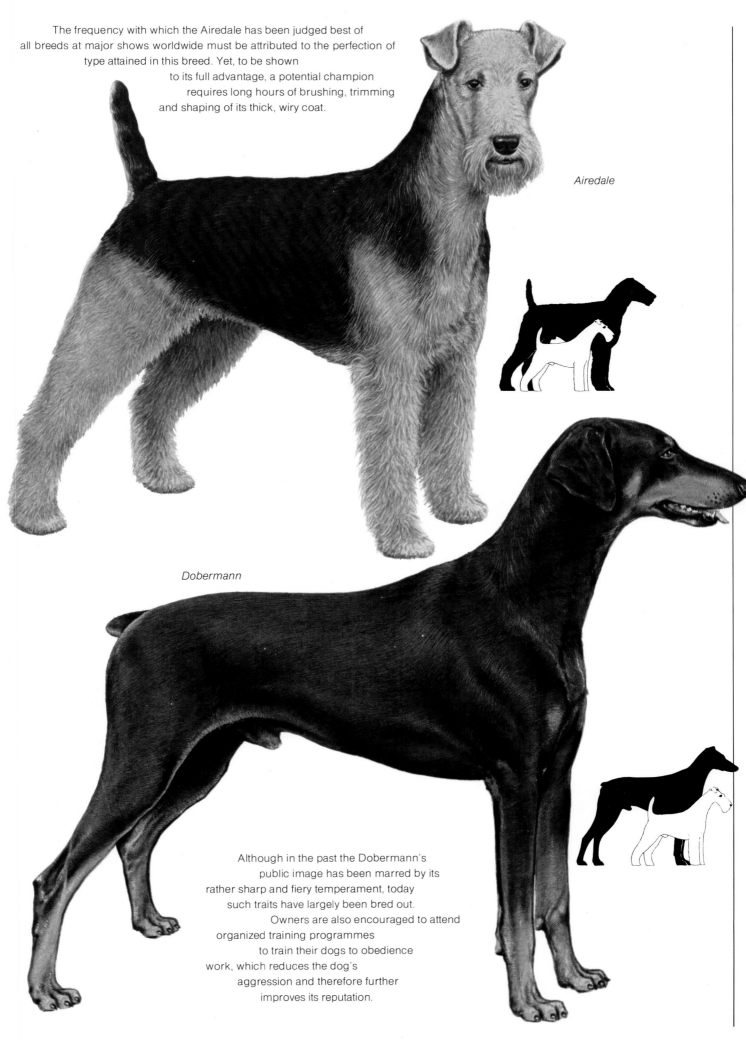

The frequency with which the Airedale has been judged best of all breeds at major shows worldwide must be attributed to the perfection of type attained in this breed. Yet, to be shown to its full advantage, a potential champion requires long hours of brushing, trimming and shaping of its thick, wiry coat.

*Airedale*

*Dobermann*

Although in the past the Dobermann's public image has been marred by its rather sharp and fiery temperament, today such traits have largely been bred out. Owners are also encouraged to attend organized training programmes to train their dogs to obedience work, which reduces the dog's aggression and therefore further improves its reputation.

# BEARDED COLLIE

## Good points
● *Devoted pet*
● *Good with children*
● *Intelligent*
● *Natural herder*
● *Playful*

## Take heed
● *Needs plenty of exercise*

The Bearded Collie is not so well known as other Collies in Britain, and was almost extinct after the Second World War. Now, however, numbers of this delightful breed are increasing. It is a lovable dog, ideally suited for family life, but retaining its herding capabilities. It is easily trained and reliable with children, and proves a willing, lively playmate.

## Size
Ideal height at the shoulder: dog 53-56cm (21-22in), bitch 51-53cm (20-21in).

## Exercise
Not suitable for a confined existence. Needs plenty of exercise, including off-the-lead runs.

## Grooming
Daily brushing. Bathing and chalking are necessary for show.

## Feeding
One to 1½ cans (376g, 13.3oz size) of a branded meaty product, with biscuit added in equal part by volume; or 3 cupfuls of a dry food, complete diet, mixed in the proportion of 1 cup of feed to ½ cup of hot or cold water.

## Origin and history
The lovable Beardie bears a keen resemblance to the Old English Sheepdog, or Bobtail, and is reckoned to be one of the oldest herding dogs in Scotland. It is said to be of Polish origin, being derived from purebred Polish Lowland Sheepdogs — two bitches and a dog were exchanged on a trading voyage to Scotland in 1514, for a ram and a ewe. It has also been said to have Magyar (Hungarian) blood.

Luckily the survival of the breed was assured when Mrs G. Willison, of the former Bothkennar Kennels, acquired a Beardie bitch puppy (then without pedigree) in 1944, and, after a fruitless search for a Beardie dog, found one playing with its owners on the beach at Hove, Sussex. They were willing to sell and from this pair, 'Jeannie' and 'Bailie', all to-day's Beardies are descended.

## SHOW SUMMARY
**General appearance.** An active dog with a long, lean body, and none of the stumpiness of the bobtail: Though strongly made, it shows plenty of daylight under the body and does not look too heavy. The face should have an enquiring expression. Movement should be free and active.

**Colour.** Slate grey or reddish fawn, black, all shades of grey, brown and sandy, with or without white collie markings.
**Head and skull.** Broad, flat skull with ears set high; fairly long foreface with moderate stop. Nose should be black except with brown or fawn coats, when brown is permitted.
**Tail.** Set low, should be moderately long, with abundant hair or brush; carried low when the dog is quiet, with an upward swirl at the tip; carried gaily when the dog is excited, but not over the back.
**Feet.** Oval in shape, soles well padded, toes arched and close together; well covered with hair, including between the pads.

A dog that bears a fairly strong resemblance to the Beardie is the Dutch Schapendoes, which has Beardie blood in its veins, as well probably as that of the Bergamasco, Puli and Briard. It is a popular sheepdog, guard and house-dog in Holland, but is little known in other countries.

*Below: The Dutch Schapendoes.*

# SMOOTH COLLIE
(Smooth-haired Collie)

## Good points
● *Affectionate*
● *Easily trained*
● *Excellent pet*
● *Loves children*
● *Loyal*

## Take heed
● *Not too keen on strangers*

The Smooth Collie is like the Rough Collie in temperament. It makes an ideal family pet, and is hardy and simple to groom. It is identical to the Rough-hair except in coat (see Show Summary).

## Size
Height at shoulder: dog 56-61cm (22-24in); bitch 51-56cm (20-22in). Weight: dog 20.5-29.5kg (45-65lb); bitch 18.1-25kg (40-55lb).

## Exercise
Normal daily exercise, with off-the-lead runs when possible.

## Grooming
Daily brushing will keep the coat in good condition.

## Feeding
Recommended would be 1½-2½ cans (376g, 13.3oz size) of a branded meaty product, with biscuit added in equal part by volume; or 5 cupfuls of a dry food, complete diet, mixed in the proportion of 1 cup of feed to ½ cup of hot or cold water.

## Origin and history
Every Smooth Collie and Rough Collie can trace its origin to a tricolour dog called 'Trefoil', born in 1873; and until 1974 the Smooth-coat did not have a separate standard in Britain, except for the coat. However, while the Rough-coat has maintained international popularity, the Smooth-coat is seldom seen and might have become extinct were it not for the determined efforts of dedicated breeders.

## SHOW SUMMARY
**General appearance.** The Collie should instantly appeal as gifted with intelligence, alertness and activity. It should stand with dignity, and its movements, governed by perfect anatomical formation, with no part out of proportion, should be smooth and graceful. It should give the appearance of a dog capable of working.
**Colour.** The three recognized colours are: sable and white; tricolour; and blue merle.
**Head and skull.** The head properties are of great importance and must be considered in proportion to the size of the dog. When viewed from both front and profile the head should bear a general resemblance to a well-blunted, clean wedge, being smooth in outline. Whatever the colour of the dog, the nose must be black.
**Tail.** Should be long, with the bone reaching at least to the hock joint. To be carried low when the dog is quiet but with a slight upward swirl at the tip. It may be carried gaily when the dog is excited, but never over the back.
**Feet.** Should be oval, with soles well padded. Toes arched and close together. Hind feet slightly less arched.

# ROUGH COLLIE
(Rough-haired Collie)

## Good points
● *Affectionate*
● *Easily trained*
● *Excellent pet*
● *Loves children*
● *Loyal*

## Take heed
● *Not too keen on strangers*

No breed causes so much consternation to buyers and those giving breed information as the Collie. People tend to have a fixed idea of the type of Collie they want, be it Rough, Smooth, Border, Old English or Bearded; and, having written to enquire about a Collie, they expect the recipient of their letter to be on the same wavelength. If it's a dog like the film star 'Lassie' that you want, you *are* thinking of a Rough Collie, sometimes erroneously called a Scottish Collie; the Sheltie, or Shetland, is a 'Lassie' in miniature.

The Rough Collie makes an ideal family pet, being biddable, affectionate and loyal. It is hardy and, despite its thick coat, relatively simple to groom.

## Size
Height at shoulder: dog 56-61cm (22-24in); bitch 51-56cm (20-22in). Weight: dog 20.5-29.5kg (45-65lb); bitch 18.1-25kg (40-55lb).

## Exercise
Normal daily exercise with off-the-lead runs when possible.

## Grooming
Daily brushing. Don't be afraid to vacuum clean with the smallest brush, if it gets muddy. But get the dog accustomed to the noise of the machine first.

## Feeding
As for Smooth Collie.

## Origin and history
The Rough Collie is generally spoken of as a Scottish breed. In fact, its ancestors were introduced into England and Scotland from Iceland 400 years ago. But it was as guardians of the flock that they acquired their name in Scotland, where sheep with black faces and legs were known as colleys. Queen Victoria kept a Rough Collie at Balmoral in 1860, and in the same year a breed member was exhibited in a Birmingham show.

## SHOW SUMMARY
**General appearance.** The Collie should instantly appeal as a dog of great beauty, standing with impassive dignity, with no part out of proportion to the whole.
**Colour.** Sable and white, tricolour and blue merle.
*Sable* — any shade from light gold to rich mahogany or shaded sable.
*Tricolour* — predominantly black with rich tan markings about the legs and head.
*Blue merle* — predominantly clear, silvery blue, splashed and marbled with black.
**Head and skull.** The head properties are of great importance and must be considered in proportion to the size of the dog. When viewed from the front or the side the head bears a general resemblance to a well-blunted, clean wedge, being smooth in outline. Whatever the colour of the dog, the nose must be black.
**Tail.** Should be long, with the bone reaching at least to the hock joint. To be carried low when the dog is quiet, but with a slight upward swirl at the tip. It may be carried gaily when the dog is excited, but not over the back.
**Feet.** Should be oval in shape, with soles well padded, toes arched and close together. The hind feet slightly less arched.

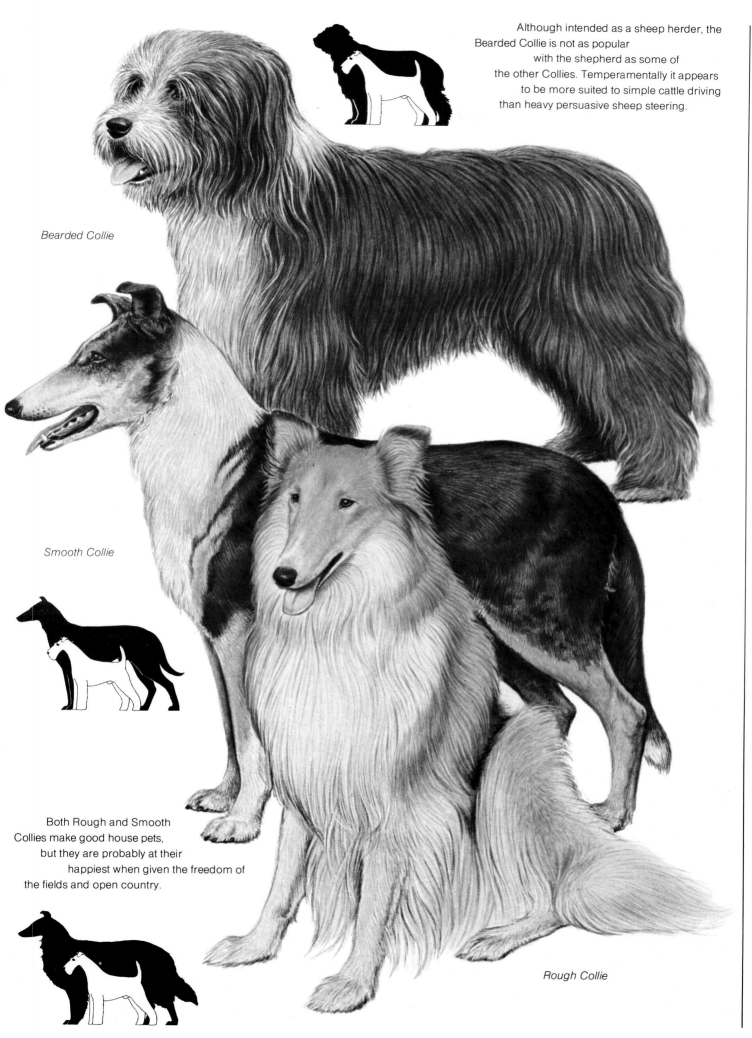

Although intended as a sheep herder, the Bearded Collie is not as popular with the shepherd as some of the other Collies. Temperamentally it appears to be more suited to simple cattle driving than heavy persuasive sheep steering.

*Bearded Collie*

*Smooth Collie*

Both Rough and Smooth Collies make good house pets, but they are probably at their happiest when given the freedom of the fields and open country.

*Rough Collie*

# GERMAN LONG-HAIRED POINTER
(Langhaar)

## Good points
- Easily trained
- Equable temperament
- Excellent gundog
- Good with children
- Makes a good household pet
- Obedient

## Take heed
- Needs plenty of exercise

The German Long-haired Pointer (or Langhaar) is, alas, almost extinct. It is a healthy dog, with a good temperament, much endurance and the swimming and hunting ability of all pointers. It is energetic and immensely loyal to its master.

## Size
Height: 61-63.5cm (24-25in) at the shoulder.

## Exercise
Should be allowed plenty of exercise.

## Grooming
Brush the coat regularly to keep it in good condition.

## Feeding
Recommended would be 1½-2½ cans (376g, 13.3oz size) of a branded meaty product, with biscuit added in equal part by volume; or 5 cupfuls of a dry food, complete diet, mixed in the proportion of 1 cup of feed to ½ cup of hot or cold water.

## Origin and history
This type varies in appearance from other pointers, in that it resembles the setter in appearance. This is not surprising, because it evolved as the result of crossing Dutch and French spaniels and local German breeds with the Gordon Setter, which at the time was greatly favoured by German huntsmen. It is an attractive dog, of great endurance, but its numbers are sadly dwindling in favour of the Wire-haired Pointer.

## SHOW SUMMARY (FCI)
**General characteristics.** A dog of robust, muscular build, but with a distinguished general appearance. The expression is one of intelligence and nobility, the character lively without any nervousness.
**Colour.** Usually self-coloured, light brown or dead leaf. The presence of red and black is penalized.
**Head and skull.** Long, lean, quite broad, divided into equal length for skull and muzzle; the upper part of the head is slightly rounded. It is the head which gives import and distinction to the general appearance. The nose is flat, more or less deep brown in colour.
**Tail.** Well set on, carried horizontally, sometimes slightly curved upward, the tail may be slightly docked if it is too long or if it is out of proportion with the rest of the body; the long hair at the midpoint of the tail should be a good fringe.
**Feet.** Well closed, of moderate length, moderately round.

# GERMAN WIRE-HAIRED POINTER
(Drahthaar)

## Good points
- Easily trained
- Equable temperament
- Excellent gundog
- Good with children
- Makes a good household pet
- Obedient

## Take heed
- Needs plenty of exercise
- Slightly more aggressive than other pointer types

In its native country the German Wire-haired Pointer is known as the Drahthaar (literally translated, this means 'wire hair') and is perhaps more spirited and aggressive than its fellow pointers, with stronger guarding instincts and a hardy physique. It is an excellent gundog.

## Size
Dog 61-66cm (24-26in), bitch smaller, not less than 56cm (22in).

## Exercise
Needs plenty of exercise.

## Grooming
Brush the coat regularly.

## Feeding
As German Long-haired Pointer.

## Origin and history
The German Wire-haired Pointer is identical to the Short-hair except in coat. There are, however, some differences in background, and although the English Pointer undoubtedly contributed to its development, the Wire-hair was also derived from other hunting breeds. It is mentioned in German medieval documents.

## SHOW SUMMARY
**General appearance.** A medium-sized hunting dog of noble bearing; very harsh hair completely covers the skin; intelligent expression; devoted and energetic.
**Colour.** Solid liver, liver and white spotted, liver and white spotted and ticked, liver and white ticked, black and white. Colour unimportant.
**Head and skull.** The head should be of medium length with a long, strong muzzle.
**Tail.** Starts high and thick, growing gradually thinner. Docked by half its length. When quiet, tail should be carried down; when moving horizontally, never held high over the back or bent.
**Feet.** Compact, close-knit, round to spoon-shaped, well padded; should turn neither in nor out. Toes well arched, heavily nailed.

# GERMAN SHORT-HAIRED POINTER

## Good points
- Easily trained
- Equable temperament
- Excellent gundog
- Good with children
- Makes a good household pet
- Obedient

## Take heed
- Needs plenty of exercise

The German Short-haired Pointer is a good all-round sporting dog, and affectionate and good with children. It is, however, happiest when in the wide open spaces, and is excellent at working wildfowl and most types of game. It is a first-rate swimmer.

## Size
Dog 58.5-63.5cm (23-25in); bitch 53-58.5cm (21-23in).

## Exercise
Needs plenty of exercise.

## Grooming
Brush the coat regularly.

## Feeding
As German Long-haired Pointer.

## Origin and history
The German Short-haired Pointer is of Spanish origin, bred from dogs imported into Germany and crossed with local hounds and, probably, with the English Foxhound for speed, the Bloodhound for nose, and the English Pointer to retain its pointing ability.

## SHOW SUMMARY
**General appearance.** A noble, steady dog showing power, endurance and speed, giving the immediate impression of an alert and energetic (not nervous) dog whose movements are well co-ordinated. Neither unduly small nor conspicuously large, but of medium size, and like the hunter, 'With a short back, but standing over plenty of ground'.
**Colour.** Solid liver, liver and white spotted, liver and white spotted and ticked, liver and white ticked, black and white.
**Head and skull.** Clean-cut, neither too light nor too heavy, but well proportioned to the body. The skull sufficiently broad and slightly rounded. Nose solid brown, wide nostrils well opened and soft.
**Tail.** Starts high and thick, growing gradually thinner. Docked to medium length by two fifths to half its length. When quiet, tail should be carried down; and when moving horizontally, never held high over the back or bent.
**Feet.** Compact, close-knit, round to spoon-shaped, well padded; should turn neither in nor out. Toes well arched, heavily nailed.

# POINTER

## Good points
- Equable temperament
- Obedient
- Good with children
- Easily trained
- Excellent gundog
- Makes a good household pet

## Take heed
- Needs plenty of exercise

The Pointer is famed for its classic pose 'pointing' with its nose and tail in the direction of the game that has been shot. It is a friendly dog, and makes an ideal household pet, getting on well with other animals. and children. But it does need a generous amount of exercise.

## Size
Desirable height: dog 63.5-68.5cm (25-27in); bitch 61-66cm (24-26in).

## Exercise
Needs plenty of exercise.

## Grooming
Brush the coat regularly.

## Feeding
As German Long-haired Pointer.

## Origin and history
There is some controversy as to whether the Pointer originated in Spain, or was produced in Britain through crossings of Bloodhounds, Foxhounds and Greyhounds. A great authority on the breed, William Arkwright of Sutton Scarsdale, England, spent his life travelling the world to check on the history and development of the breed. He believed that it originated in the East, found its way to Italy, then to Spain (where it developed its classic head) and thence to England and South America. Arkwright on Pointers is still the bible of the breed.

## SHOW SUMMARY
**Head and skull.** The skull should be of medium breadth and in proportion to the length of the foreface; the stop well defined; pronounced occipital bone. Nose and eye-rims dark, but may be lighter in the case of a lemon and white dog. The nostrils wide, soft and moist. The muzzle somewhat concave, and ending on a level with the nostrils, giving a slightly dish-faced appearance. The cheekbones should not be prominent. Well-developed, soft lip.
**Colour.** The usual colours are lemon and white, orange and white, liver and white, and black and white. Self-colours and tri-colours are also correct.
**Tail.** Of medium length, thick at the root, growing gradually thinner to the point. It should be well covered with close hair, and carried level with the back, with no upward curl. When the dog is moving, the tail should lash from side to side.
**Feet.** Oval, with well-knit, arched toes, well cushioned underneath.

Used originally for hawking and falconry, the German Long-haired Pointer is a powerful animal and a versatile gundog. Particularly useful for work with gamebirds, it is also very good in close coverts.

*German Long-haired Pointer*

*German Wire-haired Pointer*

*German Short-haired Pointer*

*Pointer*

Handsome rather than glamorous, with its deep chest, straight bones and beautifully proportioned body, the Pointer is the epitome of the working gundog.

# IRISH SETTER
(Red Setter)

## Good points
- *Affectionate*
- *Beautiful*
- *Excellent with children*
- *Hunting ability*

## Take heed
- *Lively*
- *No good as a guard; it loves everybody!*

The Irish Setter is a first-class gundog that combines this work admirably with the role of family pet. It is happiest as a housedog and has great need of affection, which it returns a hundredfold. It is intelligent and utterly reliable with children. It is, however, high spirited and lively and should not be confined in close quarters or kept by those who cannot provide adequate exercise. It often strikes up a good relationship with horses.

## Size
The Americans look for a tall dog, 63.5-68.5cm (25-27in) high, but in Britain no height is specified.

## Exercise
An exuberant dog that needs lots of exercise, either working or running in the wide open spaces.

## Grooming
Regular brushing, claw clipping, and inspection of ears.

## Feeding
Recommended would be 1½-2½ cans (376g, 13.3oz size) of a branded meaty product, with biscuit added in equal part by volume; or 5 cupfuls of a dry food, complete diet, mixed in the proportion of 1 cup of feed to ½ cup of hot or cold water.

## Origin and history
The Irish Setter has evolved from the crossing of Irish Water Spaniels, Springer Spaniels, the Spanish Pointer and English and Gordon Setters, its name being settled by the Ulster Irish Setter Club in 1876. Synonymous with the breed is the name of Edward Laverack who, prior to his death in 1877, spent almost a lifetime improving the breed.

## SHOW SUMMARY
**General appearance.** Must be racy, full of quality, and kindly in expression.
**Colour.** Rich chestnut, with no trace whatever of black; white on chest, throat, chin or toes, or a small star on the forehead, or a narrow streak or blaze on the nose or face not to disqualify.
**Head and skull.** The head should be long and lean, not narrow or snipy, and not coarse at the ears. The skull oval (from ear to ear), having plenty of brain room, and with well-defined occipital protuberance. Brows raised, showing stop. Muzzle moderately deep, and fairly square at the end. From the stop to the point of the nose should be long, the nostrils wide, and the jaws of nearly equal length; flews not pendulous. The colour of the nose snould be dark mahogany, dark walnut or black.
**Tail.** Of moderate length, proportionate to the size of the body; set on rather low, strong at the root, and tapering to a fine point; to be carried as nearly as possible on a level with or below the back.
**Feet.** Should be small and very firm; toes strong, close together and arched.

# ENGLISH SETTER

## Good points
- *Adaptable*
- *Beautiful*
- *Can live in house or kennel*
- *Reliable gundog*

## Take heed
- *Not a loner; thrives in company of humans or of other dogs*

The English Setter is the most distinctive of the three Setter varieties, Irish, Gordon and English. It has a gentle nature that makes it the ideal companion for children, at the same time being an excellent gundog. As it needs lots of exercise, it is not a suitable companion for a flat dweller. It also requires a fair amount of grooming.

## Size
Weight: dog 27.2-30kg (60-66lb); bitch 25.4-28.1kg (56-62lb). Height: dog 65-68.5cm (25½-27in); bitch 61-63.5cm (24-25in).

## Exercise
Needs at least 10 minutes of exercise a day as a 3-month-old pup and a hour in adulthood to keep it in top condition. Trains well to the gun.

## Grooming
You will need trimming scissors and a fine steel comb for daily grooming, also a good stiff brush for the coat. Take care that the feathering on the legs does not become tangled. The silky hair under the ears should be removed and also hair under the throat and below the ear down to the breast bone. Care must also be taken to remove hair that forms between the dog's pads. Any straggly hairs have to be plucked from the body before the dog goes into the show ring. The English Setter is always bathed before a show, and the coat combed flat when it is dry. American competitors are trimmed more heavily than those exhibited in the United Kingdom.

## Origin and history
It is generally agreed that the English Setter evolved from spaniels. Credit for the breed is given to Edward Laverack (1815-1877) who in his work *The Setter* wrote: 'this breed is but a Spaniel improved'. The Setting Spaniel, accepted by many modern authorities as the forerunner of the English Setter, was used as far back as the 16th century for setting partridges and quails. Through interbreeding, Laverack affected the strain so that it acquired not only the standard of excellence in the 19th century but that on which the present-day English Setter was built. To quote Sylvia Bruce Wilmore writing in *Dog News* magazine: 'About the time the Laverack strain of English Setter was at its zenith, Mr R.L. Purcell Llewellin purchased a number of Mr Laverack's best Show dogs of the pure Dash-Moll and Dash-Hill Laverack blood. He crossed these with entirely new blood which he obtained in the North of England represented by Mr Slatter's and Sir Vincent Corbet's strain, since referred to as the Duke-Kate-Rhoebe. The Llewellin strain of English Setter became immensely popular at the turn of the century, their reputation spreading to the United States and Canada where they dominated field trials for a quarter of a century, thus firmly establishing the line of breed in America.'

## SHOW SUMMARY
**General appearance.** Of medium height, clean in outline, elegant in appearance and movement.
**Colour.** The colour may be black and white, lemon and white, liver and white or tricolour (that is, black, white and tan); those without heavy patches of colour on the body, but flecked all over, are preferred.
**Head and skull.** Head should be long and reasonably lean, with a well-defined stop. The colour of the nose should be black or liver, according to the colour of the coat.
**Tail.** The tail should be set on almost in line with the back; medium length, not curly or ropy, to be slightly curved or scimitar-shaped but with no tendency to turn upwards; the flag or feather hanging in long pendent flakes.
**Feet.** The feet should be very close and compact, and well protected by hair between the toes.

# GORDON SETTER

## Good points
- *Affectionate*
- *Equable temperament*
- *Excellent gundog*
- *Good with children*

## Take heed
- *Not suitable for a guard dog*

The Gordon Setter is a fine gundog, a bird-finding dog, used to silent trekking. It does not fit the role of guard; although it will not accept strangers as readily as the Irish Setter, which could well lick the face of a burglar while presenting him with some item 'retrieved' from its mistress's wardrobe.

The Gordon makes an excellent family pet and is trustworthy with children. It does enjoy an active working life, however, and is not really suitable for apartments.

## Size
Shoulder height for dog, 66cm (26in), weight about 29.5kg (65lb); bitch, 62cm (24½in), weight about 25.4kg (56lb).

## Exercise
Ensure that it has plenty of exercise.

## Grooming
Regular brushing, and monthly nail clipping.

## Feeding
Recommended would be 1½-2½ cans (376g, 13.3oz size) of a branded meaty product, with biscuit added in equal part by volume; or 5 cupfuls of a dry food, complete diet, mixed in the proportion of 1 cup of feed to ½ cup of hot or cold water.

## Origin and history
The Gordon is a true Scot, bred at Gordon Castle, Banffshire, the seat of the Duke of Richmond and Gordon. It is the only native Scottish gundog and was originally known as the Gordon Castle Setter. Credit must go to the 4th Duke of Richmond and Gordon for establishing the breed in the late 1770s, using probably the Collie and the Bloodhound.

## SHOW SUMMARY
**General appearance.** A stylish dog, built on galloping lines, having a thoroughbred appearance consistent with its build, which can be compared to a weight-carrying hunter. Must have symmetrical conformation throughout, showing true balance. Strong, fairly short and level back. Shortish tail. Head fairly long, clearly lined and with an intelligent expression; clear colours and long flat coat.
**Colour.** Deep shining coal-black, with no sign of rustiness, with lustrous tan markings of a rich chestnut red, i.e. the colour of a ripe horse-chestnut as taken from the shell. Black pencilling allowed on toes, also a black streak under the jaw. Tan markings: two clear spots over the eyes, not over 2cm (⁴/₅in) in diameter; on the sides of the muzzle, the tan should not reach above the base of the nose.
**Head and skull.** Head deep rather than broad, but definitely broader than the muzzle, showing brain room. Nose big and broad, with open nostrils and black in colour.
**Tail.** Fairly short, straight or slightly scimitar-shaped; should not reach below the hocks. Carried horizontal or below line of back. Thick at the root, tapering to a fine point. The feather or flat, which starts near the root, should be long and straight, and grow shorter uniformly to the point.
**Feet.** Oval, with close-knit, well-arched toes, with plenty of hair between. Full toe pads and deep heel cushions.

The Setters are elegant and efficient gundogs. The name arises from the traditional practice of training such dogs to sit when they have located game by scent and sight, hence the term 'sitting' or 'setting' dogs.

*Irish Setter*

*English Setter*

*Gordon Setter*

# GERMAN SHEPHERD DOG
(Alsatian)

### Good points
- *Devoted to owner*
- *Excellent worker/herder*
- *Favoured for obedience competitions*
- *Loyal*
- *Supremely intelligent*
- *Protective*

### Take heed
- *Tendency to over-guard*
- *Not a lap dog, but a worker that needs a task in life*

The German Shepherd Dog has one of the largest followings in the world. It is also the breed that rouses the strongest emotions in the public. They either worship the German Shepherd or abhor it. If a smaller breed takes a nip out of the postman's trousers, the misdeed may go unreported; but if a German Shepherd is involved, the headlines are likely to be: 'German Shepherd Dog savages postman!'

The German Shepherd is one of the most courageous and intelligent of dogs, debatably *the* most intelligent. Breed members have fought bravely, and many lost their lives in two World Wars. They have been, and still are, used, as guide dogs for the blind (US 'seeing eye dogs'), police dogs, and military dogs. Certainly they are a very popular guard. It is this strong guarding instinct that can be their undoing, however, for a German Shepherd protecting a toddler may menace a stranger at the garden gate. It could also turn nasty through sheer boredom, if acquired as a mere pet dog. The German Shepherd deserves a job to do, whether it be in the public service, or competing eagerly in obedience and working trials.

### Size
The ideal height (measured to the highest point of the shoulder) is 56-61cm (22-24in) for bitches and 61-66cm (24-26in) for dogs. The proportion of length to height varies between 10:9 and 10:8.5.

*Below: A German Shepherd puppy with soft under-coat.*

### Exercise
Needs plenty of exercise, off-the-lead runs and, if possible, obedience exercises. It will excel at the local dog training club in 'scent' and 'retrieve'. Remember that this breed is used to sniff out illegal drug shipments, and to detect the elusive 'black box' amid the wreckage strewn over many miles after airplane crashes.

### Grooming
Daily brushing is recommended.

### Feeding
Give 1½-2½ cans (376g, 13.3oz size) of a branded meaty product, with biscuit added in equal part by volume; or 5 cupfuls of a dry food, complete diet, mixed in the proportion of 1 cup of food to ½ cup of hot or cold water.

### Health care
This is a healthy, hardy breed. However, its popularity in recent years has encouraged indiscriminate breeding, resulting in loss of temperament and form. Take care, when purchasing a German Shepherd Dog, to acquire only from registered HD-free stock. HD is an abbreviation for hip dysplasia, a malformation of the hip joint that can result in the dog being crippled before middle age. Reliable vendors do not breed from affected stock. Many people feel this defect came about through over-emphasis on that desired show dog crouch.

### Origin and history
The German Shepherd Dog is attributed by some to the Bronze Age wolf, perhaps an unfortunate suggestion in that it wrongly associates the breed with wolf-like tendencies. Certainly around the 7th century AD a sheepdog of this type, but with a lighter coat, existed in Germany; and by the 16th century the coat had appreciably darkened.

The breed was first exhibited at a dog show in Hanover in 1882. Credit for the formation of the breed is widely assigned to a German fancier named von Stephanitz, who did much to improve its temperament and physical appearance.

The German Shepherd Dog was introduced into Britain following the First World War by a small band of dedicated fanciers who had seen the breed working in Germany. These included the late Colonel Baldwin and Air Commodore Alan Cecil-Wright, President of the Kennel Club. It was thought inappropriate at that time to glorify an animal bearing a German prefix, so, as the breed had come from Alsace, it became known in the United Kingdom as the Alsatian. Only in 1971 did the British Kennel Club relent and agree to the breed being known once more as the German Shepherd Dog.

### SHOW SUMMARY
**General appearance.** In general, the Alsatian is a well-proportioned dog showing great suppleness of

*Above: An agile German Shepherd Dog successfully climbs a special barrier at a working trial.*

limb, neither massive nor heavy, but at the same time free from any suggestion of weediness. It must not approach the Greyhound type. The body is rather long, strongly boned, with plenty of muscle, obviously capable of endurance and speed and of quick and sudden movement. The gait should be supple, smooth and long-reaching, carrying the body along with the minimum of up-and-down movement, entirely free from stiltiness.

**Colour.** The colour of the Alsatian is in itself not important: it has no effect on the character of the dog or on its fitness for work, and should be a secondary consideration for that reason. All white or near white, unless possessing black points, are not desirable, however. The final colour of a young dog can be ascertained only when the outer coat has developed.

**Head and skull.** The head is proportionate to the size of the body, long, lean and clean cut, broad at the back of the skull, but without coarseness, tapering to the nose with only a slight stop between the eyes. The skull is slightly domed and the top of the nose should be parallel to the forehead. The cheeks must not be full or in any way prominent, and the whole head, when viewed from the top, should be much in the form of a V, well filled in under the eyes. There should be plenty of substance in the foreface, with a good depth from top to bottom. The muzzle is strong and long and, while tapering to the nose, it must not be carried to such an extreme as to give the appearance of being overshot. It must not show any weakness, or be snipy or lippy. The lips should be tight fitting and clean. The nose must be black.

**Tail.** When at rest the tail should hang in a slight curve, and reach at least as far as the hock. During movement and excitement it will be raised, but under no circumstances should the tail be carried past a vertical line drawn through the root.

**Feet.** The feet should be round, the toes strong, slightly arched and held close together. The pads should be firm, the nails short and strong. Dew-claws are neither a fault nor a virtue, but should be removed from the hind legs at 4-5 days old, as they are liable to spoil the gait.

# BELGIAN SHEPHERD DOG
(Groenendael [Belgian Sheepdog], Laekenois, Malinois [Belgian Malinois], Tervueren [Belgian Tervuren]).

### Good points
- *Alert and agile*
- *Excellent guard*
- *Handy, medium size*
- *Intelligent*
- *Physically robust*

### Take heed
- *Best suited to the open spaces, so won't take kindly to apartment living*
- *Needs firm but kind handling*

There are four types of Belgian Shepherd Dog—the Groenendael, the Laekenois, the Malinois and the Tervueren—all of which are similar to the German Shepherd.

Basically, they are hunting and herding dogs, but they have also served as Red Cross messengers in war-time, are vigilant guards and kindly protectors of children.

### Size
The desired height for the dog is 61-66cm (24-26in) and for the bitch 56-61cm (22-24in). This applies to all four types.

### Exercise
The Belgian Shepherd Dog is a working dog that excels in defending master and property. It is oblivious to bad weather, and enjoys being out of doors, so adequate exercise is vital.

The breed has done well in working trials and in various obedience competitions; a Belgian Shepherd Dog, in the hands of an experienced trainer, will soon learn all that is required of it. Conversely, rough handling will benefit neither owner nor dog, but may turn a forthcoming, eager pup into a nervous animal.

### Grooming
Little grooming is needed other than a good surface brushing. Bathing is not recommended, even for exhibition, unless the dog has got its coat into a filthy condition. As it has a double coat, combing out the under-coat will result in a dog with only half a coat.

### Feeding
The Belgian Shepherd Dog should be fed similarly to other dogs of its size. Basic daily rations might be 1½ to 2 cans of branded dog food (376g, 13.3oz size), with an equal volume of biscuits, or 5 cupfuls of a dry food, complete diet, mixed in the proportion of 1 cup to ½ cup of hot or cold water.

### Origin and history
At the end of the 19th century there were Shepherd Dog varieties of all colours and sizes in Belgium, but in about 1890, Monsieur Rose of the Café du Groenendael discovered a black, long-coated bitch among one of his litters.

The characteristic expression of the German
Shepherd Dog gives the impression of perpetual
vigilance, fidelity, liveliness and watchfulness, alert to
every sight and sound, with nothing escaping
attention. The German Shepherd Dog possesses
highly developed senses, mentally
and temperamentally.

German Shepherd Dog

Belgian Shepherd Dog
(Groenendael)

The black-coated
Belgian Shepherd Dog
has received high praise
for its working abilities,
particularly in the USA, where
it first appeared in 1907.

Later, he bought a similar dog from a Monsieur Bernaert and, by selective breeding and strict culling, eventually produced the Groenendael.

The origin of the modern Belgian Shepherd Dog dates from 1891, when a collection of shepherd dogs of all colours and sizes was gathered at the Brussels Veterinary University. It was decided to recognize three varieties: the rough-coated black; the smooth-coated fawn with black mask; and the wire-haired darkish grey. Since then there have been various additions to and subtractions from these types, but they have now been settled into four varieties: the Groenendael (long-coated black); the Tervueren (long-coated other than black); the Malinois (smooth-coated); and the Laekenois, or de Laeken (wire-coated).

It should be mentioned that in America only the Groenendael is known as the Belgian Shepherd Dog or Belgian Sheepdog; the Malinois and the Tervueren are registered as separate breeds, and the Laekenois—the rarest of the four—is not recognized. Incidentally, the breeds are known in America as the Belgian Malinois and the Belgian Tervuren, the latter with a slightly different spelling.

### SHOW SUMMARY
Belgian Shepherd Dog (Groenendael); Belgian Sheepdog

**General appearance.** A medium-sized dog, well-proportioned, intelligent, hardy and bred to withstand adverse weather. It should be alert and attentive with a lively and enquiring mien.

**Colour.** Black, or black with limited white as follows: small to moderate patch or strip on chest, between the pads of the feet, and on the tips of the hind toes. Frosting (white or grey) on the muzzle.

**Head and skull.** The head should be finely chiselled, long (but not excessively so) and gaunt. The skull and muzzle should be roughly equal in length, with at most a slight bias in favour of the muzzle, giving the impression of a balanced whole. The skull should be of a medium width in proportion to the length of the head, with a flattened rather than rounded forehead, and the centre line not very pronounced; seen in profile it should be parallel to an imaginary line extending the muzzle line. The muzzle should be of medium length, tapering gradually towards the nose. The nose should be black with well-flared nostrils. Moderate stop.

**Coat.** The outer coat should be long, straight and abundant. It should not be silky or wiry; the texture should be of medium harshness. The under-coat should be extremely dense. The hair should be shorter on the head, the outside of the ears and the lower part of the legs. The opening of the ear should be protected by hair. The hair should be especially long and abundant around the neck, like a ruff, particularly in the male. There should be a fringe of long hair down the back of the forearm, and long and abundant hair evident on the hindquarters and the tail. The male should be longer coated than the female.

**Tail.** The tail should be firmly set, strong at the base and of medium length. At rest the dog should carry it hanging down with the tip slightly bent backwards at the level of the hock; on the move the dog should lift it, accentuating the curve towards the tip; however, it should under no circumstances curl up or bend to one side.

**Feet.** No specific requirements are laid down in the standard.

The four varieties of Belgian Shepherd Dog vary only in coat and colour. These are the standards for the other three varieties:

Laekenois:

**Coat.** The coat should be rough, dry, untidy-looking and not curly. Any sprinkling of fluffy fine hair in locks in the rough coat is inadmissible. The length of the coat should be about 6cm (2.4in) on all parts of the body. The hair around the eyes and that on the muzzle should be fairly long. It is essential, however, that the hair around the muzzle should not be so long as to make the head appear square or heavy. The tail should not be plumed.

**Colour.** Reddish fawn with black shading, principally on the muzzle and tail.

Malinois

**Coat.** The hair should be very short on the head, the exterior of the ears and the lower parts of the legs; short on the rest of the body; and thicker on the tail and around the neck, where it should resemble a ridge or collar, beginning at the base of the ear and extending to the throat. In addition the hindquarters should be fringed with longer hair. The tail should be thick and bushy. The coat should be thick, close and of a good firm texture with a wool under-coat.

**Colour.** Dark fawn with considerable black overlay; washed-out fawn or grey is highly undesirable, as is patchy black overlay or the total absence of black overlay. Black shading on muzzle and ears is desirable.

Tervueren

**Coat.** The outer coat should be long, straight and abundant. It should not be silky or wiry; the texture should be of medium harshness. The under-coat should be extremely dense. The hair should be shorter on the head, the outside of the ears and the lower part of the legs. The opening of the ear should be protected by hair. The hair should be especially long and abundant around the neck, like a ruff, particularly in the male. There should be a fringe of long hair down the back of the forearm, and long and abundant hair evident on the hindquarters and the tail. The male should be longer coated than the female.

**Colour.** All shades of red, fawn and grey with black overlay. The coat should be characteristically double-pigmented, wherein the tip of each light-coloured hair is blackened. On mature males this blackening should be especially pronounced on the shoulders, back and rib section. The face should have a black mask, not extending above the line of the eyes, and the ears should be mostly black. The tail should typically have a darker or black tip. A small to moderate white patch or strip is permitted on the chest, between the pads of the feet and on the tips of the hind toes. Frosting (white or grey) on the muzzle. Beyond the age of 18 months a washed-out colour or a colour too black should be considered a fault.

# HOLLANDSE HERDER
(Dutch Shepherd Dog)

### Good points
- Excellent guard
- Hardy
- Intelligent
- Sound temperament

### Take heed
- No drawbacks known

The Hollandse Herder was bred in Holland as a sheepdog, but nowadays is kept mainly as a companion and guard. It is relatively unknown outside its native country, where it is used as a police dog, as a guide dog for the blind (seeing eye dog) and occasionally for farmyard duties. It comes in three coat types: short-hair, long-hair and wire-hair. The long-haired variety is almost extinct and the wire-hair is not greatly favoured; the short-hair type is the one most widely known.

### Size
Height at the withers: dog 58.5-63.5cm (23-25in); bitch 54.5-62cm (21½-24½in). In the case of the long-hairs only, the minimum is lowered to 54.5cm (21½in) for dogs, 53cm (21in) for bitches.

### Exercise
Needs plenty of exercise to keep in good health.

### Grooming
Regular brushing will keep the coat in good condition.

### Feeding
Recommended would be 1½-2½ cans (376g, 13.3oz size) of a branded meaty product, with biscuit added in equal part by volume; or 5 cupfuls of a dry food, complete diet, mixed in the proportion of 1 cup of feed to ½ cup of hot or cold water.

### Origin and history
The Hollandse Herder is closely related to the Belgian Shepherd Dog and they are of similar origin. It has, however, developed as a separate breed in its native Holland, where it has always been extremely popular.

### SHOW SUMMARY
**General characteristics.** A medium-sized dog, not too heavy; muscular, strong, symmetrical, always attentive and always in movement. The Dutch Shepherd has an intelligent expression and shows great aptitude for working with sheep.

**Colour.** *Short-hair:* Yellow, chestnut, brown, gold and silver streaked. The streaks should be sharp and distributed well over the entire body, as well as on the back of the thighs and tail. The streaking must involve the hair from root to tip. Too much black in the outer coat is a fault. The mask should be black.
*Wire-hair:* Yellow, red-brown, ash blue, streaked, grey-blue, salt and pepper.
*Long-hair:* Chestnut, gold or silver streaked.

**Head.** In good proportion to the body, without being coarse, it gives the impression of leanness. Of moderate length, rather narrow (but not of the greyhound type), more or less conical in shape. The muzzle is a little longer than the skull. The bridge is straight and parallel to the skull line; the stop is barely perceptible. The head of the wire-haired variety is squarer than for the short-haired. The tip of the nose is invariably black. The lips are well closed over the gums. The teeth are strong and regular and meet in a scissor bite.

**Tail.** In repose the tail is carried low with a slight curve, the tip not reaching the hocks. In action it is carried high but not rolled and without tending to either side.

**Feet.** Close, with well-arched toes; nails preferably black. The pads are soft and elastic, preferably black in colour.

*Below: A short-haired Hollandse Herder, showing its streaked coat. Originally bred as a sheepdog, it is now used as a companion/guard.*

The Belgian Shepherd Dogs are similar in size and appearance to the German Shepherd Dog. The four breeds begun to take their final form during the 1890s. They all take their names from villages in Belgium.

*Belgian Shepherd Dog (Malinois)*

*Belgian Shepherd Dog (Laekenois)*

*Belgian Shepherd Dog (Tervueren)*

# DALMATIAN

### Good points
● *Equable temperament*
● *Loyal*
● *Reliable with children*

### Take heed
● *Needs ample exercise*
● *That coat will shed!*

The Dalmatian has a happy nature, is loyal and devoted to its owners and rarely fights. It is easily trained and fairly simple to present in show. It is generally long-lived, and has a lively youth. Remember that it was bred to run with horse and carriage, and has the need and stamina for plenty of exercise.

### Size
Overall balance of prime importance, but the ideal height for a dog is 58.5-61cm (23-24in), for a bitch 56-58.5cm (22-23in).

### Exercise
Don't buy a Dalmatian unless you can give it plenty of exercise. It is in its element running behind a horse, but an active, open-air country life will suffice.

### Grooming
Daily brushing; occasional bathing.

### Health care
Some Dalmatians suffer from deafness. Check that a pup can hear before buying.

### Feeding
Recommended would be 1½-2½ cans (376g, 13.3oz size) of a branded meaty product, with biscuit added in equal part by volume; or 5 cupfuls of a dry food, complete diet, mixed in the proportion of 1 cup of feed to ½ cup of hot or cold water.

### Origin and history
The Dalmatian is often thought of as a British dog, mainly because of its popularity as a carriage dog in the 18th century, but in fact it originated in Yugoslavia. The breed has enjoyed an upsurge in popularity since 1959, when Walt Disney made a film of Dodie Smith's enchanting book, *A Hundred and One Dalmatians*. It is still shown on the cinema circuits during children's holiday periods, and has a healthy effect on Dalmatian registrations. Mrs E.J. Woodyatt's Champion Fanhill Faune won Best in Show at Crufts in February 1978.

### SHOW SUMMARY
**General appearance.** The Dalmatian should be a balanced, strong, muscular, active dog of good demeanour. Symmetrical in outline, free from coarseness and lumber, capable of great endurance with a fair amount of speed.
**Colour.** The ground colour should be pure white. Black-spotted dogs should have dense black spots, and liver-spotted dogs liver-brown spots. The spots should not run together, but be round and defined, 1-2cm (0.4-0.8in) in diameter, as well distributed as possible. Spots on the extremities should be smaller than those on the body.
**Head and skull.** The head should be of fair length; the skull flat, reasonably broad between the ears but refined. The nose in the black-spotted variety should always be black, in the liver-spotted variety always brown.
**Tail.** In length reaching approximately to the hocks. Strong at the insertion, gradually tapering towards the end; it should not be inserted too low or too high; free from coarseness and carried with a slight upward curve, never curled; preferably spotted.
**Feet.** Round, compact, with well-arched toes (cat feet) and round, tough, elastic pads. Nails black or white in the black-spotted variety, brown or white in the liver-spotted variety.

# WEIMARANER

### Good points
● *Does not shed*
● *Excels in obedience competitions*
● *Fine gundog*
● *Good temperament*
● *No need to brush*

### Take heed
● *Likes to have a job of work to do*
● *Thrives best if kept indoors, not kennelled*

The Weimaraner (or Silver Ghost) is an excellent gundog, which originally hunted big game. It is obedient and eminently trainable, excelling in obedience competitions, and has been used as both police dog and guard. It makes a good pet, but is happiest when given a job to do.

### Size
Height at withers: dog 61-68.5cm (24-27in), bitch 56-63.5cm (22-25in).

### Exercise
Needs plenty; has boundless energy. No need to rule out town living, but it is essential that the Weimaraner has lots of supervised freedom.

### Grooming
Needs very little brushing, if any, for its sleek coat will naturally free itself of mud. Clip nails when necessary.

### Feeding
Recommended would be 1½-2½ cans (376g, 13.3oz size) of a branded meaty product, with biscuit added in equal part by volume; or 5 cupfuls of a dry food, complete diet, mixed in the proportion of 1 cup of feed to ½ cup of hot or cold water.

### Origin and history.
The Weimaraner burst upon the British scene in the early 1950s, since when it has become popular as a family pet, show dog and contender in obedience com-petitions. It is also well thought of in the United States, the best stock being available in those two countries. But the Weimaraner is in fact no newcomer, having been purpose-bred as a gundog at the court in Weimar, Germany, towards the end of the 18th century. Bloodhounds, Pointers and the old St Hubert Hounds are said to have assisted in its make-up. Its silver-grey colour is extremely distinctive.

### SHOW SUMMARY
**General appearance.** A medium-sized grey dog with light eyes, it should present a picture of great driving power, stamina, alertness and balance.
**Colour.** Preferably silver-grey; shades of mouse or roe grey are admissible. The colour usually blends to a lighter shade on head and ears. A dark eel stripe frequently occurs along the back. The whole coat gives an appearance of metallic sheen.
**Head and skull.** Moderately long and aristocratic, with moderate stop and slight median line extending back over the forehead. Expression should be keen, kind and intelligent.
**Tail.** Docked at a point such that the tail remaining shall just cover the scrotum in dogs and vulva in bitches. The thickness of the tail should be in proportion to the body and it should be carried in a manner expressing confidence and sound temperament. In the long-haired Weimaraner the tip of the tail should be removed.
**Feet.** Firm and compact. Toes well arched; pads closed and thick. Nails short, and grey or amber in colour. Dew-claws allowable on imported dogs only.

# BOXER

### Good points
● *Brave*
● *Clownish*
● *Good guard*
● *Loves children*
● *Loyal*

### Take heed
● *Enjoys a scrap and respects opponents smaller than itself!*

The Boxer is a delightful animal that takes longer than most to grow up. It loves children and is a faithful protector of the family. However, it is an exuberant, fairly powerful dog, deserving a reasonable-sized home and garden and owners prepared to spend the necessary time on exercising and training. It has served in the armed forces and as a guide dog for the blind (seeing eye dog). Its tail is docked, and when pleased it tends to wag its whole body with pleasure.

### Size
Height at the withers: dog 56-61cm (22-24in); bitch 53-58.5cm (21-23in). Weight: dogs around 58.5cm (23in) should weigh about 30kg (66lb); and bitches of about 56cm (22in) should weigh about 28.1kg (62lb).

### Exercise
Good daily walks and off-the-lead runs are recommended.

### Grooming
Daily brushing will keep the coat in good condition.

### Feeding
Recommended would be 1½-2½ cans (376g, 13.3oz size) of a branded meaty product, with biscuit added in equal part by volume; or 5 cupfuls of a dry food, complete diet, mixed in the proportion of 1 cup of feed to ½ cup of hot or cold water.

### Origin and history
The Boxer is traceable to the old holding dogs of Molossus or Mastiff type, which the Cimbrians took into battle against the Romans. Like the Bulldog, its jaw is undershot, a trait common in bull-baiters. The Brabant bull-baiter, from which the English Bulldog evolved, also played its part in the evolution of the Boxer, which retains its fighting spirit to this day.

### SHOW SUMMARY
**General appearance.** The Boxer is a medium-sized, sturdy, smooth-haired dog of short, square figure and strong limb. The musculation is clean and powerfully developed, and should stand out plastically from under the skin. Movement should be alive with energy. Its gait, though firm, is elastic; the stride free and roomy; carriage proud and noble.
**Colour.** The permissible colours are fawn, brindle and fawn in various shades from light yellow to dark deer red. The brindle variety should have black stripes on a golden yellow or red-brown background. The stripes should be clearly defined.
**Head and skull.** The head imparts to the Boxer a unique individual stamp peculiar to the breed. It must be in perfect proportion to the dog's body; above all it must never be too light. The muzzle is the most distinctive feature. The greatest value is to be placed on its being of correct form and in absolute proportion to the skull. The nose, broad and black, very slightly turned up. The nostrils should be broad with a naso-labial line between them. The two jaw-bones should not terminate in a normal perpendicular level in the front, but the lower jaw should protrude beyond the upper jaw and bend slightly upwards. The boxer is normally undershot. The upper jaw should be broad where attached to the skull, and maintain this breadth except for a very slight tapering to the front.
**Tail.** Attachment should be high. The tail should be docked and carried upwards, and should be not more than 5cm (2in) long.
**Feet.** Should be small, with tightly arched toes (cat feet) and hard soles. The rear toes should be just a little longer than the front toes, but similar in all other respects.

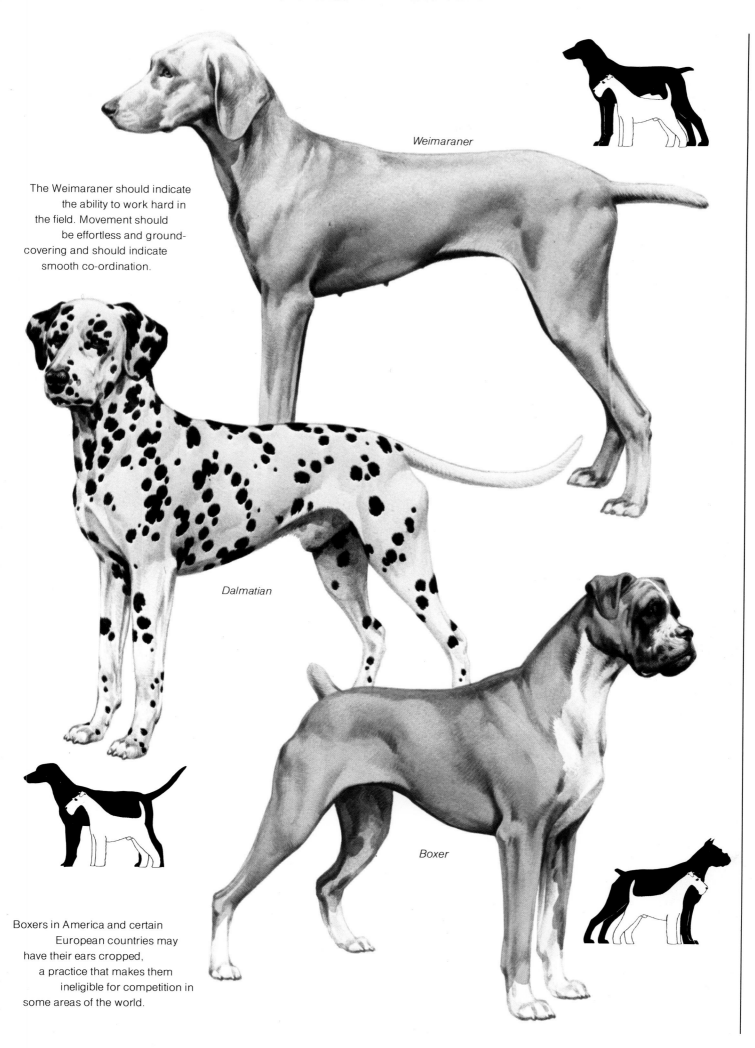

*Weimaraner*

The Weimaraner should indicate the ability to work hard in the field. Movement should be effortless and ground-covering and should indicate smooth co-ordination.

*Dalmatian*

*Boxer*

Boxers in America and certain European countries may have their ears cropped, a practice that makes them ineligible for competition in some areas of the world.

# GOLDEN RETRIEVER

## Good points
● *Excellent gundog*
● *Gentle with children*
● *Sound temperament*

## Take heed
● *No drawbacks known*

The Golden Retriever cannot be too highly recommended as a breed to suit all the family. It will romp with the children, enjoy a day's shooting with the man of the house, and happily accompany the mistress on a shopping trip, or for a session at the dog training club. This is a trustworthy breed, which can be kennelled, but individuals are happiest sharing the fireside with their family. They love to retrieve and will enjoy nothing better than carrying the newspaper home, or wandering around the house with an old chewed slipper. They are often used as guide dogs (seeing eye dogs) for the blind.

## Size
The average weight in good hard condition should be: dog 31.8-36.3kg (70-80lb); bitch 27.2-31.8kg (60-70lb). Height at shoulder: dog 56-61cm (22-24in); bitch 51-56cm (20-22in).

## Exercise
Needs at least an hour's exercise every day, and free runs, also an ample garden.

## Grooming
Regular brushing will keep the coat in good condition.

*Below: A Golden Retriever with pups, the ideal pet for all the family.*

## Feeding
Recommended would be 1½-2½ cans (376g, 13.3oz size) of a branded meaty product, with biscuit added in equal part by volume; or 5 cupfuls of a dry food, complete diet, mixed in the proportion of 1 cup of feed to ½ cup of hot or cold water.

## Origin and history
There is some controversy as to the origin of this breed. Did it, as many like to believe, develop from a troupe of Russian shepherd dogs found by Lord Tweedmouth performing in a Brighton circus in 1860, or did it begin with a litter of golden-haired pups of retriever/spaniel ancestry born on his Scottish estate? Romanticists like to believe the tale that Lord Tweedmouth was so greatly impressed with the Russian shepherd dogs that he bought the entire troupe and bred from them, adding Bloodhound blood to develop the nose. It is a theory that still has enthusiasts arguing.

## SHOW SUMMARY
**General appearance.** Should be a symmetrical, active, powerful dog, a good level mover, sound and well put together, with a kindly expression, not clumsy or long in the leg.
**Colour.** Any shade of gold or cream, but neither red nor mahogany. The presence of a few white hairs on the chest is permissible. White collar, feet, toes or blaze should be penalized. Nose black.
**Head and skull.** Broad skull, well set on a clean and muscular neck; muzzle powerful and wide; not weak-jawed; good stop.
**Tail.** Should not be carried too gaily or curled at the tip.
**Feet.** Round and cat-like, not open or splay.

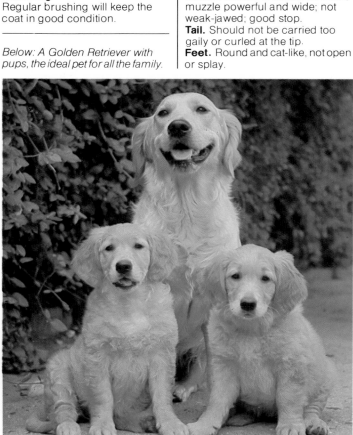

# LABRADOR RETRIEVER

## Good points
● *Equable temperament*
● *Excellent gundog*
● *Good family pet*
● *Kind with children*

## Take heed
● *No drawbacks known*

Like the Golden Retriever, the Labrador Retriever cannot be too highly recommended as a breed tailor-made to suit the whole family. It is an excellent retriever, can be trusted with the children and will give a good account of itself in obedience training competitions. The Labrador Retriever is a breed much favoured as a guide dog (seeing eye dog) for the blind.

## Size
Height: dog 56-57cm (22-22½in); bitch 54.5-56cm (21½-22in).

## Exercise
Needs an hour a day at least, with free runs, also an ample garden.

## Grooming
Regular brushing will keep the coat in good condition.

## Feeding
Recommended would be 1½-2½ cans (376g, 13.3oz size) of a branded meaty product, with biscuit added in equal part by volume; or 5 cupfuls of a dry food, complete diet, mixed in the proportion of 1 cup of feed to ½ cup of hot or cold water.

## Origin and history
The Labrador Retriever came to Britain with fishermen from Newfoundland (not Labrador) in the 1830s, the dog's task in those days being to land the nets of the fishermen; their ability to swim has

*Above: Yellow Labrador Retrievers, now more popular than black.*

survived. Among the most popular British gundogs, they are also much sought after as family pets in many parts of the world.

## SHOW SUMMARY
**General appearance.** The Labrador should be a strongly built short-coupled, very active dog, broad in the skull, broad and deep through the chest and ribs, broad and strong over the loins and hindquarters. The coat is close and short, with a dense undercoat and free from feather. The dog must move neither too wide nor too close in front or behind; it must stand and move true all round on legs and feet.
**Colour.** Generally black or yellow, but other whole colours are permitted. The coat should be free from any white markings but a small white spot on the chest is allowable. The coat should be of a whole colour and not of a flecked appearance.
**Head and skull.** The skull should be broad with a pronounced stop so that the skull is not in a straight line with the nose. The head should be clean cut without fleshy cheeks. The jaws should be medium length, powerful and free from snipiness; the nose wide and the nostrils well developed.
**Tail.** A distinctive feature of the breed; it should be very thick towards the base, gradually tapering towards the tip, of medium length and practically free from any feathering, but clothed thickly all round with the Labrador's short, thick, dense coat, thus giving the peculiar 'rounded' appearance that has been described as the 'otter' tail. It may be carried gaily, but should not curl over the back.
**Feet.** Should be round and compact, with well-arched toes and well-developed pads.

Golden Retrievers were first shown under that name in the United Kingdom in 1913 and first registered in the United States in 1925. Since that time, the breed has undergone an explosion in popularity, both as a gentle and trustworthy pet and as a reliable and intelligent working dog.

*Golden Retriever*

Recognized by the British Kennel Club as a distinct breed in 1903, the Labrador Retriever has been much celebrated around the world for its intelligence, even temperament and all round ability.

*Labrador Retriever*

# CHESAPEAKE BAY RETRIEVER

## Good points
- *First-class retriever*
- *Sportsman's favourite*
- *Usually good with children*

## Take heed
- *Occasionally aggressive*

The Chesapeake Bay is a favourite with American sportsmen but has to date few devotees in the United Kingdom. It is an excellent swimmer and an unsurpassed retriever of wild duck. It is generally good with children, but can be a little headstrong and difficult to train. Distinguishing features are the breed's yellow eyes and web feet. Its coat is water-resistant.

## Size
Weight: dog 29.5-34kg (65-75lb), bitch 25-29.5kg (55-65lb). Height: dog 58.5-66cm (23-26in), bitch 53-61cm (21-24in).

## Exercise
Needs plenty of hard exercise to stay in good condition.

## Grooming
Normal brushing is sufficient.

## Feeding
Recommended would be 1½-2½ cans (376g, 13.3oz size) of a branded meaty product, with biscuit added in equal part by volume; or 5 cupfuls of a dry food, complete diet, mixed in the proportion of 1 cup of feed to ½ cup of hot or cold water.

## Origin and history
This is an American retriever of British origin. An English brig went aground off the coast of Maryland in 1807 and was rescued by an American ship, the *Canton*. Aboard the brig were two pups, which were named 'Canton', after the rescue ship, and 'Sailor'. They were subsequently trained to retrieve duck, and crossed with Otterhounds and the Curly-coated and Flat-coated Retriever. The pups are said to have been Newfoundland in origin. Americans seem to want to retain the breed as a sporting dog, which is why it has not found its way into many homes as a pet. People either rave about the merits of the Chesapeake Bay, or are completely put off by their oily coats, not unpleasant oily odour, and yellow-orange eyes.

## SHOW SUMMARY
**General appearance.** Should show a bright and happy disposition and have an intelligent expression, with general outlines impressive and indicative of a good worker.
**Colour.** Any colour varying from dark brown to faded tan, or dead-grass colour of any shade from tan to dull straw.
**Head and skull.** Broad, round, with medium stop; nose medium; muzzle pointed but not sharp; lips thin, not pendulous.
**Tail.** Of medium length, in the dog 30-38cm (12-15in), in the bitch 28-35.5cm (11-14in). It should be fairly heavy at the root. Moderate feathering on tail and stern is permissible.
**Feet.** Well-webbed hare feet of good size. Toes well rounded and close; the pasterns slightly bent.

# CURLY-COATED RETRIEVER

## Good points
- *Beautiful*
- *Equable temperament*
- *Excellent guard*
- *Fine swimmer*
- *Good nose/retriever*
- *Stamina*

## Take heed
- *No drawbacks known*

The Curly-coat is an excellent worker on land and in water, and will retrieve any game. It is a hardy dog, of good temperament and fine appearance. One wonders why its numbers have diminished.

## Size
Weight: 31.8-36.3kg (70-80lb). Height: 63.5-68.5cm (25-27in).

## Exercise
Thrives on liberal amounts of vigorous exercise.

## Grooming
Don't brush and comb this breed. Just damp the coat down and massage with circular movements. Seek advice on trimming.

## Feeding
As for Chesapeake Bay Retriever.

## Origin and history
The Curly-coat was one of the earliest British retrievers. It was exhibited at dog shows in England as early as 1860 and was depicted in many sporting prints beforehand. Its popularity seems to have waned since the beginning of the First World War and, despite its superb working ability, it has never been in great demand since. The early Labrador obviously played a part in its make-up and, to hazard a suggestion, the Water Spaniel, which, with its tight curly coat, it resembles.

## SHOW SUMMARY
**General appearance.** A strong, smart, upstanding dog, showing activity, endurance and intelligence.
**Colour.** Black or liver.
**Head and skull.** Long, well-proportioned flat skull; jaws strong and long but not inclined to snipiness. Nose black in the black-coated variety, with wide nostrils. Coarseness of head to be deprecated.
**Tail.** Moderately short, carried fairly straight and covered with curls; tapering towards the point; gay tail not desirable.
**Feet.** Round and compact, with well-arched toes.

# HOVAWART

## Good points
- *Excellent guard*
- *Home-loving*
- *Fond of children*
- *Loyal*
- *Obedient*

## Take heed
- *Slow to mature*
- *Tends to be a one-person dog*
- *Will fight if challenged*

The Hovawart is an old German breed which, like so many of similar origin, was not bred for a specific purpose. It is, and always has been, just a loyal companion dog and protector of the home.

It is generally obedient, loves children, and has utter loyalty to its master, tending to be a one-person dog, although defending the entire family with its life. It is good natured, but will fight well if put to the test.

## Size
Height: 63.5-68.5cm (25-27in); Weight: 29.5-40.8kg (65-90lb); bitches less.

## Exercise
Normal regular exercise.

## Grooming
Regular brushing will keep the coat in good condition.

## Feeding
As for Chesapeake Bay Retriever.

## Origin and history
The Hovawart was already a popular companion dog in Germany during the Middle Ages. In fact, the name Hovawart means 'house guard'. It resembles the Kuvasz in stature and looks like a large Collie. The breed seems to have suffered a period of unpopularity, but after the First World War such specimens as could be found were crossed with Leonbergers and Newfoundlands to perpetuate a once famous breed.

## SHOW SUMMARY
**General appearance.** A robust working dog of medium weight, the Hovawart is strong and highly weather-resistant, a good runner and jumper, brave, attentive and quick to react. It is a splendid guard dog. Sexual characteristics should be clearly evident. The voice is deep, full and powerful.
**Colour.** Black, black and tan (small white ticking permissible), flaxen (with a dark shade preferred). Eyes, nose and nails to be of a colour consistent with the basic colouring of the coat, but not too light.
**Head.** Strong, with a broad, convex forehead. The muzzle is straight, neither too long nor too short. Maximum muzzle length should be equal to the distance from the occipital bone to the stop. Tight lips, well-formed muzzle. Teeth should be strong, with a scissor bite. A pincer (level) bite is allowed but is counted a fault in show.
**Tail.** Reaches beyond the hocks but not to the ground, well feathered, carried low in repose and high when the dog is excited.
**Feet.** No dew-claws. Hard pads on the forefeet.

# FLAT-COATED RETRIEVER

## Good points
- *Can live kennelled or as a housepet*
- *Easy to train*
- *Good with children*
- *Hardy*
- *Natural retriever*

## Take heed
- *No drawbacks known*

The Flat-coated Retriever is likely to enjoy renewed popularity since attaining the coveted Best in Show award at Crufts in 1980. It is a natural retriever, used for picking up game; it is hardy and easily trained, and makes a good household companion if you wish, being very good with children.

## Size
Should be 27.2-31.8kg (60-70lb).

## Exercise
Thrives on plenty of exercise.

## Grooming
Regular brushing and tidying up.

## Feeding
As for Chesapeake Bay Retriever.

## Origin and history
The Flat-coat probably owes its evolution to the Labrador Retriever, the Collie and certain spaniels. It was at one time known as the Wavy-coated Retriever, and it is thought that Collie blood was introduced to produce the Flat-coat. Prior to the First World War the Flat-coat was perhaps the best-known gundog in Britain, but it was over-shadowed in the post-war era by the Golden Retriever and Labrador Retriever, whose appeal has remained constant, not, however, to the detriment of the quality of the Flat-coat breed.

## SHOW SUMMARY
**General appearance.** A bright, active dog of medium size with an intelligent expression, showing power without lumber, and raciness without weediness.
**Colour.** Black or liver.
**Head and skull.** The head should be long and nicely moulded; the skull flat and moderately broad. There should be a depression or stop between the eyes, slight and in no way accentuated, so as to avoid giving either a down or a dish-faced appearance. The nose of a good size, with open nostrils. The jaws should be long and strong, with the capacity for carrying a hare or pheasant.
**Tail.** Short, straight and well set on, carried gaily, but never much above the level of the back.
**Feet.** Should be round and strong, with toes close and well arched; the soles thick and strong.

Curly-coated Retriever

Chesapeake Bay Retriever

Flat-coated Retriever

Hovawart

# JAPANESE AKITA

## Good points
- *Easily trained*
- *First-class guard*
- *Good temperament*
- *Intelligent*

## Take heed
- *No drawbacks known*

The Japanese Akita is the best-known of the Japanese Spitz breeds but has only recently come on the international scene. The breed has been exhibited in recent years in the United Kingdom and America, and the Japanese are doing all possible to improve their purebred stock. Bred as a hunter of wild boar, deer and even black bear, the Akita is undoubtedly capable of ferocity, but it is easily trained and generally has an equable temperament.

## Size
Height: dog 53-61cm (21-24in), some bigger; bitch 48-53cm (19-21in). Weight: 38.6-49.9kg (85-110lb).

## Exercise
Does not require a great deal of exercise. Incidentally, it has webbed feet and is a fine swimmer and a good water dog.

## Grooming
Normal daily brushing.

## Feeding
Recommended would be 1½-2½ cans (376g, 13.3oz size) of a branded meaty product, with biscuit added in equal part by volume; or 5 cupfuls of a dry food, complete diet, mixed in the proportion of 1 cup of feed to ½ cup of hot or cold water.

## Origin and history
The Akita resembles a smooth-coated Chow and is the largest of the known Japanese Spitz breeds. It is bred in its native land as a hunter of wild boar and deer, and is obviously related to the Icelandic breeds. However, it has bred true in Japan's Akita Province for more than 300 years, and its exact origin is obscure.

## SHOW SUMMARY (FCI)
**General appearance.** A solidly-built dog, well proportioned, with an imposing appearance of great distinction. Prudent, docile, intelligent without sacrificing an impetuous temperament.
**Colour.** Salt and pepper, reddish salt and pepper, black pepper, streaked, white, or white with markings.
**Head.** The skull is large, with a broad forehead; the medial furrow is well marked. The stop is well defined. The cheeks are well formed. The muzzle is strong and pointed, the bridge straight and short. The teeth are solid and must meet in a bite free from overshot effects. The nose is large and black (white dogs may have a pink nose). The lips are rather thin and well fitted over the gums.
**Tail.** The tail is stout and strong, reaching the hocks when straight. It is carried over the back in a ring which can be shifted from one side to the other. Sometimes the tail is a screwtail, at others a spiral curl; in either case the curl should be a complete turn.
**Feet.** The feet are large, with close toes. The nails are hard and dark. Pads should be hard and rugged.

# CHOW CHOW

## Good points
- *Beautiful*
- *Good endurance*
- *Loyal*
- *Odour-free*

## Take heed
- *Formidable opponent*
- *Needs firm gentle handling*
- *Strong willed*
- *One-man dog (but will accept owner's family)*

The Chow Chow, whose name is perhaps derived from the Chinese Choo Hunting Dog, is a member of the Spitz family known for over 2000 years, lion-like in appearance and famed for its black tongue. It is odour-free and makes an incredibly loyal companion, tending to devote itself to one member of the family though accepting and returning the affection of other household members. It needs quiet but firm handling: with its aloof temperament it is unlikely to deign to walk at your heel without persuasion. It does not take kindly to strangers and is a fearsome fighter if provoked.

## Size
Minimum height for Chows is 46cm (18in), but in every case balance should be the outstanding feature and height left to the discretion of the judges.

## Exercise
Most Chow owners seem to manage with regular on-the-lead walks with runs in permitted areas. However, mindful of the Chow's prowess as a hunter of wolves, game and anything that moves, it seems unfair to keep it in confined surroundings or to deprive it of the open spaces that it relishes.

## Grooming
About 5 or 10 minutes' brushing a day and about an hour each weekend with a wire brush should maintain the Chow gleaming.

## Feeding
One to 1½ cans (376g, 13.3oz size) of a branded meaty product, with biscuit added in equal part by volume; or 3 cupfuls of dry, complete food mixed in the proportion of 1 cup of feed to ½ cup of hot or cold water. Perhaps not surprisingly, they also do well on rice or on tripe, chicken and lean beef.

## Origin and history
Although there are other black-mouthed dogs, the Chow is the only dog with a black tongue, although small bears — to which it has some resemblance — share this characteristic. Reputed to be the original Lama's Mastiff, the Chow Chow must be one of the oldest members of the Spitz family and was bred variously for its flesh — which in many parts of Asia is considered a delicacy — and for its fur and as a useful hunter of game. In early Chinese writings, it was known as the Tartar Dog, or Dog of Barbarians. The first breed members imported into England, in 1760, were exhibited in a zoo. Sadly, a reputation for ferocity has come down with the Chow, yet it is an affectionate, devoted animal. It is unlikely to fight unless provoked, but then it will be a formidable opponent. The Chow Chow Club was formed in England in 1895 and today around 600 or 700 breed members a year are registered with the British Kennel Club, and interest in the breed is constantly growing.

## SHOW SUMMARY
**General appearance.** An active, compact, short-coupled and well-

*Above: The beautiful, lion-like Chow is a one-man dog, but it keeps on friendly terms with the rest of the household. Delightful as a puppy, the adult Chow can be single-minded and aloof. A stunning sight in the show ring.*

balanced dog, well knit in frame, with tail carried over the back.
**Colour.** Whole-coloured black, red, blue, fawn, cream or white, frequently shaded but not in patches or parti-coloured (the underpart of tail and back of thighs are frequently of a light colour).
**Head and skull.** Skull flat and broad, with little stop, well filled out under the eyes. Muzzle moderate in length, broad from the eyes to the point (not pointed at the end like a fox). Nose should be black, large and wide (with the exception of creams and whites, in which case a light-coloured nose is permissible, and in blues and fawns a self-coloured nose); but in all colours a black nose preferred.
**Tail.** Set high and carried well over the back.
**Feet.** Small, round and cat-like, standing well on the toes.

Outside its native country, the Japanese Akita is especially popular in the United States; many specimens were brought back by American servicemen at the end of World War II.

*Japanese Akita*

Now appreciated in the Western world mainly as an outstandingly successful show dog, the Chow Chow is an ancient breed with great scenting and hunting ability. It was first exhibited in the USA in 1890.

*Chow Chow*

# ALASKAN MALAMUTE

## Good points
- Affectionate
- Fast and strong
- Fine sled dog
- Loves children
- Sociable

## Take heed
- No drawbacks known

The Alaskan Malamute is an Arctic Spitz-type little known outside Alaska and the United States. It is a sociable dog, capable of being driven in sled races by children. It is highly prized as a sled dog, and capable of immense speed. Don't be put off by the wolfish appearance: the kindly expression is genuine!

## Size
Height: dog 63.5-71cm (25-28in); bitch 58.5-66cm (23-26in). Weight: 38.6-56.7kg (85-125lb).

## Exercise
Needs plenty of vigorous exercise to stay healthy.

## Grooming
Regular brushing will keep the coat in good condition.

Below: The Alaskan Malamute is, in fact, a very sociable breed.

## Feeding
Recommended would be 1½-2½ cans (376g, 13.3oz size) of a branded meaty product, with biscuit added in equal part by volume; or 5 cupfuls of a dry food, complete diet, mixed in the proportion of 1 cup of feed to ½ cup of hot or cold water.

## Origin and history
The Alaskan Malamute is named after a native tribe called the Mahlemuts. The origin of the dogs is obscure, but the breed is obviously closely related to other Spitz-types, such as the Samoyed.

## SHOW SUMMARY
**General appearance.** The breed is primarily a working sled dog of the Arctic, used for hauling heavy freight, and therefore it should be a heavily boned and powerfully built animal, not too compact and never appearing low on the leg.
**Colour.** From light grey through the intermediate shadings to black, or from gold through the shades of red to liver, always with white on the underbody, feet, parts of legs, and part of mask markings. The markings on the face should be either cap-like or mask-like: combination of cap and mask is not unusual. A white blaze on the forehead, a white collar, or a spot on the nape is acceptable. Heavy mantling of unbroken colour is acceptable, but broken colour extending over the body in spots or uneven splashings is undesirable. The only solid colour allowable is the all-white.
**Head and skull.** The head should be broad and powerful, not coarse, and in proportion to the size of the dog. The skull should be broad between the ears, gradually narrowing to the eyes; moderately rounded between the ears, flattening on top as it approaches the eyes, and rounding off to the cheeks, which should be moderately flat. There should be a very slight but perceptible stop. The muzzle should be large in proportion to the size of the skull, scarcely diminishing in width or depth from the stop. Nose black except in red-and-white dogs, when it should be brown.
**Tail.** Moderately high set and follows the line of the spine at the start. Well-furred and carried over the back when the dog is not working; not tightly curled to rest on the back, nor short-furred and carried like a fox brush, but with the appearance of a waving plume.
**Feet.** Large and compact; tightfitting toes, well arched; thick, tough pads; toe-nails short and strong. There should be a protective growth of hair between the toes.

# ESKIMO DOG
(And Greenland Dog)

## Good points
- Beautiful
- Can become devoted
- Endurance
- Excellent sled dog
- Strong
- Fine guard

## Take heed
- Rarely lives indoors
- Suspicious of strangers

The Eskimo Dog is one of several regional sled dogs of different names, few of which are well known outside the polar area. It is hardy, and accustomed to fending for itself, living out of doors and often having to find its own food.

The Greenland Dog is so similar that controversy rages as to

Above: Strong and beautiful, two Greenland Dogs in sled harness.

whether they should be separately classified. Usually the Eskimo Dog is a little shorter in the back than the Greenland, and weightier generally, but without extra height.

## Size
Height at shoulder: dog 58.5-68.5cm (23-27in); bitch 51-61cm (20-24in). Weight: dog 34-47.6kg (75-105lb); bitch 27.2-40.8kg (60-90lb).

## Exercise
These dogs are accustomed to pulling sleds and hauling fishing boats ashore. They would soon get bored just snoozing by the fireside all day.

## Grooming
Regular brushing will keep the coat in good condition.

## Feeding
Recommended would be 1½-2½ cans (376g, 13.3oz size) of a branded meaty product, with biscuit added in equal part by volume; or 5 cupfuls of a dry food, complete diet, mixed in the proportion of 1 cup of feed to ½ cup of hot or cold water.

## Origin and history
These polar Spitz breeds no doubt originated in Eastern Siberia and shared a common task and ancestry with the Alaskan Malamute, Siberian Husky and Samoyed. To quote the American explorer Peary, 'there is, in fact, only one sled dog'.

## SHOW SUMMARY
**Colour.** All known dog colours, or combinations of these colours.
**Head and skull.** Well proportioned, broad and wedge-shaped, with a moderate stop. Strong, flat skull and powerful jaws. Black or brown nose and lips. Muzzle of medium length, gently tapering to the nose.
**Tail.** Large and bushy. Set high and curled loosely over the back, falling to one side or the other.
**Feet.** Rather large, well spread and strong, with strong nails. Thick pads well intersected with fur.

The Eskimo Dog is recognized by the Canadian Kennel Club as a separate breed, and the FCI recognize the closely related Greenland Dog. Both are Arctic hauling dogs.

*Eskimo Dog*

The Alaskan Malamute is a tremendously powerful sled dog known for generations in its native Alaska. It has survived as a pure breed and is particularly popular in the United States for winter sports.

*Alaskan Malamute*

# OTTERHOUND

## Good points
- *Appealing*
- *Easy to groom*
- *Friendly*
- *Gentle with children*
- *Waterproof coat*

## Take heed
- *Essentially a hound rather than a house pet, and not ideally suited to suburban living*

With otter hunting now outlawed in the United Kingdom, the Otterhound could have faced extinction, had not the last Master of the Kendal and District Otterhounds, in the Lake District, set up the Otterhound Club to ensure the survival of the breed. Without the continued interest of breeders and the show world, the Otterhound would certainly die out.

The Otterhound is an amiable, friendly animal, gentle with children and responsive to affection. However, one should not lose sight of the fact that it was a pack hound bred to kill, a background that does not ideally equip it as a household pet.

## Size
Height: dogs should stand approximately 68.5cm (27in) at the shoulder; bitches approximately 61cm (24in). Weight: dogs 34-52.2kg (75-115lb); bitches 29.5-45.4kg (65-100lb).

## Exercise
The Otterhound needs a lot of exercise. A unique feature of this breed is the existence of webbing between the toes. This gives the Otterhound a decided advantage in the water. Most dogs can swim, but the Otterhound excels in that ability, and is as much at home in the water as it is on land.

## Grooming
A thorough brush and comb once a week should be sufficient to keep the Otterhound's coat in good condition. There is natural oil in the coat and, if bathing the animal for a show, it is advisable to do this a week beforehand to allow the coat to regain its correct texture. However, the head hair can be bathed the day before a show because this is of a finer texture.

Particular attention must be paid to the ears, as they are inclined to collect wax and can become a source of irritation to the animal. Care should be taken to inspect the ears regularly.

## Feeding
The Otterhound is a large dog and will need up to 2½ cans of a good branded meaty diet (376g, 13.3oz size) to which biscuit should be added in equal parts by volume; or 5 cupfuls of a dry food, complete diet, mixed in the proportion of 1 cup of feed to ½ cup of hot or cold water.

## Origin and history
The Otterhound is an extremely old breed, and its origins are somewhat obscure. Some say it descended from the old Southern Hound and others see the Bloodhound in its ancestry. Today it is most like some of the French hounds, such as the Griffon Nivernais or Griffon Vendéen, and it is quite possible that the Otterhound springs from the same origins as these French breeds.

Otter hunting was one of the earliest field sports in the United Kingdom and King John, Henry II and Elizabeth I all kept Otterhound packs, long before foxes were thought worthy to be hunted. Many monasteries also kept Otterhounds to protect their fishponds from the nightly ravages of otters.

## SHOW SUMMARY
**General appearance.** A big, strongly built hound, straight-limbed, rough-coated, with majestic head, strong body and loose, long-striding action. For a long day's work in water, the rough double coat and large feet are essential. As the animal must also gallop on land it has to be free-moving. The Otterhound requires no trimming for exhibition. Handling and presentation are natural.

**Colour.** Any recognized hound colour is permissible, with the exception of the liver and white and a white-bodied hound with black and tan patches distinctly separated. Usually, whole-coloured grizzle, sandy, red, wheaten or blue, but these may have slightly white markings on head, chest, feet and tail tip. White hounds may have slight lemon, blue or badger pied markings. Also black and tan, blue and tan, black and cream or occasional liver and tan. Pigment should harmonize, though not necessarily blend, with coat colour: i.e. a tan hound may have a brown nose and eye rims.

**Head and skull.** Clean and very imposing, it is deep rather than wide, with clean cheekbones. Skull nicely domed, not coarse or overdone, rising from a distinct though not exaggerated stop to a slight peak at the occiput. There is no trace of scowl or bulge in the forehead, the expression being open and amiable. The muzzle should be strong and deep with a good wide nose bone ending in wide nostrils, the distance from nose-end to stop being slightly shorter than that from stop to occiput. Plenty of lip and flew, though not exaggerated. The whole head, except for the nose bone, should be well covered with rough hair, ending in slight moustaches and beard, both being part of the natural face hair. A slight butterfly nose should not disqualify an otherwise good hound.

**Legs and feet.** Forelegs should be strongly boned, straight from elbow to ground, with strong slightly sprung pasterns. Feet should turn neither in nor out, being large, round, well-knuckled and thick-padded with web in evidence. They are compact when standing but capable of spreading.

Above: The Otterhound, a good retriever and excellent swimmer.

The hind feet should be only slightly smaller than the forefeet.

**Tail (stern).** Should be set high and carried up when alert or on the move, but must never curl over the back, though it may droop when standing. Thick at the base, tapering to a point and reaching to the hock; carried straight or in a slight curve, the hair under the stern being rather longer and more profuse than that on the topside.

# ITALIAN SPINONE

## Good points
- *Affectionate*
- *Fine retriever of water fowl*
- *Hardy*

## Take heed
- *No drawbacks known*

The Italian Spinone is an ancient breed of gundog, much appreciated by Italian horsemen for its ability to work in marshy and wooded country. It has a soft mouth and will point and retrieve. It is good-natured and well established in its own country.

## Size
Height: dog 60-65cm (23½-25½in); bitch 54.5-60cm (21½-23½in).

## Exercise
Needs plenty of vigorous exercise.

## Grooming
Daily brushing will keep the coat healthy.

## Feeding
Recommended would be 1½-2½ cans (376g, 13.3oz size) of a branded meaty product, with biscuit added in equal part by volume; or 5 cupfuls of a dry food, complete diet, mixed in the proportion of 1 cup of feed to ½ cup of hot or cold water.

## Origin and history
The Spinone originated in the French region of Bresse but later found its way to Piedmont in Italy, its evolution being attributable to the French Griffon, French and German Pointers, the Porçelaine, Barbet and Korthals Griffon. What has emerged is a reliable gundog with a pleasing appearance, somewhere between a Pointer and a Foxhound.

## SHOW SUMMARY
**General appearance.** The Spinone has a body that is square in outline. It is a solid, vigorous country dog, with strong bone and well developed muscles; the breed is characterized by its excellent fast trotting gait.

The breed's facial expression is intelligent and shows power and courage. Its eyes are expressive with a markedly sweet, almost human expression. It is exceptionally hardy and enters nonchalantly into brambles and deep, cold water; for such work being protected by its thick skin and hard, thick coat.

**Colour.** Permissible colours include: white; white with orange markings; solid white peppered with orange; white with brown markings; white speckled with brown hairs (brown roan), with or without larger brown markings.

**Head and skull.** The head is large with fairly broad, domed skull; the stop is not accentuated, but the muzzle is well developed and square.

**Tail.** Thick at the base and set on as a continuation of the croup line; carried horizontally or down; should be docked at 15-25cm (6-10in) from the root.

**Feet.** Compact and round, with well-closed toes that are well arched and covered with short, thick hair, including the spaces between the toes.

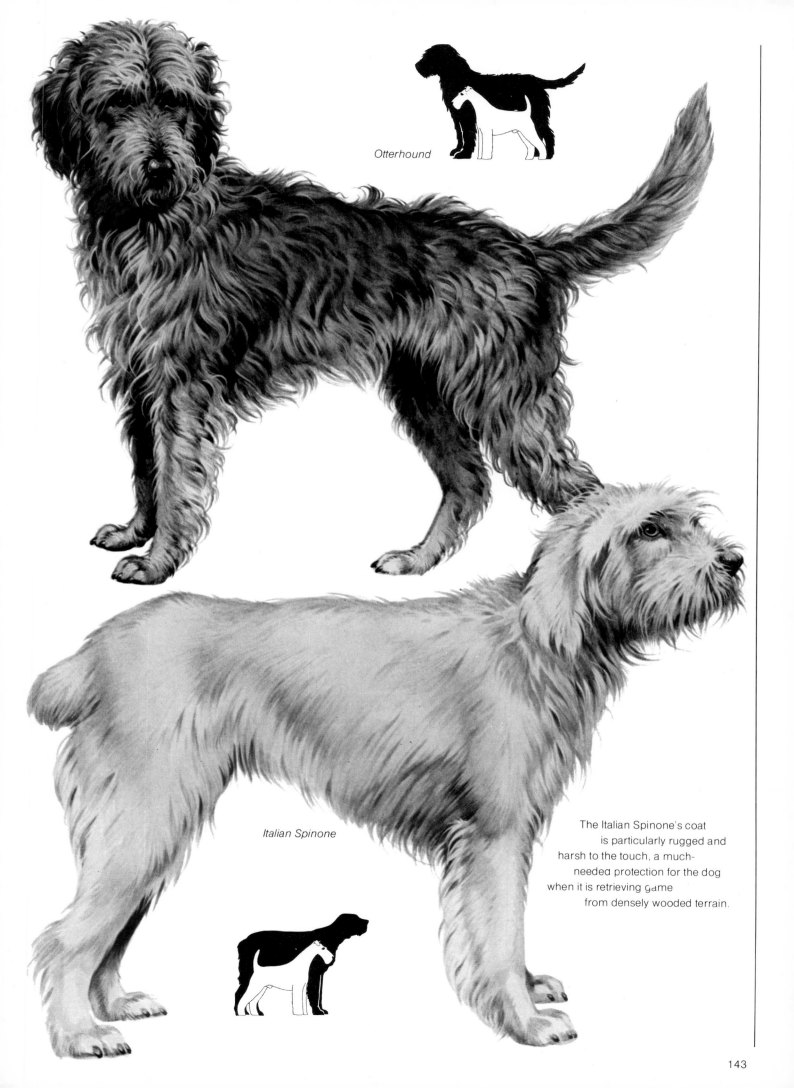

Otterhound

Italian Spinone

The Italian Spinone's coat is particularly rugged and harsh to the touch, a much-needed protection for the dog when it is retrieving game from densely wooded terrain.

143

# ROTTWEILER

## Good points
- *Good temperament*
- *Intelligent*
- *Makes a good household companion/guard*
- *Reliable working dog*

## Take heed
- *Responds best to kind, firm handling – not being chained or kennelled in a back yard*

The Rottweiler is a German working dog of high intelligence and good temperament. It has been a draught dog and herder, and is still used as guard, police dog, sled dog and mountain rescue dog. In many countries it is sought after as a companion/ pet and guard. It is a popular contender in the show ring and does well in obedience tests.

## Size
Height at shoulder: dog 63.5-68.5cm (25-27in); bitch 58.5-63.5cm (23-25in).

## Exercise
Regular walks and runs.

## Grooming
Daily brushing will keep the coat in good condition.

## Feeding
Recommended would be 1½-2½ cans (376g, 13.3oz size) of a branded meaty product, with biscuit added in equal part by volume; or 5 cupfuls of a dry food, complete diet, mixed in the proportion of 1 cup of feed to ½ cup of hot or cold water.

## Origin and history
The Rottweiler is a butcher's dog. It comes from the West German town of Rottweil in Württemberg, where it is known as the Rottweiler Metzgerhund or Rottweil butcher's dog.

It was known in the Middle Ages as a hunter of wild boar, and later as a revered and trusted cattle dog as well as a draught dog that would draw carts for butchers and cattle dealers. Just before the first World War its abilities were recognized as a police dog and guard.

Thelma Gray of the Rozavel Kennels introduced the breed into Britain in 1936. It was developing a following until World War II, when breeding ceased, and it was not until a Captain Roy-Smith, serving with the Occupation Army in Germany, brought home a dog and bitch that a sound breeding programme was re-established, since when a few breed devotees have produced many good specimens.

## SHOW SUMMARY
**General appearance.** The Rottweiler is an above average sized stalwart dog. Its correctly proportioned, compact and powerful form permits of great strength, manoeuvrability and endurance. Its bearing displays boldness and courage; and the tranquil gaze manifests good nature and devotion.

**Colour.** The animal is black with clearly defined markings on the cheeks, muzzle, chest and legs, as well as over both eyes and the area beneath the tail. The markings range from rich tan to mahogany brown.

**Head and skull.** The head is of medium length; the skull between the ears is broad. The forehead line is moderately arched as seen from the side. The occipital bone is well developed but not conspicuous. Cheeks are well muscled but not prominent, with the zygomatic arch well formed. The skin on the head should not be loose, although it is allowed to form moderate wrinkle when the dog is attentive. Muzzle fairly deep with topline level, and length not more than that from stop to occiput.

**Tail.** Carried horizontally; short, strong and not set too low. It should be docked at the first joint.

**Feet.** Strong, round and compact, with the toes well arched. The hind feet are somewhat longer than the front ones. The pads should be very hard, and the toenails short, dark and strong. Rear dew-claws are removed.

# RHODESIAN RIDGEBACK

## Good points
- *Affectionate*
- *Obedient*
- *Good with children*
- *Superior intelligence*
- *Sense of fun*

## Take heed
- *Will guard you, and your possessions, with its life!*

The Rhodesian Ridgeback is a handsome, muscular, medium-sized dog of the hound group, with a short tan-coloured coat, pendulous ears and a long, uncropped tail.

The breed is named after the line of hair, shaped like the blade of a broadsword, that grows in the reverse direction along the back, with two crowns at the shoulder and the point towards the tail. This ridge is a very distinctive marking that is not found in any other breed of dog.

Although the ridge may appear to be a superficiality, created for the show ring or as a talking point, in fact it is far from recent and has come down through the centuries by way of the African Hottentot Hunting Dog.

The Rhodesian Ridgeback is of a quiet temperament and rarely barks; it enjoys spending hours curled up lazily in the corner of a room, stretched out in the summer sun, or basking in front of an open fireplace. Although its exploits as a hunter of African game first brought it recognition, the breed was developed as a dual-purpose dog, as a hunter and

*Above: A Rhodesian Ridgeback and her pup. The ridge can be seen on the puppy's back.*

a gentle guardian of the families of the early white settlers. More and more people are discovering the tranquil temperament of this breed, its affectionate disposition and desire for human companionship. The Ridgeback likes nothing better than to lean against you, or to sit on your feet. And if you own a diamond, this is just the dog to guard it!

## Size
The desirable weight is: dog 36.3kg (80lb), bitch 31.75kg (70lb), with a permissible variation of 2.3kg (5lb) above and below these weights. A mature Ridgeback should be a handsome, upstanding animal; dogs should be of a height of 63.5-68.5cm (25-27in) and bitches 61-66cm (24-26in). Minimum bench standard: dog 63.5cm (25in), bitch 61cm (24in).

## Exercise
This large, sleepy and apparently slow-moving animal with its characteristic love of lazing, contrasts sharply with its action when alerted. In a flash, it is converted into a graceful streak of rhythmic motion, a pleasure to watch as it quickly overtakes a rabbit or a squirrel in full flight. This is a pet that should have a large garden to run in, and deserves a master able to give it a good walk every day.

## Grooming
Daily grooming with a hound glove, coupled with correct feeding and plenty of exercise, will keep the Ridgeback in healthy and gleaming condition.

## Feeding
About 1½-2½ cans of branded dog food (376g, 13.3oz size), supplemented by biscuit, should be sufficient for your Ridgeback. Or, if you prefer, 5 cupfuls of a dry food, complete diet, mixed in the proportion of 1 cup of feed to ½ cup of hot or cold water. And of course, like most breeds, the Ridgeback will enjoy meat scraps and the occasional bone.

Remember that suggested quantities are only a guide, and should be increased or decreased according to the desired weight of your dog. Watch it carefully, and if it appears to be putting on undue weight, cut down on the biscuit.

## Origin and history
Long before Europeans settled in South Africa, the members of the Hottentot tribe had, as a companion who accompanied them on their hunting expeditions, an animal that has since been called the Hottentot Hunting Dog, a distinct characteristic of which was the ridge of hair growing in the reverse direction along its back.

During the 16th and 17th centuries, Dutch, Boers, Germans and Huguenots migrated to South Africa and, as these people were pioneers in a new and uncivilized country teeming with fierce wild animals, they brought with them their own European medium-sized and large working and hunting dogs. Probably by chance, the white settlers' dogs became crossed with the tough Hottentot Hunting Dogs, and the superior quality and vigour of their offspring were quickly recognized, the presence of the ridge identifying the most desirable dogs.

This blending over 200 years of the best qualities of many European breeds with those of the Hottentot Hunting Dog formed the immediate ancestor of today's Ridgeback, which has many of the characteristics usually associated with other hounds.

## SHOW SUMMARY
**General appearance.** The Ridgeback should be a strong, muscular, active dog, symmetrical in outline, and capable of great endurance with a fair amount of speed. Movement should be similar to the Foxhound's gait.

**Colour.** Light wheaten to red wheaten. Head, body, legs and tail should be of a uniform colour. A little white on the chest is permissible but excessive white hairs here, on the belly, or above the paws should be penalized. White toes are undesirable. Dark muzzle and ears are permissible.

**Head and skull.** Should be of a fair length, the skull flat and rather broad between the ears, and should be free from wrinkles when in repose. The stop should be reasonably well defined and not in one straight line from the nose to the occiput bone, as required in a Bull Terrier. The nose should be black or brown, in keeping with the colour of the dog. No other-coloured nose is permissible. A black nose should be accompanied by dark eyes; a brown nose by amber eyes.

**Tail.** Should be strong at the insertion and generally tapering towards the end, free from coarseness. It should not be inserted too high or too low, and should be carried with a slight curve upwards.

**Feet.** The feet should be compact, with well-arched toes and round, tough elastic pads protected by hair between the toes and pads.

Because the Rottweiler was long used
by butchers in the region of Rottweil,
southern Germany, to drive cattle to
market (and to guard its newly enriched
master when the cattle had been sold!),
it was known there as the Rottweiler
Metzgerhund, or Rottweil butcher's dog.
As a show dog, it was established
in the USA a little earlier than in
Britain, the breed being
recognized by the American
Kennel Club in 1935, and it is
steadily increasing in
international popularity.

*Rottweiler*

The characteristic ridge of hair
along the back of the Rhodesian
Ridgeback should be clearly defined,
tapering and symmetrical, and extend
from immediately behind the
the shoulders to the haunches.
It must have an average width of
5cm (2in), and contain two
identical crowns, the lower
edges of which must not extend
down the ridge further
than one-third of its length.

*Rhodesian Ridgeback*

# BOUVIER DES FLANDRES

### Good points
- *Can be kept as a pet*
- *Easily trained*
- *Impressive guard*
- *Loyal to owner's family*
- *Trustworthy*

### Take heed
- *Fierce appearance, especially with cropped ears as in country of origin*
- *One-person family dog*

The Bouvier des Flandres is a Belgian cattle dog, hardy, trustworthy, and—when its ears are cropped, as in its country-of-origin—looking the epitome of ferocity. It can be kept as a pet, but tends to be a one-person dog, though that means guarding their family as well!

### Size
Weight: dog 34.9-39.9kg (77-88lb); bitch 27-34.9kg (59½-77lb). Height: dog 62-68.5cm (24½-27in); bitch 58.5-65cm (23-25½in).

### Exercise
Needs plenty of exercise. Not ideally suited to town life.

### Grooming
Regular brushing will keep the coat in good condition.

### Feeding
Recommended would be 1½-2½ cans (376g, 13.3oz size) of a branded meaty product, with biscuit added in equal part by volume; or 5 cupfuls of a dry food, complete diet, mixed in the proportion of 1 cup of feed to ½ cup of hot or cold water.

### Origin and history
The Bouvier was derived from a number of working Belgian breeds with the purpose of producing a good all-purpose dog, suitable for the rough shoot, for herding, and also as a draught dog. It was not until 1912 that a meeting was held to discuss a possible standard for the Bouvier; no agreement was reached, and devotees had to wait until after the First World War for a standard to be drawn up by the Club National Belge du Bouvier des Flandres and efforts made to improve future stock of the breed.

### SHOW SUMMARY
**General appearance.** Rather short-legged and cobby, the body set on well-muscled, strong legs, giving the impression of great strength without clumsiness.
**Colour.** Usually fawn or grey, often brindled or shaded. Black is also permissible, and no colour shall have preference. Light, washed-out shades are undesirable.
**Head and skull.** The head should appear big, the moustache and beard making it appear even more so, in proportion to the body and height. When handled it should be found to be well-chiselled. Well-developed and flat, the skull should be slightly broader than it is long. The lines of the underside of the skull and the top should be parallel. The proportion of the length of the skull to the muzzle should be 3:2. A very slight furrow in the forehead. The stop not very deep, but appearing so, due to the heavy eyebrows. The muzzle broad, strong and bony, rectangular when seen from the front, gradually narrowing towards the nose, but never becoming pointed. The circumference, measured just in front of eyes, should be approximately equal to the length of the head. Extending the foreface in a slightly convex line towards its tip, the nose should be very well-developed, rounded at its edges and always black. Nostrils wide. Cheeks flat and clean.
**Tail.** Docked to 2-3 vertebrae. It should continue the normal line of the vertebral column and be carried gaily when moving. Dogs born tail-less should not be faulted for this.
**Feet.** Short, round and compact. Toes tight and well-arched. Nails black, strong. Thick, hard pads.

# BRIARD

### Good points
- *Easy to train*
- *Family pet and/or farm worker*
- *Gentle nature*

### Take heed
- *No drawbacks known*

The Briard is the best-known of the four French sheepdogs—the others being the Beauceron, the Picardy and the Pyrenean Mountain Dog—although the latter won Best in Show at Crufts in 1970. Briards are good-natured, and can be kept happily either as an affectionate family pet, or for work around the farm; quite a number are finding their way into the show ring.

### Size
Height: dog 58.5-68.5cm (23-27in); bitch 56-65cm (22-25½in).

### Exercise
Regular, and not just a walk around the park.

### Grooming
Regular brushing. The Briard takes pride in cleaning itself.

### Feeding
Recommended would be 1½-2½ cans (376g, 13.3oz size) of a branded meaty product, with biscuit added in equal part by volume; or 5 cupfuls of a dry food, complete diet, mixed in the proportion of 1 cup of feed to ½ cup of hot or cold water.

### Origin and history
The Briard comes from the Brie area of France, where it is also known as the Berger de Brie or Chien de Brie. It has been known since the 12th century. There is an entertaining 14th century French legend of how the Briard was given its name: in the year 1371 Sir Aubry de Montdidier was assassinated. His killer was hunted down by his dog, and it was ordained by the king that a battle should take place between the man, named Macaire, and the dog. The battle took place on the Isle of Notre Dame, and the dog proved the victor. Macaire then admitted his crime and was beheaded. It is likely that from then on, the Briard became known as the Chien d'Aubry, and a shield sculpted in stone was placed in the church at Montdidier, bearing a likeness of a dog's head that looks similar to the Briard of today.

### SHOW SUMMARY
**General appearance.** A dog of rugged appearance; supple, muscular and well-proportioned, gay and lively.
**Colour.** All solid colours are correct except those mentioned below. The darker shades are preferred. Incorrect colours are white, chestnut, mahogany and bicolour. Bicolour should not be confused with the slightly lighter shading at the extremities due to the beginnings of uneven pigmentation. This lighter shading should be of the same tone as the rest of the coat, e.g. light fawn on dark fawn, light grey on dark grey. Occasional white hairs through the black coat are acceptable and do not designate a bicolour.
**Head and skull.** Head strong, fairly long, with a well-defined stop placed exactly mid-way in the length of the head. The head should carry hair forming moustache, beard and eyebrows that slightly veil the eyes. The muzzle should be neither narrow nor pointed. The nose should be large square, and always black, no matter what colour the dog. The forehead slightly rounded, the skull rectangular in shape.
**Tail.** Long, well covered with hair, and with an upward hook at the tip. Carried low and deviating to neither one side nor the other. The bone of the tail should reach at least to the point of the hock.
**Feet.** Strong and slightly rounded, about mid-way between a cat foot and a hare foot. Nails should always be black. Pads should be firm and hard, and the toes close together.

*Below: A Briard suckles her pups. This French sheepdog is used for herding, and it also makes an affectionate family pet. It is good-natured, easy to train and is very successful as a show dog.*

The name of the Bouvier des Flandres stems from the French word for a cowherd or oxherd, reflecting its function as a working dog in the later 19th century. The fact that the Bouvier's coat — rough, tousled and unkempt in appearance — requires regular brushing is perhaps reflected in another early name for the breed: Vuilbaard, or 'dirty beard'.

*Bouvier des Flandres*

It is believed that the Briard was first brought into North America by either the Marquis de Lafayette or Thomas Jefferson, both heroes of the American Revolution of the later 18th century. No litter was registered with the AKC until 1922; foundation of the Briard Club followed in 1928.

*Briard*

# HUNGARIAN VIZSLA

## Good points
- *First-class gundog*
- *Makes an excellent family pet*

## Take heed
- *No drawbacks known*

The Vizsla is Hungary's national dog and one of the purest breeds in the world. It is an excellent all-purpose gundog, with a keen nose, and well able to point, set and retrieve. Despite its hunting abilities it adapts happily to life as a family pet, and its temperament is sound.

## Size
Height at withers: dog 57-63.5cm (22½-25in); bitch 53-60cm (21-23½in). Weight: 22-30kg (48½-66lb).

## Exercise
Needs plenty of vigorous exercise.

## Grooming
Regular brushing will keep the coat in a healthy condition.

## Feeding
Recommended would be 1½-2½ cans (376g, 13.3oz size) of a branded meaty product, with biscuit added in equal part by volume; or 5 cupfuls of a dry food, complete diet, mixed in the proportion of 1 cup of feed to ½ cup of hot or cold water.

## Origin and history
The Hungarian Vizsla was no doubt developed by the Magyar nobles and great care has been taken to avoid introducing new blood. It is a pure breed of outstanding ability and quality.

## SHOW SUMMARY
**General appearance.** A medium-sized dog of distinguished appearance, robust and not too heavily boned.
**Colour.** Russet gold. Small white marks on chest and feet, though acceptable, are not desirable.
**Head and skull.** The head should be gaunt and noble. The skull should be moderately wide between the ears, with a median line down the forehead and a moderate stop. The muzzle should be a little longer than the skull and, although tapering, should be well squared at the end. The nostrils well developed, broad and wide. The jaws strong and powerful. The lips should cover the jaws completely and be neither loose nor pendulous. The nose should be brown.
**Tail.** Of moderate thickness, set rather low, with one third docked off. Whilst moving should be held horizontally.
**Feet.** Rounded, with toes short, arched and well closed. A cat-like foot is desirable and a hare foot is objectionable. Nails short, strong and a shade darker in colour than the coat; dew-claws should always be removed.

*Above: The Hungarian Vizsla, one of the purest breeds in the world.*

# SLOVAKIAN KUVASZ

(Tsuvatch)

## Good points
- *Brave*
- *Intelligent*
- *Keen, alert watchdog*

## Take heed
- *Predominantly a working dog and guard*

The Slovakian Kuvasz is a lively and intelligent dog, ever watchful, and with acute hearing. Its characteristics are similar to those of the Hungarian Kuvasz.

## Size
Height at shoulder is around 61cm (24in), but should not exceed 71cm (28in) for a dog, 66cm (26in) for a bitch.

## Exercise
Needs plenty of vigorous exercise to stay healthy.

## Grooming
Regular brushing is necessary to keep the coat in good condition.

## Feeding
One to 1½ cans (376g, 13.3oz size) of a branded meaty product, with biscuit added in equal part by volume; or 3 cupfuls of a dry food, complete diet, mixed in the proportion of 1 cup of feed to ½ cup of hot or cold water.

## Origin and history
The Slovakian Kuvasz is little known outside its own country. It would seem to be related to the Hungarian Kuvasz and bears resemblance also to the Owczarek Podhalanski, an ancient Polish herding breed. Indeed, Bo Bengtson and Ake Wintzell in their *Dogs of the World* suggest that the three breeds could be said to be local varieties in their respective countries of the same herding breed. The Polish and Slovakian types are sometimes known as 'Tatry' dogs, after the mountain range that stretches through both countries and where each has existed for a long time.

## SHOW SUMMARY
There is not a recognized standard in Britain for this breed. However, the most desirable colour is certainly pure white. (White animals were always desired by huntsmen, as their colour would distinguish them from their prey.)

# HUNGARIAN KUVASZ

## Good points
- *Excellent guard*
- *Loyal*

## Take heed
- *Tends to be a one-person dog*

The Hungarian Kuvasz may be kept as a pet and is loyal and devoted to its owner and family. It is, however, essentially a guard and will be ever watchful for intruders. It is an intelligent dog, and its name comes from a Turkish word meaning 'guardian of the peace'. It is a natural herder and has been used for big game hunting. However, its role in life is predominantly that of protector.

## Size
Height at withers: dog 71-75cm (28-29½in); bitch 66-70cm (26-27½). Weight: dog 39.9-52.2kg (88-115lb); bitch 30-42.2kg (66-93lb).

## Exercise
Needs plenty of exercise to stay healthy.

## Grooming
Regular brushing will keep the coat in good condition.

## Feeding
Recommended would be 1½-2½ cans of a branded meaty product (376g, 13.3oz size), with biscuit added in equal part by volume; or 5 cupfuls of a dry food, complete diet, mixed in the proportion of 1 cup of feed to ½ cup of hot or cold water.

## Origin and history
The Kuvasz has existed in Hungary for centuries, and as early as the 1490s was protecting Hungarian nobility against possible assassins. It became known as the guard dog of the privileged, only the high-born being permitted to keep one. It is a breed that has to date attained greater popularity in the United States than in Great Britain, where there are very few.

## SHOW SUMMARY
**General appearance.** A big dog of nobility and power. The various parts of the body are well-proportioned, neither excessively long nor too compact. The body outline is roughly square. The muscles are lean, the bone structure is strong without coarseness. Joints are lean. The regular positioning of the limbs, the deep chest, the slightly hollowed croup, allow the Kuvasz to work tirelessly. The teeth are very strong. The coat is rough and wavy in a way that is characteristic of the breed.
**Colour.** Invariably white; ivory is at present accepted.
**Head.** The most attractive feature of the Kuvasz, the head denotes nobility and power. The nose is pointed and black, as are the inner lips and eye-rims. The bridge is long, broad and straight. The lips fit closely to the gums and have a saw-toothed closure. The muzzle tapers from base to nose, but must not be too pointed at the tip. The forehead medial furrow continues to the muzzle. The teeth are well developed, regular and strong; the jaws close in a scissor bite. The stop is gently sloping and broadly curved. The skull is long but not pointed, of medium width, with a broad occiput. The ears are set on fairly high, close to the rather flat skull. The supra-orbital ridges are of moderate development.
**Tail.** Set on quite low, a continuation of the croup. It hangs down approximately to the height of the hocks; the tip is curved slightly upward, but without forming a ring. When the Kuvasz is excited or alerted, the tail is held above loin level.
**Feet.** The hind feet are longer than the forefeet but just as strong. The pads are tight and elastic, the nails well developed and slate grey in colour. Dew-claws must be removed.

*Below: The Hungarian Kuvasz is a natural herder and makes an excellent guard. It has also been used for big game hunting.*

A dog resembling the Hungarian Vizsla is shown on a Magyar rock carving dating from around AD 1000, but the Vizsla became known outside its native country only after World War II, when many dogs were taken out of Hungary by refugees.

*Hungarian Vizsla*

*Slovakian Kuvasz (Tsuvatch)*

A grave decline in the indigenous Hungarian Kuvasz breed, caused by two World Wars and a Communist takeover, has fortunately been outweighed by increased interest abroad.

*Hungarian Kuvasz*

# BERNESE MOUNTAIN DOG
(Bernese Sennenhund)

### Good points
- *Beautiful*
- *Easily trained*
- *Excellent watchdog*
- *Good with other animals and people*
- *Suitable as a pet*

### Take heed
- *No drawbacks known, but it is a big dog to have around the place*

The Bernese Mountain Dog is the most internationally known of the four Swiss Mountain Dogs, the others being the Great Swiss Sennenhund (or Mountain Dog), the Appenzell Sennenhund and the Entlebuch Sennenhund. It is used as both draught dog and companion in its country of origin, but elsewhere it is gaining popularity as pet and show dog, being easy to train despite its size and strength, loyal, affectionate and docile with both other animals and humans. It is a beautiful dog, with something of the Collie in its appearance.

### Size
Height at the withers: dog 63.5-70cm (25-27½in); bitch 58.5-66cm (23-26in).

### Exercise
Needs a reasonable amount of exercise and is not ideally suited to town life.

### Grooming
Regular brushing will keep the coat in good condition.

### Feeding
Recommended would be 1½-2½ cans (376g, 13.3oz size) of a branded meaty product, with biscuit added in equal part by volume; or 5 cupfuls of a dry food, complete diet, mixed in the proportion of 1 cup of feed to ½ cup of hot or cold water.

### Origin and history
The Bernese has been used as both herder and draught dog for centuries, and many a visitor to Switzerland returns with a snapshot of a Sennenhund pulling a milk cart. The types of Sennenhund are named after the regions in which they were found. They have Mastiff characteristics and are believed to have Molossian ancestry. The St Bernard, Rottweiler and Newfoundland are also related.

Above: Two Bernese puppies, showing the white tips to their tails.

### SHOW SUMMARY
**General appearance.** Above medium size; a strong, active working dog; alert, well boned, and of striking colour.

**Colour.** Jet black, with rich reddish brown on the cheeks, over the eyes, on all four legs and on the chest. Slight to medium-sized symmetrical white head marking (blaze) and white chest marking (cross) are essential. Preferred but not essential are white paws, the white not reaching higher than the pastern, and a white tip to the tail. A few white hairs at the nape of the neck and a white anal patch are undesirable but tolerated.

**Head and skull.** Strong with flat skull and slightly developed furrow; well-defined stop; strong, straight muzzle; lips slightly developed.

**Tail.** Bushy, reaching just below the hock. When alert may be carried gaily, but should not curl or be carried over the back.

**Feet.** Short, round and compact.

NB The Great Swiss Sennenhund stands up to 71cm (28in), and is short-haired, black with a red brand and white markings; the short-haired, Appenzell Sennenhund is smaller (maximum 58.5cm, 23in) but identical except for a curled tail; and the Entlebuch Sennenhund stands no more than 46cm (18in), is short-haired, and has a stump tail and a black coat with yellow to brown and white markings.

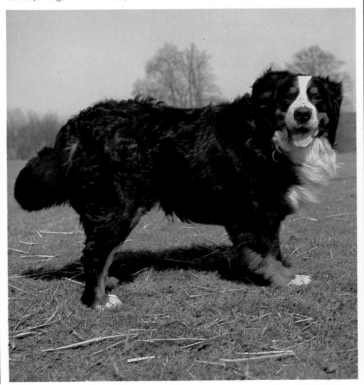

Below: The Bernese, used as a draught dog for centuries.

Below: The Great Swiss Mountain Dog, bred to herd cattle.

Appenzeller
Mountain Dog

Entlebucher
Mountain Dog

Great Swiss
Mountain Dog

Bernese Mountain Dog

# POLISH SHEEPDOG

(Owczarek Podhalanski, Owczarek Nizinny)

## Good points
- *Excellent guard*
- *Hardy*
- *Generally good-natured*
- *Intelligent*

## Take heed
- *No drawbacks known. However, the Nizinny is generally thought to be the more docile of the two varieties*

There are two varieties of Polish Sheepdog, the Lowlands Shepherd Dog (Owczarek Nizinny), which looks something like the Old English Sheepdog, and the Tatry Mountain Sheepdog (Owczarek Podhalanski), a bigger type that has something of the Retriever or Kuvasz about its appearance. They are both intelligent, good-natured, generally docile and have a keen memory.

## Size
Height: Tatry Mountain Sheepdog 66cm (26in); Lowlands Shepherd Dog 40.5-51cm (16-20in).

## Exercise
Liberal exercise necessary to keep the dogs fit and healthy

## Grooming
Regular brushing; the Lowlands type will need combing with a steel comb also.

## Feeding
Recommended would be 1½-2½ cans (376g, 13.3oz size) of a branded meaty product, with biscuit added in equal part by volume; or 5 cupfuls of a dry food, complete diet, mixed in the proportion of 1 cup of feed to ½ cup of hot or cold water.

## Origin and History
The Tatry Mountain Sheepdog bears a strong similarity to the Hungarian Kuvasz, and both varieties are credited with having been introduced to Poland in the 4th or 5th century. They are little known outside their homeland.

# OLD ENGLISH SHEEPDOG

## Good points
- *Excellent with children*
- *Gets on well with other animals*
- *Sound temperament*

## Take heed
- *No drawbacks known*

The Old English Sheepdog, or Bobtail, is an extremely popular breed, being a devoted friend and guardian of children, with a sound, sensible temperament. It will live contentedly in a fairly small house despite its bulky appearance.

## Size
Height: dog 56cm (22in) and upwards; bitch slightly less.

## Exercise
Regular walks of average length—perhaps two good walks of 20 minutes duration per day; and, of course, you need a garden.

## Grooming
Daily brushing and weekly combing with a steel comb. The hair is brushed forward to cover the eyes. I don't know how, but it *can* see! White parts are powdered for showing.

## Health care
Check the ears for canker, and take care that dead, matted hair does not accumulate around the feet. Some Bobtails are born with that stumpy tail; otherwise it is docked to a length of 5cm (2in).

## Feeding
Recommended would be 1½-2½ cans (376g, 13.3oz size) of a branded meaty product, with biscuit added in equal part by volume; or 5 cupfuls of a dry food, complete diet, mixed in the proportion of 1 cup of feed to ½ cup of hot or cold water.

## Origin and history
The Old English Sheepdog is often, for obvious reasons, known as the Bobtail. How it came to England is a subject of conjecture, for the breed is said to have evolved through the crossing of the Briard with the large Russian Owtscharka, a dog related to the Hungarian sheepdogs. It was used in England as a cattle dog and guard, but nowadays is kept mainly as a much loved pet. Because of the Bobtail's reliability with children, a number have found their way into schools for handicapped youngsters. The first breed club for the Old English Sheepdog was established in Britain in 1888 and the standard has altered little in the intervening years.

## SHOW SUMMARY
**General appearance.** A strong, compact-looking dog of great symmetry; absolutely free of legginess; profusely coated all over; very elastic in a gallop, but in walking or trotting it has a characteristic ambling or pacing movement; its bark should be loud, with a peculiar 'pot casse' ring in it. All round, it is a thick-set, muscular, able-bodied dog, with a most intelligent expression, free of all Poodle or Deerhound character.

**Colour.** Any shade of grey, grizzle, blue or blue merle, with or without white markings; any shade of brown or sable is considered distinctly objectionable and not to be encouraged.

**Head and skull.** Skull capacious and rather squarely formed, giving plenty of room for brain power. The parts over the eyes should be well arched and the whole well covered with hair. Jaw fairly long, strong, square and truncated; the stop should be defined, to avoid a Deerhound face. Nose always black, large and capacious.

**Tail.** Puppies requiring docking should have the operation performed within a week of birth, preferably within four days.

**Feet.** Small and round; toes well arched, and pads thick and round.

*Below: It is easy to see why Old English Sheepdogs make such popular pets. This pup will grow into a playful and even boisterous young dog, excellent with children and perfectly happy to live in a small house – with a garden.*

*Polish Sheepdog (Lowlands)*

The coat of the Old English
Sheepdog should be profuse
and of good, hard
texture; not straight, but
shaggy and free
from curl.

*Old English Sheepdog*

# ANATOLIAN KARABASH

(Anatolian Sheepdog, Turkish Shepherd's Dog)

## Good points
● *Affectionate*
● *Hardy*
● *Intelligent*
● *Independent*
● *Loyal*
● *Trainable*

## Take heed
● *Not suited to town life or limited space*
● *Will accept others, but main loyalty remains with owner*

The Anatolian Karabash is a shepherd's guard dog of ancient lineage. It is a large, fast, vigorous outdoor working dog with a self-sufficient temperament. Such dogs are found from the Anatolian plateau of Turkey right across Afghanistan. The shepherds of Central Asia crop their dogs' ears and give them massive iron-spiked collars to help defend the flocks from predators.

The Anatolian Karabash can live outside all day, but it is much better to allow it in the house as part of the family, when it will become more amenable and a good companion.

This is a dog that will automatically identify with one person as its owner. It will accept other members of the family, and friends who have been introduced, but its main loyalty will remain with its owner.

It needs and responds to a great deal of love, and should be taken around and socialized at an early age, otherwise it may become too possessive. The Anatolian Karabash's natural inclination is to be friendly with other animals and it has a very long memory. Incidentally, when it leans heavily against you, this means that you have been totally accepted.

## Size
Weight: dog 49.9-64kg (110-141lb); bitch 41-59kg (90½-130lb). Height: dog 73.5-81cm (29-32in) at the shoulder; bitch 71-78.5cm (28-31in) at the shoulder.

## Exercise
As a pet the Karabash is not suited to town life, because it needs plenty of space in which to work off its energy. This it will do on its own, so normally there is no need to walk it in the conventional way. Indeed, it is said that a man would have to walk all day to give such a dog enough movement for it to be able to develop its superb body. The breed is naturally active and playful and will be happy in a large and well-fenced garden.

For such a big dog, the Anatolian Karabash moves remarkably quickly and gracefully, and speeds of 55kph (34mph) have been clocked up by the breed.

## Grooming
The natural inclination of the Anatolian Karabash is to get up at intervals, especially at night, and patrol the area, bedding down in a different spot each time. This keeps its coat remarkably clean, odourless and free of parasites. However, it will benefit from regular brushing.

## Feeding
The canned food requirement for a dog of this size is approximately 3 cans per day (376g, 13.3oz size), with biscuit supplement in equal part by volume, or the fresh meat equivalent, so they are by no means cheap to feed. Incidentally, all so-called soft bones may be given and are probably a necessity for the animal's proper development.

However, it is of interest that in their own country they can exist on very little, and shepherds have recounted with pride how their dogs remained with the flocks for up to a week without food or water. They have two strange behavioural adaptations to help them survive, one being an alert 'hibernation' in the cruel midday Turkish sun, the other an ability to dig up gophers — a kind of prairie dog or marmot-like animal — for food.

## Origin and history
Since Babylonian times, there existed in this area a breed of large, strong dogs with a heavy head. They were employed as war dogs, and for hunting big game such as lions and horses. Some spectacular examples can be seen on the very well preserved bas-reliefs in the Assyrian Room of the British Museum in London.

In their native Turkey the dogs do not herd the sheep, but patrol around them, often seeking higher ground to get a better view and a breeze. The dogs patrol the ground ahead of the flock, checking out every bush and irregularity of the terrain for potential trouble. Should they notice anything, even a moving car, they will, silently at first, split up and converge upon it at great speed. These ambush tactics are inborn and fascinating to watch.

## SHOW SUMMARY
**General characteristics.** An active working breed used originally as a guard dog for sheep, unsuited for town life. Hardworking, capable of enduring extremes of heat and cold. Steady and bold without undue aggression, naturally independent, very intelligent and trainable.
**Colour.** All shades of fawn. White socks and chest blaze commonly occur. Characteristic black mask varies in extent, from a wholly black head and ears, to a slight blackness around the muzzle.
**Head and skull.** Large and broad between the ears with slight stop. Mature males have a broader head, the females have a slighter and more feminine head. Foreface one third of total head length. Slightly pendulous black lips. Square profile. Nose black.
**Tail.** Long bone reaching at least to hock joint. Set on rather high. When relaxed, carried low with slight curl; when alert, carried high with end curled over back, especially by males.
**Feet.** Good strong feet with well-arched toes. Nails blunt, grey or black depending on coat colour.

# ESTRELA MOUNTAIN DOG

(Rafeiro do Alentejo)

## Good points
● *Excellent sheepdog*
● *Good temperament*
● *Popular show dog in its own country*
● *Useful dray animal*

## Take heed
● *No drawbacks known*

The Estrela Mountain Dog is a hardy animal, of great power, used for both herding sheep and pulling carts. It is a popular show dog in Portugal.

## Size
Weight: dog 39.9-49.9kg (88-110lb) bitch 15.6-20.2kg (34½-44½lb). Height: dog 66-73.5cm (26-29in); bitch 63.5-70cm (25-27½in).

## Exercise
Needs plenty of exercise to stay healthy.

## Grooming
Regular brushing will keep the coat in good condition.

## Feeding
Recommended would be 1½-2½ cans (376g, 13.3oz size) of a branded meaty product, with biscuit added in equal part by volume; or 5 cupfuls of a dry food, complete diet, mixed in the proportion of 1 cup of feed to ½ cup of hot or cold water.

## Origin and history
This is a dog that has existed for centuries in the Estrela mountains of Portugal. It resembles the St Bernard, but is of lighter stature, with something of the Mastiff in its make-up. It was bred as a herding dog.

## SHOW SUMMARY
**General appearance.** A large dog of powerful build, a sober farm animal of fairly (but not excessively) long, stout configuration.
**Colour.** Black, wolf, tawny or yellow, mixed with white; bicoloured, roan or dappled; very often streaked or grizzled.
**Head and skull.** A bear-like head, in good proportion to the overall body structure. The skull is broad, with a slight medial furrow above and between the eyes. The stop is not accentuated. The upper longitudinal axes of muzzle and skull are divergent. The occipital protuberance is not very pronounced. The muzzle is rounded, with a straight profile, not so long as the skull and moderately broad. The lips are slightly rounded in front, well cut and overlapping; they are thin and solid, and give a slight curve to the lower profile. The jaws are strong, well muscled and well opposed. The nose is oval, its tip blunted from above to below and from forward back, and dark in colour.
**Tail.** Set on moderately high, slightly curved at the end, and of good length. When the dog is at rest, the tail is carried between the hocks and reaches below them. It may curl moderately when the dog is in action.
**Feet.** Must not be flat; well closed and long, with stout toes that are barely arched. The colour varies with the colour of the coat. Pads thick and tough.

# TIBETAN MASTIFF

## Good points
● *Excellent guard dog*
● *Reliable temperament unless provoked*

## Take heed
● *No drawbacks known*

The Tibetan Mastiff bears a strong resemblance to the St Bernard. It is an excellent guard dog, but is good-natured unless provoked. It can be kept happily as a companion/guard.

## Size
Height at shoulder: dog 63.5-68.5cm (25-27in); bitch 56-61cm (22-24in).

## Exercise
Needs regular vigorous exercise.

## Grooming
Daily brushing will keep the coat in good condition.

## Feeding
Recommended would be 1½-2½ cans (376g, 13.3oz size) of a branded meaty product, with biscuit added in equal part by volume; or 5 cupfuls of a dry food, complete diet, mixed in the proportion of 1 cup of feed to ½ cup of hot or cold water.

## Origin and history
The Tibetan Mastiff is regarded as a British breed, but it originated in Central Asia, where its job was to guard flocks. Like other mastiffs, it is likely to have descended from the Roman Molossus.

## SHOW SUMMARY
**General characteristics.** A powerful, heavy-boned dog, docile and aloof. A good guard dog.
**Colour.** Black and tan, or golden.
**Head.** Broad, massive head and smooth face. Perfectly level mouth, with powerful jaws. Muzzle of mastiff type, but lighter than that of the English Mastiff.
**Tail.** Set on high, curled over back to one side; very thick and bushy.
**Feet.** Smooth, large, strong and compact.

The Anatolian Karabash breed developed its extreme hardiness as a result of centuries of herding on the rough and arid plateau which extends over most of Turkey.

Anatolian Karabash

Estrela Mountain Dog

Tibetan Mastiff

Although now seldom seen in Britain, the Tibetan Mastiff was quite well-known during the 19th century, when King George IV imported the breed.

# BORZOI

### Good points
- *Aloof*
- *Beautiful and graceful*
- *Intelligent*
- *Faithful*

### Take heed
- *A dignified dog, not ideal as a children's playmate*

The Borzoi is an animal of great beauty and grace used in Russia from the 17th century for wolf hunting and coursing. Today it is often regarded more as a fashion accessory: the fur-clad silent film star accompanied by two Borzois was not a rarity!

They are dignified, good-natured animals, but somewhat aloof and not likely to enjoy playing wild games with children.

### Size
Height at shoulder: dog from 73.5cm (29in) upwards; bitch from 68.5cm (27in) upwards.

### Exercise
The Borzoi needs a great deal of exercise, but remember that this dog is a hunter: it is essential that it should be allowed to run only when far from livestock.

### Feeding
Recommended would be 1½-2½ cans (376g, 13.3oz size) of a branded meaty product, with biscuit added in equal part by volume; or 5 cupfuls of a dry food, complete diet, mixed in the proportion of 1 cup of feed to ½ cup of hot or cold water.

### Origin and history
The Borzoi was maintined for centuries by the Czars and noblemen of Imperial Russia for hunting the wolf. During the 15th and 16th centuries it was crossed with the sheepdog to provide strength, and later with various hounds to obtain more speed. However, it was from the strain developed by the Grand Duke Nicolai Nicolayevitch that the present-day standard evolved. Information on present-day Borzois in the USSR is sketchy. There would appear to be more Borzois in fashionable capital cities of the world such as New York, London and Paris.

### SHOW SUMMARY
**General appearance.** A very graceful, aristocratic and elegant dog, possessing courage, muscular power and great speed.
**Head and skull.** Head long and lean; well filled in below the eyes. Measurement equal from the occiput to the inner corner of the eye, and from the inner corner of the eye to the tip of the nose. Skull very slightly domed and narrow; stop not perceptible, inclining to Roman nose. Head fine so that the direction of the bones and principal veins can be clearly seen. Bitch's head should be finer than the dog's. Jaws long, deep and powerful; nose large and black, not pink or brown, nicely rounded,

neither cornered nor sharp. Viewed from above the skull should look narrow, converging very gradually to tip of nose.
**Tail.** Long, rather low set. Well feathered, carried low, not gaily. In action may be used as a rudder, but not rising above level of back. From the level of the hocks may be sickle-shaped but not ringed.
**Feet.** Front feet rather long, toes close together; well arched, never flat, turning neither in nor out. Hind feet hare-like, i.e. longer and less arched.

# BLACK AND TAN COONHOUND

### Good points
- *Fine nose*
- *Good temperament*
- *Strong and hardy*

### Take heed
- *No drawbacks known*

The Black and Tan Coonhound is a fast, hardy, strong working hound that, like the Bloodhound, does not kill its prey. It is similar to the Bloodhound in appearance, but you can detect the Coonhound by its lack of wrinkles, characteristic of the Bloodhound.

### Size
Height at the shoulder: dog 63.5-68.5cm (25-27in): bitch 58.5-63.5cm (23-25in).

### Exercise
It is a working dog and needs plenty of vigorous exercise.

### Grooming
Daily grooming with a hound glove. Regular ear inspection is advocated.

### Feeding
Recommended would be 1½-2½ cans (376g, 13.3oz size) of a branded meaty product, with biscuit added in equal part by volume; or 5 cupfuls of a dry food, complete diet, mixed in the proportion of 1 cup of feed to ½ cup of hot or cold water.

### Origin and history
The Black and Tan Coonhound is essentially an American breed, though a close relation of the Bloodhound, being identical in size and often in colour. It traces back from the Talbot Hound to the Bloodhound and the Virginia Foxhound. The Black and Tan is one of six types of Coonhound recognized in America, and is used for hunting opossum and racoon. It is a working hound not often seen on the show bench.

### SHOW SUMMARY
**General appearance.** The Black and Tan Coonhound is fundamentally a working dog, capable of withstanding the rigours of winter, the heat of summer, and the difficult terrain over which it is required to work. Judges are asked by the club sponsoring the breed to place

great emphasis upon these factors when evaluating the merits of the dog. The general impression should be that of power, agility and alertness. The expression should be alert, friendly, eager and aggressive. The dog should immediately impress with its ability to cover the ground with powerful, rhythmic strides.
**Colour.** Coal black, with rich tan markings above the eyes, on the sides of the muzzle, and on chest, legs and breeching, with black pencil markings on the toes.
**Head and skull.** Should be cleanly modelled, with medium stop occurring midway between occiput bone and nose. The head should measure 23-25cm (9-10in) in males and 20-23cm (8-9in) in females. Viewed in profile, the line of the skull is practically on a parallel plane to the foreface or muzzle. The skin should be devoid of folds or excess dewlap. The flews should be well developed, with typical hound appearance. Nostrils well open and always black. Skull should tend toward an oval outline. Teeth should fit evenly with a slightly scissor bite.
**Tail.** Strong, with base slightly below level of back line, carried free and, when in action, at approximately a right angle to the back.
**Feet.** Should be cat-like, with compact, well-arched toes and thick, strong pads.

# BLOODHOUND

### Good points
- *Charming to look at*
- *Good with children*
- *Great tracker and trailer*
- *Ideal family pet – if you have room*

### Take heed
- *Easily hurt – use only voice control*

The Bloodhound is a delightful animal with a nose that is second to none. It follows its quarry, but does not kill. Indeed, it is loved by children, who can accompany it on the lead, and is often kept as a family pet. Bloodhounds are popular show dogs, but individuals are still often called in by police for tracking purposes; a number have appeared in films.

### Size
Height: dog 63.5-68.5cm (25-27in); bitch 58.5-63.5cm (23-25in). Weight: dog 40.8kg (90lb); bitch 36.3kg (80lb).

### Exercise
Needs plenty. These dogs have to gallop. Best to join a Bloodhound club if you become an owner, and take part in organized events.

### Grooming
Daily grooming with a hound glove. Regular ear inspection is advocated.

### Health care
Bloodhounds are subject to torsion (stomach gases building into a bloat). A large proportion

are affected and it can prove fatal if not treated by a vet within minutes. Best to be aware of this, and ready to seek immediate help.

### Feeding
Recommended would be 1½-2½ cans (376g, 13.3oz size) of a branded meaty product, with biscuit added in equal part by volume; or 5 cupfuls of a dry food, complete diet, mixed in the proportion of 1 cup of feed to ½ cup of hot or cold water.

### Origin and history
The Bloodhound is said to have been brought to England by William the Conqueror in 1066, and to be one of the oldest and purest of the hound breeds. Bloodhounds in Britain are popular show ring contenders.

### SHOW SUMMARY
**General appearance.** The expression is noble and dignified, and characterized by solemnity, wisdom and power. The gait is elastic, swinging and free, the stern being carried high, scimitar fashion.
**Colour.** The colours are black and tan, liver and tan (red and tan) and red. The darker colours are sometimes interspersed with lighter or badger-coloured hair, and sometimes flecked with white.
**Head and skull.** The head is narrow in proportion to its length and long in proportion to the body, tapering only slightly from the temples to the muzzle, thus (when viewed from above and in front) having the appearance of being flattened at the sides and of being nearly equal in width throughout its length. In profile the upper outline of the skull is in nearly the same plane as that of the foreface. The length from the end of the nose to the stop (midway between the eyes) should not be less than that from the stop to the occipital protuberance (peak). The brows are not prominent, although owing to the deep-set eyes they may have that appearance. The foreface is long, deep and of even width throughout, with a square outline when seen in profile. The head is furnished with an amount of loose skin, which in nearly every position appears superabundant, but more particularly so when the head is carried low; the skin then falls into loose pendulous ridges and folds, especially over the forehead and sides of the face. The nostrils are large and open. In front, the lips fall squarely, making a right angle with the upper line of the foreface; behind, they form deep hanging flews, and, being continued into the pendant folds of loose skin about the neck, constitute the dewlap, which is very pronounced.
**Tail.** The stern is long and thick, tapering to a point, set on high with a moderate amount of hair underneath. It should be carried scimitar fashion, but not curled over the back or corkscrew at any time.
**Feet.** Should be strong and well knuckled up.

Borzoi

Black and Tan Coonhound

Bloodhound

The Bloodhound's
extremely long ears
must receive regular
attention. Thin and soft to the touch,
they are set on very low and fall
in graceful folds, the lower parts curling inwards
and backwards.

# IRISH WOLFHOUND

### Good points
● *Marvellous with children*
● *Good guard*
● *Happiest as a housedog*

### Take heed
● *Gentle when stroked, fierce when provoked*

The Irish Wolfhound, variously known as the Wolfdog, the Irish Greyhound and the Great Dog of Ireland, is a gentle giant, fierce only when provoked. It is intelligent, intensely loyal and slow to anger. Irish Wolfhounds do, nonetheless, have a mind of their own, so firm, gentle discipline is advocated in puppyhood.

### Size
The minimum height and weight of dogs should be 78.5cm (31in) and 54.4kg (120lb); of bitches 71cm (28in) and 40.8kg (90lb). Anything below this should be heavily penalized. Great size, including height at shoulder and proportionate length of body, is the target to be aimed for, and ideally the breed should average 81-86cm (32-34in) in dogs, showing the requisite power, activity, courage and symmetry.

### Exercise
Despite its size, the Irish Wolfhound does not require more exercise than smaller breeds, but it should have ample space in which to gambol. Let it have unrestricted play during puppyhood, but do not force it to take lengthy walks, rather allowing it to 'muscle up' by its own joyful activity. Irish Wolfhounds are usually taught both to walk and to move at the trot while being led; as they are so powerful, obedience is essential.

### Grooming
Brush regularly, and remove long, straggly hairs from ears, neck and

*Below: Irish Wolfhound puppies need firm but gentle discipline.*

underside with finger and thumb. This is a natural-looking breed, which is not difficult to groom.

### Feeding
At least 2½ cans (376g, 13.3oz size) of a branded meaty product, with biscuit added in equal part by volume; or 5 cupfuls of a dry food, complete diet, mixed in the proportion of 1 cup of feed to ½ cup of hot or cold water.

### Origin and history
The Irish Wolfhound is the national dog of Ireland, and its original role was to kill wolves. It is spoken of in many legends, but almost certainly came from Greece with the invading Celts, circa 279 BC. The best-known story of an Irish Wolfhound concerns the dog Gelert, given as a gift to Llewellyn, Prince of Wales, by King John of England around 1210. Prince Llewellyn went hunting, leaving the faithful Gelert in charge of his baby son. On his return he could see only Gelert, with blood on its mouth, and, thinking it had killed the child, he drew his sword and slew the dog. It was only then that he saw, nearby, the body of a wolf, and heard the happy chuckle of his child. Gelert had killed the wolf and saved the child. Full of remorse, Prince Llewellyn ordered a statue to be erected in memory of Gelert, and the dog's name has lived on through the centuries.

### SHOW SUMMARY
**General appearance.** The Irish Wolfhound should not be quite so heavy or massive as the Great Dane, but more so than the Deerhound, which in general type it should otherwise resemble. Of great size and commanding appearance; very muscular, strongly though gracefully built, movements easy and active; head and neck carried high; the tail carried with an upward sweep with a slight curve towards the extremity.
**Colour.** The recognized colours are grey, brindle, red, black, pure white, fawn, or any colour that appears in the Deerhound.
**Head and skull.** Long; the frontal bones of the forehead very slightly

raised, and very little indentation between the eyes. Skull not too broad. Muzzle long and moderately pointed.
**Tail.** Long and slightly curved; of moderate thickness, and well covered with hair.
**Feet.** Moderately large and round, turned neither inwards nor outwards. Toes well arched and closed. Nails very strong and curved.

# DEERHOUND
(Scottish Deerhound)

### Good points
● *Graceful and beautiful*
● *Happy to be with humans and to please*
● *Loving*
● *Sound temperament*

### Take heed
● *No drawbacks known, if you have sufficient space*

The Deerhound is a creature of grace and beauty, mentioned frequently in the novels of Sir Walter Scott. It is strong and healthy, anxious to please and asks no more than to be its owner's devoted companion.

### Size
Weight: dog 38.5-47.6kg (85-105lb); bitch 29.5-36.3kg (65-80lb). Height at shoulder: dog not less than 76cm (30in); bitch 71cm (28in).

### Exercise
Needs a great deal of exercise.

### Grooming
Requires very little trimming, just removal of extra shaggy hairs for show, and regular brushing. Its coat is weather-resistant, and this breed rarely feels the cold — in fact, it seems to prefer it.

### Feeding
Recommended would be 1½-2½ cans (376g, 13.3oz size) of a branded meaty product, with biscuit added in equal part by volume; or 5 cupfuls of a dry food, complete diet, mixed in the proportion of 1 cup of feed to ½ cup of hot or cold water. Will need extra feed if used for coursing.

### Origin and history
The Deerhound was purpose-bred to hunt with its master by day and to grace his sumptuous dining hall at night. With the advent of breech-loading rifles, the need for the hunting Deerhound ceased, as did its popularity; in Britain, it is now kept only by devotees of the breed. It is said that once you have owned a Deerhound, never again do you wish to own another breed. It is truly a gentle giant.

The breed has much of the Greyhound in its make-up, and it seems that until the 19th century the Irish Wolfhound and the Deerhound were of a similar type. Today it is easy to distinguish between the two, the Deerhound being a sleeker, lighter dog.

*Above: The graceful Deerhound makes a devoted companion.*

### SHOW SUMMARY
**Colour.** Much a matter of fancy. But there is no doubt that the dark blue-grey is the most preferred, because quality tends to follow this colour. Next come the darker and lighter greys or brindles, the darkest being generally preferred. Yellow and sandy red or red-fawn, especially with black points, i.e. ears and muzzle, are also in equal estimation, this being the colour of the oldest-known strains, the McNeil and Cheethill Menzies. White is condemned by all the old authorities; a white chest and white toes, which occur in a great many of the darkest dogs, are not so greatly objected to, but the less the better, as the Deerhound is a self-coloured dog. A white blaze on the head or a white collar should be heavily penalized. In other cases, an attempt should be made to get rid of white markings. The less white the better, but a slight white tip to the stern occurs in the best strains.
**Head and skull.** The head should be broadest at the ears, tapering slightly to the eyes, with the muzzle tapering more decidedly to the nose. The muzzle should be pointed, but the lips level. The head should be long, the skull rather flat than round, with a very slight rise over the eyes, but with nothing approaching a stop. The skull should be coated with moderately long hair, which is softer than the rest of the coat. The nose should be black (though in some blue-fawns the colour is blue) and slightly aquiline. In the lighter coloured dogs, a black muzzle is preferred. There should be a good moustache of rather silky hair, and a fair beard.
**Tail.** Should be long, thick at the root, tapering, and reaching to within about 4cm (1½in) of the ground. When the dog is still, dropped perfectly straight down, or curved. When in motion it should be curved when excited, in no case to be lifted out of the line of the back. It should be well-covered with hair on the inside, thick and wiry; on the underside, longer; and towards the end, a slight fringe is not objectionable. A curl or ring tail is very undesirable.
**Feet.** Should be close and compact, with well-arranged toes. Nails strong.

After a history spanning some 2000 years, the Irish Wolfhound was almost extinct as a breed by the mid-19th century. It was restored by Captain George A. Graham of the British Army, who in 1885 was able to supervise the establishment of the first standard for the breed.

*Irish Wolfhound*

The Deerhound should be shaggy but not over-coated, and never wooly. The hair on the body, neck and quarters should be harsh and wiry, about 7.5-10cm (3-4in) long; that on the head, breast and belly is much softer.

*Deerhound*

# LEONBERGER

## Good points
● *Derived from sound breeds*
● *Handsome*

## Take heed
● *Little known outside Germany, Holland, France and Belgium*

The Leonberger is a strong, sound dog, used for protecting livestock and as a draught dog in Western Germany and certain other European countries. It was derived from animals of sound temperament, and is beginning to create interest internationally. A breed member was exhibited at Crufts soon after World War II, but it is doubtful if any specimens were bred in England.

## Size
Height: dog 76cm (30in); bitch 70cm (27½in).

## Exercise
Would need adequate space and exercise.

## Grooming
Normal daily brushing.

## Feeding
Recommended would be 1½-2½ cans (376g, 13.3oz size) of a branded meaty product, with biscuit added in equal part by volume; or 5 cupfuls of a dry food, complete diet, mixed in the proportion of 1 cup of feed to ½ cup of hot or cold water.

## Origin and history
The Leonberger is a German dog derived through crossing the Landseer-type Newfoundland with the Pyrenean Mountain Dog, the result being a most attractive, light-coloured animal (see Show Summary) that is still little known except in Germany and the bordering countries.

## SHOW SUMMARY
**General appearance.** The Leonberger is a big dog, extremely muscular yet elegant and well proportioned, with a lively temperament.
**Colour.** Light yellow, golden yellow to reddish brown, with a black mask that is highly desirable without being imperative. There may be dark or even black points on the coat. Particularly in the south of Germany there are dogs whose coats are sandy, silver grey (wolf grey) or yellow-red with dark points (wolf yellow). White is absolutely inadmissible and should be completely eliminated in breeding. A small white star on the chest is allowed, as is a little light or white hair on the toes. The colour of the tail is the same as the rest of the coat.
**Head and skull.** The upper part of the head is moderately domed, but it must never approach the length and depth of the St Bernard's head. It must appear generally longer than it is wide. The nose is less obviously open than in the St Bernard. The lips should be well fitted and not pendulous as in the St Bernard, and there must be no slavering. The skin on the head and muzzle must always be close-fitting, and there should be no wrinkles on the forehead. The muzzle is moderately deep, sufficiently well proportioned and never pointed. The cheeks are not greatly developed. The teeth are very strong, with good adaptation between lower and upper jaws. The stop is not pronounced; the bridge is proportionately broad, continuous and slightly arched.
**Tail.** Bushy; always carried 'at half mast'; not too high and never curled over the back.
**Feet.** Well closed and quite rounded; hare feet are not acceptable. The toes are almost invariably webbed; generally the Leonberger loves the water and is a good swimmer.

# PYRENEAN MOUNTAIN DOG
(Great Pyrenees)

## Good points
● *Can be kept indoors or outdoors*
● *Easy to train*
● *Family protector*
● *Gets on well with other animals*
● *Intelligent*

## Take heed
● *A working dog, happiest with a job to do*
● *Does not like strangers taking liberties*
● *Needs plenty of space*

The Pyrenean Mountain Dog is a natural shepherd dog bred to guard flocks in the Pyrenees. Nonetheless it has become a popular household pet with those who have the space and income to keep such a large dog. Mr and Mrs Prince's Bergerie Knur won Best in Show at Crufts in 1970.

They are hardy and good-natured, and become devoted to the entire family. They are not keen on approaches from strangers, however, and accidents have occurred when show visitors have been tempted to give a pat.

## Size
Height at shoulder: dog at least 71cm (28in); bitch at least 66cm (26in). Weight: dog at least 49.9kg (110lb); bitch at least 40.8kg (90lb).

## Exercise
Normal requirements. Strangely, for such a big fellow, the Pyrenean will adapt to town or country, and be content with walks of average length.

## Grooming
Regular brushing will keep the coat in good condition.

## Feeding
Recommended would be 1½-2½ cans (376g, 13.3oz size) of a branded meaty product, with biscuit added in equal part by volume; or 5 cupfuls of a dry food, complete diet, mixed in the proportion of 1 cup of feed to ½ cup of hot or cold water.

## Origin and history
The Pyrenean was a royal favourite in the French court before the revolution. It has never regained the same popularity, though it is widely known and frequently exhibited. It comes from the area from which it takes its name and was once used to guard sheep, and also fortresses, wearing a spiked collar like that of the mastiff. The breed became known when shepherds found a ready market for their pups with tourists.

## SHOW SUMMARY
**General appearance.** The Pyrenean should possess great size, substance and power, giving an impression of an immensely strong yet well-balanced dog. These qualities should be accompanied by a certain elegance resulting from a combination of the attractive coat, the correct head and a general air of quiet confidence. It is of the utmost importance that nervousness or unprovoked aggression should be heavily penalized by judges.
**Colour.** Mainly white with patches of badger, wolf-grey or pale yellow; and white. These colours are of equal merit and judges should show no preference for either. Areas of black hair, where the black goes right down to the roots, are a serious fault. The coloured markings can be on the head, the ears and at the base of the tail; a few patches on the body are permitted. The nose and eye-rims should be black. The presence of liver pigmentation or pink is to be considered a serious fault.
**Head and skull.** It is very important that the head should give an impression of strength with no sign of coarseness; it should not be too heavy in proportion to the size of the dog. The top of the skull, as viewed from front and side, should show a definite curve so as to give a somewhat domed effect, and the breadth of the skull at its widest point should be about equal to the length from occiput to stop. The sides of the head should be nearly flat and of a good depth. There should be no obvious stop and only a slight furrow so that the skull and muzzle are joined by a gentle slope. The muzzle should be strong, of medium length, and with a slight taper near its tip. The nose should be absolutely black. When viewed from above, the head should have the general form of a blunt V, well filled in below the eyes.
**Tail.** Should be thick at the root, tapering gradually towards the tip; for preference, should have a slight curl. It should be of sufficient length to reach below the hocks, and the thick coating of fairly long hair should form an attractive plume. In repose, the tail should be carried low with the tip turned slightly to one side, but as the dog becomes interested the tail rises, and when the animal is fully alert the tail should be curled high above the back in a circle.
**Feet.** Short and compact, the toes being slightly arched and equipped with strong nails.

*Below: The large and elegant Pyrenean Mountain Dog, seen here with pup, can adapt quite happily to town living.*

The Leonberger takes its name from the town of Leonberg in southern Germany, where it was bred by a certain Herr Essig who, it is said, aimed to produce a dog resembling the lions on the town's coat of arms! It was first shown in Paris in 1907.

*Leonberger*

In keeping with its great size and dignity, the gait of the Pyrenean Mountain Dog should be unhurried, giving observers the impression of a powerful animal moving steadily and smoothly, yet well able to produce bursts of speed.

*Pyrenean Mountain Dog*

# MAREMMA SHEEPDOG

## Good points
- *Has stamina*
- *Beautiful*
- *Intelligent*
- *Natural guarding instinct*

## Take heed
- *Will treat its master as an equal—this breed is not renowned for obedience*

The Italian Sheepdog, known in England as a 'Maremma', has a double name in Italy, where two regions claim it as their own—the Maremma (that is, the land that follows the coast roughly from Cecina down to Rome) and the mountains of Abruzzi. In the past some people called the breed Pastore Abruzzese, other Pastore Maremmano, thinking that there was a difference between them. About 20 years ago, following a meeting in Florence, the late Professor Giuseppe Solaro drew up the present breed standard; and as both regions were so proud of their sheepdog, it was decided that henceforth it should have the double name of Pastore Maremmano Abruzzese, which made everybody happy.

The task of this breed was never to work sheep as would a Collie or German Shepherd Dog, but to defend the flocks from wolves, bears and thieves.

The Maremma is a dog that cannot tolerate discipline and, although it becomes fond of its master, it would consider it a weakness to show it. The dog will guard the entrance to its master's home, but will not lie across his feet. It will not forget kindness, or forgive injury, and will protect the family.

## Size
Some latitude in size is permitted, with a minimum height of 65cm (25½in) for a dog and 60cm (23½in) for a bitch.

## Exercise
Exercise is a necessity for the breed's well-being in its formative years, but excessive exercise is not a vital need when the animal is mature. Rather than covering a long distance, their daily walks should be made as varied and interesting as possible, and — despite the fact that they are not particularly obedient — it is important that they should have some off-the-lead freedom. Walking on a hard surface will help to keep the dog's nails in condition. Rain will not have an adverse effect on the Maremma's coat. All it needs after a soaking is a good rub down. The dog will clean itself and soon be gleaming white again!

## Grooming
Grooming should be carried out regularly, preferably with a wire dog brush and the occasional use of a good cleansing powder. A bath should be given once a year—more often if absolutely necessary—but this is a scrupulously clean breed that attends to its toilet fastidiously. During grooming the ears should be checked carefully for any possible sign of infection.

## Feeding
The diet of the Maremma must contain adequate calcium, which can be given in either tablet or powder form. It is very necessary because of the extraordinary growth rate of Maremma puppies. Two meals daily are recommended for the breed, with perhaps some 'goodnight' biscuits. Recommended would be 1½-2½ cans of a branded canned product (376g, 13.3oz size), with biscuit added in equal parts by volume; or 5 cupfuls of a dry food, complete diet, mixed in the proportion of 1 cup of feed to ½ cup of hot or cold water.

## Origin and history
It is believed that the Maremma sheepdog may have evolved from the ancient white working dog of the Magyars, and they have been bred exceedingly true to type on the Maremma plains and hills by Tuscan farmers.

The first known record of what is believed to be the Maremma was made 2000 years ago when Columbella (about AD 65) mentioned a white dog, and Marcus Varro (116-27 BC) gives a standard for a sheepdog that would seem to describe the Maremma of today.

## SHOW SUMMARY
**General appearance.** The sheepdog of Central Italy is of large size, lithe, strongly built, of outdoor appearance, and, at the same time, majestic, distinguished, sturdy, courageous without being aggressive, lively and intelligent. Any tendency to nervousness to be penalized by show judges. Movement should be free and active, giving the impression of a nimble dog, able to move easily over rough ground and to turn quickly.

**Head and skull.** The head should appear large and of conical shape, but in proportion to the size of the body. The skull should be rather wide between the ears, and should narrow towards the facial area. The occipital ridge should be very slightly less than that of the cranial area. The muzzle should tend to converge without showing snipiness. The jaws should be powerful and there should be plenty of substance in the foreface. The lips should be little developed, close fitting and not pendulous. Pigmentation of the lips and nose should be black.

**Tail.** The tail should be set low and carried low in repose, but should curl into the horizontal at hock level in normal carriage. It may be carried above the level of the back in excitement. It should be well provided with thick hair.

Another Italian Sheepdog, little known outside its country of origin, is the Bergamasco, or Bergamaschi Herder, a working dog descended from the herding dogs of Roman times, which have lived and worked for centuries in the mountains of Northern Italy.

# KOMONDOR

## Good points
- *Hardy*
- *Will live indoors or in a kennel*
- *Loyal*
- *Excellent guard*
- *Seldom sheds*
- *Has little doggie odour*
- *Good with other animals (in family)*

## Take heed
- *Will not tolerate teasing*
- *Wary of strangers*

The Komondor (pronounced Koh-mohn-dohr—the plural is Komondorok) is a large white dog of imposing bearing, very strong and agile for its size. Nobody can mistake a grown dog for any other breed. It is covered with a full coat falling in tassels or cords and looks like an old-fashioned string mop.

This is a loyal dog whose purpose in life is to guard the property and charges in its care. It does not attack without provocation but trespassers will not be tolerated.

## Size
Weight: dog about 49.9-61.2kg (110-135lbs); bitch about 36.3-49.9kg (80-110lb). Height: dog average 80cm (31½in), minimum 66cm (26in); bitch average 70cm (27½in), minimum 60cm (23½in). Of the Komondor it can be said that there is no maximum height, but height should always be taken into consideration with the overall picture of the dog, which should be strong and well balanced, and give the impression of vast strength.

## Exercise
Puppies are large and active and require a lot of exercise for good development. A grown dog is maintained in good condition on a moderate amount of exercise. In a city this will have to be given on a lead.

## Grooming
The Komondor has a thick, heavy, double coat; the shorter undercoat is woolly and soft, the outer coat longer, coarse and wavy. The combination of the two types of hair forms naturally into tassel-like cords, the cords being a type of controlled matting. The coat feels felty to the touch. It is unique, and once you get used to the adult coat, it is a pleasure to maintain and to live with. It is never brushed or combed. It forms naturally, with the owner aiding by controlling the size of the cords in areas where matting is too large: this must usually be done on the ears and the area behind them, and especially in areas where limbs join the body.

Bath the Komondor when it gets dirty, wetting the coat thoroughly and using a canine shampoo; rinse thoroughly, and wring with towels. A grown dog will take a long time to dry. Cords do not come out when you wash the dog; indeed, they will tighten up with age and washing. The dog requires standard care for eyes, pads and nails. If the eyes or ears run this can cause staining on the coat.

## Feeding
Recommended would be 1½-2½ cans of a branded canned product (376g, 13.3oz size), with biscuit added in equal parts by volume; or 5 cupfuls of a dry food, complete diet, mixed in the proportion of 1 cup of feed to ½ cup of hot or cold water.

Remember that working dogs need more energy than a house dog of the same size. The same general feeding pattern should be used for working dogs, but most of their extra energy can be provided by biscuit, and it is better to increase this part of the diet more than the meat part.

## Origin and history
The Komondor was bred for centuries to guard flocks and property from thieves and predators on the Hungarian plains. It has worked with and without other dogs, first herding the semi-wild Hungarian sheep, later protecting whatever herds and property required a large and commanding dog as guard. Bred into the dog is an instinct to guard and to take responsibility for making decisions. The Komondor naturally protects whatever is entrusted to it—if not sheep, then goats, cattle, and chickens on a farm or ranch, or cats, dogs and children if it is a family companion.

## SHOW SUMMARY
**General appearance.** A large muscular dog, with plenty of bone and substance. Powerful in conformation.

**Colours.** Always white. Ideally the skin should be grey; pink skin is acceptable if there is no evidence of albinism.

**Head and skull.** The head should look somewhat short in comparison with the wide forehead. The skull should be slightly arched when viewed from the side. Stop moderate, muzzle slightly shorter than the length of the skull. Broad, rather coarse muzzle, not pointed. Nostrils wide. Nose black, though a dark grey or dark brown nose is acceptable (but not desirable).

**Tail.** Continuation of rump line, should reach down to the hocks, slightly curved at tip; when excited, raised in line with body.

**Feet.** Strong, large and compact; well-arched toes. Claws strong, grey or black; toes slightly longer on hind feet. Pads hard, elastic and dark.

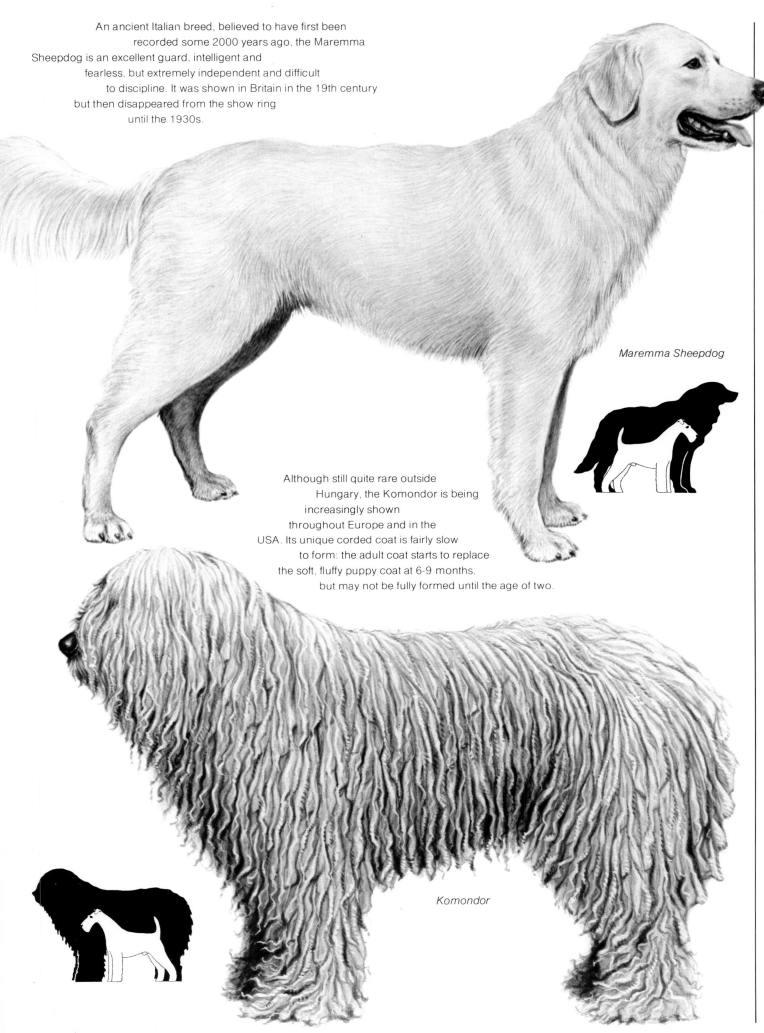

An ancient Italian breed, believed to have first been
recorded some 2000 years ago, the Maremma
Sheepdog is an excellent guard, intelligent and
fearless, but extremely independent and difficult
to discipline. It was shown in Britain in the 19th century
but then disappeared from the show ring
until the 1930s.

*Maremma Sheepdog*

Although still quite rare outside
Hungary, the Komondor is being
increasingly shown
throughout Europe and in the
USA. Its unique corded coat is fairly slow
to form: the adult coat starts to replace
the soft, fluffy puppy coat at 6-9 months,
but may not be fully formed until the age of two.

*Komondor*

# BULLMASTIFF

## Good points
- *Affectionate*
- *First-class guard*
- *Good with children*

## Take heed
- *Remember its ferocious past; if you have one, make sure it is trained and temperamentally sound*

The Bullmastiff is an extremely strong breed, obtained through crossing the Mastiff with the Bull-dog. At one time it had an almost unequalled reputation for ferocity, but today's specimens tend to be lovable and trustworthy, despite their power and size.

## Size
Height at shoulder: dog 63.5-68.5cm (25-27in); bitch 61-66cm (24-26in). Weight: dog 49.9-59kg (110-130lb); bitch 40.8-49.9kg (90-110lb).

## Exercise
Needs regular exercise. A child or lightweight adult would not be able to hold on to the lead.

## Grooming
Regular brushing will keep the coat in good condition.

## Feeding
Recommended would be 1½-2½ cans (376g, 13.3oz size) of a branded meaty product, with biscuit added in equal part by volume; or 5 cupfuls of a dry food, complete diet, mixed in the proportion of 1 cup of feed to ½ cup of hot or cold water.

## Origin and history
The Bullmastiff is said to have been evolved 200 or 300 years ago by crossing the Mastiff with the Bulldog, as a guard dog against poachers, the bulk of the dog weighing down intruders without actually harming them. It was not until later that they attained their reputation for ferocity, despite novelist Charlotte Brontë's loving references to her Bullmastiff Tartar. Nowadays the breed has become a big softie whose appearance alone would deter. However, such large dogs need skilful handling.

## SHOW SUMMARY
**General appearance.** The Bullmastiff is a powerfully built, symmetrical dog, showing great strength, but not cumbersome.
**Colour.** Any shade of brindle, fawn or red, but the colour to be pure and clear. A slight white marking on the chest is permissible but not desirable. Other white markings are a fault. A dark muzzle is essential, toning off towards the eyes, with dark markings around the eyes, giving expression. Dark toe-nails are desirable.
**Head and skull.** The skull should be large and square, viewed from every angle, with fair wrinkle when interested, but not when in repose. The circumference of the skull may equal the height of the dog measured at the top of the shoulder; it should be broad and deep with good cheeks. The muzzle short, the distance from the tip of the nose to the stop should be approximately one third of the length from the tip of the nose to the centre of the occiput, broad under the eyes and nearly parallel in width to the end of the nose; blunt and cut off square, forming a right angle with the upper line of the face, and at the same time proportionate with the skull. Under-jaw broad to the end. Nose broad with widely spreading nostrils when viewed from the front; flat, not pointed or turned up in profile. Flews not pendulous, and not hanging below the level of the bottom of the lower jaw. Stop definite.
**Tail.** Set high, strong at root and tapering; reaching to the hocks, carried straight or curved, but not hound fashion. Crank tails a fault.
**Feet.** Not large, with rounded toes; well arched (cat feet); pads hard. Splay feet a fault.

# NEAPOLITAN MASTIFF

## Good points
- *Excellent guard*
- *Friendly*

## Take heed
- *Make sure the specimen you buy is physically sound*

The Neapolitan Mastiff is a large, imposing dog, usually depicted wearing a spiked collar. It is an excellent guard, but is reputed to have a docile and friendly temperament, being unlikely to attack except on command.

## Size
Height: dog 65-72.5cm (25½-28½in), bitch 60-68.5cm (23½-27in). Weight: 49.9-68kg (110-150lb).

## Exercise
Like most dogs of its size, it is happiest when given a job to do and with a reasonable area in which to exercise.

## Grooming
Regular brushing will keep the coat in good condition.

## Feeding
Recommended would be 1½-2½ cans (376g, 13.3oz size) of a branded meaty product, with biscuit added in equal part by volume; or 5 cupfuls of a dry food, complete diet, mixed in the proportion of 1 cup of feed to ½ cup of hot or cold water.

## Origin and history
One scientific classification of the Neapolitan Mastiff puts it in the Molossoid group. It is a guard and defence dog, a police dog and a tracker, of Italian origin, more specifically Neapolitan. Whether Italy's Mastiff ever did battle in the arenas of Rome is debatable, but geographical evidence gives credence to this theory.

## SHOW SUMMARY
**General appearance.** The large Neapolitan Mastiff is strongly built, vigorous, of rustic but at the same time majestic appearance, robust and courageous, intelligent in expression, and having good mental balance, with a docile, unaggressive character; it is a matchless defender of its master and his property. The general conformation is that of a heavy mesomorph, with a body longer than the height at the withers.
**Colour.** Permissible are black, lead, mouse grey, streaked, sometimes with small white spots on the chest or on the tip of the toes.
**Head.** Massive, with a broad, short skull. The total length of the head is about 35 percent of the height at the withers; the length of the muzzle should be one third of the total length of the head. The skin is abundant, forming wrinkles and folds.
**Tail.** Thick at the root, robust and slightly tapered toward the tip. In repose the tail should be carried as a sabre tail: that is, hanging for the first two thirds of its length and slightly curved in the lower third. It is never carried straight up or curled over the back, but horizontal or very slightly above the backline when the dog is in action. Its length is equal to or slightly more than the distance to the hock. It is docked to about two thirds of its length.
**Feet.** Oval (hare feet), with close, arched toes; the pads are lean and hard, and dark in colour. The nails are strong, curved and dark.

# MASTIFF

## Good points
- *Brave*
- *Excellent guard*
- *Intelligent*
- *Loyal*
- *Quietly dignified*

## Take heed
- *Likes to have a job to do*

The Mastiff is a large, powerful dog that makes a formidable guard and loyal companion, becoming devoted to its owners. It is suspicious of strangers, and happiest when given a job to do.

## Size
Height at shoulder: dog 76cm (30in), bitch 70cm (27½in).

## Exercise
Regular normal exercise, but preferably with a purpose.

## Grooming
Daily brushing will keep the coat in good condition.

## Health care
Their size can contribute to limb joint problems. Check with your veterinarian if you suspect trouble.

## Origin and history
The Mastiff is an ancient breed that was treasured by the Babylonians, fought in the arenas of Rome, and has lived in Britain since the time of Julius Caesar. In the Middle Ages the Mastiff was used as a guard dog and also for hunting. St Bernard blood has been introduced, in an effort to restore the Mastiff to something of the size of its early splendour. Numbers today are fairly low though the author has come across one or two guarding the traditional British public house with powerful dignity.

## SHOW SUMMARY
**General appearance.** Large, massive, powerful, symmetrical and well-knit frame. A combination of grandeur and good nature, courage and docility. The head in general outline gives a square appearance when viewed from any point. Breadth is greatly to be desired, and should be to the length of the whole head and face in the ratio of 2:3. Body should be massive, broad, deep, long and powerfully built, on legs wide apart and squarely set. Muscles sharply defined. Size is greatly prized, if combined with quality. Height and substance are important if both points are pro-portionately combined.
**Colour.** Apricot or silver, fawn or dark fawn-brindle. In any case, muzzle, ears and nose should be black, with black around the orbits and extending upwards between them.
**Head and skull.** Skull broad between the ears; forehead flat, but wrinkled when excited. Brows slightly raised. Muscles of the temples and cheeks well developed. Arch across the skull of a rounded, flattened curve, with a depression up the centre of the forehead, from the median line between the eyes, to half-way up the sagittal suture. Face or muzzle short, broad under the eyes, and keeping nearly parallel in width to the end of the nose; truncated, i.e. blunt and cut off squarely, forming a right angle with the upper line of the face; of great depth from the point of the nose to under-jaw. Under-jaw broad to the end. Nose broad, with widely spreading nostrils when viewed from the front; flat (not pointed or turned up) in profile. Lips diverging at obtuse angles with the septum, and slightly pendulous so as to show a square profile. Length of muzzle to whole head and face in the ratio of 1:3. Circumference of muzzle (measured mid-way between the eyes and nose) to that of the head (measured before the ears) in the ratio of 3:5.
**Tail.** Put on high up, and reaching to the hocks or a little below them; wide at root and tapering to the end; hanging straight in repose, but forming a curve with the end pointing upwards (but not over the back) when the dog is excited.
**Feet.** Large and round. Toes well arched up. Nails black.

_Bullmastiff_

_Neapolitan Mastiff_

The Neapolitan Mastiff is only rarely seen outside its native Italy, where it has a strong and enthusiastic following and is regularly shown. In spite of its forbidding appearance, which is sometimes accentuated by close-cropped ears, it is a gentle, friendly animal.

_Mastiff_

The Mastiff should have a wide chest, deep and well let down between the forelegs, with arched, well-rounded ribs. The dog's girth should be one third greater than its height at the shoulder, and its back and loins wide and muscular.

# GIANT SCHNAUZER

## Good points
- *Easy to train*
- *Excellent with children*
- *Fearless*
- *Fine guard*
- *Good-natured*
- *Playful*

## Take heed
- *Slow to mature*
- *Wary of strangers*

The Giant Schnauzer is the largest of the three Schnauzer varieties, (the other being Miniature and Standard), with which it shares the qualities of good humour, intelligence and devotion. It has been used for security and as a messenger in the armed services; it works well in obedience competitions, and is a good ratter—ratting was, after all, the Schnauzer's original job. However, this giant variety is little seen in America or Great Britain, where the Miniature variety is popular, but the Standard Schnauzer less so.

## Size
Height: dog 65-70cm (25½-27½in); bitch 60-65cm (23½-25½in).

## Exercise
Needs plenty of vigorous exercise.

## Grooming
This is a breed that requires a certain amount of care if it is to do its owner justice. Daily grooming with a wire brush or glove is necessary, and those quizzical whiskers have to be combed. The coat has to be stripped with a serrated stripping comb, or the dead hair plucked out with finger and thumb. Ask the breeder for a grooming chart, or at least a demonstration, before tackling the job yourself—especially if your heart is set on the show ring.

## Feeding
Recommended would be 1½-2½ cans (376g, 13.3oz size) of a branded meaty product, with biscuit added in equal part by volume; or 5 cupfuls of a dry food, complete diet, mixed in the proportion of 1 cup of feed to ½ cup of hot or cold water.

## Origin and history
Descended from German sheepdogs and cattle dogs, this, the largest Schnauzer, was evolved through interbreeding with the smaller Schnauzer varieties. It was first shown in Munich in October 1909 under the name 'Russian bear Schnauzer', the breed being classified as a working dog in Germany in 1925.

## SHOW SUMMARY
**General appearance.** The Schnauzer is a powerfully built, robust, sinewy, nearly square dog (length of body equal to height at shoulder). Its temperament combines high spirits, reliability, strength, endurance and vigour.

*Above: The bristly moustache and chin whiskers of the Giant Schnauzer require combing daily.*

Expression keen and attitude alert. Correct conformation is of more importance than colour or other purely aesthetic points.
**Colour.** All pepper and salt colours in even proportions, or pure black.
**Head and skull.** Head strong and elongated, gradually narrowing from the ears to the eyes and thence forward toward the tip of the nose. Upper part of the head (occiput to base of forehead) moderately broad between the ears, with flat, creaseless forehead and well-muscled but not too strongly developed cheeks. Medium stop to accentuate prominent eye-brows. The powerful muzzle formed by the upper and lower jaws (base of forehead to tip of nose) should end in a moderately blunt line, with a bristly, stubby moustache and chin whiskers. Ridge of the nose straight and running almost parallel to the extension of the forehead. The nose is black and full. Lips tight and not overlapping.
**Tail.** Set on and carried high; cut down to three joints.
**Feet.** Short, round, extremely compact with close-arched toes (cat's paws), dark nails and hard soles. The feet deep or thickly padded, pointing forward.

# GREAT DANE

## Good points
- *Devoted*
- *Gets on with other animals*
- *Good-natured*
- *Easy to train*
- *Family dog*

## Take heed
- *Not the dog to have a rough and tumble with—it might take it seriously!*
- *Not renowned for longevity*

The Great Dane is a wonderful companion, devoted to the family, slow to anger and ready to accept other pets. Despite its size, it does not object to apartment life, provided it has plenty of walks. It is easily trained. Regrettably this is a breed that is not renowned for its longevity.

## Size
Minimum height: dog 76cm (30in); bitch 71cm (28in). Weight: dog 54.4kg (120lb); bitch 45.4kg (100lb).

## Exercise
Regular exercise on hard ground.

## Grooming
Daily grooming with a body brush. *NB* The Great Dane needs warm sleeping quarters.

## Feeding
Recommended would be 1½-2½ cans (376g, 13.3oz size) of a branded meaty product, with biscuit added in equal part by volume; or 5 cupfuls of a dry food, complete diet, mixed in the proportion of 1 cup of feed to ½ cup of hot or cold water.

## Origin and history
The Great Dane has existed in Britain for many centuries and is thought to be a descendant of the Molossus hounds of Roman times. In the Middle Ages they were used to chase wild boar, to bait bulls and as body guards.

Interest in the breed was roused in Germany in the 1800s by Bismarck, who had a penchant for the Mastiff, and by crossing the Mastiff of southern Germany and the Great Dane of the north produced a Dane similar to the type known today. It was first exhibited at Hamburg in 1863, being shown under the separate varieties of Ulmer Dogge and Dänisch Dogge. In 1876, it was decided that they should be shown under the single heading of Deutsche Dogge, and they were acclaimed as the national dog of Germany. This breed is sometimes referred to as the Apollo of the dog world.

## SHOW SUMMARY
**General appearance.** The Great Dane should be remarkable in size and very muscular, strongly though elegantly built; the head and neck should be carried high, and the tail in line with the back, or slightly upwards but not curled over the hindquarters. Elegance of outline and grace of form are most essential to a Dane; size is absolutely necessary, but there must be that alertness of expression and briskness of movement without which the Great Dane character is lost. It should have a look of dash and daring, of being ready to go anywhere and do anything. The action should be lithe, springy and free, the hocks move freely, and the head be carried high except when galloping.
**Colour.** Brindles must be striped, ground colour from the lightest yellow to the deepest orange, and the stripes must always be black;

eyes and nails preferably dark. Fawns, varying from lightest buff to deepest orange; darker shadings on the muzzle and ears and around the eyes are by no means objectionable; eyes and nails preferably dark. Blues, varying from light grey to deepest slate. Black. (In all the above colours, white is admissible only on the chest and feet, but it is not desirable even there. The nose is always black, except in blues. Eyes and nails preferably dark). Harlequins, pure white ground with preferably black patches (blue patches are permitted), having the appearance of being torn. In harlequins, wall eyes, pink noses or butterfly noses are permissible but not desirable.
**Head and skull.** The head, taken altogether, should give the idea of great length and strength of jaw. The muzzle or foreface is broad, and the skull proportionately narrow, so that the whole head, when viewed from above and in front, has the appearance of equal breadth throughout. The entire length of head varies with the height of the dog; 33cm (13in) from the tip of the nose to the back of the occiput is a good measurement for a dog of 81cm (32in) at the shoulder. The length from the end of the nose to the point between the eyes should be about equal to, or preferably of greater length than, that from this point to the back of the occiput. The skull should be flat and have a slight indentation running up the centre, the occipital peak not prominent. There should be a decided rise or brow over the eyes but no abrupt stop between them; the face should be well chiselled, well filled in below the eyes with no appearance of being pinched; the foreface long, of equal depth throughout. The cheeks should show as little lumpiness as possible, compatible with strength. The underline of the head, viewed in profile, should run almost in a straight line from the corner of the lip to the corner of the jawbone, allowing for the fold of the lip, but with no loose skin to hang down. The bridge of the nose should be very wide, with a slight ridge where the cartilage joins the bone. (This is a characteristic of the breed.) The nostrils should be large, wide and open, giving a blunt look to the nose. A butterfly or flesh-coloured nose is not objected to in harlequins. The lips should hang squarely in front, forming a right angle with the upper line of the foreface.
**Tail.** Should be thick at the root, and taper towards the end, reaching to or just below the hocks. It should be carried in a straight line level with the back, when the dog is in action, slightly curved towards the end, but in no case should it curl or be carried over the back.
**Feet.** These should be cat-like, and should turn neither in nor out. The toes well arched and close; nails strong and curved. Nails should be black but light nails are permissible in harlequins.

As a herd dog in Germany in the later 19th century, the Giant Schnauzer was known as the Münchener, since the finest specimens were found in the Munich-Augsburg region. Its progress as a show dog has been impeded, especially in the USA, by the long-continuing popularity of the German Shepherd Dog, and it is still seldom seen.

*Giant Schnauzer*

*Great Dane*

The coat of the Great Dane should be short, dense and sleek-looking; it should never incline to roughness. The dog's ears should be small, set high on the skull, and carried slightly erect with the tips falling forward.

# ST BERNARD

## Good points
- *Adores children*
- *Easy to train*
- *Supremely intelligent*

## Take heed
- *No drawbacks except, perhaps, that the breed is not renowned for longevity*

The St Bernard is a gentleman; powerful, but gentle. It adores children and is loyal and affectionate, coupled with which it is supremely intelligent and proves very easy to train.

## Size
The taller the better, provided that symmetry is maintained; thoroughly well proportioned, and of great substance.

## Exercise
Do not give the young St Bernard too much exercise. Short, regular walks are advocated, rather than long, tiring ones.

## Grooming
Daily brushing will keep the coat in good condition.

## Feeding
Recommended would be 1½-2½ cans (376g, 13.3oz size) of a branded meaty product, with biscuit added in equal part by volume; or 5 cupfuls of a dry food, complete diet, mixed in the proportion of 1 cup of feed to ½ cup of hot or cold water.

## Origin and history
The St Bernard is a descendant

*Below: A young St Bernard needs regular exercise but should not be taken for long, tiring walks.*

of the Roman Molossian dogs. It is named after the St Bernard Hospice in the Swiss Alps, to which it was introduced between 1660 and 1670, where it became famed for rescuing climbers in the Alps. One dog, Barry, is credited with saving 40 lives between 1800 and 1810. The first St Bernard to come to Britain arrived in 1865. The breed had a boost in popularity in the 1950s, when a St Bernard played a prominent role in the British film *Genevieve*, and it is also associated by almost everyone with advertisements for a well-known brandy.

## SHOW SUMMARY
**General appearance.** Expression should show benevolence, dignity and intelligence. Movement is most important, and St Bernards have often failed in this respect, the hind legs being especially prone to faults.
**Colour.** Orange, mahogany-brindle, red-brindle; white with patches on the body of any of the above-named colours. The markings should be as follows: white muzzle, white blaze up the face, white collar around the neck, white chest, white forelegs, feet and end of tail; black shadings on face and ears.
**Head and skull.** Large and massive, circumference of skull being rather more than double the head length from nose to occiput. Muzzle short, full in front of the eye, and square at nose end. Cheeks flat; great depth from eye to lower jaw. Lips deep, but not too pendulous. From nose to stop perfectly straight and broad. Stop somewhat abrupt and well defined. Skull broad, slightly rounded at the top, with somewhat prominent brow. Nose large and black, with well-developed nostrils.
**Tail.** Set on rather high; long, and in long-coated variety well

feathered; carried low when in repose, and when excited or in motion should not be curled over the back.
**Feet.** Large and compact, with well-arched toes; dew-claws should be removed.

# NEWFOUND-LAND

## Good points
- *Excellent guard, but fierce only when provoked*
- *Fine swimmer*
- *Marvellous with other animals and children*

## Take heed
- *No drawbacks known*

The Newfoundland is a gentle gian a protector of children and family, that gets on well with other animals and makes a thoroughly reliable companion and guard; it is slow to attack unless provoked.

## Size
Average height at shoulders: dog 71cm (28in); bitch 66cm (26in). Weight: dog 63.5-68kg (140-150lb); bitch 49.9-54.4kg (110-120lb).

## Exercise
Regular exercise on hard ground.

## Grooming
Daily brushing with a hard brush.

## Feeding
Recommended would be 1½-2½ cans (376g, 13.3oz size) of a branded meaty product, with biscuit added in equal part by volume; or 5 cupfuls of a dry food, complete diet, mixed in the proportion of 1 cup of feed to ½ cup of hot or cold water.

## Origin and history
The Newfoundland is the traditional life-saving dog, an animal with the over-powering instinct to carry anything in the water safely ashore. It originates from the north-east of Canada, into whose protective harbours fishing boats of other nations have habitually come to avoid bad weather. It is believed that ships' dogs mated with the local working dogs, whose ancestors probably included Red Indian dogs and Basque sheepdogs, to produce the

*Above: The Newfoundland is a life-saving dog and will rescue almost anything from the water.*

Newfoundland. Particularly famous is the Landseer variety, with black and white markings; it is so named because of its portrayal by the British painter Sir Edward Landseer (1802-73).

## SHOW SUMMARY
**General appearance.** The dog should impress the eye with its strength and great activity. It should move freely on its legs, with the body swung loosely between them, so a slight roll in gait should not be objectionable. Bone is massive throughout, but not to give a heavy, inactive appearance.
**Colour.** Dull jet black: a slight tinge of bronze or a splash of white on chest and toes is acceptable; black dogs having only white toes, white chest and white top of tail should be exhibited in classes for blacks.
Brown: can be chocolate or bronze; should in all other respects follow the black; a splash of white on chest and toes is acceptable; brown dogs to be exhibited in classes for blacks. White with black markings only (Landseers): for preference a black head with a narrow blaze, an evenly marked saddle and a black rump extending on to the tail; beauty in markings to be taken greatly into consideration; ticking is not desirable. These are the only permitted colours.
**Head and skull.** Head should be broad and massive, the occipital bone well developed; there should be no decided stop; the muzzle should be short, clean cut, rather square in shape and covered with short, fine hair.
**Tail.** Should be of moderate length, reaching down a little below the hocks. It should be of fair thickness and well covered with hair, but not to form a flag. When the dog is standing still and not excited, the tail should hang downwards with a slight curve at the end; but when the dog is in motion it should be carried up; and when excited, straight out with only a slight curve at the end. Tails with a kink or curled over the back are very objectionable.
**Feet.** Should be large and well shaped. Splayed or turned-out feet are objectionable.

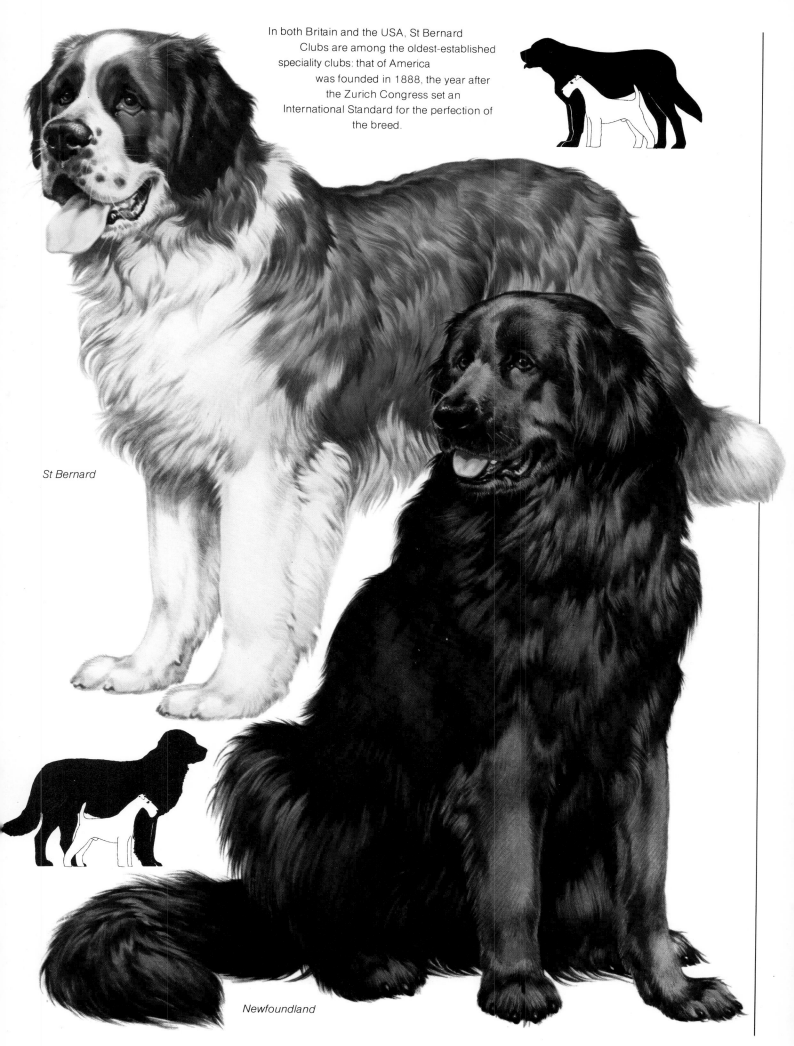

In both Britain and the USA, St Bernard Clubs are among the oldest-established speciality clubs: that of America was founded in 1888, the year after the Zurich Congress set an International Standard for the perfection of the breed.

St Bernard

Newfoundland

169

*Below: The tartar that builds up on a dog's teeth can be carefully removed with a moist cotton bud dipped in tooth powder.*

# Part Two
# PRACTICAL SECTION

*Essential information for everyone with a dog
or thinking of buying one.*

It is a sad fact that many practical, well-meaning people bring puppies into their homes without really considering their responsibilities or the basic needs they must provide if the pet is to lead a happy, healthy life. A puppy is like a new-born baby: it needs care and attention, especially during its first few months of life; it needs a basket and a corner it can call its own, where it can rest and recover from over-curious children; and it needs good-quality food and the right sort of exercise for its growing body. And, as it matures, it will benefit from discipline and sensible training, so that it can become a responsible and well-loved companion for its owners.

Just as expectant mothers and anxious fathers-to-be need sound practical advice to help them prepare for their 'happy event', so prospective dog owners should know something of the tasks and possible problems that will face them. It is to provide such basic advice that this part of the book has been prepared. It consists of seven chapters, written by acknowledged experts in the dog world.

The first chapter raises the all-important question of what sort of dog to choose, and suggests some of the points the would-be dog owner should consider before finally making a choice. This is followed by a detailed account of how to feed and exercise a dog to keep it in tip-top condition, including recommended diets for invalid dogs. The all-important subject of training is covered

in the next chapter by an experienced dog trainer and veterinarian who recommends that basic discipline should be instilled in the very young pup by the owner acting as a substitute 'pack leader'. All the standard training routines are described and clearly illustrated, including general advice on the use of whistles and hand signals.

Grooming and health care are the subjects of the next chapter, which explains first how to keep a dog looking smart and then how to safeguard its health, with sections on vaccinations, regular health checks, common diseases and ailments, first aid measures and the correct way to give medicines. For owners with their sights set on entering their dogs in the show ring, Chapter 5 gives detailed information on how shows are organized, what all those confusing terms really mean, how to buy, care for and train a show dog, and how to make show day an enjoyable and trouble-free experience for owner and dog alike. How to breed dogs is covered in the following chapter, with details of the breeding cycle of the bitch, the timing and mechanism of mating, how the owner can assist at the time of birth, aftercare of the puppies, and advice on the various forms of contraception available.

The last section explains the legal responsibilities every prospective dog owner should consider carefully before taking that final step into what should be a rewarding and enjoyable relationship.

# 1

# CHOOSING A DOG

BY JOAN PALMER

There can be few more pleasurable outings than when one goes to buy a pup. Yet sadly, many such pups end up in a dogs' home, because they were bought on the spur of the moment, their buyers giving little thought to the breed's suitability for their home, overlooking the likes and dislikes of a partner, or ignoring the wishes of a landlord or other authority.

There are times when a change of lifestyle is inevitable and the dog bought with good intent cannot, after all, remain with us for its 10- to 14-year lifespan. Owners may find themselves bereaved, divorced, or the victims of ill-health. Their financial circumstances may change and subsequently the type of home they occupy. But, misfortunes aside, it is essential to realize, when choosing a dog, that we are assuming responsibility for a life — a life that will need correct feeding, exercise, comfort, veterinary care and, perhaps the most important ingredient, love, for without the latter no pet can reach its true potential.

**Think before you buy**

In choosing a dog there are many points to consider. Do you want a small breed or a large one? Would your minuscule apartment be better suited to a tiny Pomeranian or Pekingese? Do you want a short-haired breed or a long-haired one, mindful that long-hairs are bound to need more grooming and, with a light-coloured coat, there are bound to be hairs on the carpet.

Breeds such as the golden retriever offer the ideal all-purpose dog for a family where Dad wants a companion to take for a day's shooting, the kids

*Above: The dainty and affectionate Papillon, an ideal toy breed for someone with limited space who wants a lively and resilient pet.*

*Left: The whole family takes a young Afghan Hound for a country walk. Owning a dog can bring a new dimension to family life.*

want a dog to romp with, and Mum wants a largish dog about the place for protection and to take for walks. The Airedale Terrier, despite its size, does not need a great deal of space, is good with children, but can look sufficiently forbidding to deter the boldest intruder, a trait shared with the stout-hearted little Dachshund, which hides a big bark within its small frame.

Toy dogs make devoted companions and, despite their small stature, will defend their owners quite heedless of their own safety. They are superb for town dwellers, the elderly, and those who do not relish the thought of long country treks. They are not, however, quite so suitable for young

children, who may treat them as playthings with disastrous effect on fragile canine bones.

Boxers adore children and so, in common with many other breeds, do the St Bernard, the Old English Sheepdog and the smaller Cavalier and King Charles Spaniels. Indeed, most dogs have an affinity with children, especially if brought up with them from puppyhood; trouble occurs only when a breed with a particularly strong protective instinct begins to overguard.

Don't be put off if you come across a dog whose personality holds little appeal. We don't get on with all people and, similarly, there will be animals whose personality and characteristics clash with your own, and others with which you develop an immediate rapport.

**A pet or a show dog?**

Having decided on the breed you want, the next thing to consider is quality. If you want a purebred dog with a certificate of pedigree you must make up your mind whether you are looking merely for a healthy, attractive specimen of the breed, or for a show dog. A common mistake among first-time buyers is to imagine that any dog with a pedigree is a likely show candidate. Disappointment, and even recriminations, can follow when, on entering their pet in a show, they discover that it falls well below the show standard for the breed. This does not mean that the breeder has cheated them. All it does prove is, that they have been sold an animal of 'pet' rather than show quality, and probably at a lower price than they would pay for show stock.

The fact that the dog is just a pet in no way reflects on its breeding or soundness. All it means is, that the animal falls below the standard of perfection laid down for its breed. It may be slightly taller, or shorter, than it should be, or it may have one of several other small defects that, though barring it from a successful show career, have no bearing whatsoever on its suitability as a healthy, lovable and desirable pet.

The earliest age at which a pup should leave its mother is between eight and 10 weeks, which is when most litters are advertised for sale. However, it is hard to determine, at such an early age, which animals have show potential. This is why breeders tend to 'run on' promising pups in the hope that they will develop along show lines. So if you want to be 'sure' of purchasing a show dog you may well have to dispense with the joys, and tribulations, of coping with those first six months or more of puppyhood.

No breeder worth his or her salt will object to a veterinary examination as a condition of purchase. You should receive a certificate of pedigree with the pup, and the breeder should provide a signed form for Transfer of a Registered Dog, thus enabling you, for a modest fee, to register the dog in your name (instead of the vendor's or breeder's name) with the Kennel Club. It is vital to obtain these documents, because without registration your dog cannot be exhibited in other than Exemption shows, and resultant progeny could not command purebred prices.

Most reliable breeders provide the buyer with a diet sheet. They also give information on whether the pup has been wormed, received its preventative inoculations, and so on. Often a certificate of insurance goes with the pup, usually for the first three months of life, following which the insurance company contact you inviting renewal of the policy.

### A dog or a bitch?
An important decision is whether you want a dog or a bitch. Undoubtedly the bitch is preferred for competitive obedience work, generally proving more amenable than the dog. There is also the factor that she is uninterested in the sex act except during her twice yearly season, unlike the dog, which is always an ardent suitor. However, there are those, like myself, who enjoy the company of a male dog and prefer its more rumbustious approach to living.

On the plus side of owning a bitch is her ability to reproduce her own kind; on the debit, the necessity of coping with her 21-day season every six months — a time when the normally most complacent bitch will develop into an escape artist and indulge in every ploy to find a mate. It is possible to have her spayed — that is, to undergo the canine equivalent of a hysterectomy — a step that is being widely recom-

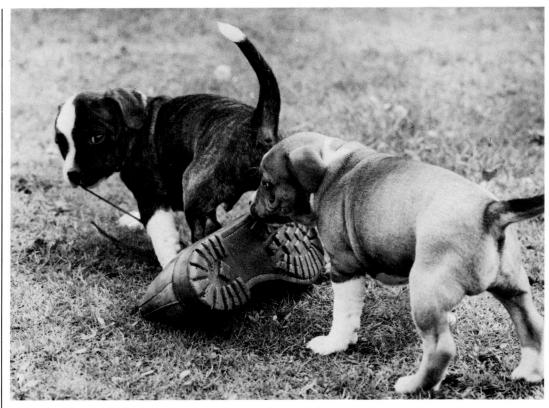

*Above: These Staffordshire Bull Terrier puppies will grow into surprisingly gentle adults despite their fierce appearance.*

*Below: This girl obviously loves her pet Schnauzer, a breed that can be recommended as a good-natured companion for children.*

mended among the pet-owning fraternity to avoid unwanted matings. However, it is a step that is irreversible.

### Where to buy a puppy
Pups are advertised in the classified advertisement columns of national and provincial newspapers, in pet magazines and elsewhere. They are also to be found on sale in pet shops of both superior and inferior quality.

Generally it is more sensible to buy from a breeder who specializes in the breed of your choice, who can pick out the pup that fits your requirements and advise on its care. Also, if you are able to see the pup's dam (mother), if not the sire (father), you should have an idea of how your choice is going to turn out.

Unless the breed you choose is extremely popular, there may not be a breeder in your area, but surely it is better to journey to another locality than to buy a Great Dane when really you wanted an Affenpinscher.

Every breed has its own breed club. The Secretary will put enquirers in touch with members likely to have stock for sale, and of course provide details of membership. Addresses of these clubs, and of breeders, can be obtained from the Kennel Club in London, the American Kennel Club, and similar organizations throughout the world.

In Great Britain, The National Dog Owners' Association, based in Hampshire, can also provide information on breed clubs and breeders, and arranges veterinary and third party insurance, but registration matters can be dealt with only by the Kennel Club, under whose jurisdiction all dog shows in Britain are held.

The Kennel Club, in Clarges

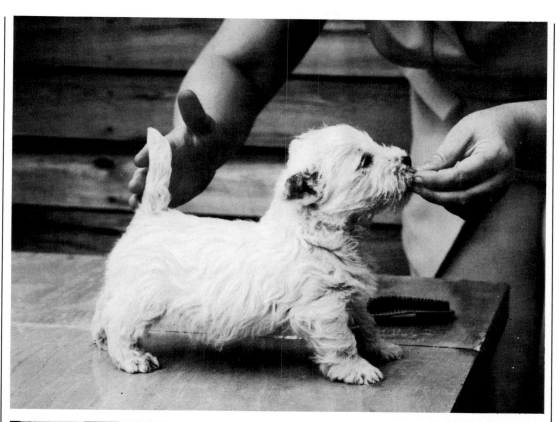

Street, Piccadilly, London, was founded in 1873 under the patronage of the Prince of Wales, later King Edward VII. It is the parent club on which all others have been modelled, although the American Kennel Club followed hot on its heels, coming into existence only a year later.

## How much will it cost?
To suggest the figure one should pay for each breed is impossible. This can depend on the popularity or rarity of a breed, on location, and also on supply and demand. In Britain prices vary between those charged in London and the south, and those in more remote parts of the country.

Generally, prices of purebred dogs range from £60 to £80 for a popular breed, rising quickly to £100, or very much more, for show dogs and rare breeds. But whereas one breeder will tell you that, 'The price is whatever you can get!' another will declare that, 'Soon the £200 dog will no longer be a rarity'. You cannot say, with any degree of conviction, that the price of a certain breed is x pounds or dollars, because in pricing dogs it just isn't so.

## Collecting your dog
Don't go to buy your dog without taking a puppy harness, but remember that the pup must not be put down in the street or come into any contact with other dogs until it has had its inoculations. Make sure that a comfortably lined basket, of some unchewable substance, is awaiting your arrival at home; and don't forget to have an identity disc engraved, which you can affix to your new pet's collar, just in case it should be stolen or stray.

Before you buy, do please make sure that the rest of the family want a dog too. Never buy a dog as a present without checking that the recipient will appreciate the gift, and do make sure, rather than risk heartbreak later, that you *are* permitted to keep a dog where you live.

Most important, don't take the decision to buy a dog lightly. Much as you may admire an Afghan Hound, it is not the dog to live happily in a small apartment, any more than an energetic terrier is suitable for an elderly lady, or a Chihuahua is the ideal choice for a man who wants a hunting dog.

There are bound to be a number of breeds that would suit your home and your way of life, and that would also be happy with you. It is essential to make the right choice, for your sake and the dog's, too!

*Right: The classic picture of man and dog; the sportsman with his attentive gundog, in this case the versatile Labrador Retriever.*

# 2

# FEEDING AND EXERCISE

BY KAY WHITE

The first food many owners think of giving to their dogs is muscle meat, particularly beef. In fact an all-meat diet can quickly kill a dog through overstraining the kidneys. It is all too easy to make a dog addicted to meat by assuming that no other foods will be acceptable, but the wise owner at once establishes a balanced diet containing proteins, starches, fats, minerals, and vitamins, accompanied by water.

Meat is not even an essential part of the dog's diet; a good-quality vegetable protein can adequately take the place of animal protein, and will be increasingly necessary as animal meat becomes scarcer and more expensive. My own dogs have been fed exclusively on a soya bean based complete diet for more than 10 years; in fact, many of the tinned and prepared meats that look so 'beefy' contain a proportion of soya protein.

## The basic facts

The dog is best described as an omnivore, having lived with man so long that it has adapted to human diet. A dog's meals can be fitted in with the tastes of its human family, although an appetite for sugar and chocolate should be discouraged. Just like us, however, dogs need energy-giving fats and carbohydrates; body-building proteins; water; and small amounts of vitamins and minerals to keep healthy.

The newly bought puppy should arrive with a complete diet sheet from the breeder. For at least two weeks after the puppy's arrival keep strictly to the breeder's schedule, even to the quality of milk if this is being given. Leaving the litter and changing homes is traumatic enough for an eight-

*Above: Puppies feed most easily from a flat plate. A disposable one ensures that the dog does not share crockery with the family.*

*Left: Taking the dogs for a walk can become a family outing. Keep adult dogs on a lead in restricted areas and carry young puppies.*

week-old dog without courting an intestinal upset by giving the puppy unfamiliar foods.

Water is the first essential of life. From three weeks old, puppies should be offered water several times a day, even if they are having milk feeds. Older dogs should have access at will to a water bowl in some convenient position. An earthenware bowl is most hygienic and is not known to cause allergies; it should be refilled several times a day, and washed once daily to rid it of accumulated saliva. Dogs should be prevented from drinking from stagnant pools or vessels left in the garden in case of contamination by rodents, birds, or fall-out from pesticide sprays.

Milk is not essential for dogs

that have been weaned and many are unable to digest the lactose in milk after early puppyhood. A bowl of milk given to a dog may give rise to a very loose bowel movement. Bitch's milk is considerably richer in fats than cow's milk or goat's milk. If newly born puppies must be bottle fed, a reliably branded bitch-substitute milk should be used according to the manufacturer's instructions; time-expired powdered milk intended for human infants is not good enough for puppies. The nutritional balance is wrong, and powdered milk has a comparatively short shelf life: puppies need food as fresh and chemically pure as human babies do.

A successful home-made formula for puppies can be concocted from 800ml (28fl oz) of whole, full-cream cow's milk, with the addition of 200ml (7fl oz) of single cream and one egg yolk. Add two drops of a multi-vitamin preparation, store in the refrigerator, and warm small amounts slowly to blood heat, feeding every two hours for the first week of life if the mother is not available. If she has some milk, small amounts of the formula may be offered to any puppies seeming to need more than they are obtaining.

The milk should be given in a bottle designed for premature babies, with a teat appropriate in size to the puppy. A dropper is unsuitable because it injects too much air.

The pregnant bitch does not need to drink milk to make milk for her puppies; extra protein is the very best food to promote maximum lactation.

## What kind of meat?

Meat of any kind may provide the protein in a dog's diet. You can use very lean steak to make balls of scraped meat in order to give tiny puppies their first taste of food other than bitch's milk, but as soon as they are eating actively their meat should contain a proportion of fat minced with lean.

Years ago, gamekeepers used to feed dogs on stew containing whole rabbits complete with fur. There is no doubt that this rather primitive mess provided roughage, protein, and calcium on which dogs throve, provided they got bread and hound meal too; but this diet would not please today's owner.

Feeding the pet animal is an important expression of the relationship between it and the owner, and in fact many manufactured pet foods are coloured and presented to appeal to the owner rather than the dog. This is not quite so misguided as it sounds, for if the owner finds serving the dog's food distasteful or repulsive this factor may contribute to rejection of the pet.

Offals such as raw and unwashed tripe are much enjoyed by dogs, and kennels buy them cheaply from the slaughterer, but handling such meat is unpleasant and may be dangerous to human health if the meat is cut up in the family kitchen. All meats fed to the companion dog are best cooked, and the knives and boards on which they are cut up should be kept especially for the purpose and sterilized after use. Liver should be limited in the dog's diet as it is so laxative, but dogs are very fond of liver, and slivers of this meat are often used in the show ring to persuade dogs to pose alertly.

Cooked lamb, chicken, and turkey meats may also be fed to dogs, but pig meat is unsuitable. Cooked fish and eggs, hard cheese and prepared foods based on soya beans are other valuable sources of protein.

### Balancing the diet
The amount of protein necessary varies with the growth stage of the dog and its activity. For fully grown companion dogs receiving little exercise, protein can account for only 18% of the diet; large-breed puppies growing rapidly may require twice as much. A lactating bitch will want four times her usual ration when the puppies are taking large quantities of milk.

The carbohydrate part of the diet can be supplied by stale brown or wholemeal bread, or by a prepared dog meal, but it is important to ensure that the meal is 100% wheatmeal, lightly cooked, and excluding any dried meat or other addition that would throw the dog's diet out of balance.

Fruit and vegetables are not essential for dogs with access to grass, but many enjoy fruits, especially apples and raspberries picked straight from the bush. Liquidized vegetables and the liquor they were cooked in form an appetizing gravy that helps to make complete diets more palatable. In theory yeast extracts containing the B vitamins should be

## Feeding Your Dog

| Food | Preparation | Age of Dog |
|---|---|---|
| **Beef** | Scraped | From 2½ weeks |
| | Minced | From 3 weeks according to breed |
| | 1.25-2.5cm (½-1in) cubes or larger | From 3 months (according to breed) until elderly or teeth are lost, then minced again |
| **Lamb** | | From 3 months |
| **Pork** | Never. Danger of Aujeszky's disease from condemned pig meat, and hookworm from pig carcases | |
| **Rabbit** | Cooked | From 4 weeks |
| **Chicken** | Cooked | From 4 weeks |
| **Chicken heads, necks** (said to be good food value for hound breeds) | | From 6 months |
| **White fish** | Cooked | From 4 weeks |
| **Herring** | Cooked, boned | From 8 weeks |
| **Tripe** | Washed, minced | From 4 weeks |
| | Unwashed | From 3 months |
| **Rice** | Plain boiled | Invalid diet from 5 weeks |
| **Rice pudding** | | From 3½ weeks |
| **Cottage cheese** | | From 3½ weeks |
| **Hard cheese** | Grated | From 3½ weeks |
| **Eggs** | Cooked | From 3½ weeks |
| **Egg custard** | | From 3½ weeks |
| **Madeira cake** | | In illness, from 4 weeks |
| **Baby rusks** | | From 4 weeks |
| **Baby cereal** | Pre-cooked | From 3 weeks |
| **Glucose** | Dissolved in boiled water | From birth for fluid therapy |
| **Dog biscuits** | | From 3 months |
| **Heart** | | From 4 weeks |
| **Lung, Spleen, Kidney** | | From 6 months |
| **Liver** (restricted amounts) | | From 6 months |
| **Potatoes** | Cooked | From 3 months |

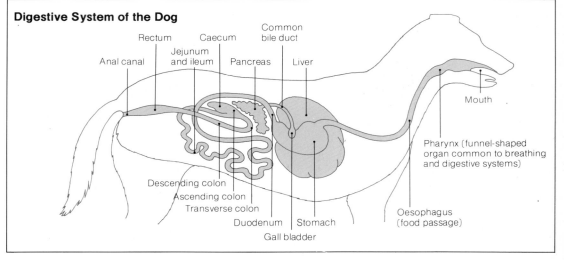

**Digestive System of the Dog**

Rectum · Caecum · Common bile duct · Jejunum and ileum · Anal canal · Pancreas · Liver · Mouth · Pharynx (funnel-shaped organ common to breathing and digestive systems) · Descending colon · Ascending colon · Transverse colon · Duodenum · Stomach · Oesophagus (food passage) · Gall bladder

useful for gravy but many dogs dislike the salty taste.

When the owner can happily arrive at a diet on which the dog thrives and produces regular formed motions, he should use that diet every day except when physical illness requires a modification. Dogs do best on the food their intestinal flora has become accustomed to; adding nutritious household scraps provides variety enough.

### The choice of menu
Here is a list of five possibilities.
1. Beef, lamb, chicken, or turkey bought fresh and cooked at home, with bread or biscuit meal, vitamin supplement, plus nourishing household scraps.
2. Deep-frozen meat loaf prepared for dogs, used in the same way

as the fresh meat, with the same additions.
3. Tinned meat without cereal content, plus bread or biscuit meal, plus nourishing scraps. Vitamin and mineral supplement is not usually necessary, as this is added by the manufacturer.
4. Tinned meat with cereal content, providing a complete meal. Note: this means using extra tins to make up the bulk provided by biscuit and bread in the other diets.
5. Complete dried diet, available as flakes or expanded chunks, usually based on soya protein with meat by-products added, plus fat and minerals. Such diets are said to contain everything a dog needs. In experimental kennel units bitches

have certainly bred well, raised puppies, and lived to a great age on complete dried diets and water only. However, the opportunities for exercise and even the expenditure of mental energy are limited in such kennels, so in a home situation we have found that a little extra protein and gravy enhances palatability, and for breeding bitches we add up to 15% more protein in the form of minced meat or cheese.

Complete diets may be fed dry or pre-soaked. If the diet is given dry, abundant fresh water must be available throughout the 24 hours, as dogs need to drink at night if they are fed in the evening.

The transition from wet food to dry diet should be made over three weeks, and you will notice that

| Food | Preparation | Age of dog |
|---|---|---|
| Bread | | From 3½ weeks |
| Sweet biscuits | | From 4 weeks |
| Yoghurt | | Especially after antibiotic treatment, from 3½ weeks |
| Sardines | | In illness, from 3 months |
| Pilchards | | In illness, from 3 months |
| Cabbage, Carrots | Cooked | From 6 months |
| Cow's milk (unfortified) | | From 8 weeks |
| Cow's milk (fortified) | 800ml (28fl oz) full-cream cow's milk plus 200ml (7fl oz) single cream plus one egg yolk | From birth for orphan pups |
| Apples, Oranges, Raspberries, Blackberries | Small quantity if liked | From 4 months |
| Soya substitute meat | | From 4 weeks |
| Tinned dog food (both with and without carbohydrate) | | From 5 weeks |
| Complete diets | | |
| Expanded | Provide abundant water, unless diet is pre-soaked | From 3 weeks |
| Flaked | As above | From 4 months |
| Soft-moist | As above | From 3 months |
| Onions. | Never. Antisocial | |
| Garlic. | Never. Antisocial | |
| Ham (salted and spiced) | Best avoided | |
| Sausages (salted and spiced) | Best avoided | |
| Beer | | From 6 months |
| Brandy | | Small quantities in illness from birth |
| Tea with milk | | From 5 weeks |
| Rose hip syrup | | If Vitamin C lacking, from 3½ weeks |
| Bones | Very large | From 4 weeks |
| Ice-cream | | From 4 months |
| Water | | From weaning time, 3½ weeks |

## Types of Dog Food

**1 Plain biscuit meal** Ideal to mix with any type of meat or fish to provide essential carbohydrate.
**2 Meaty canned dog food** Made with animal products not in demand for human diet, together with 'meat-like' chunks made from vegetable protein. Feed with equal volume of biscuit.
**3 Meat and cereal canned food** Costs less initially, but you will need to feed twice as much as food 2. Do not add more biscuit.
**4 Canned puppy food** Formulated for puppies and gives them an excellent start in life. No extra vitamins are needed with foods 2, 3 and 4.
**5 Large dog biscuits** Provide good jaw exercise for medium and large dogs. Ensure biscuits are fresh and uncontaminated.

**6 Bone-shaped biscuits** Ideal for dogs to carry about, and not so hard as large ones. Useful to satisfy fast-growing dog between meals.
**7 Small dog biscuits** Available in various shapes and flavours. Good for rewards and retrieving games.
**8 Expanded complete food** Dry chunks containing all essential nutrients. Can be fed mixed with milk, water or broth, or dry with water available.
**9 Flaked complete food** Good for soaking in gravy, milk or hot water. Do not allow dry diets to go rancid in storage; buy little and often.

**10 Soft-moist complete food** Made of partly dehydrated chunks of meat substitute. Feed straight from the sachet in which it is packed. Easy to carry and convenient when you and your dog are away from home.
**11 Water** Essential to life. Dogs with free access to water adjust their drinking according to the moisture content of their food. This is why you must provide adequate water at all times and especially for dogs feeding on dry diets that have not been pre-soaked. The best container for water is an earthenware bowl — it is heavy enough not to tip and can be cleaned easily. Rainwater is enjoyed by dogs but ensure that it is collected from a completely uncontaminated source.

faeces produced by dogs on these diets are exceptionally bulky at first. This is not necessarily a bad thing, as undigested cellulose and other roughage passing through the intestines keeps a dog active and healthy. Constipation used to be a hazard of keeping toy dogs but sensible feeding regimes have reduced this problem.

When examining the content of a complete diet, pay attention to the fat component. If this is above 20% it slows digestion, keeping the food in the stomach long and improving palatability; but fat-rich products have a relatively short shelf life and go rancid rather easily. In fact the storage conditions of any foods bought in bulk warrant inquiry; you sometimes find sacks contaminated by rats in store, or biscuit meal kept next to garden chemicals.

While all dogs do well (if expensively) on a fresh meat and biscuit diet, and most enjoy tinned meats, some types of dog are at their best on a particular diet; you can always get hints from the breeder. Smooth-coated dogs thrive on a high-fat-content diet, or with extra vegetable oil added to a complete diet; Labrador Retrievers and Beagles live well on the cheapest and plainest of foods; an unpelleted, complete diet containing a good proportion of flaked maize seems to suit the German Shepherd (Alsatian). Very tiny breeds need a greater proportion of protein to carbohydrate than larger breeds, which can take more bulk.

### The vegetarian's dog
Where the household is totally vegetarian, it will be a disagreeable chore to handle meat for the dog. An active 34kg (75lb) dog will thrive on the following diet:
2 teaspoonfuls (10ml) of vegetable oil
1 cooked egg (preferably boiled)
2 cups (480ml) of cooked vegetables, put through a blender with sufficient milk to make a smooth mousse
1 tablespoon (15ml) of nutritional yeast
Bulk in the form of bread, left-over cereals, beans and cheese. Feed once daily according to appetite, and for growing puppies add a breakfast of wholemeal bread and peanut butter.

### Vitamins
It is important to read the labels on tins, especially bargain offers. You discover just what you are feeding your dog, and whether or not you need extra cereal. Check that each tin contains those vital A, B, and D vitamins together with trace minerals. Vitamin E for fertility

*Left: This display shows examples of the main types of dog food available. Some canned meaty products have cereal added; others should be given with extra biscuit meal. The dry complete diets should be mixed with water or given dry with water available.*

must be bought as a separate component. Only relatively few dogs need extra Vitamin C, and you can best give this as rosehip syrup. A dog's Vitamin C requirements are normally considered to be synthesized from sunlight.

When feeding a diet based on fresh meat you must supply the basic vitamins too. You can do this most conveniently by buying a complete vitamin supplement formulated for dogs and made up in tablet form by a pharmaceutical company whose name you trust. Dogs find some such tablets very palatable, and they may serve as titbits or rewards for behaviour and training, provided that you keep to the dosages prescribed. Using pre-formulated tablets ensures giving more accurately measured doses than adding cod liver oil, yeast, calcium salts, and so on to the dog's dinner. Many dogs dislike powder on their food, and great care must be taken when measuring cod liver oil, which supplies vitamins A and D, as over-dosage can be just as damaging as deprivation of these vitamins.

When there is need for additional vitamins (during rapid growth or pregnancy, for instance) the number of tablets given can be increased in accordance with the maker's directions. During pregnancy and lactation the bitch needs extra calcium, as her own bodily reserves can be dangerously depleted by the demands of her puppies. Special tablets are available to supply the need; one brand is cheese-flavoured and proves especially acceptable.

An enormous amount of research goes into the formulation of dog foods by the major companies; nearly all maintain big colonies of dogs on feeding trials, rearing, breeding, and keeping dogs into old age. Products are frequently quality tested, and the factories are kept at least as clean as those preparing foods for human use. The origin of the meat used in tinned dog food is not usually stated, but most of the big brand names in dog food are well aware of public concern to conserve endangered species and accordingly avoid these animals.

### Allergies
A very few dogs have carbohydrate intolerance or gluten sensitivity. The first condition calls for a low-carbohydrate diet; for gluten intolerance remove wheat cereals and bread. Other allergens found among certain dogs are milk, beef, horsemeat, liver, kidney, and heart. In cases of persistent loose bowel movements it is worth considering allergies with your veterinarian.

### Amount to feed
There is no fixed amount of food for dogs of the same size or breed. As with humans, metabolism varies, so enough food to make one individual grossly fat may be just right for another of the same breed, weight and sex. Obesity in dogs is as great a problem as it is

*Above: If puppies are fed from separate dishes make sure that each gets a fair share and there is no poaching by dominant rivals.*

*Above: A tall dog will find it more comfortable to eat from a plate on a low bench. A sick dog will also appreciate not having to bend.*

for people, perhaps more so, for complete strangers seem to have a compulsive urge to offer food to dogs whenever they encounter them. Training rewards can also significantly boost the daily intake.

Activity level and environmental temperature as well as a dog's size and metabolic character influence its food needs. A working sheepdog or hunting dog, active all day and sleeping in an unheated kennel at night, will need 50-60% more food (broken into two meals) than a retired Greyhound that lies on its bed in a centrally heated house and takes only a short walk on a lead. A growing dog needs more food than an adult dog of the same weight; in fact a four-month-old Labrador puppy weighing 18kg (40lb) needs twice as much food as an adult Bull Terrier of the same

weight. This is why any feeding chart gives so much latitude in recommendations and only the owner can really decide how much food his dog should have.

Points for consideration are maintaining weight or growth, and whether the dog is contented or persistently worrying for food hours before a meal is due. The well-fed dog has a shiny coat, glowing eyes, alert carriage and a happy demeanour. Sluggishness and lack of enthusiasm for exercise in the absence of any physical disease may indicate an overfed dog. A perpetually haggard look with sharply outlined ribs (except

where kennel club standards call for this in certain breeds) tells you that the dog could do with extra feeding. A dry and scurfy coat may well respond to extra vegetable oil in the diet.

Sometimes food intake varies with external factors: a male dog obsessed by nearby bitches in season will lose weight dramatically; a sensitive dog will 'fade' in a boarding kennel or even when there is sadness and disharmony in the family. A guard dog aware of its responsibility will wear away its fat when there are decorators in the house or strangers continually on the property. Dogs in these situations need increased rations, supplied in two or three meals; but discontinue extra feeding once the time of stress is over.

It is probably best to think of your dog's food, as we do our own, in terms of calories. A growing puppy will need 220 calories a day per kg (2.2lb) of body weight, but a lethargic elderly dog needs only 55 calories per kg. A 376g (13.3oz) can of one of the leading brands of tinned meat contains 303 calories, but you would also feed biscuit meal at 3550 calories per kg (1610 per lb). Using premium-grade canned dog meat, comprising meat, vitamins and minerals in jelly, you can use the following formulas based on rations for one day. (Measuring the biscuit meal into the emptied meat can saves the need for weighing.)
1. For a toy dog weighing up to 4.5kg (10lb):
   ½ can of meat, ¾-1½ cans of biscuit meal, and water.
2. For a dog of 4.5-9kg (10-20lb):

Above: Holding the food bowl is good for long-legged pups, but may cause the puppy not to eat unless its owner is in attendance.

Below: Clean eating. The spaniel's ears fall outside its bowl; the Afghan's ears hide in a cap; the St Bernard has a snood and bib.

Above: These dogs have begged for tit-bits too often; they are now grossly fat. Overweight dogs do not live as long as lean ones.

## Table Manners for Dogs

A spaniel bowl

A mob-cap for ears

A snood and bib

between six weeks and five months. But after this age, when the teeth and jaws have become powerful, it is best to give no bones at all. Many veterinary emergencies have been caused by swallowed bone splinters.

### Feeding the old dog
Decaying teeth often affect the appetite of middle-aged to elderly dogs and general health may be much improved by a visit to the veterinarian for the removal of bad teeth. Older dogs sometimes suffer from indigestion, due probably to reduced motility of the gut. Small, light meals served frequently will help. You must also remember that age may impair the sense of smell.

### Feeding the invalid dog
A dog that is in pain or mentally or physically uncomfortable will stop eating. This may help its condition if the animal has transient diarrhoea or vomiting. A dog recovering from illness may respond to slivers of cooked chicken, sardines, Stilton cheese, or creamed cheese. A cheese-flavoured egg custard will often appeal, and a canned diet commercially formulated for the convalescent dog is extremely popular. After surgery, when a dog has had a breathing tube passed down its throat during anaesthesia, the throat may be sore, so ice-cream, meat essences or puréed baby foods may be used for a day or two. Remember, if you are using a milk-based food you may be creating a loose bowel problem that has nothing to do with the original disease.

The larger breeds of dog, especially those with a deep chest and small waist, seem particularly prone to minor digestive upsets. As often as once a week you may find an otherwise healthy

1 can of meat, 1¼-2¼ cans of biscuit meal, and water.
3. For a dog of 9-23kg (20-51lb): 1½ cans of meat, 2-3½ cans of biscuit meal, and water.
4. For a large dog of about 50kg (110lb):
2½-3 cans of meat, up to 6 cans of biscuit meal and water.
In addition to these rations most dog appreciate two or three hard, small biscuits in the morning if they are fed the main meal at night.

There is now available a 'soft moist diet' for dogs, marketed in sachets and designed to be fed direct from the packet as the only food, although of course you still give water. This food is attractive and convenient, but a great change for a dog previously fed in other ways. It is thus unsuitable unless gradually introduced. Dogs

with diabetes should not be fed on soft moist diets, as these have been preserved with sugar.

### Complete whole diets
The following weights are a guide to daily rations of dry complete diets. A 4.5kg (10lb) dog typically needs 150g (5.3oz); an 11kg (24lb) dog needs 227g (8oz); a 23kg (51lb) dog needs 370g (13oz); and a 45kg (100lb) dog needs 624g (22oz). Note that a Newfoundland dog weighing 65kg (143lb) needs 3000 calories a day, a generous amount for a woman of that weight. Plenty of fresh water must be available.

If you wish to give a fresh-meat complete diet, base it on the following formula:
½kg (1.1lb) cooked meat
½kg (1.1lb) biscuit meal or dried brown bread

2 teaspoonfuls (10ml) of sterilized bone flour
2 drops of fresh cod liver oil, or a commercially formulated vitamin preparation.
This formula would feed an active large dog of Boxer size. For smaller breeds the amounts should be reduced proportionally, with vitamins in tablet form if the quantity required is less than one drop. Sterilized bone flour is the best source of calcium if you wish to give it separately, with fresh cod liver oil as the catalyst. The biscuit meal should be lightly soaked in hot water, and freshly prepared for each meal, as wet grain rapidly turns sour.

### Bones
Large, unsplintered marrow bones may be given to puppies while they are cutting their teeth,

dog refusing food, bringing up white froth, and producing rumbling noises in the gut. The use of a low residue diet (fish, lamb or tripe with plain boiled rice) for one or two days, together with an absorbent such as bismuth or charcoal biscuits, seems to help. Lamb and boiled rice is the standard diet for any dog recovering from disease of the stomach or intestine.

## EXERCISE

It is a great pity that the myth that dogs need a great deal of exercise has so much currency. The unattractive prospect of plodding around the streets on a wet winter night with a bored dog on the end of a lead deters many people from seeking the companionship of an animal. The truth is that dogs are as adaptable as humans in their exercise requirements, and generally speaking neither really enjoys road walking. Dogs need activity and interest in their lives but they do not need mileage, although they will certainly accompany their owner in whatever form of exercise he wishes to take. While it is true that dogs and humans are the fitter for walking several miles a day, many people seldom achieve this target yet remain healthy; the same applies to dogs.

Dogs survive surprisingly well on little or no exercise. A dog imported into a country where quarantine regulations are in force must spend several months in quarantine kennels, where its exercise is confined to a kennel run smaller than the smallest garden or patio. Yet dogs come out of quarantine in good show condition, as evidenced by the prizes some gain almost immediately. During quarantine each dog has the interest of watching the staff go about their duties, and ample opportunity to run up and down the cage in response to the actions of neighbouring dogs. Its day is not boring and that is largely the secret of good health in less than ideal circumstances.

There is a rapidly growing feeling that it is civically irresponsible to walk a dog through streets so that it can pass urine against other people's gate-posts and deposit faeces at the entrance to buildings. In many places heavy fines are imposed upon owners who allow their pets to soil pavements; there is no doubt that such regulations will multiply, and quite rightly so. Elimination should take place on the owner's property or some other place convenient for clearing faeces. If the dog is taught to eliminate in its own garden, then the walk is solely for pleasure, and pleasure it should be for both owner and dog, and not undertaken as a duty.

One deprivation that does seem cruel is denying free outdoor access to dogs kept in apartments. Even the smallest dog should have the freedom to go in or out, to sit in sun or shade, to hunt moles or play at jungles. The dog that can only be *taken* out, however dutiful its owner may be, spends all its

*Above: Children should take care not to overtax young puppies at play, and should wash their hands to reduce the slight risk of infection.*

*Right: These two Yorkshire Terriers from the same owner are allowed to share their quarantine. A friendly kennelmaid keeps them active.*

time under human domination. A tiny patch of garden, securely fenced, provides some element of choice and the opportunity occasionally to be an independent animal, instead of perpetually an extension of the human race. Free outdoor access is, in my opinion, essential to the physical and mental health of any dog.

Most dogs like to keep busy, especially small terriers and the guarding breeds. They enjoy having access to all the rooms of an apartment, and dashing from one door to another to warn off pretended intruders. Two dogs will exercise each other, in play fights or trials of strength of all kinds.

Dogs are amazingly adaptable: they can walk for miles on fine days and do little for the rest of the week. But this attribute must not be abused. Young puppies and old, arthritic dogs alike must not be over-exercised to suit their owners. Boxers, Bullmastiffs, Bulldogs, Bostons and other brachycephalic dogs—those with high foreheads, broad skulls, and shortened faces — must not be asked to take a lot of exercise in hot, humid conditions; such breeds faint easily under stress and become a liability on a long walk in warm weather.

### Exercising puppies
Puppies should not be exercised while they are very young. There is great temptation, especially among children, to take out a newly acquired pet so as to show it off; but apart from the risk involved to growing limbs, tugging a dog along on a lead is the quickest way to instil bad lead habits. Puppies are best taught lead control in the garden. In any case, they should not be out on public ground until their course of primary inoculation is completed, at three and a half to four months.

Unfortunately, this advice conflicts with the need to accustom a puppy to traffic noise and to meeting people. The best compromise is for an adult to carry the puppy in his arms for short journeys through busy places, so that road walking holds fewer terrors when the dog is old enough to be on the lead.

Avoid formal exercise for large-breed puppies until they are six months old, and it is much better for their development if you can stop them jumping and climbing stairs and banks. It is all too easy to get their shoulders over-developed in an ugly way through too much early exercise.

### Other forms of activity
There are several valuable kinds of special exercise. Swimming is an excellent activity, especially to help a bitch regain her figure after whelping. Teaching a minimal water retrieve is a lot of fun with any breed, and familiarity with water may save a dog's life one day. Teaching a dog to jump over low obstacles is a great game for children, although dogs that must be kept in compounds or fenced gardens should not be encouraged to scale-jump.

Agility tests of all kinds can be devised by sensible older children; teaching a dog to crawl under a weighted tarpaulin, climb short ladders, jump through a suspended car tyre, and catch thrown articles fills many hours and offers the opportunity for humans and dogs to discover a lot about each other. A rubber quoit is a safer toy to play catch with than a ball, which may go far down the dog's throat and lead to tragedy.

On stormy and rainy days much activity is possible within the home. Play hide-and-seek with your dog, creeping surreptitiously upstairs, then calling it to come to you, and praising when it tracks you down. Make sure you conduct all play with laughter and a merry voice to help the dog to learn the difference between play situations and those that call for aggression and guarding. Animals signal 'play' to one another by distinctive body movements and possibly by scent. Humans have to make their purpose very clear by tone of voice.

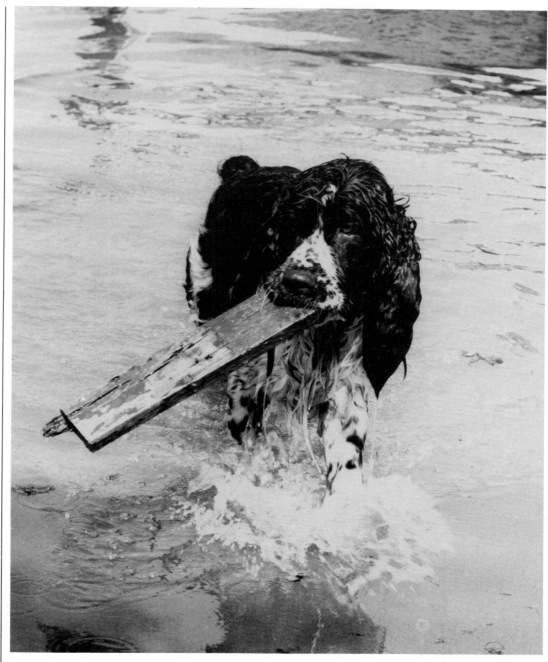

Above: Swimming is a healthy and enjoyable exercise for dogs; this spaniel combines splashing with a natural instinct to retrieve.

But you can use your dog's power of scent discrimination by playing 'hunt the slipper' in increasingly difficult places, or devising a treasure hunt with pieces of biscuit. You can also train your dog to choose which hand holds the goody.

### The beginnings of training
Simple obedience tasks are best taught indoors. A dog will learn the commands 'sit', 'beg', 'down', 'stand again', 'down and roll' from someone sitting in an armchair — or a wheelchair for that matter. First, though, the trainer must teach the animal to concentrate its attention on one person by talking to it, calling it and offering a small food reward.

Where a large covered space is available one or two active adults can play countless games with a dog, and this kind of exercise involves more profitable interaction with the dog than lead walking. Far more behaviour control is possible when a dog is part of a three-cornered football game than when it is ambling at your side on the third mile of damp road. Play in a confined area develops attachment, so that when you take your dog on a country ramble it is more likely to stay within range and come back when you call.

The really tired or chairbound person can still do a lot for the dog, especially the young puppy or the old and arthritic dog that is also disinclined to move around. Gently move your hands all over the dog's body; while you are at leisure you will have the opportunity to detect lumps if they arise, to find knots in the coat, or to see the early signs of visitation by fleas. Massage the muscles of the hind- and fore-limbs of the elderly dog to increase the blood supply. Examine the feet and nails, teeth and ears, not as a deliberate onslaught on dignity and liberty, which the dog may resent, but as a pleasurable grooming activity, of the kind monkeys and other animals indulge in. You may well discover conditions that need

attention to make life more comfortable for the old dog, and you will accustom the puppy to having sensitive areas handled, making its future veterinary visits easier for both dog and veterinarian.

In a growing puppy it may be advantageous to massage the jaw or ears in the way you hope they will develop. Use your fingers to disentangle knots in the coat instead of pulling at them with the comb you use in normal grooming; some corded coats can be encouraged into locks while the dog lies on your lap. Incidentally a dog's smell at close quarters helps to indicate its state of health.

Having built up a close relationship with your dog and developed a number of its skills during the winter season, you will find your walks in good weather give far more pleasure to you both.

# TRAINING YOUR DOG

## BY JOHN R. HOLMES

Many a would-be dog owner daydreams of proudly owning a 'wonder' dog like a keen-nosed St Bernard, able to find people lost in deep snow; a beast with the brains of the movie dog Lassie; or a powerful bodyguard such as a German Shepherd (Alsatian). Before you choose your own dog, stop for a minute and think why you really want one at all. For most of us the answer is simple: companionship and understanding. Whatever its breed, shape, size or sex, this is what keeping a dog is all about. If you are thinking of choosing a dog of a particular breed just because it looks beautiful or as 'one-upmanship' to impress the neighbours, I suggest you grow prize roses or put in a new swimming pool instead: you are likely to get more satisfaction and suffer fewer disappointments.

These introductory words are meant to help you clarify your objective as a potential dog owner. The aim of the rest of this chapter is to help you attain that objective — companionship — by training. It is essential for the sake of your household and friends that you have some sort of control over your animal. It is equally essential for your pet companion to learn that it cannot please itself on its passage through life; dogs that do are insufferably antisocial. Also they do not get the full enjoyment from life that all dogs deserve.

Any kind of dog can be trained, to a certain degree, but if you want one that will win obedience competitions or act as a shooting companion, make sure you choose a breed with the appropriate mental or physical capacity. Mongrels or cross-breeds are doubtful prospects for such purposes. The expert may be able to get just what he wants from dogs

*Above: Turning right with your dog walking to heel, a reasonably easy exercise to teach your dog once it responds to basic commands.*

*Left: Teaching your dog to sit is one of the first essentials in dog training. Tone of voice is just as important as a guiding hand.*

of unknown breeding, but there are few experts about. Here, though, we shall be dealing simply with basic training for the average family dog, whatever its pedigree.

### Think dog!
Training should be based on 'thinking dog'. I cannot over-emphasize the importance of this phrase from the outset. The difference between a dog and a human being is that a person is capable of analysing and sifting complex thoughts, whereas a dog is highly developed in the fields of stamina, scent, eyesight and hearing, but designed to learn only simple things. The trouble with humans as trainers usually stems from their inability to use their

superior brain power from the dog's point of view. They find it difficult to realize that training is relatively simple once they can 'think dog' and anticipate a dog's reactions to a given set of circumstances, instead of expecting the creature to behave as they would.

Above all, owners must realize that wild dogs are pack animals, and domesticated dogs inherit behaviour patterns geared for life in a pack. A dog's simple instincts are to feed, sleep and breed in a regular pattern dictated by the Sun, Moon, weather and food availability. As a young pup it plays and fights with the litter in a manner that simulates adult conditions. When introduced to the pack a wild dog at first has its mother's protection but soon learns that father, uncles and aunts are intolerant brutes. Adult dogs and bitches show displeasure by a sharp snap of the teeth, and the pup learns to submit by lying on its back until the dominant animal walks away.

As it grows up in the pack it learns who are its superiors, inferiors and equals. If a male, at around a year old he will probably challenge the pack leader only to be put firmly in his place. This dominance may have to be reinforced from time to time. If he wins, he will become leader, allowed to develop all the natural aggressive tendencies required of a pack leader in order to protect the group. Bitches develop on similar but less positive lines and will show the same tendencies.

These biological facts have a direct bearing on your own dog-training problems. Remember that your dog is at heart a pack animal; learns fast by repetition and example; and at some stage will almost certainly challenge for leadership, but will be content once its place in the pack is firmly established. In your case your family represents the pack and you, and maybe other family members, represent the pack leader (for there can be more than one). 'Thinking dog' again, your animal must be made to feel that its place is below you and possibly other members of the family, provided they earn that position in the dog's eyes. Thus all aspects of early training can be related to enforcing basic pack rules. If you accept this you will find far fewer training problems arising than you expected.

Taking this broad view of pack laws has enabled me to train to a fine degree many dogs of various breeds, while making allowance for individual variations of temperament. I shall develop this theme later on in this chapter, for it is possible to take different dogs through the same phase in training using entirely different tones or types of command yet achieve the same ultimate response. The rules are fairly basic and simple, but the handler must never forget that once known they may be broken or at least bent by the individual dog and handler. The good handler (the one who has a good relationship with his dog) keeps the capacity to learn and the humility occasionally to be taught by his dog. There is limited scope for dogma in dog training!

At this stage you may uneasily recall some apparently knowledgeable 'doggy' acquaintance condemning training for making dogs 'soft, stupid, submissive' and so on. Take heart: such criticism is founded on ignorance. Training has no harmful effect. I know of some wonderfully cunning and powerful police dogs who play entirely naturally with the children of the household when off duty. That excellent British society the Guide Dogs for the Blind Association trains dogs fully and it is wonderful to see such a dog using its eyes and brain to direct its blind human companion safely through streets and around obstacles. Training directs energy in a positive manner.

### Some basic facts
In the past few paragraphs I have attempted to gear your thinking to the habits and ways of dogs. Continuing with the same theme, let us assume you have decided to get your dog or bitch from a reputable source, and are ready to learn to tackle the problems ahead. You will usually get your puppy at eight weeks old. The dog should look active and fit and be one fat bundle of potential mischief. If in any doubt about its state of health, talk to your nearest veterinarian who may well prove reassuring and help you relax. This is important, for even a puppy of those tender weeks can sense a neurotic owner, and the indecisiveness of such owners does more than anything I know to make puppies difficult and unstable. This disaster can happen early in a dog's life.

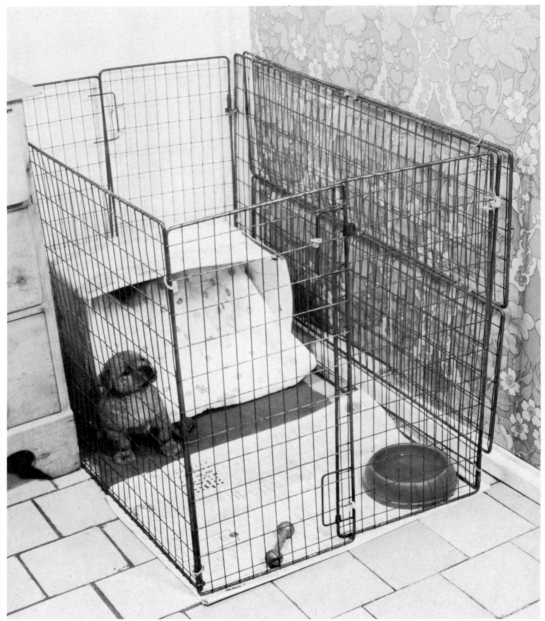

*Above: A makeshift den provides a puppy with a safe retreat; a place of its own in which to eat, sleep and play with the odd bone.*

*Right: A puppy soon learns to come for its food and early training can then begin. Commands should be simple and consistent.*

A two-month old puppy spends a lot of time sleeping and some time playing. About four times daily it fills its stomach and twice as often empties it. Bearing in mind this routine, you should provide a comfortable basket, box or makeshift den. This must be kept in the same place, where your puppy can feel safe and rest in peace. Secondly, allow a play area. Thirdly, supply food at roughly regular intervals. Fourthly, at regular and frequent intervals show it a place where it can defecate and urinate at will.

### The den
Let's now look at these points in more detail. Besides affording a sleeping place, the den (or basket) provides somewhere secure

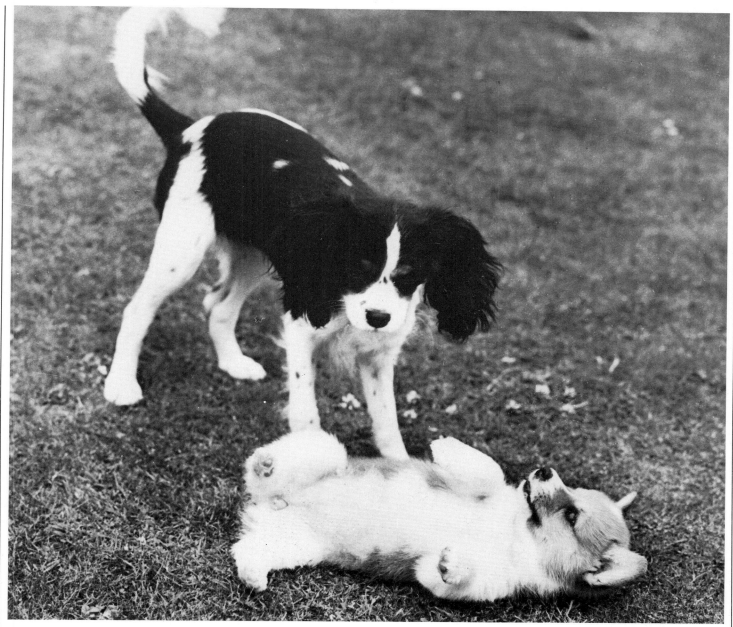

where the puppy can chew or inspect a bone, old shoe or retrieved article. Actions like this play an important part in the pup's education. Only on rare occasions should a pup be removed from this environment for scolding or reprimand. Removal reduces the sense of security and makes the puppy nervous. If you have children, dissuade them from persistently interfering with puppies in a box, as this can make them overtired and fractious. Tell your children to wait until the pups come out.

Incidentally, I am against putting puppies in outdoor kennels, as they fret and whine. They do not learn to socialize and integrate, and it is unnatural in terms of pack law for dogs to be alone.

**Play areas**
Many a kitchen makes a good play area. Here the puppy learns to manoeuvre around such obstacles as the legs of chairs and a table. It may also meet opposition from the family cat, which it will have to learn to respect. This encounter may be painful, but keep 'thinking dog': your pup will

be much more circumspect about the second encounter, if there is one, and will therefore not get injured in the future. It must learn by experience.

If you have another dog, pack law applies, and it will be fascinating to watch the fierce show put on by the older dog, and the fawning, submissive behaviour of the new puppy, lying on its back and licking the older dog as a sign of non-aggressive intent. As the pup grows in age and confidence you can gradually extend its play or living area by letting it into the garden, or nearby parks or fields.

**Feeding times**
Feeding times at this early part of the pup's life are very important. These occasions give you a fine opportunity to begin painless training. The rattle of a food dish is good news to the puppy and should be accompanied by high-pitched cries of 'Pup! Pup! Pup!' or the pup's name repeated. The creature will learn to respond to your calls within a couple of days. Much later you will substitute 'Come!' in the tone of a recall command, which should ensure

instant obedience if correctly carried out. Incidentally your early high-pitched cries are the equivalent of the high-pitched whines or squeaks often uttered by a bitch when entering the den with food.

At this quite early stage you can also get the pup used to sitting for its food by saying 'Pup, sit!' or substituting its name, at the same time firmly but gently pressing its buttocks on the ground. It will soon learn to come for its food and sit on command before the food is placed on the ground.

Your puppy's brain is very receptive to simple commands expressed in a consistent and repetitive manner. Remember it is important not to be too clever: you will get only a token dropping of the buttocks at this stage and should ask for no more. But by making the pup learn reflex responses to the commands 'Sit!' and 'Come!' you will save a lot of time and trouble later. You are also getting the pup to associate your voice with the important events of feeding times. In these ways, then, you have already begun asserting your dominance over the pup before it even realizes.

*Above: A new puppy will submit to an older dog in the house with signs of non-aggression. As the pup grows, roles may reverse.*

**Toilet training**
A pup is naturally clean in its habits. It first passes all in the den, and the mother cleans up. At three or four weeks it relieves itself during excursions out of the den, although accidents happen and again the bitch cleans up. Next the pup begins making efforts to get to its place of relief before emptying itself. This pattern continues through life, intervals between evacuations getting longer as the creature matures.

When you obtain your puppy encourage regular, frequent visits to the yard or garden, especially in the five minutes following feeding, when it is certain to pass something. If you live in a flat you should put newspapers by the back door and your pup will learn to use these as occasion demands if encouraged to do so by being picked up and placed on the paper each time you can see an action starting.

*Above: Teaching a puppy to retrieve is a natural extension of its own instincts. It is a useful starting point for more formal training.*

It is important not to reprimand at this stage, although it is hard not to if you find yourself paddling through puddles and treading on stools when you enter the kitchen each morning. Think dog, clear up the mess and try to show that you accept your pup's welcome.

Quite soon the dog will be clean, in our sense of the word, although in nature a dog and its bowels often become active at dawn, long before we are awake! I repeat, take no positive action against your puppy about these unfortunate occurrences. Time and training will solve the problem and repri-

mand will not be understood. It will only cause nervousness and later troubles.

**A part of the family**
Your pup is now established in the home as a member of the family. It is important that all members of the family handle the pup, make a fuss of it and cuddle it at times. This helps it to feel secure in its new home and part of the 'pack'.

You can try to put a collar around its neck, so that it gets used to the idea. Most puppies do not object if you start this early enough and for short periods at a time. You can also assist at this stage by calling the puppy's name in a high tone when entering the room, at the same time stooping and patting your knees. You can also say 'Pup, come!' using the same

tone and actions; it invariably works and the puppy enjoys it.

**Tone of voice**
If we analyse what I have just said we find some important general points to take into the next stages of training. One is the role of voice in securing control. To achieve different results we use different words of command, like: *come, sit, down, no, stay, leave* and *heel.* But just as important or more so is the way in which tone of voice varies according to the command. It is vital to be consistent in this. I have often seen a handler in a fairly advanced class fail to obtain a reponse from his dog simply because he used the same tone for every command.

Of the two first commands that you teach, 'Come!' should be a

slower, more drawn-out command than the short and sharp 'Sit!' 'Down!' is best spoken with the voice low and hard. (I shall deal with this command later.) A similar command is a sharp hard 'No!' which in dog terms means 'Whatever you are doing or about to do, stop at once or trouble will follow'. It is a command of displeasure. 'Stay!' is nearly as positive but less severe and virtually means 'Continue with the last command until told otherwise'. 'Heel!' is taught later when the pup is able to walk on the lead naturally. The dog is confined to the left-hand side of the handler and not allowed to put its nose much in front of the handler's knee. Success requires much practice and patience, and as lessons progress you can teach the dog to walk to

## Fitting a Check Chain

**1** *A check chain consists of a length of smooth-linked chain with a ring at each end. To form a loop, begin with the lead on the right.*

**2** *Holding the bottom ring in your left hand, let the chain fall through to form a loop. Make sure that the chain slides easily through the ring.*

**3** *With the lead in your right hand open out the chain loop as shown. Below: Place over the dog's neck with the ring loop hanging down.*

proceedings just before the pup gives up the object, and already it is learning a smooth sequence of actions in response to commands.

### Be patient and stay calm

Several points are important at this stage of training. From two months old until its first birthday a dog is at its most receptive stage of development. But at 8-10 weeks old it is still very young and can easily get bored and tired. I suggest that even if you have a very bright pup you should not repeat the first few exercises more than three or four times without giving it a rest. Five minutes a day are enough at this stage — the time can be increased as the dog's physical and mental capacity improve, by the age of four or five months.

Quite the worst thing you can do at this stage is to make the pup apprehensive. Each early training session should be treated as a time for fun in which you both join. Praise for all things done correctly is very important: your pup is keen to please you and will respond to your praise by repeating the exercise with greater enthusiasm at ensuing attempts.

It is also very important not to use any form of reprimand. Your pup will not understand it properly, if at all, and is likely to disappear into the safety of its box and be worried about the next performance. That would be a very retrograde step, so at all costs avoid it.

Another important point to remember is that your bearing and manner may reflect the stresses and strains that affect your own life. Your pet can sense this and will react accordingly. If you need companionship or sympathy it will respond easily, but if you are tense or bad tempered or just out of patience you will be well advised to forget about training until you feel completely better, for all training requires patience and tolerance from the handler, especially in the early stages. Also much harm can be done by short-tempered reactions and oversharp tone and criticism.

So far you have shown your pup interest and tolerance and have just started to guide its exuberance and natural vivacity into particular channels. At this stage you should have produced a dog that is keen to see you and takes pleasure in trying to please you.

### Fitting a collar and lead

Make sure you buy a leather collar that fits. If you slip it on the dog's neck just before its meal, with any luck the creature accepts it without making a fuss. Whether you leave it on permanently or only fit it occasionally does not matter provided the puppy gets used to it.

When the pup is around five months of age you should lbuy a chain collar and attach a lead to one end. Such collars are often called 'chokers' but are more correctly known as 'check chains'. 'Choker' gives an impression of strangulation, whereas 'check chain' implies, as it should, the ability to administer a short sharp

heel without the restriction of a lead, as well as other variations which we shall come to later.

### Teaching to retrieve

Most of us want our dog to retrieve things for us. Whether this is just for fun, or for use as a party trick or in recovering game, does not really matter. The degree to which you use this natural attribute is up to you but it is a great game for most dogs. It seems to be a natural development of their instinct to find food and return with it to their den. A young puppy that finds a bone or old slipper will invariably take it to its box. If out in a field or garden it will tend to bring its find to you in place of the den. Training should develop along these lines.

You can teach a puppy to retrieve from a very early age by

throwing something like a furry toy or ball of suitable size a short distance across the room. The pup will naturally run after it and almost certainly pick it up. Saying 'Come!' while you stoop forward and pat your knees rapidly and repeatedly will encourage the pup to bring it back. When it does, put a caressing but firm hand under its neck and make a great fuss of it, with much praise. This can be followed by the command 'Give!' or 'Drop!' or some other of your own choice, and the object should be gently removed from the pup's mouth — never snatched away. You can then put the object out of reach, saying 'Leave!' and prevent the pup from snatching at it. Repeat the process if you wish.

As time and the pup progress you can insert 'Sit!' into the

**Wrong!**

*Above: This loop is upside-down; the chain will not slacken when released and may choke the dog.*

check to the dog as a reminder that it can no longer always please itself. For training, I do not recommend the use of nylon or leather slip leads and consider them suitable only for the trained dog.

### Dog-training clubs

Once your pup has accepted a collar and you are beginning to come to a mutual understanding, I strongly advise those of you in urban areas to find a dog-training club. This will save the amateur much aggravation and will help him to train his dog under the guidance of experts, so that the whole process becomes clear and simple. The company of other dogs also helps to socialize your puppy so that it shows no more than curious interest in other dogs and happenings around. Such nuisances as aggressiveness towards others or over-excitement in the form of yapping and hysterical barking can then be checked and controlled in the proper manner. The handler can also learn the correct method of further training by watching the more advanced class and can apply its methods to his own animal. Do remember that class lessons should be applied to you and your dog at home or anywhere else.

### Walking to heel

Assuming that your puppy sits moderately well for food, retrieves, and can now wear a collar you must advance your control with some 'Heel!' work. With the dog sitting on your left, the check chain should be looped and applied so that the chain extends from your hand over the dog's neck and back underneath. This allows the

## Walking to Heel

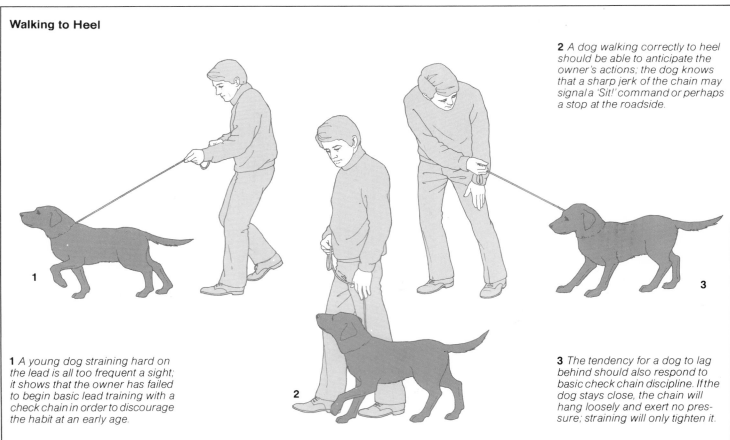

**2** A dog walking correctly to heel should be able to anticipate the owner's actions; the dog knows that a sharp jerk of the chain may signal a 'Sit!' command or perhaps a stop at the roadside.

**1** A young dog straining hard on the lead is all too frequent a sight; it shows that the owner has failed to begin basic lead training with a check chain in order to discourage the habit at an early age.

**3** The tendency for a dog to lag behind should also respond to basic check chain discipline. If the dog stays close, the chain will hang loosely and exert no pressure; straining will only tighten it.

chain to hang slack when no pressure is applied to it. The dog must learn that if it jerks forward or back the check chain will pull tight and cannot be slipped. In fact you should ensure, by jerking at exactly the right moment, that the chain does serve as a true check.

If you walk along slowly saying 'Heel!' all the time, keeping the dog on your left and with the lead in your right hand, you are likely to make a jerky progression but this will get smoother as the dog begins to understand and obey your command. The chain collar pulls tight only if the dog does not think or tries to escape by pulling forward or backward.

This is an important advance as the animal now has to think about what is required in response to your wishes. This stage should be carried out as gently as possible, but with firm insistence. Teach for short periods each day until the lesson is firmly learnt.

Once a dog can walk easily on a check chain you must develop the habit of stopping with the command 'Sit!' and using a jerk of the chain (with as little force as necessary) to ensure that this is done promptly. Then walk on again, giving the 'Heel!' command and repeat it frequently.

This can be done each day as you both walk to an exercise ground, where your dog may run free. Anticipation of this free play time will make it more keen to accept discipline on the way.

---

*Left: At a dog-training club, owners are about to walk away from their Briards to teach them to stay down until they are called.*

Do not allow your dog to urinate on lamp-posts or excrete on the path. This should be done at free exercise or by moving the dog into the gutter so that it does not foul the pavement.

### Teaching 'Sit' and 'Stay'

Your young dog should now be intelligently looking forward each day to its game of 'fetch' with some favourite object. Now introduce a slight variation. Stoop down by it, put a restraining hand under its neck and give a 'Sit!' command. Still restraining it, throw the object but check the puppy, saying 'Stay!' in a low tone. Hold the dog for a few seconds before continuing the 'Fetch!' routine as before. Also put your hand in front of its face at the same time as you say 'Stay!'

As soon as your puppy learns to stay, take your hand a few centimetres away from its face each time until it learns to stay still on both the command and the hand signal. Make sure that it cannot escape past you if it decides not to listen. If it should move, grab it firmly and positively, replace it on the original spot and start again. If your reactions are not quick enough to stop it, use the check chain attached to your wrist and let the dog come up against the check with a bang—then replace the dog firmly without showing any of the sympathy you may feel!

Avoid this exercise if you are jaded. Short-tempered action may replace what should be simple persistence. Do not carry on for too long at a time.

Once the lesson is adequately learnt you can begin teaching the animal to sit and stay as you

gradually increase your distance from it. If the dog breaks away start again, but nearer to it.

By now at six to eight months old your puppy knows the basic commands and is prepared to obey them most of the time. From this basic training we can proceed to more advanced levels if we wish to, but the hard work has already been done, and with no unpleasant confrontation.

### More advanced training

The lessons already outlined set the style for advancing the training of your animal as it rapidly develops into a young adult and grows capable of more rapid and sustained learning. As handler you must insist that lessons learned are carried out. You will have to assert your dominance as pack leader over the young adult. Before the first birthday he or she will test your resolution by trying to disobey, just to see how strong you are—and it is up to you to put your dog firmly in its place.

There is no need for cruelty, and I do not recommend beating. But when I am certain that disobedience is deliberate, I grab the dog with both hands under the jowl and shake it, cursing loudly to show extreme displeasure. (Do not apply this form of reprimand to any recently acquired untrained dog. Dogs that have not been adequately dominated from puppyhood may resent this treatment and react by biting the handler.) I then start the exercise again from the beginning. Even if it yelps, no harm is done provided the punishment is not repeated and that it is truly deserved: think pack leader if in doubt.

### Teaching Sit/Stay

**1** *Teaching your dog to sit and stay is a good basic exercise that may prevent a roadside accident or be the first step to more advanced routines. With your dog sitting, hold a hand in front of its face.*

**2** *Still holding your hand up, give a 'Stay!' command and move round in front of the dog. Keep a firm hold on the check chain and be ready to jerk it should the dog break away. If it does, start again.*

**3** *When you feel the dog understands your wishes, release the lead and move away slowly. Remember to keep you hand up high where the dog can see it clearly and repeat the 'Stay!'*

*command as often as needed. As your dog gets used to this routine, you can increase the distance you move back each time. Try this for short periods only to avoid stress to you and your dog.*

## Teaching Down/Stay

**1** *Having familiarised your dog to the sit/stay routine, it is an easy step to teach down/stay. With your dog sitting, slide the front legs forward by pushing firmly from behind with your hand and arm.*

**2** *As your dog reaches the down position, give a 'Down!' command in a low tone of voice. If the dog tries to get up, repeat 'Down!' and add 'Stay!' as emphasis. Try not to push too much.*

**3** *When your dog has settled in the down position, move round and hold your hand in front of the dog's face and give the 'Stay!' command as necessary. Move away, making the hand signal clearly.*

### Teaching the 'Down' command

The 'Down!' command is quickly taught as an extension of 'Sit!' You can teach it at an early stage with an apt pupil but I find it easier with a more mature puppy.

Give 'Sit!' and 'Stay!' commands as previously described. Repeat the 'Stay!' then return to your dog, press the shoulders down with one hand and slide the legs forward to the 'down' position. You should now be saying 'Down!' in a low tone. If the dog tries to get up, repeat the command and add 'Stay!' until the message gets across. I am not in favour of too much pushing with the hands: it is much better to dominate by voice.

Once 'Down!' is understood, extend the exercise to garden or open space and use the *sit-stay-down-stay* sequence until obedience is second nature. Then move away from the animal and walk around it at varying distances repeating 'Down!' as necessary. I usually find that this exercise can be learned in one day and perfected in three or four days by repetition.

### Jumping over obstacles

It is also simple to teach a jumping command such as 'Up!' or 'Over!' Suit yourself which you use, but stick to the same one. Sit your dog in front of a wall, plank or artificial obstruction, give a 'Stay!' command, then walk to the other side of the obstruction repeating 'Stay!' as necessary. Start with something low and not too ambitious — say 30cm (12in) high as an average. Pat the top of the wall with your hand and say 'Come — up!' It may work easily, in which case just say 'Up!' and extend the exercise by making the dog jump from the same side as you.

If it should try to run around the obstruction, put on a check chain and lead and, using the same method, gently pull the dog over, with the usual great praise at the end of a successful exercise.

### Turning right and left

Heel work should now be extended. You should be able to walk your dog at left heel using 'Sit!' 'Down!' and 'Stay!' at will. In fact your dog should automatically sit every time you stop and it is often unnecessary to give the command.

Now go back to using the check lead and teach right turn. All you do is pat your left side repeatedly to get the dog's attention, say 'Heel!' repeatedly, turn right and walk off. Once the exercise is repeated your dog will learn that the 'Heel!' command means a change of direction, and it will be with you or even slightly anticipating your action.

Having firmly fixed this idea in your dog's mind, do the left turn in the same manner, being careful not to tread on the dog as you turn towards him. You can do it in slow motion at first. This exercise can be extended easily to about turns in both directions.

### Using hand signals

During these last few exercises we should have started using alternative forms of command, namely hand signals.

Your dog should now be watchful and fairly obedient. The 'Stay!' command can now be reinforced with your hand held immediately in front of you, palm toward the dog. Ultimately, you can use just the hand signal.

Next, take the dog to open ground, give a 'Sit — stay!' (or 'Down — stay!') command and walk away 30m (100ft) or so. Call 'Come!', and when the dog is half way toward you, 'Down!' Repeat the command as necessary and get the dog to drop as soon after

## Jumping Over Obstacles

**1** *To teach your dog to jump over an obstacle, start with a safe example such as a low wall or a fallen tree. Using a check chain* and lead, give a 'Sit!' command and move to the other side. To encourage the dog to jump, pat the top and say 'Up!' or 'Over!'

**2** *As the dog jumps remember to keep the lead loose. If the dog is unwilling, gently pull it over the obstacle and show great praise as* it completes the exercise. Once your dog feels confident, try the routine without a lead and with the dog jumping from your side.

the command as possible. Reinforce your voice with one hand held high in the air, and, if necessary, put a foot forward and stamp hard on the ground. Your whole attitude should be slightly threatening and noisy until the dog learns instant obedience to 'Down!' commanded by voice, tone, hand and foot.

I consider it vital to secure instant obedience to this command as in emergencies a swift response can prevent a dog fight or even a road accident. (But however well trained a dog may be, you should always keep it on a lead in traffic.)

It is also useful to teach your dog to sit at heel when you are stopping. Do this by a tap of the foot. Your dog will be quick to pick up the vibrations through the ground and foot tapping is a useful alternative command. (This method is not allowed in advanced obedience trials).

### Commands by whistle

Commands may be given by a whistle instead of by the methods already outlined. I have seen people use various complex techniques involving different whistles, but the handler could be in trouble if one of the whistles got lost. I prefer a single whistle, preferably a so-called silent whistle too high-pitched for people to hear but well within the dog's hearing range.

I use three basic commands. One long continuous blast is substituted for the voice command and hand signal for 'Down!' Repeated short blasts are used for 'Come!' And I give two short blasts to attract the dog's attention and then signal a direction command with arm and body. If I want the dog to move left I put out my left hand and lean my body that way. To make the animal move right I put out the right arm and lean

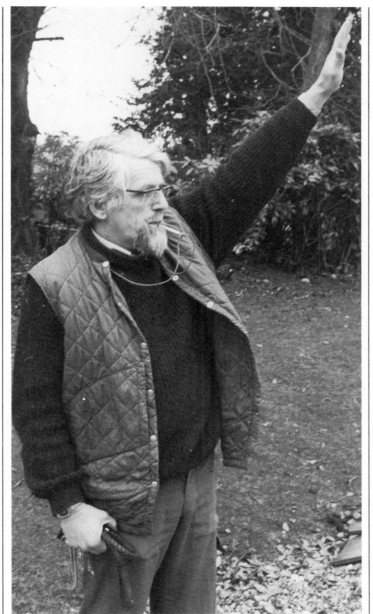

*Left: With a high-pitched silent whistle and hand signals you can direct your dog at a distance. Here the signal is to move left.*

accordingly. If necessary, I walk in the direction that I want the dog to take to make my intention clear.

If you notice your dog getting worried or confused by these advanced exercises do remember that the 'Down!' command is absolute and puts the dog in a comfortable position. While the dog rests you may want to rethink the exercise, or decide to leave it until you have worked it out yourself for another day.

There is an infinite variety of advanced exercises that you can devise and apply, given thought and care; all will add to the dog's enjoyment and sense of purpose in life and should help to give both you and your charge satisfaction and companionship.

### Dos and don'ts

If you meet problems, try to solve them in the dog's terms, always remembering pack law. For instance when you answer the door make your dog walk with you at heel and sit while you open the door. If all is well your dog will welcome your guest. If you are frightened the dog will sense your fear and be there to support you.

**Don't** let your dog hurl itself at the door in a frenzied manner when the bell goes. This may be amusing in a pup but it may also lead to biting when the dog is an adult. You may understand its attitude after my comments, but I doubt if your friends will.

**Don't** let your pet be a nuisance in cars. At an early stage in training command 'Down!' and 'Stay!' so that it rests on the floor.

**Don't** let the creature jump up at people. Muddy claws ladder stockings and spoil clothes. Teach it to accept praise by patting it at its own level. If jumping up starts, bring your knee up smartly into the dog's chest as it jumps up and preferably say nothing. You will not have to do it more than two or three times before the dog realizes.

**Don't** let your dog scratch at a door. If it does, leave the door open and balance an opened can of dried peas on top of the door. The peas will fall on a hard floor with a tremendous drumming sound when the door is pushed. This scare usually solves the problem straight away. Of course the peas do not harm the dog if they fall on it.

**Do** take your dog around with you as much as possible when it is young. It will get bored and mischievous if left alone indoors for long periods.

**Don't** let your dog run away after a reprimand — in its own eyes it will have won the contest, or at least not lost. Make sure it stays until you are ready to release it.

**Do** a little training every day.

**Do** enjoy your training and don't take it too seriously. It is supposed to give both of you simple pleasure and make you and your dog acceptable in the community.

### Turning Right and Left

**1** *With your dog walking to heel, pat your leg to attract the dog's attention and turn right, repeating 'Heel!' as you go.*

**2** *Only attempt to teach right and left turns when your dog can walk to heel correctly, close to your side and anticipating your moves.*

**3** *Turning left is slightly more difficult because of the risk of treading on your dog as you turn towards it. Try it slowly at first.*

# 4

# GROOMING AND HEALTH CARE

BY MICHAEL FINDLAY

Grooming is an essential part of the daily routine, undertaken by responsible owners from the day they acquire their dog or puppy. It is important not only to groom enthusiastically, but to use the right brushing and combing technique; to know what equipment is required; and to be reasonably well informed about toilet preparations such as shampoos.

Why is it necessary to groom dogs daily? In addition to improving the appearance, daily grooming removes old, dead hair and so reduces the amount of loose hair falling on carpets and other furnishings. Frequent grooming also prevents matting or felting of the coat in long-coated breeds, and simplifies the work of the dog-clipper or groomer in breeds such as Poodles that require to be formally clipped or stripped at intervals. Properly performed brushing and combing also removes dirt and parasitic insects from fur, and by stimulating the blood supply to the skin produces a healthier and more supple coat. Grooming is even alleged to improve muscle tone in the back and limbs in the same way as massage benefits the human body.

Furthermore, regular grooming helps the owner to detect skin ailments and some other conditions at the outset. This makes possible early veterinary diagnosis and advice, leading to a cure after a relatively short period of treatment, and therefore a saving in cost. It is amazing how many dogs are presented at surgery in an advanced state of matted fur or with very overgrown nails, purely because routine grooming has been neglected by the owners.

Dogs can be subdivided conveniently into long-coated dogs such as Old English Sheepdogs,

*Above: Grooming a short-coated dog using a wire brush. A comb, a bristle brush for finishing, and powder are at hand.*

*Left: Grooming a long-coated dog using a stiff brush for coat penetration. Combing is also essential to unmat the long hairs.*

Afghans and Yorkshire Terriers, and short-coated dogs such as Boxers, Dachshunds and Labrador Retrievers.

### Grooming equipment
Buy dog-grooming equipment designed for that purpose, rather than using combs or hair brushes made for human hair. Selection of tools will depend on the hair type of the dog. Advice can be freely obtained from pet shops and dog shows, where a vast range of suitable equipment can be seen. Also, the breeder from whom you obtain your puppy may tell you of his or her own preferences.

Generally speaking, short-coated dogs should be brushed daily with a firm brush. This should be used in long sweeping strokes, following the lie of the fur, and it is easiest if the owner always follows the same sequence, for example: back, belly, chest, limbs and tail. Care must be exercised when grooming the head or around other sensitive areas such as the sheath or vulva.

With the long-coated dogs, brushing alone does not suffice, because only the top coat will benefit, while the under-coat — usually responsible for matting or felting — remains untouched. For these dogs, then, you need not only a bristle brush but a wire brush or a metal comb that will penetrate through to the skin. But it is unwise for an inexperienced owner to use a de-matting comb, designed to remove already-formed mats. If used incorrectly, combs of this type may cause severe skin lacerations. Veterinary surgeries and grooming parlours use de-matting combs only as a last resort, in cases of severe neglect, and often with the animal sedated or under an anaesthetic.

As with short-coated dogs, long-haired dogs should be groomed systematically. Use the comb for the soft fur behind the ears, on the feathers down the back of the limbs, the tail, the armpits, and any other sites where the fur tends to tangle and knot.

Professionals also include in their grooming kit a pad of silk or velvet to produce a brilliant shine when their brushing and combing is complete; you will see this in use at dog shows, especially on short-coated dogs immediately before the animals enter the ring.

### Cleaning your dog
Few people seem to know how often to bath their pets. Regular bathing, using a shampoo or

## Basic Grooming Equipment

1. Dual-purpose (double-sided) brush for general use.
2. Dematting comb. Use with care to prevent laceration.
3. Metal comb — fine teeth for short coats, coarse for long.
4. Glove brush (hound glove), worn on hand to follow body.
5. Nail cutters — human toe-nail type for curled nails.
6. Double-sided comb combines coarse and fine teeth.
7. Insecticidal dusting powder, from veterinarian or pet store. Follow instructions.
8. Talcum powder (French chalk) for general cleansing.
9. Soap — cosmetic for cleansing, insecticidal against fleas.
10. Shampoo-like soap, for cleansing or anti-parasitic use. Follow instructions.
11. Nail cutters (guillotine type), for comfortable cutting.
12. Thinning scissors, used to thin coats with minimal cutting.
13. Trimming scissors for general coat shortening.
14. Bristle grooming brush for general use, with strap.
15. Medicated skin dressings, supplied by a veterinarian. Use does not de-oil coat.
16. Curved (Mayo) scissors for trimming, especially feet.
17. Stripping knife for terrier coats. Use 2-3 times per year.
18. Wire brush. Good general tool combining brush/comb.

detergent, undoubtedly removes the oils in the coat, taking away its natural waterproofing and thereby often making the animal more sensitive to chills and muscular rheumatism. But there are times when you just must bath a dog because it gets in a mess, often by rolling on an unsavoury substance such as a long-dead rabbit or a cow pat or by wallowing in mud. In such cases, the dog may be bathed with impunity.

Many dogs of the short-coated varieties may go through their lives without a bath, particularly if the daily grooming is adequate. Breeds such as Poodles, which are clipped at six- to eight-week intervals, are invariably bathed during this process to assist the clipper, and therefore rarely require supplementary baths.

Long-coated dogs, especially those being shown, will probably benefit from baths at intervals of not less than one month to stop

*Left: Grooming a short-coat using a hound glove. The brush shapes to the contours of the dog comfortably to tone up its muscles.*

Left: Bathing. Shampoo in plastic, unbreakable container. Large dogs must be bathed in a domestic bath, unless you have a very big sink, or bath-time can be messy.

them smelling 'doggy'. But bathing a long-coated dog with incipient matting may make the matting much worse. Frequency of bathing will also depend on the size and co-operation of the dog, and the bathing and drying facilities that you have available.

The dog should be groomed continuously while it is drying, preferably section by section under a hair-drier. Most of the domestic hair-driers are simply not powerful enough for this purpose, and you may need one built for commercial use.

Regarding the choice of shampoo, a medicated or insecticidal shampoo is needed where external parasites such as fleas are present or in summer when the risk of infestation is high. The selection of such a shampoo is often best entrusted to the local veterinarian, whose staff will advise. (Alternatively, aerosol sprays or dusting powder can be satisfactorily substituted for a bath where parasites are seen.) For general cleansing purposes a wide range of dog shampoos is available on the market, though many authorities believe it is best to use a mild, good-quality human shampoo—for example, baby shampoo—and this is often considerably cheaper than proprietary dog preparations.

Your veterinarian may prescribe other types of shampoo for various skin conditions, and these should be used exactly according to instructions and destroyed when the treatment is complete. As with other medications, it is dangerous to store and subsequently use left-over shampoos.

A further alternative to bathing, and one particularly useful for pale-coated dogs, is dusting talcum powder (French chalk) into the coat. Talcum powder particles have the power to absorb dust and dirt. Such preparations have the disadvantage of being messy, and it is important to brush out every trace of powder after it has been in the coat for 15-30 minutes. Care should be taken to ensure that the dog does not inhale the talcum powder particles.

**Regular inspections**
Many conscientious owners allot a small amount of time at, say, weekly intervals, to attend to various other parts of their dogs. For instance they check whether the anal glands (scent glands) need to be emptied, as some dogs require this to be done frequently. Owners can be shown how to do this straightforward and simple task, but because it is rather

Left: Drying. Have adequate towels to hand before bathing. Remove excess water and finish with hot-air drier, or exercise until dry.

unpleasant many prefer to have it done by veterinarian or groomer.

Weekly checks on the length of the nails will ensure that these do not grow either so long that they risk snapping off or so curved that they resemble rams' horns and stick into the flesh. Pay particular attention to the dew-claws that many dogs have on the inside of their front or hind legs a few inches above the ground. Because these claws never come into contact with the ground they are not worn down like the main nails of an active dog exercised on a hard surface. In active dogs the nails seldom need trimming.

The teeth should also be checked, and small amounts of tartar can be carefully removed by a cotton bud moistened and dipped in a tooth powder. Teeth with severe tartar deposits, however, require veterinary attention, usually under anaesthetic.

The ears should be checked at least once a week, but the owner should not be tempted to probe around any parts of the ear that cannot be clearly seen. Similarly, it is unwise to use ear drops except as prescribed by a veterinarian. A drop of almond oil or olive oil may be safely instilled in each ear the day before the ears are to be cleaned out: this will help to soften and loosen any wax.

Eyes usually require no attention, except in certain breeds such as the Pekingese, where there may be an overflow of tears that result in streaks down the cheeks. You can cleanse these tear streaks once or twice daily, using a pad of cotton wool moistened with a human eyewash.

The final piece of equipment invaluable to many dog owners is a pair of curved, blunt-ended scissors (Mayo scissors), which can be employed usefully to trim the fur, especially on the soles of the feet between the pads.

A well-groomed dog is a delight and a credit to its owner, who has the added reassurance of a fully cared-for pet.

## HEALTH CARE

In general, dogs are healthy animals, but of course all are liable to accident and injury and there are problems specific to certain breeds. Such problems include respiratory disease in short-nosed varieties such as Pugs and Bulldogs; lameness in large breeds such as German Shepherds (Alsatians), Labradors and St Bernards; and heart disease in Pekingese and Cavalier King Charles Spaniels. It is also true that a number of inherited conditions are found in specific breeds.

Before you acquire a dog you should therefore ask a reputable breeder or veterinarian about the possible risks. It is also a wise safeguard to have your new puppy checked for signs of such ailments within days of purchase, and if necessary to make such a purchase conditional on the animal's being found free from congenital disorders. Congenital ailments are those with which puppies are

*Above: Regular dental care. Small films of tartar may be removed with a cotton bud moistened and dipped in toothpowder.*

*Left and below: Cutting nails. Hold foot firmly and cut safely below the quick to avoid bleeding and pain. The quick can be seen in white nails, but is masked in black.*

**Trimming Nails**

Quick

Recommended cut

Above: Cleansing the ear with a slightly moistened cotton bud. Never attempt to probe into the ear recesses that you cannot see.

Left: Mayo scissors are used to remove sticky material adhering to the long fur between the toes. Take care not to cut the web or pad.

born, and may or may not be inheritable when breeding.

Many puppy problems can be quickly discovered and remedied. But some serious conditions believed to be inherited cannot be diagnosed with certainty in very young animals. For example a dog must be at least six months old before it can be examined for signs of progressive retinal atrophy and hip dysplasia. However, one can minimize the likelihood of acquiring dogs with these conditions by buying from breeding stock already certified clear.

## Vaccinations

Where possible, prevention is better than cure. A number of reliable vaccines free from side effects have been in use for many years to protect against specific illnesses, notably distemper (hard pad) and canine infectious hepatitis (a liver inflammation, which used to be called Rubarth's disease). Two forms of a serious disease affecting the kidneys and liver are also preventable by vaccination. These are leptospirosis canicola and leptospirosis icterohaemorrhagia (Weil's disease). The latter is considered a public health risk for it can be transmitted to humans, so all dog owners should ensure that their pet is vaccinated against it.

In most countries rabies is present and vaccination against it is essential for the sake of the dog and the family. At the time of writing, rabies does not occur in certain parts of the world, notably Australasia and the United Kingdom. Here vaccination is not required, and vaccine is not widely available. If you are in doubt, the safest plan is to discuss this subject with your veterinarian, who will advise according to the regulations in effect where you live.

As a rule, vaccination against distemper, hepatitis and leptospirosis (DHL) is commonest at about 9-10 weeks of age; normally two injections, with an interval of two to three weeks, are required to give full protection. Since the immunity given by the initial vaccination can wane, boosters should be given at intervals suggested by your veterinarian. That usually means a yearly trip to the clinic, but anyway this is a good chance for your veterinarian to give the dog a general check and for you to ask any questions that have been at the back of your mind. Most authorities consider that booster vaccinations should be given throughout a dog's life, since there is no reliable evidence to show that age makes dogs less susceptible to the above diseases. Vaccinations are usually free from side effects, and it is rare for these to be bad enough to preclude giving boosters.

## Worms

Worming is an extremely important and underrated aspect of health care. Dogs can suffer from various tyes of worms: roundworms, tapeworms, hookworms, whipworms and (in some areas of the world) heartworms.

The common dog roundworm (*Toxocara canis*) is a great problem in some communities, for the sticky eggs voided by infected dogs may be swallowed by people — especially children. When the eggs hatch and the larvae travel through the human body the results are a variety of unpleasant and serious symptoms.

Inexpensive worming preparations against roundworms are easily available from veterinarians. Regular dosing of dogs in contact with children is advocated, with commonsense hygiene such as removing faeces, washing children's hands, and giving the dog its own feeding and drinking receptacles. The dose of such tablets is proportional to the animal's weight, and the dog must be weighed so that the proper dose can be calculated.

Particularly at risk are young puppies, and bitches before whelping and while suckling their litter. Many veterinarians will therefore recommend worming at two-weekly intervals in these cases; otherwise once every three to six months may be enough.

Tapeworms are generally regarded as less of a problem, except for the beef and sheep tapeworm(*Echinococcus granulosus).* This is a particular problem in dogs fed on raw condemned offal, especially where sheep farming is intensive, as in much of New Zealand. Again, the remedy is simple: excluding all such undesirable parts of the diet and regular worming (say every 6-12 months) with a drug effective for tapeworms. A commoner tapeworm in dogs is *Dipylidium caninum,* acquired by swallowing fleas while self-grooming. This tapeworm is thought to produce few, if any, ill effects. It, too, is cleared by using a drug toxic to tapeworms. There are now drugs that are effective against both tapeworms and roundworms.

**Dog Worms with Eggs**
(Not to scale)

**1** *Roundworm (Toxocara canis)*
**2** *Tapeworm (Dipylidium caninum)* **3** *Whipworm (Trichuris vulpis)* **4** *Hookworm (Ancylostoma caninum)*

In the United Kingdom hookworms seem of little significance except in certain kennels, where the problem is endemic. Thus you are likely to encounter them only if buying a puppy from such an establishment. In some areas of the world hookworms cause a much greater problem. They will respond to roundworm medications.

Whipworms are basically a parasite of foxes, but are occasionally encountered in dogs. Fortunately they are easily treated.

Dogs that have been in the tropics may suffer from heart-worm, which can give rise to circulatory problems. Treatment is by means of a specific drug available only from veterinarians.

**Diet**
With improved education and acceptable prepared foods, dietary deficiencies are rarely encountered nowadays. Virtually all leading pet-food manufacturers have taken a responsible attitude in ensuring that their products are not only tasty but nourishing, with essential minerals and vitamins as well as protein and carbohydrate. However, getting the best from such foods means carefully following the feeding instructions on the can or packet.

In general, prepared food can be divided into moist canned, semi-moist and dry; the type selected depends largely on the preference of the owner or the foibles of the dog. Some dogs with digestive problems do better on semi-moist or dry food. Also, the offal content of some tins may result in diarrhoea because the protein level is too high.

Feeding fresh meat or butcher's scraps is less common than it once was, partly because of high cost and because fresh meat does not keep well. If using this method you may need to add certain vitamin and mineral supplements. Usually such supplements are unnecessary where animals are fed on prepared foods, but young growing dogs, especially those of large breeds, may need extra calcium, phosphorus and vitamin D until at least six months old, preferably until the age of nine months or a year. Similar recommendations are frequently given for bitches during the latter half of pregnancy and right through lactation. In all these cases the supplements largely reflect a much increased need for calcium, either for bone formation or to replace calcium drawn from the bitch's milk.

Very old animals and those recovering from a major illness or operation also benefit from a food supplement containing vitamins and minerals. There are many reliable brands on the market, in liquid, powder or tablet form to suit the convenience of the owner and the preference of the dog.

Feeding can also influence coat condition. Owners frequently complain of their dogs' poor coats. Possible factors include frequency of swimming, bathing or grooming, and the temperature of the dog's environment. Too warm an environment, especially a centrally heated house, can produce poor coat quality, but this can often be remedied by feeding unsaturated fatty acids. The best sources are vegetable oils, available as liquids and in soft margarine. Giving too much may cause diarrhoea, so restrict amounts to alternate-day doses related to the size of the dog. Vegetable oils improve coat oil production and enhance overall condition. A word of warning: animal fats such as butter and milk will not produce this effect.

*Above: Exercise is essential for all dogs. Always exercise on a lead unless your dog is safe from traffic and will return on command.*

**Exercise**
All dogs need exercise, some more than others. It is a fallacy that the amount of exercise varies directly with the size of the dog: for example, Great Danes are happy with considerably less exercise than terriers. Although breeds such as the Jack Russell Terrier are frequently advocated for the city dweller, this is not good advice unless they can have large areas in which to run free.

Generally speaking, the amount of exercise required varies according to the original purpose for which the various breeds were developed. Game dogs such as spaniels and retrievers were bred for a 12-hour working day in the season, and accordingly need plenty of exercise. Boxers, on the other hand, were originally bred as guard dogs, and tend to enjoy a more sedentary life. It is a great mistake to carry toy breeds everywhere, for Chihuahuas, Pekingese and Yorkshire Terriers enjoy walking and need the exercise.

It is possible to over-exercise dogs, especially puppies of the large breeds up to the age of six months. This can result in permanent deformity of tendons and ligaments. Bitches in the latter half of pregnancy should be allowed whatever exercise they select themselves. Old dogs may suffer from rheumatism or arthritis; they should still be given exercise, but

*Above: Cleansing the eye-lid area using moistened cotton wool. Use a new pad for each eye. Cleanse carefully, using a gentle eyewash.*

judiciously. If such animals are allowed to rest all the time they stiffen up; most seem greatly improved after short walks, which can be given frequently throughout the day. In the heat of summer, individuals with heart conditions or breeds such as Pugs and Bulldogs with difficulty in breathing should be exercised only in the cool of early morning or late evening, to allow them to rest during the hottest part of the day.

Swimming is an integral part of exercise for many breeds and should be encouraged if the dog shows interest. It is, of course, wise to avoid dirty ponds or oil-polluted sea water. Similarly, you should keep your dog on a leash near dangerous waters such as rivers in flood, in case the animal plunges in and gets into difficulties. Domes-

*Above: Weighing the average-sized dog on bathroom scales. Subtract owner's weight from the combined owner/dog weight. Check weekly.*

tic swimming pools can be dangerous because of their structure; dogs can easily get in but may fail to get out without help.

### Regular health checks
Like cars, dogs need regular checks. Grooming time is a convenient point, especially for long-coated dogs, which should be groomed daily and fastidiously. Paws should be checked for length of nails, and for flint, glass or thorns sticking in the pads; any grass seeds found in the web or between the toes should be removed, and foreign material

such as chewing gum or plasticine should be carefully clipped from between the pads. If you suspect that your dog has stood in an irritant substance such as paraffin or wet road tar, smother the feet in an emulsifying agent such as oil or butter to soothe and to soften the irritant, and then wash thoroughly in washing-up liquid.

Teeth need examining for signs of discoloration, as tartar frequently builds up on the tooth surface, especially in dogs that are reluctant to chew, and those with narrow 'bites', for example Yorkshire Terriers and Toy Poodles. Many dogs allow their owners to clean the teeth, a task you need not do very often. The easiest method is using a cotton bud moistened and dipped in ordinary tooth powder. Watch for signs of broken teeth, teeth with incipient holes, receding gums, inflamed gums or loose teeth (except in puppies aged between four and six months, when baby teeth are being cast to make room for the adult teeth). Any of these indicates a trip to the veterinarian for expert treatment before the animal develops toothache or mouth pain.

Regularly check the eyes for opacity in the cornea and for inflammation. Severe inflammation will cause the eye to be kept half-closed and to water profusely. Dogs so affected will often rub the inflamed eye.

When checking the ears, watch for signs of squelching when rubbing around them, and examine under each flap for signs of excessive wax production. If you find this, have the ears checked by your veterinarian to establish the cause; similarly if the ear canals smell unpleasant. If the animal seems unduly irritated by either ear seek help without delay.

Grooming should also include paying attention to the areas around the anus and urinary region, for problems here are often first detected by the observant owner. Such problems

include diarrhoea and cystitis.

In the coat itself, notice the general condition, watch for local hair loss producing baldness, and look out for those external parasites, fleas, lice and ticks.

### Signs to note
There are various general points to bear in mind in inspecting your dog — points that in sickness may greatly help your veterinarian to reach a diagnosis. Does the dog suddenly seem to have gained or lost weight? Weigh your dog at regular intervals, say weekly. This is easily accomplished in all but the largest breeds by lifting the dog and stepping onto bathroom weighing scales; then, still standing on the scales, put the dog down. The difference in the two readings gives a fairly accurate indication of the dog's weight. For very small dogs and puppies, kitchen scales may be easier; and for very large dogs, a public weighbridge should be used.

Appetite and thirst should also be noted, with any preference changes — for example, eating biscuit meal and refusing meat, or vice versa. If in doubt about fluid consumption, measure out water or milk daily and keep a record of the quantity consumed. Letting your dog also drink puddle or pond water would distort the overall intake (and, in any case, this is a possible source of infection that should be avoided).

Signs of vomiting and diarrhoea should be carefully noted, as these can be a valuable guide. All animals, including man, have the occasional stomach upset, but if this is persistent or combined with undue lassitude and a refusal to eat, veterinary attention is needed.

Intolerance to exercise or downright unwillingness to walk is important as this may be the first indication of heart disease, especially if it is combined with a persistent soft, dry cough.

It goes without saying that any departure from normal behaviour should be carefully watched. If in doubt, telephone your veterinarian and describe the signs that are worrying you. He or she will either put your mind at rest, or — if in doubt — ask to examine the animal.

## A Simple First-Aid Kit

1   Bland eye ointment. If in doubt, seek advice from your veterinarian.
2   Suitable cream or balm for grazes and scalds.
3   Sedative tablets (these should be supplied by a veterinarian, with details of dosage).
4   Aspirin tablets, preferably the soluble variety – one tablet treats a 9kg (20lb) dog.
5   Surgical or methylated spirit for cleansing and sterilizing.

6/7   Adhesive plaster roll.
8   Crepe bandages for sprains and injured limbs.
9   Suitable antiseptic solution, safe for use with dogs – e.g. antiseptics designed for use with babies.
10   Stomach mixture, e.g. kaolin or bismuth for sickness and diarrhoea.

11   Wound powder. Antiseptic powder for cuts and grazes or after operations. Easy to apply from plastic puffer.
12   White open-wove cotton
to   bandages for dressing cuts
14   and wounds.
15   Lint or sterile dressings for cuts and grazes.
16   Nail clippers.

17   Blunt-ended tweezers, such as eyebrow tweezers, to remove thorns, ticks, etc., from the skin.
18   Cotton wool for dressings and bandages.
19   Curved, blunt-ended scissors (Mayo scissors) useful for trimming fur and removing foreign materials from between the pads.
20   Cotton buds for cleansing purposes.

### Simple first aid

It is useful to build a simple dog's first-aid kit. You may never need some of the items but just having them handy can be a comfort. Shown on this page is a basic kit of equipment and materials.

The kit excludes splints because they are rarely required. If you ever suspect a limb fracture you can probably improvise splints from household materials, pending veterinary treatment.

### Ailments of different body systems

The following paragraphs deal briefly with afflictions grouped under the affected parts of the body. This summary may help owners to recognize whether or not veterinary treatment is required, and if so, how urgently. Where possible, we outline first-aid measures. Remember that it is often impossible for the veterinarian to diagnose by telephone.

**Skin.** The commonest problems encountered with skin are probably the direct result of parasites, of which fleas are by far the commonest. Usually found along the back of the dog, fleas leave their droppings (but not their eggs) in the coat, and therefore can be detected easily by little coal-like particles in the fur. Fleas themselves are readily visible to the naked eye; they are brownish and flattened from side to side, and scatter speedily through the hair. If you see fleas give prompt insecticidal treatment in the form of a special shampoo, dusting powder or aerosol. Repeat at suitable intervals if the dog becomes infested again.

*Right: Four common types of external parasite. Lice and their eggs (nits) are found mostly on the head; fleas, ticks and mites may be found on the body.*

### Common Dog Parasites

Dog flea *(Ctenocephalides canis)*

Dog tick *(Ixodes ricinus)*

Dog louse *(Linognathus setosus)*

Follicular mite *(Demodex canis)*

If left untreated, dogs may become allergic to flea bites and may scratch persistently or bite at themselves until a patch of self-inflicted wet eczema appears. This patch can vary from 1-2cm (²/₅-⁴/₅in) in diameter to almost a quarter of the body if left untreated, and, as the name suggests, has a shiny moist-looking surface. Although requiring veterinary attention, wet eczema can sometimes be minimized by applying a soothing cream and administering a sedative or aspirin tablet, which helps to curb scratching and biting.

Lice are greyish-blue creatures usually found on the ear flaps. They hardly move and they cement their eggs (nits) to the fur. Insecticidal treatment is essential, for many lice on one dog can cause anaemia by sucking large quantities of blood.

Ticks embedded in the skin are unsightly and may in certain areas of the world cause problems by transmitting disease. If there are many ticks, insecticidal treatment will clear them; if just one or two, they can be smothered in spirit and a few minutes later removed, using tweezers. Ticks usually let go and leave the dog once they have had sufficient food (i.e. by sucking blood).

Grazes cause little problem and should be cleaned with an antiseptic, followed by the application of a suitable soothing ointment. If the dog persists in licking, seek treatment. Cuts vary greatly in depth, length and position. If you can apply a firm bandage this will usually control bleeding, but stitching is required for any cuts longer than 2cm (⅘in). Bathe cuts with disinfectant, but you should not apply any ointment.

**Ears.** Ear troubles generally require expert diagnosis and treatment; home treatment does not work satisfactorily. One rather dramatic condition is aural haematoma, a blood blister of the ear flap. This must be drained surgically and the flap secured to prevent recurrence while the flap heals. Aural haematomas are usually caused by an animal excessively shaking or scratching an ear flap.

**Eyes.** Although it is safe to bathe the dog's eyes in lukewarm water or with an ordinary proprietary eyewash, it is extremely unwise to delay seeking professional advice and such a delay could result in permanent loss of vision. A bland ointment may help, however, until such time as professional assistance can be sought.

**Nails.** These may need to be cut occasionally, especially the dewclaws, which do not come into contact with the ground and therefore do not get worn down. If left unchecked they frequently curve and dig into the flesh; they also stand a good chance of catching in undergrowth and wire fencing. All nails contain a blood vessel and nerve, and

**Anal Glands**

Anus

Enlarged anal gland

Normal anal gland

*Above: Anal (scent) glands may be emptied by applying gentle pressure with thumb and second finger just below and to either side of the anus.*

*Left: Dogs have two scent or anal glands, each about the size of a cherry. They may enlarge if overfilled with secretion or infected. Untreated, such abscesses will burst like a boil to the exterior. They can be surgically removed.*

cutting should be left to experienced people unless you are quite sure what you are doing. Broken nails usually need to be removed by a veterinarian to save the animal distress and pain.

**Digestive system.** It is a good plan to watch animals regularly while they are eating, because signs of mouth pain usually show in the way the animals tackle their food. Apart from a suitable temporary analgesic such as aspirin, little can be done to help except seeking professional attention.

Uncomplicated vomiting is common in dogs. The vomit is usually fluid, and often described as a froth, which may be white or yellowish. If solid food is returned, this may indicate inflammation of the stomach (gastritis) or mild food-poisoning caused by eating food that is 'off'. But if vomiting is persistent, especially in a young dog with a tendency to swallow

stones, there is the possibility of an obstruction and you should seek veterinary attention as soon as possible. In cases of gastritis it is usually effective, or at least helpful, to withhold food from the dog for a period of 24 hours, allowing only small frequent drinks of boiled water.

Liver failure is encountered quite often in dogs and usually requires veterinary treatment and advice. It is undoubtedly aggravated by foods rich in fat; therefore special diets may be needed to minimize the symptoms.

Failure of the pancreatic gland to work efficiently may well result in a dog that eats voraciously yet loses weight and condition. Again, avoid fats; also seek veterinary help to remedy the enzyme deficiency that is the usual cause of the symptoms.

Diarrhoea is probably one of the commonest signs of illness seen at a veterinary surgery. There are

many possible causes: an unsuitable diet or a low-grade bowel infection are the commonest, and withholding food for 24 hours followed by a light diet of white meat, such as chicken, veal or fish, will cure mild cases. If the condition persists or recurs, however, qualified treatment by a veterinarian is strongly indicated.

**Anal glands.** These are a constant source of worry to some dogs. The little scent glands are situated on either side of the anus. If they become overfilled they will cause irritation, and if this is not relieved they may become infected and eventually form abscesses, which usually burst on the outside like a boil. Anal glands can be emptied by the owner once a veterinarian has shown how this should be done. Prompt attention may well help to avoid prolonged treatment and the risk of the animal self-inflicting other lesions such as wet eczema in the process of trying to soothe the discomforted part of its body.

**Heart and circulation.** These give rise to few problems in young animals, except for rare cases of inherited heart disease. However, dogs of some breeds tend to develop heart murmurs and other signs, usually exercise intolerance, a dry cough of increasing frequency and severity, and progressive lassitude. Veterinary treatment is, of course, necessary, but owners can help by exercising affected dogs at the coolest times of the day during hot weather, providing adequate ventilation indoors, and preventing their pets becoming overweight.

**Respiratory system.** Fortunately, most dogs have a robust respiratory system. There are few cases of bronchitis and even fewer of pneumonia except when associated with the distemper virus. A troublesome condition against which vaccines are available in some parts of the world is kennel cough, an inflammation of the windpipe (tracheitis). Usually this is not serious except in very young, ill or old animals; and the owner can complement veterinary treatment by giving cough preparations—even the old-fashioned honey and lemon seems to help.

**Musculo-skeletal system.** One of the commonest conditions is pain in a limb, leading to limping. There are many possible causes. The owner should inspect the pads for signs of an imbedded piece of glass or a thorn. Until help is obtained the owner should rest the animal, possibly giving some support to the affected limb in the form of a crepe bandage.

Dogs, like humans, can tear muscles, ligaments and tendons by tripping or jumping awkwardly; and in an older animal, joint disease such as arthritis or muscular rheumatism may well cause limping. In such cases the degree of lameness is often linked with climatic conditions, damp cold weather being the worst. Drugs will help, and in the early stages many veterinarians simply prescribe aspirin, which seems to work well.

Broken limbs are fortunately uncommon and are usually the result of a major trauma such as a road accident. Until professional help is obtained, the golden rules are:

1. Give nothing by mouth.
2. Move the animal as little as possible.
3. Try to immobilize the broken limb or limbs by a splint or by using a bandage to tie it to its partner on the opposite side of the body.

A stretcher of any description helps to reduce pain while the animal is taken to a surgery or hospital. A jacket or coat can be used as an emergency stretcher. The limb will be set, using stainless steel pins or an external plaster of Paris cast, depending on the site of the fracture and the preference of the surgeon.

A common injury to a back leg is tearing a small but important ligament in the knee. Rest may help, but usually the ligament must be replaced, using nylon, or a skin graft to strengthen the knee.

Hip dysplasia (abnormal hip development) is widespread among dogs, especially the large breeds. The abnormality seldom shows up while dogs are young. As they age, however, sufferers become stiffer, probably as a result of a superimposed arthritis in the joint, and have difficulty in rising, jumping or walking any distance. In most cases it is possible to remove the malformed hip joint, but various techniques are used to relieve the pain of hip dysplasia and these depend on the surgeon's preference.

Another bone condition is spondylitis, a progressive disease affecting the spinal cord and producing progressive paralysis of the hindquarters, sometimes linked with incontinence. Regrettably this is incurable.

**Urinary system.** The main problem here is often the state of the kidneys, for without their effective working the whole body system collapses. Fortunately as leptospirosis vaccination has become more widespread, kidney disease has apparently grown rarer. But through wear and tear, the nephron units of the kidneys become damaged anyway and renal disease develops in many dogs as they age. There is no cure, but veterinary help may ensure years of useful, happy and pain-free life. Symptoms are usually a marked increase in water intake, progressive loss in weight, decreasing appetite and a tendency to vomit—especially water after copious drinking. Diagnosis is usually by urine and blood tests; veterinary treatment and dietary advice are helpful.

Cystitis, or inflammation of the bladder, is a more acute condition

and must be promptly tackled to save discomfort. It can originate in a simple infection or in combination with bladder tumours, polyps or stones (calculi). Diagnosis and treatment must be left to the professionals. Signs include increased frequency of urination, in dogs of either sex. Difficulty and pain on urinating are usual. Veterinarians can sometimes feel causative calculi in bitches, and those in male dogs are often detected when a catheter is passed in the clinic. If stones are present, they must be removed to secure long-term relief. Blood passed in urine is also a significant sign. Total

*Right: The normal hip is a perfectly smooth fit between the top of the thigh bone and the pelvis, like a ball and socket. In dysplasia, close contact is lost and the edges of the ball and socket become rough and uneven, causing uneven gait, pain and weakness.*

## Bandaging a Limb

*After applying a dressing to the foot, place a double layer of bandage round the top and bottom.*

*Continue the same bandage, winding round the leg from the bottom up. Overlap each turn.*

*Apply at least two layers to give comfort and protection. Take care not to wrap the limb too tightly.*

*Split the tail of the bandage; double-knot round the leg. It is risky to use safety or other pins.*

*Apply two strips of adhesive plaster crosswise over the foot, then up the bandage, sticking to fur.*

*The final bandage should be neat, strong and waterproof. It should be firm, comfortable and not too tight.*

### Normal Hip

Smooth cartilage — Pelvis

Thigh bone — Short ligament

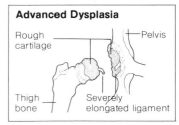

### Advanced Dysplasia

Rough cartilage — Pelvis

Thigh bone — Severely elongated ligament

## Applying a Tape-muzzle

*A tape-muzzle ensures your safety with a vicious, nervous or injured dog. Using a length of bandage or*

*pyjama cord, form a wide loop and pass this well over the snout from a safe distance and pull really firm.*

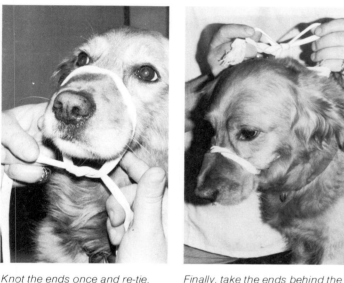

*Knot the ends once and re-tie, this time under the muzzle. Again, pull tight to ensure effectiveness.*

*Finally, take the ends behind the dog's crown and tie in a bow. The muzzle should not dislodge.*

## Improvising a Splint and Stretcher

*Limb injuries can be made more comfortable by tying the damaged leg to the opposite one.*

*Use strips of bandage to tie it firmly to the lower, intact, limb at 3 or 4 points to limit movement.*

*A coat, jacket or blanket held at all four corners by two people is a useful means of transportation.*

*This minimises struggling and any worsening of the damage. Roll dog gently onto this stretcher.*

---

inability to pass urine—especially in a male dog—merits the fastest possible veterinary treatment.

**Reproductive system.** This system gives little trouble in male dogs but can cause serious problems in bitches. The only organ likely to worry a male dog is the prostate. As in older men, this enlarges, giving rise to difficulty in passing urine or faeces. Fortunately this problem responds readily to drug treatment.

Not so, necessarily, an inflammation of the female womb—a condition often referred to as metritis. The result may be sterility, and a severe attack can even hazard the animal's life. Though this condition may respond to antibiotics, it is often safest to opt for an entire ovaro-hysterectomy. Danger signs include a progressive vulvar discharge coupled with increasing thirst, decreasing appetite and a tendency to vomit.

One of the commonest and annoying conditions encoun-

tered in bitches is false pregnancy. About two months after season, the bitch behaves as if she had been mated, and will nest, lactate, and foster mock pups such as socks, cushions and toys. In severe cases treatment is required, but it is helpful to remove all make-believe pups and to prevent self-licking of milk glands (which in itself stimulates milk production). You can do this by painting with distasteful materials such as vinegar and bitter aloes.

**Nervous system.** Infection of the brain by distemper virus may result in fits that are sometimes controllable by medication. Epilepsy also occurs, and again this is usually treated with a human anti-convulsant drug. Spinal-disc injuries are common, especially in long-backed dogs such as Dachshunds. They may be treated by drugs or surgery. It is important to discourage sufferers from jumping on and off chairs, or climbing and descending stairs.

**Various medical conditions**
We end this section on illness with an account of miscellaneous medical conditions and suggestions for combating them.

**Tumours.** Some dog owners have an unwarranted horror of all tumours. An experienced veterinarian can dismiss many a swelling as harmless, to the owner's relief. In fact most lumps are benign, for instance, fatty lumps (lipomas), warts (fibromas) and cysts. These do not spread from the site of origin and many can be removed without trouble if this seems desirable. That is particularly true of skin masses and bitches' tumours of the mammary glands. However, as in humans, some benign growths are inoperable because of their position: it is impossible to detach them from surrounding vital tissues.

Cancerous tumours may present a similar problem, and anyway these may not be worth removing if some of their cells

have spread through the body to other tissues, or organs such as the lungs. It would be pointless to remove the primary growth only to find inoperable secondary growths elsewhere. A surgeon may use X-rays and laboratory tests to determine the type of tumour and the chance of surgical success. He may also take a small sample (biopsy) to get an expert pathologist's assessment. This is also often done after removal to confirm the nature of the mass.

**Shock.** Dogs may suffer shock after a road accident, following surgery, or in any condition involving extensive internal or external bleeding. Treatment is prompt, skilled veterinary care. In mild cases a small dose of a stimulant such as brandy may be a help, though this can be risky, especially if the dog has to undergo surgery or anaesthesia. Never, of course, give anything by mouth to an unconscious dog: it may choke and die if you do.

**Poisoning.** Many substances toxic to dogs may be swallowed accidentally or given deliberately. Probably the greatest risk is from rodenticides and garden chemicals—especially slug bait and weedkillers. When using one of these always observe the container's instructions about safety. If you know that a dog has been poisoned, cause it to vomit by making it swallow a crystal of washing soda like a tablet, a strong salt solution or mustard in water. This works only if done minutes after the dog took the poison. If possible take the poison container to the veterinarian when you seek treatment; it may help him or her to choose the right remedy quickly.

### Common dog diseases

The following diseases include some mentioned earlier, most under the topic of vaccination.

**Distemper** is caused by a virus that can attack virtually all of a dog's body tissues—the eyes and nose, causing discharges; the bowel, causing diarrhoea; the lungs, causing a cough; and the brain, causing encephalitis that may result in a twitch, paralysis or fits. Distemper can also cause crusting of the nose and pads, hence its old name 'hard pad'. Vaccination has reduced the incidence of this often fatal disease.

**Virus hepatitis** can affect all ages but is particularly dangerous to pups. Signs vary from persistent vomiting, lack of appetite and possibly jaundice, to Fading Puppy Syndrome and sudden death. As with distemper, affected dogs are obviously ill and prompt treatment must be sought.

**Leptospirosis** is another acute disease caused by either of two micro-organisms. Both will damage kidneys and liver, causing collapse, vomiting, high fever and coma, or a distinct yellowing of the whites of the eyes. One form of leptospirosis is usually contracted from rats and should be taken expecially seriously as, under the name Weil's disease, it can affect humans.

**Rabies** is a grave virus disease present in many countries; dogs or people bitten by a rabid dog or other mammal are likely to die in agony. Where the disease is present, dogs must be vaccinated; you should never befriend stray dogs and you must keep pet dogs isolated from such possible sources of infection. Signs range from 'dumb', when an affected dog is subdued and the mouth hangs open dribbling saliva as if a bone were lodged in the throat, to 'furious', which is less common: the affected dog becomes noticeably aggressive and will attack live or inanimate objects, even its owners. Hydrophobia, or fear of swallowing water, is not a symptom among dogs.

**Kennel cough** is caused by a variety of germs that spread readily from dog to dog, especially where they are confined together (hence the name). Despite a

persistent cough there are rarely other or more serious symptoms.

**Canine parvovirus** causes sudden death in puppies up to 8-9 months due to infection of heart muscle. Adult dogs infected exhibit signs of a severe gastro-enteritis (vomiting and diarrhoea, often with blood present). Currently protection is given using cat pan-leucopaenia vaccine.

**Tonsilitis** is common and may be uncomplicated or occur with other illness, e.g. gastritis. Signs may be gulping, difficulty in swallowing or a soft cough (often with a noticeable tendency to eat grass) and retching. Response to antibiotics is normally good and it is rarely necessary to remove the tonsils surgically.

**Hormone disease** occurs in individual dogs and is not trans-

*Top: Grip pill or capsule between thumb and forefinger and push to the back of the throat. Release jaws and allow dog to swallow.*

*Above: Keep the mouth closed when giving liquids, pouring into flap formed by the lips. Allow to swallow before releasing.*

missible to other animals. Signs vary depending on the gland affected, but weight gain, hair loss and change in the nature of the coat are frequent, especially in older animals and in bitches during the active part of the oestrus cycle and immediately after. Sometimes surgery is opted for, but more commonly gland extracts will cure these diseases.

**Diabetes** is not uncommon. As with many diabetic people, affected dogs show increased thirst and appetite with an associated weight loss. Treatment of diabetes may involve your giving

the dog daily insulin injections.

**Pancreatic disease** is quite common. It involves a failure to digest food properly, caused by inability to produce a digestive enzyme. Characteristic signs are ravenous appetite, marked decline in weight and general condition, and bulky, pale (putty-like) faeces.

**Anal gland disease** is frequently troublesome and due to overfilling, infection or abscess formation affecting the anal glands. Irritation of the anal region occurs and there is real pain. Surgical removal may be needed if the problem recurs after treatment.

*Above: Small dogs can be given tablets with forceps or tweezers, reducing the chance of getting bitten or choking the dog.*

*Above: To apply eye medications, hold the head against your body, keep lids open and pipe ointment onto the eye. Hold tube clear.*

### Giving medicines

At some time most owners have to give their pets medicines under the direction of a veterinary surgeon. With all but the most vicious animals this should be accomplished easily. But medicines given by mouth should not be mixed with food: the dog may be too ill to eat all its rations, or may detect that its food has been 'doctored' and leave it; or, if fed with other animals, may swap bowls. It is much better to give it a direct dose of the specified quantity to ensure that this is swallowed and therefore effective.

Few medicines come in powder form except those that are palatable and designed to be mixed with the food. When giving powders do not be tempted to pour these into the mouth neat—the dog is sure to cough them up again. Instead, mix them with water, milk, butter, jam or honey, and smear the resulting palatable paste on the tongue or lips. The patient usually swallows this enthusiastically.

Tablets, pills or capsules should be given, singly or in multiples, by pushing them to the back of the throat and holding the mouth closed until you see the dog gulp them down. If the dog protests, get an assistant to hold the patient securely during dosage. Lubricating the medicines by dipping in oil or butter may make them easier for the dog to swallow.

Liquid medicines usually should not exceed one teaspoonful (5ml) per dose. Sit the dog and hold the jaws closed with the head tilted well back. Pull out the flap of the lip on one side to form a natural funnel, and pour in the liquid. Do not release the head or jaws until the dog is seen to swallow.

*Above: To instil ear drops, steady the head, lift flap and aim the drops down the widest canal. Close flap and massage the ear.*

As with all medicines, ointments, creams and lotions must be applied to the affected areas at prescribed frequencies. It is essential to rub such preparations well into the skin unless otherwise directed. The natural tendency for animals immediately to lick off such applications is reduced if little remains on the skin surface. A good time to apply these medicines is just before taking the dog out for a walk: your pet's attention will be distracted while the drug does its work. If you have to rub the stuff on at, say, bedtime, when you cannot prevent the dog licking, it is a good idea to apply a protective bandage or sock.

Ear drops should be instilled down the largest visible opening to the vertical canal. Being liquid, they will work their way around the ear's nooks and crannies to reach the trouble spot. A little gentle external massage to the ear will assist, and thereafter even frantic head-shaking will not dislodge the drops. Ear powders clog, and a veterinarian will have to remove them by syringeing or other cleansing, so unless these are specially prescribed never be tempted to pour or puff powder inside a dog's ears.

Eye drops or ointments need special handling which owners often find difficult. Always steady the dog in a sitting position with its head slightly raised, if necessary getting someone to help. Eyes are very delicate and will not withstand accidental rough treatment. Hold the head firmly with one hand, using thumb and index finger to keep the lids open. With the dropper bottle or tube in the other hand, drip the required number of drops onto the open eye. Squeeze ointment from a tube as you would pipe cream onto a cake, but make sure that the tube nozzle does not touch the eye—especially the clear structure (cornea). The natural blinking that follows treatment will spread the preparation over the front of the eye; do not allow the dog to rub with its front paws for a few minutes after application.

In conclusion, a few words of warning about medication. Never administer drugs not specifically made for animal use without the guidance and blessing of your veterinarian. Such amateur doctoring may cause undue and protracted suffering to your dog and possibly injure, maim or even kill. For this reason proprietary medicines bought from chemists or pet stores are rarely to be commended. Also always store canine medicines somewhere safe from snooping children, who might use them to experiment on themselves; and safely dispose of drugs left over when treatment is completed. Otherwise they may become useless or even dangerous. Of course your veterinarian may dispense some drugs that you can safely keep inside your canine medicine chest for future use against specified conditions. If you have medicines like this, clearly mark the container with dose amount and frequency and the particular condition for which the drugs are to be used.

# 5

# SHOWING YOUR DOG

### BY MURIEL SHEARWOOD

What is the dog-showing game? Exactly that: a game — one with an element of chance. We take a gamble by pitting one dog's beauty and conformation against another's. The rules and regulations are laid down by the Kennel Club.

But showing means much more besides. Shows provide a shop window for the individual breeder's wares; and a market for dog-related products, from dog collars, breed badges and feeding bowls to commercial kennels; from cottage crafts to exotic artwork; from protective clothing to à la mode. Thus showing plays no small part in national and international economics.

The 'game' itself involves qualities of leadership, skills of organization and the hard preparatory work of those participating. It has its own language. It evokes feelings of joy, sorrow, bewilderment and anger. It can be likened to an addictive drug. The writer can say so with authority — she tried to kick the habit, experienced merciless withdrawal symptoms, gave in and is happily unashamed of her failure!

### The breed standard

Showing is an opportunity for people interested in specific breeds to get together socially; but above all, through the element of competition, it is the means by which breeds are kept true to type — to their respective standards.

Breed standards, or breed points, are drawn up by specialist breed clubs. Each carefully describes a specific breed — its conformation; movement; eye shape and colour; type and colour of coat; temperament. This description makes plain exactly what is desirable in a particular

*Above: Examining skeletal make-up, coat colour and texture. The handler keeps a hold on the lead to prevent a disqualifying bite!*

*Left: Judging the movement of a Samoyed. The handler controls the pace, taking care to keep out of the judge's line of sight.*

breed and what is not. The specification also sets out the breed's original function. The wish to preserve this is what first leads a group of devotees to form a specialist breed club and to fix breed standards. With minor changes these have remained the same for certain breeds for more than 70 years.

This original determination to keep breeds true to type so that they could continue to fulfil their original functions largely explains why we are not now left with a product mediocre in height, weight, colour and temperament, and just describable as 'a dog'. This does not decry the worth of the many much-loved, mixed-

race Fidos. Rather it explains the choice we have available between say, the benign and dignified Newfoundland and the extrovert and cocky Yorkshire Terrier.

The breed standard is the blueprint that helps prevent exaggeration of breed idiosyncrasies. Over-accentuating these invites genetic changes, making the breed incapable of fulfilling its original function, or even rendering the breed extinct through skeletal malformaton.

Interpreting the breed standard is a fascinating task, for sometimes the wording is vague or ambiguous. Weights and heights can be defined precisely thanks to scales and measures, but each breeder and judge may interpret terms such as 'small, dark brown eye' in a slightly different way. Meeting in competition helps to remove this ambiguity, for competitors can see if 'small' gets too small or if 'dark' is growing paler, thus altering the characteristic expression of the breed.

In the United Kingdom, each judge may award no more than one Challenge Certificate (the highest award for the best dog and best bitch in each breed at a Championship show) to a breed within a 9-month period. This allows for the entry of one new generation, so judges can note whether a particular point of a breed is improving or deteriorating and so help to maintain balance.

### Types of dog show

There are seven distinct types of dog show in the United Kingdom:
1. **Exemption** The only show exempt from nearly all Kennel Club show rules and regulations. Usually held at fund-raising efforts, with pedigree and non-pedigree classes.

## Open and Championship

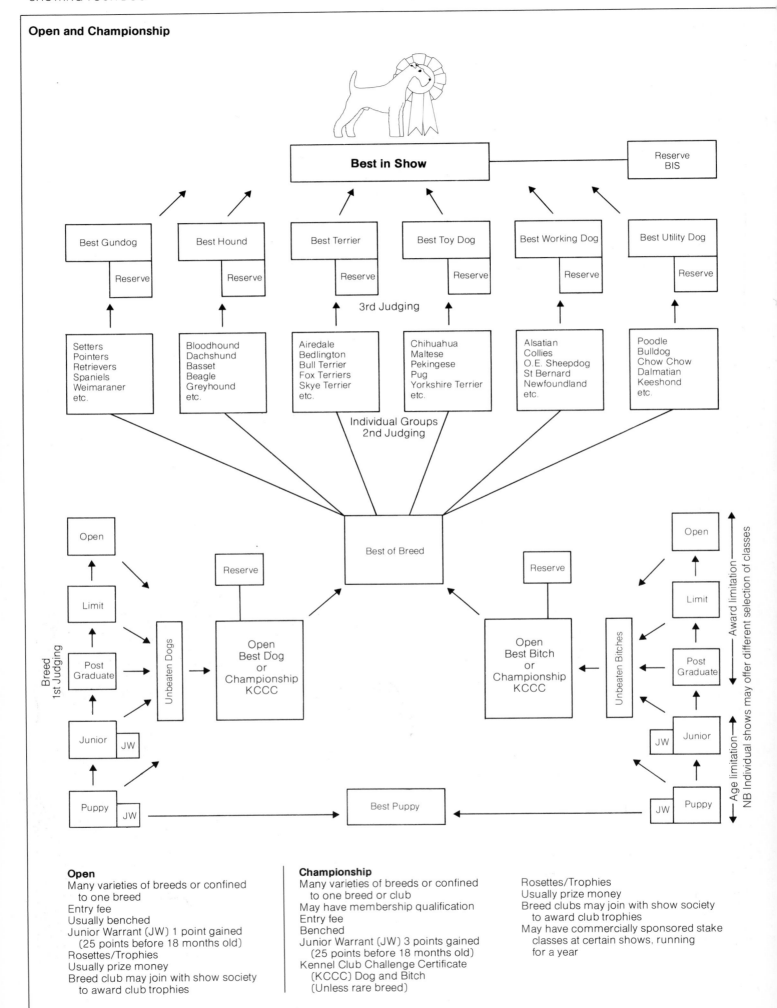

**Best in Show** — Reserve BIS

Best Gundog — Reserve
Best Hound — Reserve
Best Terrier — Reserve
Best Toy Dog — Reserve
Best Working Dog — Reserve
Best Utility Dog — Reserve

3rd Judging

Setters
Pointers
Retrievers
Spaniels
Weimaraner
etc.

Bloodhound
Dachshund
Basset
Beagle
Greyhound
etc.

Airedale
Bedlington
Bull Terrier
Fox Terriers
Skye Terrier
etc.

Chihuahua
Maltese
Pekingese
Pug
Yorkshire Terrier
etc.

Alsatian
Collies
O.E. Sheepdog
St Bernard
Newfoundland
etc.

Poodle
Bulldog
Chow Chow
Dalmatian
Keeshond
etc.

Individual Groups
2nd Judging

Best of Breed

Open
Limit
Post Graduate
Junior — JW
Puppy — JW

Breed 1st Judging

Unbeaten Dogs

Reserve

Open
Best Dog
or
Championship
KCCC

Open
Best Bitch
or
Championship
KCCC

Reserve

Unbeaten Bitches

Open
Limit
Post Graduate
JW — Junior
JW — Puppy

Award limitation
Age limitation
NB Individual shows may offer different selection of classes

Best Puppy

**Open**
Many varieties of breeds or confined
  to one breed
Entry fee
Usually benched
Junior Warrant (JW) 1 point gained
  (25 points before 18 months old)
Rosettes/Trophies
Usually prize money
Breed club may join with show society
  to award club trophies

**Championship**
Many varieties of breeds or confined
  to one breed or club
May have membership qualification
Entry fee
Benched
Junior Warrant (JW) 3 points gained
  (25 points before 18 months old)
Kennel Club Challenge Certificate
  (KCCC) Dog and Bitch
  (Unless rare breed)

Rosettes/Trophies
Usually prize money
Breed clubs may join with show society
  to award club trophies
May have commercially sponsored stake
  classes at certain shows, running
  for a year

## Some typical classes offered at Open and Championship Shows

**Puppy:** For dogs of six and not exceeding twelve calendar months of age on the first day of the Show.

**Junior:** For dogs of six and not exceeding eighteen calendar months of age on the first day of the Show.

**Maiden:** For dogs which have not won a Challenge Certificate at an Open or Championship Show (Puppy, Special Puppy, Minor Puppy and Special Minor Puppy classes excepted).

**Novice:** For dogs which have not won a Challenge Certificate or three or more First Prizes at Open and Championship Shows (Puppy, Special Puppy, Minor Puppy and Special Minor Puppy classes excepted).

**Undergraduate:** For dogs which have not won a Challenge Certificate or three or more First Prizes at Championship Shows (Puppy, Special Puppy, Minor Puppy and Special Minor Puppy classes excepted).

**Graduate:** For dogs which have not won a Challenge Certificate or four or more First Prizes at Championship Shows in Graduate, Minor Limit, Mid Limit and Open Classes, whether restricted or not.

**Post Graduate:** For dogs which have not won a Challenge Certificate or five or more First Prizes at Championship Shows in Post Graduate, Minor Limit, Mid Limit, Limit and Open Classes, whether restricted or not.

**Minor Limit:** For dogs which have not won two Challenge Certificates or three or more First Prizes in all at Championship Shows in Minor Limit, Mid Limit, Limit and Open Classes, confined to the breed, whether restricted or not, at shows where Challenge Certificates were offered for the breed.

**Mid Limit:** For dogs which have not won three Challenge Certificates or five or more First Prizes in all at Championship Shows in Mid Limit, Limit and Open Classes, confined to the breed, whether restricted or not, at shows where Challenge Certificates were offered for the breed.

**Limit:** For dogs which have not won three Challenge Certificates under three different judges or seven or more First Prizes in all, at Championship Shows in Limit and Open Classes, confined to the breed, whether restricted or not, at shows where Challenge Certificates were offered for the breed.

**Open:** For all dogs of the breeds for which the class is provided and eligible for entry at the Show.

**Veteran:** For dogs of an age specified in the schedule but not less than five years on the first day of the Show.

**Brace:** For two exhibits (either sex or mixed) of one breed belonging to the same exhibitor, each exhibit having been entered in some class other than Brace or Team.

2. **Primary** Confined to breed clubs. Not more than eight classes. No class higher than Maiden, Puppy classes excepted. No First Prize winners may enter.

3. **Match Meeting** This is a shadow of the old dog-fight days. It is a knock-out system with up to 32 dogs meeting in couples.

4. **Sanction** Up to 25 classes. Some are confined to specific breeds, some to varieties of breeds and some to groups of breeds.

5. **Limited** Like the Sanction shows and Match Meetings, this is limited to members of the canine society holding the show. Dogs with Challenge Certificates, or which have won a certain number of prizes of specified value, are not eligible to compete at this type of show. Sanction and Limited shows are often used by exhibitors to give their new show prospects much-needed experience.

6. **Open** Open to all, with no membership qualification. Competition is fierce. Winning first prize brings a young dog under 18 months one point nearer the coveted Junior Warrant (which we shall discuss later). An Open show is sometimes held in conjunction with an agricultural or county show, which helps to make the event part of a family outing.

7. **Championship** Some Championship shows are specifically confined to breed clubs, e.g. The Newfoundland Club Championship Show; others are open to many varieties of breeds. They are geographically distributed by the KC, so that each part of the country gets a fair 'quota'. This is where a winning exhibit may gain a Challenge Certificate (CC), which are only awarded at Championship shows. Open and Championship shows often cover two or three days.

## A glossary of showing terms

To the uninitiated, the terminology of the showing world can be confusing. Here are some basic terms in Kennel Club usage.

**Sire** and **Dam**. A puppy's father and mother.

**Affixes.** The **prefix** is the first part of a dog's Kennel Club registered name, identifying and exclusive to the breeding kennel. For example, a bitch's pet name may be 'Nana' but her registration would read something like 'Caladh Bahr Gossamer of Gerahmeen' — Caladh being the breeding kennel, and the **suffix** Gerahmeen, the owning kennel.

**Class** is an undefined number of dogs in a competition, which may or may not have sex, age or award limitations. A breed class allows for the entry of one specific breed. A group class embraces several breeds with, say, a common original function, for instance hounds or terriers. A variety class has completely different breeds.

An **exhibit** is a dog or a bitch competing at a show. Males should be **entire**: with two developed testicles in the scrotum. Bitches should not be spayed.

The **owner, handler** or **exhibitor** need not be the same person. A dog or bitch may be registered at the Kennel Club in the ownership of more than one person. It may be exhibited or handled by one member of that partnership. Any exhibit may be handled — i.e. controlled in the ring — by a friend or professional handler, so long as there is a verbal understanding or written agreement.

The **ring** is the area designated for a particular class or breed competition. **Ring numbers** are allocated to individual dogs. Its ring number is a dog's only identification for the judge, and is used for class checking and benching.

**Benching** is a dog's kennel for the day. It may be a small closed cage or an open-fronted structure on trestles. Both types are provided by commercial agencies. Some shows bear benching costs; at others a small fee is paid by the exhibitor. A Kennel Club rule states that a dog must be on its bench unless being prepared for, or required in, the ring, or unless there is a veterinarian or show committee decision to remove it from the bench. No dog is allowed off the bench for more than 15 minutes at a time for exercise and other activities. (Accordingly a packet of tissues tucked into a bag or pocket is a useful standby against natural emergencies!)

**Stewards** come in both sexes and their title may be prefixed 'judge's' or 'ring'. Often one steward plays both roles: shepherding exhibits and their handlers to the ring, checking class lists, distributing ring numbers, calling exhibits in for judging and announcing winners. Stewards also assist the judge with paper work and keep rings clear of the results of dog's 'other activities'. The efficiency of any show depends upon the stewards, although their labour often goes unrecognized and unrewarded.

**Judges** come in both sexes and two types: 'specialist' and 'all-rounder'. A specialist judge is usually a devotee of one breed, having bred many champions or been involved with that breed in various ways for many years. The 'all-rounder' judge will be know-

*Below: Ambition achieved! The result of many hours of patient training, this English Setter maintains the required show pose.*

BEST IN SHOW

## Exemption

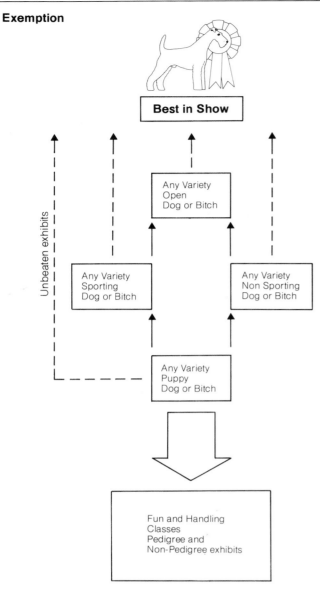

**Best in Show**

Unbeaten exhibits

Any Variety
Open
Dog or Bitch

Any Variety
Sporting
Dog or Bitch

Any Variety
Non Sporting
Dog or Bitch

Any Variety
Puppy
Dog or Bitch

Fun and Handling
Classes
Pedigree and
Non-Pedigree exhibits

## Match Meeting

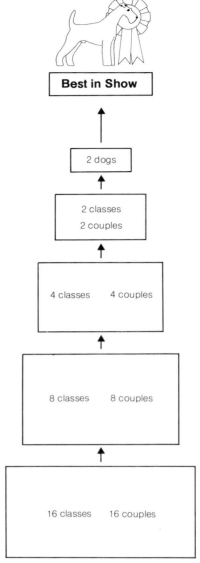

**Best in Show**

2 dogs

2 classes
2 couples

4 classes     4 couples

8 classes     8 couples

16 classes     16 couples

**Exemption**

No dogs under 6 months old
No dogs with Challenge
  Certificates (CC)
Not more than 12 classes
Pedigree and non-pedigree
  classes
Dogs need not be registered
  at the Kennel Club

Small entry free
Unbenched
Individual class judging by
  one judge
Unbeaten dogs compete for
  Best in Show
Rosettes as prizes

**Match Meeting**

No dogs under 6 months old
No dogs with Challenge
  Certificates (CC)
Up to 32 dogs
Confined to membership
Small entry fee
Unbenched
Social occasion

*Left: A long-haired Dachsund
'alone' with the judge. If your dog
is inexperienced, remember to
keep hold of the lead; a sudden
jump could lead to serious injury.*

ledgeable about many breeds, and you will meet him or her in variety classes. Probably both types of judge will have gained experience by, perhaps, first stewarding, then judging small shows before the Kennel Club allows them to award Challenge Certificates. Five years' experience is the minimum prerequisite for this in the United Kingdom.

The judge's task is to determine how close each exhibit comes to his or her mental image of the breed standard compared with other exhibits in the class. The judge closely examines each indi-

vidual, then its handler moves the animal away from and back to the jduge at a gait suitable for the breed. The line taken may be straight, triangular or circular, perhaps all three: each judge has a preference. Except in cases of fraud, misrepresentation, breach of rules or genuine mistake, the judge's decision is final. But then there is always another show—another judge!

A **Challenge Certificate** (CC) is the highest award given at a Championship show; it is awarded to the Best Dog and Best Bitch in each breed.

In the United Kingdom the number of Challenge Certificates allocated to a breed by the Kennel Club depends on the number of entries in breed classes at all Championship Shows for the previous three years, i.e. if entries are low, the breed may forfeit a CC, if high, it may gain one.

In order to win the title Champion an exhibit must gain three Challenge Certificates from three different judges, including one certificate awarded after the age of 12 months.

An **International Champion** is an exhibit that has gained a breed championship in more than one country.

A **Junior Warrant** (JW) is an award granted (on application) by the Kennel club to an exhibit gaining 25 points before the age of 18 months. One point comes from each first prize won in a breed class at an Open show and three points are gained from every first prize won in a breed class at a Championship show.

The magical **Best in Show** is determined by the type of show. Smaller shows will have all unbeaten dogs competing in the ring, so here the Best in Show and Reserve Best in Show will be chosen from a miscellany of shapes, sizes and colours. Open and Championship shows may warrant the 'group' system. In the breed classes the Best Dog and the Best Bitch compete for Best of Breed. The Best of Breed competes in its respective group. Then the group winners compete against each other, and at last one stands alone to receive the accolade of the day.

The **group** system used for showing dogs is based on their original roles. The six groups used for judging in the United Kingdom are as follows:

| Terriers | Gundogs |
|----------|---------|
| Toys | Working dogs |
| Hounds | Utility dogs |

The **Stud Book** is a register compiled by the British Kennel Club of awards given to dogs at shows. In the United Kingdom a dog or bitch winning a first, second or third prize in the Open class of its breed class has its achievement registered as a number in the Stud Book. This number is then quoted on the dog's pedigree.

A **pedigree** is a dog family tree, showing at least five generations of Kennel Club registered names. Champions will be written or underlined in red.

The **schedule** is a contract created between the show society and exhibitors when the exhibitor pays the entry fee and the show society accepts it. The schedule should contain all the information required: details of prize money (or the lack of it); instructions for travelling by rail or in a coach party; list of judges; number and types of classes available to the breeds; catering and parking arrangements; perhaps a tenting plan. The schedule also states the latest time when the exhibitor may arrive at the show and the earliest for leaving. (Before you set off remember [a] that your dog will now be part of a public exhibition; [b] to leave money for your newspaper boy and make arrangements for your children after school!)

**Catalogues** are on sale at shows. These list all the exhibits

and the owners' names and addresses. They may also have information on trade stands and other amenities plus private and commercial 'doggy' advertising.

So much for our short glossary of show jargon. Now for those of you who feel drawn in that direction, some hints on how to tread the thorny path toward show-ring stardom for a dog of your own. But before you start make no mistake; you will be adding a time-consuming and increasingly expensive hobby to the already large responsibility that comes with owning a dog.

**Sanction and Limited**

**Best in Show**

Any Variety Open or Post Graduate

Any Variety Non-Sporting Dog or Bitch

Any Variety Sporting Dog or Bitch

Any Variety Utility Dog or Bitch

Any Variety Gundog Dog or Bitch

Any Variety Working Dog or Bitch

Any Variety Terrier Dog or Bitch

Any Variety Toy Dog or Bitch

Any Variety Hound Dog or Bitch

Unbeaten exhibits

Any Variety Puppy Dog → Best Puppy ← Any Variety Puppy Bitch

Puppies may also enter the above classes

| Sanction | | Limited | |
|----------|--|---------|--|
| No dogs under 6 months | Small entry fee | No dogs under 6 months | Small entry fee |
| No dogs with Challenge Certificates (CC) | Unbenched | No dogs with Challenge Certificates (CC) | Unbenched |
| Up to 25 classes | Usually individual class judging by one judge | Limited to number of classes designated by Kennel Club | Usually individual class judging by one judge |
| No class above Post Graduate | Rosettes/Cards | | Rosettes/Cards |
| Membership qualification | Trophies/Prize money | Membership qualification | Trophies/Prize money |
| | Commercial donations | | Commercial donations |

*Right: Another aspect of showing. An English Setter gently held while the judge inspects its mouth. She will hope to find clean teeth and correct jaw formation.*

## Specialty and All-Breed (USA)

**Best in Show**

Sporting Group | Hound Group | Working Group | Terrier Group | Toy Group | Non-Sporting Group

Group Judging

Best of Winners | BEST OF BREED Competition | Best of Opposite Sex

Reserve Winners Dog | WINNERS DOG (Only Dog to receive Championship points) | Champions | WINNERS BITCH (Only Bitch to receive Championship points) | Reserve Winners Bitch

Specialty (Breed) Judging

Open

Puppy 6-9 months 9-12 months | Novice | Bred by exhibitor | American-bred

DOGS

Open

Puppy 6-9 months 9-12 months | Novice | Bred by exhibitor | American-bred

BITCHES

## Specialty and All-Breed

At any sanctioned AKC show, there are five regular classes in which dogs seeking points toward a Championship can compete:
1 Novice
2 Bred-by-exhibitor
3 American-bred
4 Open
5 Puppy:— frequently subdivided into puppies 6-9 months of age and 9-12 months.

After the judge has judged these five classes, the winners (those having won first place in each class) are brought back to compete against each other. This is called the Winners class. The dog selected best is the Winners Dog

This male receives the Championship points at the show. The same process is repeated among the females in the classes mentioned. The winning female is referred to as Winners Bitch, the only female of the breed to receive Championship points at the show.

The judge must then judge one more class and make three more awards. The Best of Breed class has in it all the recorded champions competing, both male and female, and the Winners Dog and the Winners Bitch. The judge goes over all the animals and selects one he considers to be the best, known officially as Best of Breed

(BOB). From the Winners Dog and the Winners Bitch, the judge selects a Best of Winners. If either the Winners Dog or the Winners Bitch is selected Best of Breed, it automatically becomes Best of Winners. The judge then finishes the breed judging by selecting a Best of Opposite Sex to the Best of Breed.

At an all-breed show, this same process of elimination takes place in every breed. Then each Best of Breed winner competes in its group. Four placements are awarded in each group, but only the first place winner remains to go forward in the competition.

Finally the six group winners are brought into the ring and a Best in Show winner is selected. At the largest all-breed shows, as many as 4000 animals are narrowed down to the Best in Show winner in the course of the day.

No dog may enter a competition at a dog show if it has been surgically altered, i.e. spayed or neutered. Tail docking or ear cropping are not considered to be surgical alterations.

Dogs from other countries can enter American shows, as long as they are registered with the American Kennel Club. Such dual registration is not uncommon.

## The American system

The same 'show fever' that grips the enthusiast can be found in any country where dogs are shown. The euphoria of the win, the frustration of the loss—the new-found friends, the gala pageantry and the frazzled nerves all add up to one word: fun! It may be difficult for the beginner to understand at first; but it usually takes only one match or show for the 'bug' to enter the life of the dog enthusiast. From that point on, the enthusiast finds that he or she has entered into a new lifestyle that includes weekends away from home at a dog show or match.

To understand the American system, one must understand the difference between a *dog show* and a *dog match*. Although each is conducted in the same manner, no points toward championship or obedience degrees are awarded as the result of a win at a match. A match is a training ground for both dog and owner. Winners usually receive trophies and/or ribbons for their effort, but it's all in fun. In fact, matches are generally referred to as 'fun matches.'

At a match, some dogs will compete in obedience trials at various levels, and others will compete in the conformation rings. That is, some dogs are judged for their ability to perform various obedience exercises, and others are judged for their conformity to the breed standard as set forth by the American Kennel Club.

Matches are fun, and it is certainly recommended that the beginner enrol in as many matches as possible before ever entering a dog show. A show, though still fun, is also serious business. A dog can earn points toward obedience degrees or the title of Champion.

As in the United Kingdom, there are two types of show: specialty, and all-breed. In a specialty show, only dogs of a designated breed can be entered. An example of this would be a specialty show sponsored by the German Shepherd Club; entrants are restricted to German Shepherd Dogs only. An all-breed show is open to all purebred dogs registered with the American Kennel Club.

Animals competing in conformation must earn 15 points to receive the title of 'Champion'. Points earned at each show are based upon the number of dogs in the competition; the more dogs, obviously, the more points the winner earns. An animal may win from one to five points at a show. The 15 points required must be won under at least three different judges. Only one male and one female of each breed can win points at a show. There is no intersex competition: males compete against males, females against females.

Animals competing for obedience degrees must score 170 points or more in three separate shows, under three different judges.

Obedience trials are divided into four levels of competition. These are Companion Dog (CD), Companion Dog Excellent (CDX), Utility Dog (UD), and Utility Dog, Tracking (UDT). Each level is more difficult and more complicated than the level below. An owner and dog will enter shows and compete until the first degree is completed (CD), then continue in quest of the higher levels.

In addition to conformation and obedience trials, field trials are held specifically for certain breeds. These are working tests for owner and dog as a team. Field trials expressly test the ability of a breed to perform the function for which that breed was created — either by nature or by man.

In field trials, hounds are tested on their ability to pursue rabbits, either in packs or in pairs. The pointing breeds must assist the hunter in the field by stopping and pointing the moment they scent the presence of a game bird. Retrievers are tested for their ability to search for feathered game within gunshot range of the hunter; the animal then flushes the bird into the air, and retrieves it on command if the bird is shot.

To win — whether at a fun match or at a point show — requires dedication to training and to the hobby. The reward for the effort comes at that magic moment when the judge points his finger at a particular dog and exclaims, 'That's our winner!' Imagine the thrill for you when that day finally arrives when the judge's finger points towards your dog. But then, you knew all along that you had the best dog anyway, didn't you!

### The Continental system

It is rather difficult to generalize about the rules governing dog shows in Europe, because they vary slightly from one country to another. But they are all very similar in most respects, because, instead of each country having its own rules, all are governed by the regulations laid down by the FCI (Fédération Cynologique Internationale). Each country has its own national equivalent of the Kennel Club, but for shows each must stick to the rules laid down by the FCI.

Speaking generally, shows are either of Championship status or much smaller shows — usually held by the breed clubs — more in the nature of fun shows or matches.

At a Championship show, the judge has to write a critique on every exhibit, and also give it a grade: Excellent, Very Good, Good or Sufficient. Any dog that tries to bite is disqualified. Generally, the critique has to be written on the spot, and it is then handed to the exhibitor by the judge. In the Netherlands there is slightly less pressure on the judge, because the local rules lay down that such critiques must be sent to the Dutch Kennel Club within 14 days of the show. This kind of judging obviously takes a long time, so it is as well that the classes in European shows are neither as numerous nor as well filled as they are in the UK and the USA. Usually there are only Youth, Open and Championship classes, although additional classes are permitted. Occasionally there are Brace or Team classes. But it is very rare to find a European show that has any of the featured Variety classes that are staged in Britain and America. Whether this is a good thing or not depends upon your point of view; but it certainly takes away some of the appeal of the show to the general public.

Only a dog that has received the grading Excellent may be taken into account for the award of Best of Sex. Many countries do not

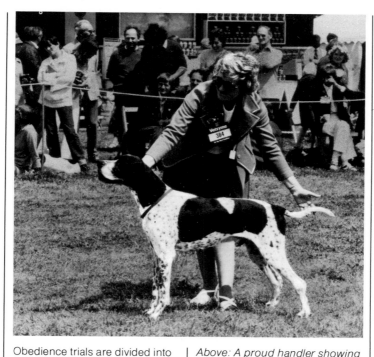

*Above: A proud handler showing off a Pointer at an outdoor show. This handsome breed has achieved great success in shows around the world.*

permit the award of an Excellent grade to a dog in the Youth class, but some do allow this. The Youth class is governed by age limits, and this is usually from 9-24 months.

It is rare for a European show to have an award for Best of Breed, though this occasionally happens. Without the award of Best of Breed, there cannot be any Group or Best in Show judging, which is a great pity, as there is then no great final climax to the show, and the onlookers tend to melt away disconsolately towards the end of the day.

After all the dogs have been graded, some may be awarded the CACIB (Certificat d'Aptitude au Championat International de Beauté) or the CAC (Certificat d'Aptitude au Championat). The CACIB is awarded only at an International Championship show. A certificate may be awarded to the winner of the grading Excellent, but not necessarily so, because a judge may not consider such a dog, even though Excellent, to be of such outstanding merit as to warrant the award of a certificate. Because a dog in the Youth class may not receive the grading Excellent, it may well happen that, in one of the few countries that allow an award for Best of Breed, the judge may put the Youth class winner above the winner of a certificate.

To obtain the title of Champion, a dog must obtain three certificates, either CACIB or CAC, under two different judges; and the first and last certificates must be won with an interval of 12 months between them. They can be won in any country that is affiliated to the FCI, and since movement of dogs is not restricted between most continental European countries by regulations regarding rabies, there is a fairly large area from which an exhibitor can choose a show.

Most UK and USA shows are thought to be fairly 'cut-throat' in their outlook, but European exhibitors seem to have a different attitude to their shows, and there is a feeling that they are even more 'out for blood'. There are fewer dogs competing, yet the owners appear to take a much more serious view of what happens to them: they confront one another with grave faces and troubled brows, and there is little chatter until all the judgments have been declared.

Shows in Europe are also rather more rigorous in their attitude to permitting removal of exhibits; you will never find a show that says participants may go home at 3.00 p.m., even when there is no real need to stay longer. Perhaps, as there are far fewer shows than in Britain and the USA, the organizers want the dogs to remain so that they can be seen by the late-comers.

But wherever they take place, dog shows are always interesting and usually fun too, and it is from this point of view that a wise owner should regard them.

### The Scandinavian system

The Scandinavian showing system is a mixture of the Continental and British systems. There are three main classes: Junior (for exhibits 8-15 months old), Open (for exhibits over 15 months old), and Champion classes (for exhibits that have already obtained the title of Swedish, Finnish, Danish, Norwegian or International Champion).

In the Junior and Open classes exhibits are graded on their own merits; they are not in competition against each other. The gradings are: 1st prize (a very good specimen of the breed), 2nd prize (a moderately good specimen), 3rd prize (an exhibit lacking in construction), and 4th prize (a very untypical exhibit).

All those that gain a 1st grading in Junior then compete against each other and are placed in order of 1st to 4th. The 1st prize winners in the Open class enter a Winners class and are also placed 1st to 4th.

Some breeds with a well-defined original function have to be highly placed at trials to test that function before they can enter Winners classes, e.g. Field Trials for Retrievers.

The International Championship Shows in Scandinavia approved by the FCI award the CACIB and the CACIT (Certificat d'Aptitude au Championat International de Travail). An International Champion has to gain four CACIBs from three different judges and in three different countries. Between the first and last CACIB there must be an interval of 12 months.

### The Australian System

In spite of, or perhaps because of a strong anti-dog movement in Australia, there is a tremendous enthusiasm among dog owners for basic training, and huge membership of training and breed clubs. Obedience training is on a par with everyday sit/stay/heel UK training, with Companion Dog (CD) awarded on a points system at trials.

Most breeds have specialist breed clubs, which use the UK Kennel Club breed standards.

The Australian states have individual kennel control organizations overseen by an advisory Australian Kennel Control Council. The availability of dog shows, field trials and obedience tests varies from state to state, and is determined by the number of pedigree dogs in the area.

The Royal Agricultural Societies of Australia all have dog show sections. The Melbourne Show, for example, runs over 11 days, with only a few breeds judged each day. These shows also cater for breed club obedience displays. Show stewards are professional people and have to pass stringent examinations before taking up their duties.

At these larger shows, the classes usually offered are: Baby puppy (pups may be shown from three months of age), Minor

puppy, Puppy, Junior, Intermediate, Novice, Graduate, Limit, State-bred, Australian-bred, and Open. These are self-explanatory or similar to the UK classification. The group classification is: Toys, Terriers, Gundogs, Hounds, Working, and Non-sporting.

Australian champions have to gain 100 points from at least four different shows and from at least four different judges. The method by which a champion gains its crown is complicated, but ensures that a superb specimen of a numerically small breed stands an almost equal chance with a superb specimen of a popular breed.

After all the breed classes have been judged, the first prize winners in each sex over six months old compete for the Challenge Certificate (CC). The winner gains five points plus one point for each competing exhibit of the same sex over six months old, to a maximum of 25 points. (A winning bitch would gain five points for the CC on its own merit, and if the total entry of bitches over six months old is 10 this would result in 15 points towards the Championship of that particular bitch.) The dog CC and bitch CC then compete for Best of Breed (BOB).

At multi-breed shows the Best of Breed then enters the group judging. The winner of each group receives five points plus one point for every exhibit in the group, to a maximum of 25 points. The six group winners then compete for

*Above: The daily routine—getting a West Highland White Terrier used to being handled on a table. For this breed, grooming for the show ring includes the use of a chalk block to highlight the white coat.*

*Below: The Maltese—with a coat to challenge the 'whiter than white' commercials! Careful grooming is a must. Two plaits, one or two top knots, tied with small ribbons make a neat finish to its appearance.*

Best in Show, from which the winner gains five points plus one point for every other exhibit entered in ordinary classes, to a maximum of 25 points. No exhibit may receive more than 25 points in one show.

Once 100 points have been gained, the record of the animal's wins is checked by its respective state control, the appropriate fee is paid, and an Australian Champion Certificate is issued.

### Buying a show dog

The first step is to find an animal with show potential. There are several ways of doing this. The local press may report the success of a nearby kennel. Write to it asking if it has any show-type puppies for sale. Remember to enclose a stamped addressed envelope. Courtesy is the key to immediate and future assistance. Do not telephone—the owner might be up to the elbows in feeding bowls, a litter of new puppies, or a veterinary visit. To owners, downing tools to answer verbal queries is not a popular pastime.

A second avenue is through the show secretary of your local canine society, whose advertisements will include the secretary's name and address. Write inquiring about successful kennels in the area. Do not telephone—if the secretary does not have a kennel full of dogs, he or she may well be working on the schedule for a forthcoming event or helping the treasurer balance the books. An insistent ringing sound is not conducive to concentration!

A third approach is through the Kennel Club, who will help you to track down the secretary of the breed club. This person will probably be gnashing his or her teeth over club affairs while holding pen in one hand and paper in the other, with the 'phone firmly off the hook! An inquiry here may well result in your discovering a successfully showing and breeding club member within half a day's journey from your home.

Alternatively there are useful

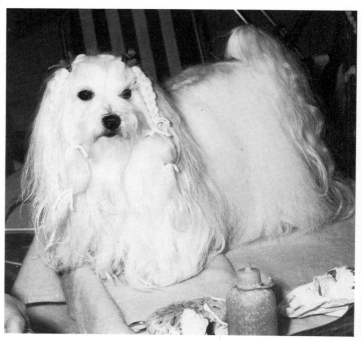

publications. The weekly British magazines *Dog World* and *Our Dogs* carry advertisements for forthcoming shows, activities of various clubs, show results and breeders' advertisements. In your local library's reference or non-fiction section you may discover an edition of *The Dog Directory*. This is a canine reference work with many aspects, and the search for an experienced exhibitor and successful breeder of your chosen breed may well end here.

Once you have found a likely breeder make a mutually convenient appointment rather than using a family excursion as the excuse for just arriving at the door. When you arrive do not be disappointed if the place is less clinically hygienic than a hospital. Look chiefly for the condition of the animals. Superb dogs in fine condition are the basis of a kennel's reputation, be that kennel an overflowing kitchen or a layout of night and day purpose-built buildings and runs. But if you notice runs deep in excreta, with stale food still in dishes, and dirty-coated dogs with running eyes, don't bother to ring the door bell.

If you press ahead, prepare to answer disconcertingly searching questions. Show the kennel proprietor you can accept advice and encouragement in the yet unknown techniques. You will need no prompting to gaze admiringly at the wall of red rosettes and green-edged Challenge Certificates, the complexities of the pedigrees and the beauty of the dogs themselves.

Consent to the asking price, and the breeder's choice of your show-potential pup. You may have to be willing to wait six months or more because current litters are probably already booked or sold. If you leave still dogless but feeling you have taken the first step in this new venture—you're hooked!

**Caring for your show dog**
The initial introduction of a pup to its new home is dealt with elsewhere in this book and is no different be it the result of a street-corner mating or the progeny of generations of champions: it will be lost, terrified and wanting its mum. The breeder will have furnished you with the pedigree and the Kennel Club registration certificate; signed and helped you to fill in the Kennel Club application for transfer of ownership certificate ready for posting; and made sure you understand the diet sheet. If the owner has been using a commercial brand of puppy food, he or she will probably sell or give you enough to last a few days, until you find your own supplier. Do not make drastic changes in the pup's diet—it will only suffer from a tummy upset, giving you extra work with mop and bucket.

Feeding a young pup is basically the same whether or not it is intended for showing. Regular meals of good-quality food, with well-balanced vitamins and minerals including trace elements, and fresh water ad lib lay sound

*Above: A young Beagle learning to show its good points: a gay tail, a straight front, good topline, hocks let down, and round, knuckled feet. Training from an early age is essential to encourage a good stance.*

foundations for the future. How much you feed depends on the size of your chosen breed. What you feed is a matter of personal choice and convenience. Not everyone will have access to raw meat supplies from a local abattoir or obliging butcher; but there are several proprietary brands of tinned and dried dog foods used with success by many exhibitors.

The kind of food that best promotes and maintains health, growth and vitality varies with each individual dog's metabolism. Experienced owners know at a glance if a feeding programme needs supplementing. Many a feeble or faddy appetite has been improved by a 'touch of seaweed powder'; many a coat has blossomed with a 'lump of rock sulphur in the drinking water'.

Vitamin and mineral compounds available under various commercial names may help to balance the chosen diet. Make sure you use the amounts advised for your dog's size; giving extra for luck may be worse for the dog's health than giving too little, and it certainly costs more.

If you have chosen a breed that needs extensive clipping or strip-

ping, ignoring experienced advice on coat preparation is the quickest way of making friends with your fellow exhibitors. The breeder will probably do the job for you or recommend a professional or competent amateur. If you are determined to do it yourself, be prepared for a non-showable result; and non-showable for at least six months.

Short-coated breeds need daily grooming, of course, and a bath two or three days before the show will freshen the coat and enable the natural oils to shine, given the aid of a silk cloth or hound glove.

Grooming once or even twice a day applies to all breeds with long or heavy coats. Again you must listen to advice, this time on what is known as 'tidying up' the feathering on legs, or ear 'stripping': too much or not enough will spoil the dog's outline.

Here it seems appropriate to mention two points of cosmetic detail. First a word of warning: the United Kingdom Kennel Club has rules about the use of artificial colouring in altering a dog's appearance to meet the breed standard requirements. The Kennel Club allows chalks and powders to be used in cleaning light-coloured coats, provided the substances are removed before the dogs enter the ring. The same applies to any oil or spray. Now the second point: I should personally like to discourage the increasingly popular cult of cutting off

muzzle whiskers. Their absence makes little difference to the dog's expression or the judge's decision.

**Training for the show ring**
Apart from helping to make your dog good to look at, you should be aiming to make it confident and happy in show conditions. The breeder or your local canine society can advise if there are ring-craft classes nearby. These classes are invaluable to the novice dog and owner. They accustom dogs to accept each other's presence, and help handlers in the techniques of showing and generally getting the best from their charges.

If you have to go it alone, borrow or buy a book about your breed. Visit one or two shows to see how the exhibitors move and stand their dogs. All toy breeds and some terriers stand for judging on a table, so if you aim to show one of these dogs use the daily grooming routine to help your dog get used to heights—working on the dog at table height will also be kind to your back muscles. Gently run your hands down its back and lift its lip with a finger; as it gains confidence, increase the pressure of your hands, and fully examine its front teeth. Ask a friend to do the same to get your dog experienced with strangers.

The larger breeds stand on the floor, and this is where daily grooming is useful. Top, sides and chest can be brushed to your crooning 'Stand! Show!' Tummy and tail can be done later. This may prevent a sudden 'roll-over' in the ring, when the judge runs his hands down the exhibit's legs.

Your dog knows right from wrong only by your reactions and voice. If it pleases you let it know; if it doesn't, growl — its dam would do just the same.

Lead training is easier said than done. The task is certainly made much less frustrating to you and your dog if you start in your own home and garden. If your garden is not big enough, try to find quiet streets, or use a neighbourhood park when the children are occupied at school. Remember, it would be dangerous to expose your pup to the health risks of lamp-posts, trees and other dogs before it has been fully immunized. The walking show dog usually keeps to its handler's left side, as in obedience training. To keep its attention happily concentrated on you use patience and encouragement, but if necessary resort to bribery or even coercion. Brute force is only for extreme emergencies. Practise in circles, triangles and straight lines. The pup will learn fastest if one person does all this initial training. When the pup is walking well, with proud head carriage, other members of the family can become involved.

Once your dog has the idea, gradually introduce it to the noise and bustle outside the home. Friends and neighbours might think you odd the first time you just acknowledge their greeting and stride on, chatting to your dog and apparently ignoring their obvious desire to talk. Be sure to explain later. They may not really understand, but explanation helps to keep them friendly, and friends make useful judge and handler substitutes! Take your dog on short journeys by car, train and bus — in fact accustom it to any kind of transport you may have to use at some time or another.

Benching is a hurdle to be overcome before the show itself. Your dog will accept this restriction in its first show all the better if it is already used to being tethered for short periods. Start at home by tying one end of the lead to the leg of a chair or table as you cook or write letters; graduate to a park or railway station bench. You can either watch the world go by, or read a book. Reassure your dog, at intervals, that you still enjoy its company; content with this knowledge, it will probably snooze.

Make haste slowly. Taking a pup straight from places it has learnt to accept and understand into the alien world of showing without adequate preparation may result in aggressiveness to humans and other dogs or to a condition known as 'being ring shy'. A ring-shy animal loves shops, travel, walks — anything but the show ring. You *may* cure the condition,

*Right: Afghan Hounds relax on their benches, waiting to enter the show ring. Adjusted chains allow enough freedom of movement.*

but probably you won't. Even dogs that usually enjoy shows can have sudden and unexpected mental aberrations. I especially remember two disconcerting occasions at different shows. Both happened in the Best in Show ring. One incident involved my small toy breed trying to devour the judge's fingers; the other time my very heavy working breed decided it had finished with the proceedings and wanted out. Neither incident recurred and both dogs seemingly forgot their lapses. But their owner's memories are vivid still!

**Helpful hints for show day**
What you need in show equipment largely depends on your choice of breed. Be sure to bring only what is absolutely necessary. You will take this advice to heart after your first long trail from the car park to your bench, dog in one hand, show clutter growing ever heavier in the other, and admission ticket in your teeth. Remember, too, that pickpockets enjoy dog shows just as much as you do, so leave all

*Right: Coats for two Greyhounds and a folding chair for their handler are sensible items for what may be a long wait at an outdoor show.*

your valuables at home.

A dog show is not the best place to wear your latest Dior creation. Comfortable clothes that allow for a change in weather will make for a happier time.

Some shows make provision for eating out, but it is often simpler and less expensive to take your own snacks and drinks. A small folding chair may save hours of standing by the crowded benches. A small bottle of disinfectant, a pair of scissors and some strips of sticking plaster may prove useful. Two plastic bags — one containing damp cotton wool, the other dry tissues — will help you cope with any show dustiness or slight accident (human or canine). Shows usually have a veterinarian on call and the services of first aiders if more help is necessary.

Your dog will need water and food bowls. If you forget them, politely decline any kindly intended offers made by other exhibitors. Go and buy more, or use your own! Virus infections have no respect for even the most cherished dog. Water and food brought from home may prevent a slight tummy upset, although dog foods are on sale at most shows. If you are tempted to give a new tasty dish just before entering the ring, do not be surprised if your dog offers it to the judge's shoes.

A most distressing and repugnant element is the occurrence of deliberate poisoning. Never leave your dog unattended on its bench, or let it accept titbits. Keep water and food in sealable containers. Vigilance is the watchword. If your dog appears abnormally sleepy, or shows signs of distress, call for veterinary aid immediately.

Toy breeds have cage-like benching, and will appreciate a flat cushion. If your dog is larger it will need a benching chain to conform to Kennel Club rules, and a rug or blanket. For either type it will be a long day: elbows soon rub on the benching surfaces. Benched dogs need a firm collar for the chain. To adjust its length use the ring set into the back of the bench. Allow the dog enough chain to lie down but not enough to get off the bench in a self-strangling attempt or to exchange quarrelsome words with its neighbour.

You may use your dog's normal collar and lead when you show it in the ring. Commercially produced leads come in various strengths, colours and designs, and personal taste determines what you buy.

On individual benches you may see cards giving the kennel name and the owner's address. Ask around until you find your card.

You will need your usual grooming kit. If you are efficient you will always keep a spare set with other show paraphernalia in a special

bag ready for the next event; but even the most experienced exhibitor will confess to last-minute hunting for a vital piece of equipment.

It is moderately easy to acquire a good dog, and experience and determination may take it to the top. But experience can only be gained by attending shows, where you must learn to listen and observe intelligently. Standing in the ring for the first time is an ordeal. You will feel convinced that every eye is on you, and it is no consolation to know that people are really concentrating on your dog. Your feelings will go right down the lead; you need not tell your dog about your nerves — it will sense and share them.

For your début, I suggest a breed show, or an Open show with breed classes. With luck you will meet a knowledgeable old hand at the showing game — someone whose advice may help you to win the first of many prize cards.

### Dos and don'ts

Finally, here are some important dos and don'ts of showing.

**Don't** take your dog to any show if there is the slightest suspicion of illness; if there is a highly infectious 'bug' in your neighbourhood; or if your exhibit is a bitch in season. It is expressly forbidden for the mating of bitches to take place within show precincts. You might not intend to have your bitch mated, but virile, experienced stud dogs will have other aims.

**Do** arrive at the show on the right day with the right dog. This reminder may seem superfluous; but exhibitors have been known to arrive on gundog or terrier day with a Toy Poodle, or to have entered a bitch in a bitch class and turn up with a dog.

**Do** allow plenty of travelling time.

**Don't** in any way attempt to influence a judge to make pre-show decisions in your favour. Bribery, if proven, may result in disqualification by the Kennel Club.

**Don't** criticize other exhibits unkindly — their owners feel about them as you feel about yours.

**Don't** be upset by unwarranted criticism of your dog by other exhibitors — they may be ignorant, jealous or incubating influenza.

**Do** give yourself and other exhibitors room to show the dogs.

**Do** allow your dog to relax when other exhibits are being judged, but keep a watchful eye on the judge in case he looks at you.

**Do** what is asked by the steward.

**Do** go to the ringside promptly

when you are requested to do so.

**Don't** charge around the ring shouting commands at your dog. It is not deaf and the judge is not interested in its name. Such demonstrations only give the other exhibitors amusement.

**Do** answer the judge's questions on age etc, but offer no other information.

**Do** accept your dog's placing in a sportsmanlike way: congratulate owners whose dogs gained higher awards than yours and commiserate with owners of pets that come off worse. If you don't get a place, there is always another show with another judge.

If you wish to talk to the judge about your exhibit or its placing, do so when his task is ended. You may be surprised to find him a little weary. He may have had more than 90 dogs to examine. If he gave each dog four minutes, he could have been bending, stretching, peering and feeling nonstop for six hours. Then, too, he may have travelled many miles to reach the show and now be wilting at the prospect of the return journey and the subsequent exercising, feeding and bedding of his own dogs. Despite all this he will find time for you.

Why? Because he's hooked!

*Right: The end of a successful day. Posing for the cameras, a determined Schnauzer and a sagacious St Bernard with their trophies.*

# 6

# BREEDING YOUR DOG

BY KAY WHITE

Wild dogs probably owe their survival at least partly to their fertility. The ability to produce young quickly and in quantity has carried over to the domesticated dog, although it seems to be waning in some of the purebred breeds. After her nine-week pregnancy, a bitch produces a litter ranging from two or three in smaller breeds to 10-14 in Labradors and Irish Setters; the really giant breeds are less fecund. The mother can give birth again six to eight months later, so without contraceptive control imposed by dog owners, in theory the world would soon be overrun by dogs if their offspring survived.

### The breeding cycle
In the wild, a bitch would breed only once a year, probably in spring; but good feeding, warmth, and the easy life of domestication have shortened the intervals at which she accepts a dog. Oestrus periods ('heats' or 'seasons') at intervals of 6, 7, 8, or 10 months may be taken as normal in the domesticated bitch, although the six-monthly interval is less frequent than many would claim. The Basenji from Central Africa, one of the breeds most recently derived from the wild, still comes into season only once a year, in autumn in the Northern Hemisphere, but in April to June in the Antipodes. Experts believe that a lack of animal protein in the diet, possibly caused by feeding vegetable-based dry diets, may delay the breeding season in the domestic bitch of most breeds.

The breeding cycle in mammals is controlled by the hypothalamus, a part of the brain sensitive to both environmental and internal stimuli. Length of available daylight has a part to play; the ken-

*Above: This mating may not succeed. A handler should support the bitch under the abdomen to allow the dog good penetration.*

*Left: A calm, relaxed bitch allowing her puppies ample room to get to her teats. Physical distress can be caused by a congested teat.*

nelled bitch kept in darkness for 12 hours daily may have a different cycle from the bitch kept in a house. A complex interplay between the hypothalamus and the anterior pituitary gland produces hormones triggering the changes that take place in the vagina of the bitch before mating, and the production of follicles that will mature, rupture, and produce eggs to be fertilized by the male. Hormones also maintain pregnancy and in due course give the signal for whelping to begin and for the mammary glands to start secreting milk for the puppies.

Female puppies come into season for the first time at 6-10 months old. If a bitch has passed her first birthday without being in

season you should consult a veterinarian in case there is some hormonal imbalance that can be adjusted. It is possible for a bitch to be mated and conceive at her first season, but she is likely to be too immature to rear a litter successfully without endangering her own health and growth potential. Most professional breeders will consider mating a bitch at her second or third season, at about the age of two or two and a half years.

The mental state of the bitch is an important factor: some bitches remain juvenile in outlook and may lack a maternal instinct for settling with their puppies and rearing them properly. The bitch that is very owner-orientated, possibly conditioned by over-association to believe that she is more human than dog, may also prove to be a poor mother, or may even refuse to be mated.

While it is possible for a bitch to have her first litter when she is quite old, this is an obvious risk to her health and to the production of healthy puppies; seek veterinary advice before mating a bitch for the first time if she is four or over. If bitches are spayed, they will go on having heats to the end of their lives; there is no menopausal state as in women.

Between any two heat periods a bitch has a long period of sexual inactivity culminating in the beginning of pro-oestrus, when the vulva will begin to enlarge and the bitch may show an alteration in temperament, ranging from over-excitement to irritability. She may lick the vulva, so masking the onset of the bloodstained discharge that marks the beginning of her next season. If the bitch is to be mated you should note the date when bloodstained discharge starts, as mating day is calculated from this time. Incidentally, the flow of bloodstained discharge cannot be compared with the human menstrual pattern. In the bitch, the surface of the very long vagina changes when the bitch is on heat and tiny blood vessels become enlarged and finally rupture.

Bleeding from the vulva increases during pro-oestrus, while the lips of the vulva enlarge and soften. During this time, which will last some 9-10 days, the bitch will be increasingly attractive to males, but she will repulse their advances. The plight of a bitch running loose at this time, pursued by a pack of eager males, is pitiful indeed. An unwilling and unready bitch can be mated only by sheer force and with considerable pain to herself.

However, the domestic bitch prepares for the time when she will be ready for copulation by altering her pattern of urination. By frequently passing small amounts of urine she informs males that something interesting is about to occur. At this time the smell of her body and urine are strong enough to be recognized by some humans and all male dogs, including those castrated as adults. So marked are the cell changes within the vulva of a bitch in season that their study may provide a basis for starting a pregnancy where this has hitherto proved impossible. A veterinarian takes a succession of vaginal-smears that are examined under a microscope. This reveals the onset of cell changes providing the right climate for mating.

### The right time for mating

The optimum day for mating and maximum fertility at conception will be just before the bitch ovulates (produces from the ovary eggs ready for fertilization by the male). The pattern of sexual readiness in the bitch is capable of infinite variation among individuals: some show no blood-stained discharge and progress by way of enlargement of the vulva straight to accepting the dog. But normally the right time for mating is when the bloodstained discharge has ceased or paled to straw colour, the vulva is grossly enlarged and tumescent, and the bitch turns her tail aside and otherwise plainly invites copulation.

It is not easy to pinpoint the right day for mating, especially where no 'teaser' dog is available to give indications. Physically the bitch may be ready, but trauma due to travelling, even nervous tension transmitted by the owner, may occlude a natural response. A bitch is usually willing to accept a dog over a period of four or five days or even more. The standard time for mating is often put at the 10th, 11th, 12th or 13th day after the bloodstained discharge started, but it would be wiser to ignore such formal time-tables and judge each bitch as an individual. Beware the common fault of trying to have bitches mated too early in their cycle.

## Signs of Readiness to Mate

*Above: Vulva of bitch, quiescent between oestrus-periods (heats). Above right: Vulva enlarged and tumescent, ready for mating.*

*Below: The duration of the oestrus cycle does vary in individual bitches. The timing given here is considered the normal.*

## The Oestrus Cycle of the Bitch

**Band 1**
**Normal cycle throughout life**

A  10 days. Pro-oestrus. Vulva swelling and bleeding.
B  5 days. Oestrus. Greatest sexual attraction and acceptance of dog.
B1 2-3 days. Ovulation at beginning of oestrus.
C  15 days. Sex attraction wanes.
E  5-7 months. An-oestrus. Sexual inactivity.

**Band 2**
**Phantom pregnancy**

A  10 days. Pro-oestrus. Vulva swelling and bleeding.
B  5 days. Oestrus. Greatest sexual attraction and acceptance of dog.
B1 2-3 days. Ovulation.
C  63 days. Phantom pregnancy.
X  Imaginary whelping.
D  10 days. Imaginary puppy rearing.
E  4½-5½ months. An-oestrus.

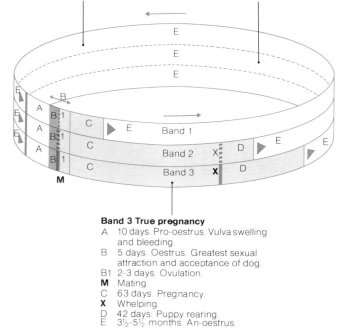

**Band 3 True pregnancy**

A  10 days. Pro-oestrus. Vulva swelling and bleeding.
B  5 days. Oestrus. Greatest sexual attraction and acceptance of dog.
B1 2-3 days. Ovulation.
M  Mating.
C  63 days. Pregnancy.
X  Whelping.
D  42 days. Puppy rearing.
E  3½-5½ months. An-oestrus.

Incidentally where several bitches are kept together, one coming into oestrus will often trigger oestrus in others. They will play simulated mating games, allowing mounting by other bitches much sooner than they would by a male. Unless the bitches become irritable with each other, such behaviour should not be curbed; by human standards it may seem unacceptable, but it represents a natural expression of a sexual urge geared to blood engorgement of the bitches' genital organs. Even neutered and spayed bitches enter into mating games, as an expression of excitement or when a meal has increased their feeling of well-being and contentment.

### The male dog

Male puppies just a few weeks old frequently practise mating behaviour as part of generalized play within the litter. When they are put into individual homes this phase is forgotten and may never again be important in the life of a dog.

There is no need for an adolescent or adult male to have sexual experience; indeed this is best avoided for a dog kept just for companionship. A companion dog used at stud on only one occasion may be disorientated by the experience, and tend to wander, show aggression toward other males, and increase marking behaviour in the home and garden with much damage to furnishings and plants. Professional stud dogs are trained to their work from about 10 months old: they become accustomed to mating bitches at intervals and to living with unready bitches, a pattern of behaviour completely foreign to companion dogs.

Sometimes young male dogs will show an upsurge of certain hormone levels between 6 and 12 months, and their mating behaviour with furniture or people may embarrass the owner. These episodes do not mean that the dog will always be hypersexual, and in the initial stages firm correction and the substitution of another form of play will often be enough to abolish what is anyway usually a transient behaviour pattern. More stubborn cases may be treated with hormones by a veterinarian and it is only rarely that the hyper-sexual dog will heed castration.

The external genitals of the male dog consist of a penis, covered in a hairy sheath, and two testicles that retain the sperm at the correct temperature for fertility. A proportion of dogs, more in some breeds than others, have only one visible testicle, the other being retained within the body; such a dog is termed a unilateral cryptorchid.

Normally both testicles are inside the body of the male puppy at birth but descend through the inguinal canal to the outside of the body at 8-16 weeks. Where only one appears by that time the undescended testicle may still appear around the age of nine months. Incidentally in the young puppy there is a tendency for a testicle to retract at times of tension. A veterinarian can tell whether an apparently missing testicle is present and likely to descend, and the buyer of an expensive pedigreed male puppy is likely to demand a certificate to this effect, particularly if the dog is intended for show or stud work.

The unilateral cryptorchid dog can be fertile and sire puppies but as the condition is thought to be hereditary, it is not desirable to use such a dog at stud. Rarely, neither testicle descends, in which case the dog is infertile. Unilateral cryptorchid dogs may be exhibited under the rules of the British Kennel Club, but American Kennel Club rules forbid this. Not only is it undesirable to perpetuate dogs with a major anatomical fault, but the retained testicle is prone to tumour formation.

### The mating

During copulation the dog's penis emerges from the hair-covered sheath and increases in size, becoming very flexible. The genitals of the family Canidae are unique in having the *bulbus*

## Male Reproductive System

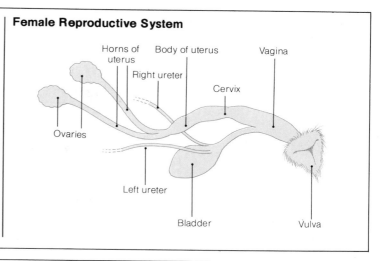

Right ureter
Prostate gland
Bladder
Rectum
Left ureter
Penis
Ductus deferens
Prepuce
Bulbus glandis of penis
Testes

## Female Reproductive System

Horns of uterus
Body of uterus
Vagina
Right ureter
Cervix
Ovaries
Left ureter
Bladder
Vulva

## The Mating Sequence

**1** *Mating should begin with a period of flirtatious play, to precipitate the correct mental and physical stimulus in both sexes.*

**2** *The dog gets the message about the state of readiness of the bitch by sniffing vaginal secretions and odours called pheromones.*

**3** *The dog mounts the bitch, clasping her behind the ribs with his forelegs and bringing his penis close to her vulva for penetration.*

**4** *After ejaculation, followed by a few moments rest, the dog will need to get down. He will turn so that the pair stand back to back.*

**5** *The tie. The dog's penis remains gripped in the vagina, partly by its own enlargement and partly by the constrictor muscle of the bitch.*

glandis, a structure that swells to balloon-like size after ejaculation and, aided by the vaginal muscles of the bitch, enables the mating pair to be locked together or 'tied' for anything up·to an hour after copulation; 20 minutes is the average time. The reason for this unique mating scheme has never been satisfactorily explained.

If the bitch is ready for mating and time is allowed for pre-mating play, she will eventually allow herself to be caught by the dog, and will then stand quietly, tail turned to one side, allowing the dog the facility for penetration. The male will mount the bitch, clasping her behind the ribs with his fore-paws. With penis inserted into the wide open vagina, the dog will make several thrusting movements, and may retract several times and remount but will finally, with shuddering movements, ejaculate sperm high into the vagina, near the cervix.

Dog ejaculate is in three fractions with a momentary pause between each; the first being a lubricating medium, the second containing several thousand sperm, and the final serving to flush the sperm onward toward the target area of the fallopian tubes.

After this phase is over, the dog will want to ease his position during the long tie; he will dismount and lift a hind leg across the back of the bitch, or be assisted to do so by handlers, so that he stands with four feet on the ground, locked together with the bitch but back to back; the dog's penis being bent at 180° within the bitch. Later, they will break away naturally and the dog will lick his genitals until the penis returns within the sheath.

It is possible to have a fertile mating without the tie if the dog has remained within the bitch long enough for the sperm-bearing factor of the ejaculate to be deposited. Eagerness to perform a mating and the ability to do so in apparently copybook fashion is no proof that the dog is fertile. He may have too little ejaculate, or the sperm may be abnormally shaped or show bent or double tails so that propulsion is lost.

The health history of the dog is also significant, as a virus infection giving a high body temperature may render a dog infertile for as long as six months although he is apparently fully recovered. It would be rare to find that over-use of a stud dog caused infertility; a dog should be capable of several matings a week over a short period of time. When a dog has mated several bitches without puppies resulting it is reasonable to suggest that a sperm count and testicular biopsy should be performed.

Some dogs are psychologically inhibited from mating bitches because of past reprimands for antisocial behaviour. Then, too, to some extent we select *away* from the most virile dogs when we choose as companions or for exhibition tractable males easily controlled in the show ring.

Every normal bitch puppy is born with some half million potential eggs in the ovary. The breeder's problems are getting a handful of eggs fertilized at the right time by normal, active sperm, and then implanted in the uterus where the resulting foetuses can be carried to term by the bitch so that she will bear viable puppies. At each oestrus period the bitch releases 4-20 immature eggs that will take hours or even one or two days to 'ripen' sufficiently for sperm to penetrate them. Fortunately, active sperm can remain alive for up to two days after mating, so there is time for sperm and eggs to meet productively.

Allowing two or even three matings gives sperm and ova the best possible chance to reach each other in peak condition. All the ova are shed at the same time, so there is no chance that whelping will be unduly prolonged even if dog and bitch run together and mate at will over six days; nor will natural matings of this type produce an abnormally high number of puppies.

### Possible problems with mating

Since the mid-1960s conditions of dog ownership and lack of kennel help have encouraged too much human interference with dog matings. After travelling hundreds of miles to bring his bitch to a carefully selected dog, many an owner frustrates his own designs by demanding instant mating. There is often neither time nor space for the two animals to become acquainted or to perform their stylized mating play. Sometimes the bitch is shackled and held down by two or more helpers, and the dog lifted on her back and manipulated until he performs the mating act. Some breeders have been known to say that dogs could not mate without human assistance, yet there is wide concern about the number of unproductive matings from apparently fertile animals.

Many veterinary experts in this field believe that more fruitful matings would follow a return to the natural running together of dog and bitch, over some days if need be, with just enough human interference to steady the bitch at the time of penetration.

However, by no means all failed matings are the owner's fault. Some bitches seem physically

**Assisted Mating (Large Dogs)**

**Assisted Mating (Small Dogs)**

ready for mating yet refuse a dog's advances. Some suffer a hormonal imbalance that makes them too masculine. Others have some abnormality of vulva or vagina causing pain or preventing penetration. Toy bitches that have been over-protected may not allow any dog to come near them, although some behave more naturally if apart from doting and fearful owners.

### Using a stud dog
Choosing a stud dog is a process demanding considerable forethought. Owners should make

*Top: An assisted mating between two large breed dogs. One of the handlers supports the bitch with his knee and also guides the dog.*

inquiries about any hereditary diseases prevalent in the breed, and the owners of both bitch and dog should be prepared to provide copies of certificates of freedom from disease if such documents are issued by their country's breed club or kennel club. It is also important to check that the bitch's current owner has correctly registered her at the national kennel

*Above: Larger brood bitches are preferred in toy breeds and the dog must be positioned on a block to increase its height.*

club, otherwise registration of the puppies may be impeded.

A stud fee is payable immediately after mating, whether or not any puppies result. A receipt and a copy of the dog's pedigree bearing kennel club numbers should be provided in return for the fee, and if the stud dog owner has to sign an official kennel club form to say that the mating has taken place, this is best done at the same time in the presence of both parties involved.

There may be some temptation to make some other arrangement; perhaps for the stud owner to take a puppy or two puppies in lieu of fee, or to buy a certain number of the puppies when they are reared. It cannot be emphasized too strongly that such agreements are full of pitfalls. For one thing the bitch owner is committed in advance to dispose of puppies about which he may feel very differently once they are born and reared. Then, too, the litter may not contain the sexes and colours needed to meet the agreement. Almost always someone ends feeling aggrieved.

It is much better to pay the stud fee outright than be bound by another's interest. However, if the stud dog's owner passes on inquiries that result in the sale of puppies it is usual to offer an additional sum. About 10% of the selling price would be about right.

Before the mating is even accomplished it is wise to find out how and where tails will be docked and dew-claws removed if these practices are customary in the breed. Veterinary opinion is hardening against such mutilations for purely cosmetic purposes and it may be that it is necessary to ask the stud dog owner or some other experienced breeder to dock the tails of the puppies when they are two to three days old if a veterinarian cannot be found to do them. In the United Kingdom a lay person may perform this operation before the puppies' eyes are open, but ear cropping — even by veterinarians — is not permitted, although in some countries in Europe and in the United States ear cropping is accepted in some breeds.

The brood bitch should be chosen from a line with full fertility on both her dam's and sire's side. Avoid lines with a history of birth by Caesarean section and low litter numbers.

**Phantom pregnancy**
Whether or not a mating was fertile or even occurred, the hormonal changes of pregnancy or closely similar changes ensue in the bitch. So great is the hormonal influence that an unmated bitch may give every impression of being pregnant, even 'thinking' herself into labour pains, producing milk and nursing some toy or household object as her make-believe litter.

It is important not to pander to such a bitch, as humouring her only prolongs the condition and she may become irritable and bad tempered in trying to protect invisible puppies. She is best distracted with increased exercise and play, and her chosen objects and whelping bed should be taken away. Extreme cases may need hormone treatment.

In a kennel situation a bitch with phantom pregnancy can be very useful for rearing another's puppies. But this condition can be distressing in the pet bitch as it tends to recur after every season; producing an actual litter is no help and the only remedy is having her spayed by your veterinarian.

**Pregnancy**
The bitch who is genuinely pregnant shows little sign for at least a month. She requires no extra food until she is two thirds of the way through pregnancy, which is calculated at roughly 63 days, but allowing for delay in fertilization and breed idiosyncrasy may last a

*Above: A pregnant Basset Hound. Pregnancy will begin to show in the fifth week. It is important to maintain good muscle tone and the bitch should continue to exercise up to the day of whelping. The pressure of several puppies on the bladder can cause incontinence.*

week longer or several days fewer. At the fifth week of pregnancy there should be some thickening of the bitch's shape behind her ribs and her mammary glands should begin to develop; there may be a little morning sickness and her appetite may vary from day to day.

From the sixth week of her pregnancy you should raise the protein content of a bitch's food by one third, with an appropriate increase in vitamin supplement. Offer meals twice, three times, or even more frequently during the day, to allow for the displacement of the stomach by the swelling uterus.

Each embryo puppy floats in fluid enclosed in a double foetal sac attached to the walls of the horn-shaped uterus by a placenta. Growth in the last three weeks of pregnancy is so rapid that the uterus may have to fold back upon itself, making a dramatic change in the outline of the bitch, and seeming to cause her a little discomfort, for bitches often seem to stop eating for a day at this time. Only at the very end of pregnancy is bone laid down in puppy skeletons, which then show up on X-ray, but toward the end of pregnancy you can see definite movements of the puppies when the bitch is resting.

A milk-like substance may be present already in the mammary glands, or may not arrive until after whelping. Owners sometimes worry because the bitch has an uneven number of teats, or because there are fewer of these than puppies born, but neither fear is justified.

## The whelping (birth)

The beginning of whelping is usually marked by a refusal of food, restlessness and a very deep, nervous panting, that seems to use up a great deal of the bitch's energy and disturbs those who hear her. This is the most distressing stage of whelping, for the actual labour pains seem to worry her far less than the initial apprehension. Left to her own devices she would seek out a secluded, dark place in which to have her puppies, and, if allowed to, will dig a burrow that will be suitable for the purpose.

A bitch with a newborn litter feels by instinct extremely vulnerable to interference, so her whelping quarters should be arranged to give her the maximum physical and psychological protection. Her whelping box should have high sides and a lid, removable if she needs help and for cleaning; she should be in a room away from household bustle and where she will not feel threatened by the sight or sound of other dogs, and no audience should be invited to witness her whelping, fascinating though this miracle always is.

The veterinarian attending should be warned when the bitch goes into first-stage labour, as veterinary services may be needed at any time, but as the average bitch's labour is so long it is not possible to have a veterinarian in attendance all the time.

The initial stage of panting and apprehension can last for 12 hours or longer and become extremely enervating; the actual expelling pains are quite short and do not seem to distress the bitch very much. Once hormonal action has induced a placenta to separate from the wall of the uterus, the puppy in its sac surrounded by another sac, filled with fluid, rotates and starts its journey through cervix and vagina and on into the outside world. Ideally it arrives head first, although many puppies are born feet first, which seldom seems to matter.

If everything is going well, one or two deep, expelling pains will bring the water bag filled with dark fluid to the vulva, and the subsequent strain will push out the puppy, still in its foetal membranes. These must now be

## Embryos Implanted in the Uterus

25 days    33 days    50 days    63 days

*Left: A section through the horns of the uterus at 30 days, showing the puppies implanted along the walls, each in two membranes.*

*Left below: Four stages in the development of the puppy within the uterus. At 50 days the embryo puppy begins to show fine hair.*

removed as quickly as possible to prevent the puppy inhaling fluid into the lungs. The bitch may instinctively bite open and eat the membranes, bite off the umbilical cord and start to dry the puppy.

If she is still so swollen with puppies that she cannot easily reach her vulva, or if she lacks the instinct to attend to her young, then the attendant owner must open the bags and dry the puppy, cutting the umbilical cord a long way from the puppy, after smoothing any blood remaining in the cord toward the pup. There is no need to tie the umbilical cord in any way.

The placenta, or afterbirth, should arrive with the puppy or very soon after. The bitch will instinctively want to eat the placenta, which looks like a piece

## The Miracle of Birth

*At birth, the puppy emerges from the vulva encased in its membranes. Each contraction expels it further, until the bitch is able to tear off the membranes and lick the mouth clear so that the puppy may take its first breath, expanding its lungs for the first time. The placenta, or afterbirth, will still be attached, or may follow very soon.*

**1** The water bag containing the puppy appears at the vulva.

**3** The bitch tears off the bag and gives the puppy a good wash.

**2** The puppy, still encased in the bag, emerges, usually head-first.

**4** The puppy's head is freed first so that it may take its first breath.

of liver, abounds in nourishment and would thus provide a valuable meal for a bitch in the wild at a time when she could not hunt. If the litter is large, the bitch may eat so many placentas that she suffers diarrhoea. Because she will be unwilling to leave her puppies until the last minute this condition can be extremely inconvenient, so the owner should try to take away at least half the placentas; it is easier to get the early ones, before the bitch realizes what she is losing. As her distended body is eased and the bitch realizes what is happening, she herself will usually attend to later arrivals in the litter.

Puppies should be born into a warm draught-free atmosphere, and must be dried quickly as they are unable to adjust their body

---

*Right: A bitch very full of puppies may require assistance to open the bags and release the puppies if she cannot reach the vulva herself.*

*Below: A Sheltie bitch snug in her insulated whelping box, with a lid that can be closed to give her a feeling of total security.*

heat to the lowered temperature of the outside world. More puppies die from chilling than from any other single cause; the most critical period is the first few hours after birth, when the dam is preoccupied with expelling other puppies, and the whelping box is continually being drenched with fluids from them. But you should not remove the first-born puppies from the bitch as this distresses her, and their presence and attempts to suckle are said to induce hormonal change that speeds up subsequent births.

The new idea of allowing puppies to be born on warm, deep polyester fur instead of newspaper has done a great deal to save puppies in the first few days of life, when fading from a multiplicity of causes is a very real and ever-present risk.

It is pleasant indeed if puppies follow each other at 40-minute to hourly intervals until the bitch is obviously empty and at rest. Unfortunately, hold-ups occur if a bitch becomes tired and loses the will to expel the puppies. Then the attendant must judge whether the interval between puppies has been unduly long (say over 90 minutes). If there are indeed still puppies to be born, continuing delay could mean they are dead, but an injection of oxytocin by a veterinarian will usually restart contractions.

Birth trouble can arise if a puppy is grossly oversized or fails to present at the cervix in a direct manner. Where the bitch is straining but making no progress with birth, delay is dangerous and a veterinarian must be consulted with a view to delivery by Caesarean section, a reasonably safe operation provided it is carried out before the bitch is exhausted.

### The early life of the puppies

Puppies will instinctively find their way to a teat, and should be encouraged to do so, as in the first few hours after birth they receive the all-important colostrum which carries antibodies for diseases that the dam has encountered, or been vaccinated against. For some weeks after whelping the bitch will have a discharge from the vulva. This emission is dark at first but later pales to bright blood red, derived from the attachment sites of the placentas. Thus there is proportionately more discharge for a large litter. Any continuation of a dark or foul-smelling discharge indicates urgent need for veterinary help, as a puppy or a placenta may have been retained, potentially with extremely grave consequences.

The bitch requires a great deal of food and water while feeding her puppies, reaching peak demand three weeks after birth. Later, in imitation of her wild ancestors, she may vomit her own partly digested food for the young puppies to eat.

Puppies are born without sight or hearing, eyes and ears being poorly developed at birth. Eyes open at around 10 days and puppies can hear at three weeks, by when they should be moving around, if a little unsteadily. The bitch licks her newborn puppies constantly to clean them and to

**Bottle-feeding the Correct Way**

*Above: Puppies may require one or two bottles a day supplementary feeding. Hold the puppy with its front legs free to 'knead', and the hind legs to stretch and kick.*

*Below: After four weeks, the bitch stands to feed her puppies, making them put extra effort into obtaining their milk. This is part of the natural weaning process.*

stimulate urination and defecation, consuming all their body wastes until weaning begins.

If the bitch has plenty of milk, weaning need not start until five or six weeks, or until the puppies start to investigate the bitch's own food, showing they are ready for more than milk. If late weaning is contemplated, the bitch should not be shut up with her puppies, unable to escape their ceaseless worrying.

Puppies are usually weaned individually on hand-fed balls of scraped meat. Later they progress to carbohydrate and milk fed from a shallow dish when they have learned to lap. Their first teeth will come through at around two to three weeks old, and the second teeth will be acquired at four to six months, probably with some minor pain. The ears are often carried at strange angles at this time, probably as a reaction to inflammation in the facial muscles.

Puppies have much to learn from the dam even after she has stopped feeding them, and although some breeders will want to remove the dam quickly so that she may regain her figure and show condition, in many ways this is a pity, for bitch and puppies enjoy each other's company so much. Ideally, the bitch should have some contact with her puppies until they leave for new homes at 8-12 weeks, the time depending on breed and size.

### Contraception

If a bitch is not required for breeding purposes, she and her owner are spared a great deal of trouble if she has her reproductive organs removed once she is adult and fully developed. The veterinarian calls this operation an ovario-hysterectomy; the popular phrase is 'having her spayed'. The bitch can then be a constant companion to her human family without the mood swings, mess and/or expense of boarding her during her seasons.

It is of no physical or mental advantage to the bitch to allow her to have one litter. This folk legend has meant that a lot of surplus puppies have been bred by people with little knowledge of the subject, inadequate premises, and inability to find permanent homes for the young.

After being spayed, the bitch need not put on weight or become lethargic: the outcome depends on owner management. Spayed bitches may be exhibited in the United Kingdom provided they have had a litter registered at the Kennel Club; the same ruling applies to castrated dogs but they are seldom in top-class competition. The American Kennel Club permits exhibition of neither spayed bitches nor castrated dogs although they may compete in field trials.

An alternative method of contraception, and one that leaves breeding options open, is giving the bitch a branded form of progesterone. This hormone inhibits ovulation in a similar fashion to the human contraceptive pill. Several versions of this drug have been marketed, to be given orally or by injection, and the much improved latest editions are perfectly safe and allow manipulation of the oestrus period so that the bitch can be brought into season and readiness for breeding at the owner's convenience.

Vasectomy (cutting the excretory duct of the testicles) is possible for the male dog. This operation should make him infertile but will not prevent active mating behaviour and urine marking of territory, so it is of little value to the pet dog owner, although a vasectomized dog might be a valuable addition to a kennel to indicate when bitches are ready for mating, especially if they are to be taken to a distant stud dog.

Castration of the male is performed much less frequently than spaying of bitches. The testicles are removed, leaving the scrotum, so that superficially the dog does not appear mutilated. Castration makes it possible for a male dog to live in the home with entire bitches; it is approaching cruelty to keep an entire male close to bitches in season. He will almost certainly stop eating and nervous tension will affect his condition to an alarming extent.

Castration is not always as effective as owners hope in curing wandering or aggressive behaviour in the adult male. A veterinarian can give injections of hormone that mimic the effect of castration for a short time. Owners can then see if the operation would cause the desired change.

Above: Six week-old pups enjoy a large marrow bone. The gnawing action helps develop the jaw and eases the cutting of teeth.

Below: The tails of certain breeds may be docked by owners at 3/4 days (before the eyes are open) to comply with breed standards.

### Tail Docking

Above: Tie a ligature tightly around the tail to reduce the blood supply and cut just below. Seal the severed end to stop bleeding.

To seal, dip the tail in finely powdered permanganate of potash, or any other recommended substance.

Above: Alternatively, cut a fine rubber band and tie tightly around the tail. After 2/3 days the lower end will wither and drop off. This method saves bleeding but may cause the puppy longer pain.

Above: A badly docked tail with protruding bone end. This tail may cause continual irritation and soreness, and it may eventually require re-docking under a general anaesthetic.

# 7

# THE LAW AND YOUR DOG

BY JOAN PALMER & BRUCE SESSIONS

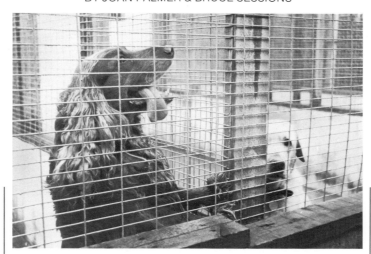

When you buy a dog you are faced with legal responsibilities as well as moral ones.

### Dog licences

In the United Kingdom, every dog over the age of six months has to be licensed. Certificates are obtainable at any post office, and cost a mere 37½ pence. If you own several dogs, you obtain one licence to keep the requisite number of dogs in the United Kingdom and pay a multiple fee based on the number of dogs. Historically, a charge for keeping dogs was first levied in Britain in 1796 to raise revenue. The rate varied, but in 1867 it was replaced by an excise duty of 5 shillings, which was increased in 1878 to 7s 6d, the equivalent in today's currency of 37½ pence. Exempt from the licence requirements are puppies under six months, hounds under 12 months (never entered in the pack), working sheep dogs, and guide dogs for the blind.

### Identity discs

Another statutory requirement is, that every dog shall, in a public place — that is, outside the home — wear a collar to which a disc is attached, clearly showing the name and address of its owner. Many owners add their dog's pet name, so that it will respond if it strays and is found by a stranger; others prefer to omit this information, believing that it could lead to the theft of the dog. The identification rule does not apply to packs of hounds, or to dogs being used for sporting purposes, for the capture and destruction of vermin, or for tending sheep and cattle.

### Stray dogs

The Dogs' Act of 1906 gave the police statutory responsibility for the capture, custody and disposal of stray dogs. The same Act allows members of the public to capture a stray, but they are required to hand it over to the police. People who lose a dog, in the United Kingdom, should report it missing at their nearest police station, where a detailed description of the animal will be taken.

Stray dogs are retained at a police station prior to dispersal to an RSPCA (Royal Society for the Prevention of Cruelty to Animals) establishment, or to various pounds. In London, dogs found straying within the Metropolitan Police area — that is, within a 20-mile radius of Charing Cross — are collected each morning from police stations all over London by the distinctive red vans belonging to the famous Dogs' Home in Battersea Park Road.

Under the law, an animal has to be kept for seven days, pending a claim, so the Home and other kennels are maintaining the animals, during this period, for the police, who pay the fee. At Battersea, however, lost and stray dogs are often maintained for several weeks, as many Londoners visit the Home to buy unwanted pets, as well as to trace lost ones.

### Rabies and quarantine

There is much anxiety in the United Kingdom that rabies will spread from Europe, where it has been moving steadily westward since the end of the Second World War. Comprehensive import control and quarantine policies have been operating for many

*Above: Dogs spend six months in approved quarantine kennels in the United Kingdom. These two dogs are separated by a double grill, which prevents them from touching.*

years with the result that there have been only two cases of animal rabies outside quarantine in the past 50 years. In the same period, 27 cases of animal rabies, of which 25 were in dogs, have been intercepted by the quarantine procedure. It is forbidden to bring a dog into the United Kingdom without an import licence, and the animal must spend six months in a quarantine kennel approved by the Ministry of Agriculture, Fisheries and Food. Smuggling in of dogs or other animals is a serious offence, leading to heavy fines and even imprisonment.

### Dogs and property

In writing earlier about choosing a dog, I mentioned the need for buyers to first ascertain that a dog might be kept on their premises. Owners of freehold property may bring home a domestic pet without concern. It is, however, not unusual for leasehold properties to contain a clause, either forbidding the keeping of any animal without the written consent of the landlord, or restricting the number to be kept; while such consent is often a pure formality, it can, if the landlord wishes, be withheld. Similarly, some councils prohibit the keeping of dogs in council-owned property, restrict permission to those tenants living in premises

that have direct access to a garden or the roadway, or insist on the tenant obtaining written approval before keeping a dog, subject to various conditions.

### The owner's responsibilities

Generally, the keeping of a dog does not present problems unless the owner allows it to become a nuisance. The owner of a persistent barker may, if neighbours complain, find himself in trouble with the local authorities. If the animal proves dangerous, its owner may be ordered to keep it under control, or a destruction order may be made against it, particularly if the dog has proved vicious on a number of occasions.

Less than 10 years ago, if a dog slipped out of the gate, took itself for a stroll, and caused an accident — perhaps by causing a car to swerve and crash into another — the dog's owner was unlikely to be taken to task. Since the Animals' Act of 1971, however, dog owners are liable for any accident or damage caused by their pet, even if the animal is out of their control at the time. Because of this Act, more and more dog owners are taking advantage of third party insurance schemes, run by specialist insurance companies and societies such as the National Dog Owners' Association.

Responsible dog owners never let their charges off the lead in a busy thoroughfare; indeed, there is a set procedure in the United Kingdom for establishing a 'designated' road, where dogs are legally prohibited, if leashless, and loose animals can be impounded as strays.

It is an offence for dogs to foul the footpath and, of course, for dogs to worry livestock. A farmer who witnesses a dog attacking his stock is legally within his rights to shoot, and frequently does; and the dog's owner is liable to make good his loss.

It is an offence to ill-treat any domestic or captive animal, or for the owner to permit such treatment; also, when a person has been convicted of cruelty to a dog, the court may disqualify him from keeping another for whatever period it considers fit.

### Transport and shops
In London, and elsewhere in the United Kingdom, dogs are permitted on buses at the discretion of the individual conductor and must, where appropriate, travel on the upper deck of the vehicle. They may also travel on both underground and overland trains, being carried free of charge if contained in a suitable receptacle; otherwise half price, or child's fare, is demanded. They may occupy a carriage, although not a seat, provided other passengers do not object, in which case they must travel in the guard's van.

There is no hard and fast rule relating to the banning of dogs from shops. Indeed, many owners consider that store proprietors, other than those trading in foodstuffs, adopt a high-handed attitude in attempting to keep out Fido. The position relating to food shops is, that the Food Hygiene (General) Regulations of 1970, made under the Food and Drugs Act of 1955 (in Scotland the Food Hygiene (Scotland) Regulations 1959), obliged food traders 'to take all such steps as may be reasonably necessary to protect the food from risk of contamination.' This places on the proprietor of a food shop the responsibility of deciding whether or not to ban dogs from that shop.

### Breeding dogs
A comparatively new law in the United Kingdom is the Breeding of Dogs Act (1973), which empowers local authorities to license breeding establishments, to inspect these premises, and to prosecute the owners for offences. Owners keeping more than two bitches for the purpose of breeding must register with their local authority and invite inspection. This law caused considerable apprehension when first introduced, but has undoubtedly done much to alleviate unhygienic, substandard breeding establishments. Animal boarding establishments also have to be registered with the local authority.

### New laws planned
The foregoing is an outline of the basic laws relating to dogs in the United Kingdom. However, following the findings of a Working Party on Dogs set up in 1974 by the Department of the Environment, and an organization called JACOPIS (Joint Advisory Committee on Pets in Society) in July 1975, there has been a move afoot to reduce the large number of strays, to raise the dog licence fee to a more realistic figure, and to

transfer responsibility for strays from the police to local authorities, who would utilize the licence fees to employ experienced and humane dog wardens who would round up strays, check licences and generally encourage responsible dog ownership. A number of councils are already employing wardens with great success, but legislation is a long time coming, and meanwhile the British are still paying the same dog licence as they have done for the past 100 years.

### International laws
The law in relation to dogs differs in various parts of the world, and it is advisable to check with the relevant Embassy as to the current position.

All European countries demand a certificate of inoculation against rabies and distemper for imported dogs, and usually a certificate of health and a statement from the appropriate Government Department that there has been no outbreak of rabies during the past 12 months.

In Australia, laws relating to the control, seizure and registration of dogs vary from state to state. There has been some general relaxation in recent years, in that German Shepherd Dogs (Alsatians) can now be imported into Australia entire, and breeding is allowed.

Guide dogs for the blind may accompany their owners into any building, or place open to the public, and on public transport.

An excellent canine registration system exists in New South Wales. Owners fill in a form, pay a fee and are issued with a receipt, registration number and a registration collar disc inscribed with the name of the area, the registration number and year of expiry.

Dogs can only enter Australia from or via the United Kingdom, New Zealand and specified Pacific Islands.

In some countries, dogs have been almost outlawed. In the People's Republic of China, for instance, the tax on dogs rose so sharply in 1947 that few people could afford to keep them. Many dogs were sent to the United States for refuge, and those less fortunate found their way to the hungry worker's table.

In recent years the dog licence fee and cost of canine food and other products has risen so steeply in Germany that the pet dog there has now become a luxury. It is a trend that is likely to spread. However, if caring and responsible ownership is encouraged by making the purebred dog expensive to buy, to keep, and to feed, few who really love dogs will complain.

### American laws
In the United States, the laws regarding dog ownership are so many, complex and varied as to require an entire book on that subject alone. Each state has the power to make rules and regulations pertaining to dog ownership. In addition, cities and counties

within a state may also enact regulations. Since each state has the power to license and regulate dogs within its boundaries, the owner of a dog must consult the law of the state, as well as the city ordinances where he is keeping his dog, in order to determine the nature and extent of licences, taxes and regulations.

Generally speaking, all dogs must be licensed upon reaching four months of age. However, in some localities, the minimum age is six months. In all cases, proof of rabies vaccination is a prerequisite for obtaining a licence. Some municipalities require such vaccinations at four months of age, others at six months. Some cities have licences that are valid for a period of one year, others for up to four years.

In some cities, there are restrictions as to how many dogs can be housed in a single family home. Because of the mish-mash of laws, it is possible that a family living on one side of the street is limited to two dogs because they live within the city limits, while neighbours across the street may be allowed four dogs because the dividing line between the city and the county is right down the centre of the street. On one side, the city laws apply, but across the street, the county's laws apply.

There are leash laws in practically every city, county and state. The extent to which these laws are enforced varies from place to place. In New York, very strict leash laws apply, as well as laws pertaining to cleaning up after one's dog. In other locales, the same 'strict' laws apply, but are seldom — if ever — enforced! The reason given most often by animal control officials is simply lack of manpower.

It is for this very reason that the United States is suffering from a severe pet population explosion — too many animals roaming loose, too few responsible dog owners, and even fewer animal control officials. In an effort to help solve the over-population problem, some areas have instituted free spay/neuter clinics. In addition, if someone desires to adopt a dog from an animal shelter, the fee for females is usually considerably higher than for males. In many cases, a portion of the adoption fee is refunded to the new owner upon submission of proof that the adopted female has been spayed.

The cost of a dog licence varies, not only from city to city, but also between male and female. In some areas, it costs less to obtain a licence for a spayed female and/or neutered male. The fees that are charged were originally intended to be a controlling method rather than a tax to generate income. Unfortunately, 50 percent of all dog owners in the United States have dogs that are not licensed, and have never been licensed. This statistic comes from an official of the Society for the Prevention of Cruelty to Animals (SPCA).

An example of the extremes in the law is a law passed in the state

of Ohio in 1965, and described as the strictest leash law in the United States. Dogs must be on a leash, tied, or fenced in 24 hours a day, except when lawfully hunting.

Whereas some states require all dogs to be leashed, however, others merely require that the dog wears a collar with a valid licence attached, when off the premises.

In some states, the strict laws whereby a dog may be killed if found roaming upon another's premises unaccompanied by its owner have been held by the courts to be constitutional. In other areas, such action would be considered as 'wanton destruction of private property'. In most states, a dog is considered 'property' just as much as a horse or a cow. An owner can sue for damages done to his dog, just as he can sue for damages done to his car. The theft of a dog can give rise to a civil action for conversion, just like the theft of a diamond ring.

In spite of the wide variances in the law relating to dogs (and in dog owners' rights), the public's right to be protected comes first. Thus, courts have upheld laws requiring that dogs be licensed, muzzled, leashed, confined and/or tagged. But the interpretation of the law varies from court to court, case by case and state by state.

The common law rule was that a property owner owed a trespasser the duty of refraining from setting traps or spring guns. In more recent times, the meaning of the word 'traps' has been extended. Many courts have held that to keep a vicious dog at large on one's property is the same as setting a trap or spring gun to catch a trespasser. A few states hold that a public warning advising of the presence of a vicious dog on private property may excuse the owner from responsibility for damage done by the dog to trespassers. Other courts hold that not even a warning justifies setting vicious dogs on a trespasser, or allowing such dogs to run at large on property when the presence of a trespasser should be known.

In some areas, the posting of a sign reading 'Beware of the Dog' is sufficient protection from the liability for damages which might be inflicted upon a person by that dog. That same sign, posted in another city, county or state, can be considered as proof that the owner of the dog knew that his dog was vicious, and therefore should be held liable. The laws are confusing, and perhaps this is one of the reasons that enforcement of existing laws is so slack.

Each dog owner should keep in mind that the laws relating to dog ownership are in effect for the protection of all concerned. Dogs that are leashed or otherwise confined seldom get run over by cars. Lost dogs with valid licence tags have a better chance of being returned to their owners. Regardless of whether existing laws are enforced, responsible dog ownership dictates that the laws should be obeyed.

# GLOSSARY

Words in *italics* refer to separate entries within the glossary

## A

**Action** The way a dog moves.

**AKC** American Kennel Club.

**Albino** Animal with pigmentation deficiency.

**All-rounder** A judge qualified to adjudicate all recognized breeds.

**Almond eyes** Oval-shaped like an almond, slanted at corners.

**Amble** A relaxed, easy *gait* in which the legs on either side move almost, but not quite, as a pair. Often seen as the transitional movement between the *walk* and the faster gaits.

**Angulation** The angles formed by a meeting of the bones: mainly, the shoulder, upper arm, *stifle* and *hock*.

**Ankylosis** The abnormal adhesion of bones, especially those forming a joint; stiffening of a joint.

**Anorchid** A male dog without testicles.

**Anticipating** In obedience training, acting before receiving a command.

**Apophysis** An outgrowth or projection, especially one from a bone.

**Apple-headed** Having a skull rounded on top. Not desirable in most breeds.

**Apron** The long hair on the throat and below the neck on long-coated dogs.

## B

**B (or b)** Abbreviation for bitch.

**Babbler** A hound that barks when not on the *trail*.

**Back** Variable in meaning depending upon standard. In some standards defined as the vertebrae between the *withers* and the *loin*.

**Bad mouth** Teeth crooked or mis-aligned; *overshot* or *undershot* bite.

**Balanced** A consistent whole; symmetrical, typically proportioned as a whole, or as regards its separate parts: e.g. balance of head, of body, or balance of head and body.

**Bandy legs** Legs bent outwards.

**Barrel** Rounded rib section.

**Barrel hocks** *Hocks* that turn out, causing the toes to turn in (also called spread hocks, or divergent hocks).

**Basewide** Having a wide footfall, resulting from a *paddling* movement, and causing body to rock from side to side.

**Bat ears** Large, stiff open ears pointing outwards (like a French Bulldog's).

**Bay** The long-drawn-out sound made by a hound in pursuit.

**Beard** The very profuse, bushy *whiskers* of the Griffon Bruxellois, as opposed to terrier whiskers.

**Beauty spot** A distinct spot, usually round, of coloured hair, surrounded by the white of the *blaze*, on the top of the skull between the ears (e.g. Boston Terrier).

**Beefy** Over-heavy development of the *hindquarters*.

**Belton** The lemon- or blue-flecked colour of certain English Setters, notably the Laverack strain. Also orange or liver belton.

**Bench show** A dog show at which the dogs competing for prizes are 'benched' (leashed on benches).

**Best in Show** The animal judged to be the best of all the breeds in a show.

**Bevy** A flock of birds.

**Bilateral cryptorchid** See *Cryptorchid*.

**Bird dog** A sporting dog trained to hunt birds.

**Bitch** A female dog.

**Bite** The position of the teeth when the mouth is shut.

**Blanket** The colour of coat on the back and upper part of the sides, between the neck and the tail.

**Blaze** A white stripe running up the middle of the face, generally between the eyes.

**Blenheim** A variety of spaniel with white and reddish markings.

**Blinker** A dog that points a bird and then leaves it, or, upon finding a bird, avoids making a definite *point*.

**Blocky** Having a square or cube-like formation of the head.

**Blooded** Of good breeding; pedigreed.

**Bloom** The glossiness of a *coat* in the very best condition.

**Blue merle** Blue and grey mixed with black. Marbled.

**Bluies** Coloured portions of the coat with a distinct bluish or smoky cast. This colouring is associated with extremely light or blue eyes, and liver or grey eye-rims, nose and lip pigment (e.g. Pembroke Welsh Corgi).

**Board** To kennel and care for a dog in its owner's absence, for a fee.

**BOB** Abbreviation for Best of Breed.

**Bobtail** (1) A naturally tailless dog, or a dog with a tail *docked* very short. (2) Common name for the Old English Sheepdog.

**Bodied up** Mature, well-developed.

**Bolt** To drive or 'start' an animal out of its earth or burrow.

**Bone** A well-boned dog is one with limbs that give an appearance and feel of strength and spring without *coarseness*.

**Bossy** With over-development of the shoulder muscles.

**Braccoid** Belonging to the *hound* family of dogs.

**Brace** A pair of dogs of the same type.

**Breastbone** Bone running down the middle of the chest, to which all but the *floating ribs* are attached; *sternum*.

**Breeching** The tan hairs on the inside and back of the thighs, seen in Manchester Terriers.

**Breed** A variety of *purebred* dog: a dog or bitch with a *pedigree*.

**Breeder** Someone who breeds dogs.

**Breeding particulars** *Sire*, *dam*, date of birth, sex, colour, Kennel Club registration details, etc.

**Brindle** A mixture of light and dark hairs, usually darker streaks on a grey, tawny or brown background.

**Brisket** The part of the lower chest that includes the breastbone.

**Brock** A badger.

**Broken colour** *Self colour* relieved by white or another colour.

**Broken-haired** A roughed-up wire coat.

**Broken-up face** A receding nose, together with a deep *stop*, *wrinkle*, and *undershot* jaw (e.g. Bulldog, Pekingese).

**Brood bitch** A *bitch* kept for breeding.

**Brush** A bushy tail; a tail heavy with hair (e.g. Alaskan Malamute).

**Brushing** A *gaiting* fault, when parallel *pasterns* are so close that the legs brush in passing.

**Bull-baiting** A cruel sport of bygone days in which a dog or dogs baited a bull.

**Bull neck** A heavy neck, well-muscled.

**Burr** The irregular inner part of the pinna of the ear.

**Butterfly nose** A nose of two colours, usually dark brown or black spotted with flesh colour.

**Buttocks** The rump or hips.

**Button ear** Ear that folds over in front, with tip drooping forward, as in the Fox Terrier.

**Bye** At *Field trials*, an odd dog remaining after the dogs entered in a *stake* have been paired in *braces* by *drawing*.

## C

**Camel back** Arched back, like that of a one-hump camel.

**Canine** Applies to dogs, foxes, wolves and jackals.

**Canines** The two upper and two lower sharp-pointed teeth next to the *incisors*; fangs.

**Canter** A *gait* with three beats to each stride, two legs moving separately and two as a diagonal pair. Slower than the *gallop* and not as tiring.

**Carinated** Keel-shaped; having a prominent central line like the bottom of a ship.

**Carpals** Bones of the *pastern* joints.

**Carp back** Arched back.

**Castrate** To remove the testicles of a male dog; to geld.

**Catch dog** A dog used to catch and hold a hunted animal, so that the huntsman can take it alive.

**Cat feet** Short, compact and round feet common to terriers, as opposed to *splay feet*.

**CD (Companion Dog)** A suffix used with the name of a dog that has been recorded a Companion Dog by the *AKC* as a result of having won certain minimum scores at three Obedience trials under three different judges.

**CDX (Companion Dog Excellent)** A suffix used with the name of a dog that has been recorded a Companion Dog Excellent by the *AKC* as a result of having won certain minimum scores in three *Open classes* at Obedience trials.

**Cephalic index** The ratio, multiplied by 100, of the greatest breadth of the dog's head from side to side, to the length from above the root of the nose to the occiput.

**Challenge Certificate (CC)** Award given, at *judge's* discretion, to best of sex of *breed* at UK Championship shows.

**Champion** A dog that has won three *Challenge Certificates* under three different *judges* at Championship shows in the UK. In the USA the title is awarded on points won at major shows.

**Character** Expression, individuality, and general appearance and deportment as considered typical of a *breed*.

**Cheeky** With cheeks prominently rounded, thick, or protruding.

**Chest** The part of the body or trunk enclosed by the ribs.

**Chicken-breasted** With a short, protruding *breastbone*.

**China eye** A clear blue eye.

**Chippendale front** Named after the Chippendale chair; forelegs out at *elbows*, *pasterns* close, and feet turned out. See also *Fiddle front*.

**Chiselled** Clean-cut in the head, particularly beneath the eyes.

**Choke chain/collar** A chain or leather collar fitted to the dog's neck in such a way that the amount of pressure exerted by hand tightens or loosens it. Also referred to as a check chain.

**Chops** The thick upper lips that hang below the lower jaw (e.g. in the Bloodhound).

**Chorea** A nervous jerking caused by involuntary contraction of the muscles, usually affecting the face or legs.

**Clip** A type of *trim*, as used on the Poodle.

**Clipping** The back foot striking the front foot during the *gait*.

**Cloddy** Low, thickset, rather heavy.

**Close-coupled** Having a short back or a short body.

**Coarse** Without refinement.

**Coat** The dog's hair covering.

**Cobby** Short-bodied, compact.

**Collar** (1) A marking around the neck, usually white. (2) A circle of leather or chain used to direct and control the dog when the leash (lead) is attached.

**Condition** Health, shown by coat, weight, general appearance and deportment.

**Conformation** Form and structure, make-up and shape; arrangement of the parts in conformance with breed *standard* requirements.

**Corky** Active, lively, alert.

**Couple** A pair of hounds.

**Couplings** The length of the body between the last rib and the pelvis.

**Coursing** The sport of chasing the hare by Greyhounds.

**Covering ground** The ratio of the distance between the ground and the *brisket* and the distance between the front and rear legs.

**Cow-hocked** With *hocks* turned towards one another.

**Crabbing** Moving with the body at an angle to the line of travel. Also referred to as side-winding, side-wheeling or yawing.

**Crank tail** A tail carried down with the tip held outwards in the shape of a crank.

**Crest** The upper, arched portion of the neck (e.g. Chinese Crested).

**Crop** To cut off the tops of the ears so that they stand erect. Illegal in some countries.

**Crossbred** The progeny of *purebred* parents of different *breeds*.

**Crossing over** Unsound *gaiting action* that starts with twisting elbows and ends with crisscrossing and toeing out. Known also as weaving and purling.

**Croup** The rear part of the back, above the hind legs.

**Crown** The highest part of the head; the top of the skull.

**Cry** The *baying* of the hounds.

**Cryptorchid** An adult dog whose testicles have not descended into the scrotum. A dog of this type cannot be exhibited. Bilateral cryptorchids are affected on both sides; unilateral cryptorchids on one side only.

**Cull** A pup that is a very inferior specimen of its *breed*.

**Culotte** The feathery hair on the backs of the legs.

**Cur** A mongrel.

**Cushion** Fullness or thickness of the upper lip.

**Cynology** The study of *canines*.

## D

**Dam** The mother of a *litter* of puppies.

**Dappled** A mottled colour – generally patches of silver and tan, black, or black and tan.

**Dead grass** Tan or dull straw colour.

**Depigmentation** Partial or complete loss of coloration.

**Derby** *Field trial* competition for young, novice sporting dogs, usually between one and two years of age.

**Dew-claw** A claw on the inside of the leg, which is usually removed in early puppyhood but retained by some breeds.

**Dewlap** Loose hanging skin under the throat and chin (as in the Bloodhound).

**Diagonals** Right front and left rear legs constitute the right diagonal; left front and right rear legs constitute the left diagonal. In the *trot*, the diagonals move together.

**Diehard** Nickname for the Scottish Terrier (or Aberdeen Terrier).

**Dish-faced** Having the nasal bone higher at the nose than at the *stop*.

**Disqualification** A decision made by a *judge* or show committee, ruling that a dog has a condition making it ineligible for further competition under the *dog show* rules or under the *standard* for its breed.

**Distemper teeth** Teeth marked, pitted, ringed and often stained, due to distemper or other severe infection.

**Divergent hocks** See *Barrel hocks*.

**Dock** To shorten the tail by cutting, usually done in early puppyhood if breed *standards* demand.

**Dog** (1) Any member of the species *Canis familiaris*. (2) A male of that species (see *Bitch*).

**Dog show** An exhibition at which dogs are judged in accordance with an established *standard* of perfection for each breed.

**Dolichocephalic** Having a dispro-portionately long head, the skull and *muzzle* both being long and the *bite* even; a skull with a *cephalic index* below 75.

**Dome** The rounded part of the skull, as in spaniels.

**Double coat** An *under-coat* of soft, thick hair to warm the body, and an outer coat of coarse, strong hair to keep out dampness and cold.

**Down-faced** The *muzzle* inclining downwards from the skull to the tip of the nose.

**Down in pastern** Weak or faulty *pastern* set at a pronounced angle from the vertical.

**Drag** A trail prepared by dragging along the ground a bag impregnated with scent.

**Drawing** Selection by lot of dogs to be run, and in which pairs, in a *Field trial stake.*

**Drive** A solid thrusting of the *hind-quarters,* denoting sound locomotion.

**Drop-eared** When the ears are pendent, and hanging close and flat to the side of the cheeks.

**Dropper** A *bird dog* cross.

**Dry neck** The skin taut; neither loose nor wrinkled.

**Dual champion** Dog that has won championships in both *Dog shows* and *Field trials.*

**Dudley nose** Flesh-coloured nose.

**E**

**Elbow** The joint between the upper arm and the forearm.

**Elbows out** Elbows pointing away from the body.

**Entropion** A condition in which the eyelid turns inward and the lashes irritate the eyeball.

**Even bite** Meeting of front teeth at edges with no overlap of upper or lower teeth.

**Ewe neck** Concave curvature of the top neckline.

**Expression** The general appearance of all features of the head as viewed from the front and as typical of the *breed.*

**Eye-teeth** The upper *canines.*

**F**

**Faking** Changing the appearance of a dog by artificial means, with the objective of deceiving the onlooker as to its real merit.

**Fall** Long hair overhanging the face.

**Fallow** Pale yellow colour.

**Fancier** Someone active in the sport of breeding, showing and judging *purebred* dogs.

**Fangs** See *Canines.*

**Fawn** A rich light golden tan.

**FCI** Fédération Cynologique Internationale.

**Feathering** Long, fine fringe of hair seen on the ears, legs, tail and body of breeds such as spaniels.

**Feet east and west** With the toes turned out.

**Femoral-tibial joint** The joining of the thigh and shin bone.

**Fetch** (1) The retrieval of *game* by a dog. (2) The command to do so.

**Fiddle face** An elongated, pinched-in *foreface.*

**Fiddle front** The front of a dog with bandy or crooked forelegs; French front.

**Field trial** A competition for certain *hound* or sporting breeds in which dogs are judged on their ability and style in finding or retrieving *game* or following a game trail.

**Field Trial Champion (Field Ch.)** A prefix used with the name of a dog that has been recorded a Field Trial Champion by the *AKC* as a result of beating strong competition in specified competitions at AKC licensed *Field trials.*

**Flag** The fringe or *feathering* found under the tails of setters and some retrievers, long at the base and shorter at the tip.

**Flank** The side of the body between the last rib and the hip.

**Flare** A *blaze* that widens as it approaches the top of the skull.

**Flat bone** The leg bone whose girth is elliptical rather than round.

**Flat-sided** (Ribs) insufficiently rounded as they approach the *breastbone.*

**Flat withers** An unattractive fault that is the result of short upright shoulder blades that join the *withers* abruptly.

**Flecked** Lightly *ticked* with other colours, as in the English Setter, and neither *roan* nor spotted.

**Flesh nose** Pink or tan nose.

**Flews** Hanging upper lips, like those of a Bulldog; usually refers to the lateral parts of the lips.

**Flexor-cubital muscle** A muscle the action of which is to flex the joint at the elbow.

**Flicking pasterns** Extremely loose movement of the lower forelegs.

**Floating rib** The last, or 13th rib, which is unattached to other ribs.

**Fluffies** A coat of extreme length with exaggerated *feathering* on ears, chest, feet and legs, underparts and *hindquarters.*

**Flush** To drive birds from cover, to force them to take flight; to spring.

**Fly-eared** Ears that should be erect fall or tilt at the tips; usually a blemish.

**Flying lips** Unsettled lips, not assuming the correct position.

**Flying trot** A fast *gait* in which all four feet are off the ground for a brief second during each half stride. Because of the long reach, the oncoming hind feet step beyond the imprint left by the front. Also called suspension trot.

**Forearm** The bone of the foreleg between the *elbow* and the *pastern.*

**Foreface** The front part of the head, before the eyes; the *muzzle.*

**Foster mother** A *bitch* used to nurse another animal's *whelps.*

**Foul colour** An uncharacteristic colour or marking.

**Foxy** Having a pointed nose and short *foreface.*

**French front** See *Fiddle front.*

**Frill** Long hair under the neck and on the forechest.

**Fringes** The *featherings* of long-coated breeds.

**Frog-face** Extending nose accom-panied by a receding jaw, usually *overshot.*

**Front** The whole front part of the body.

**Frontal bone** The skull bone over the eyes.

**Furnishings** The long hair on the *foreface* of certain breeds.

**Furrow** A groove running down the centre of the skull, as in the Bulldog; also called median line.

**Futurity stake** A class at *Dog shows* or *Field trials* for young dogs that have been nominated at, or before, birth.

**G**

**Gait** A style of movement, e.g. running or *trotting.*

**Gallop** Fastest of the dog *gaits* or *paces;* a four-beat rhythm and often an extra period of suspension during which the body is propelled through the air with all four feet off the ground.

**Game** Birds or other animals that are hunted.

**Gay tail** A tail carried straight up.

**Gazehound** A hound that hunts by sight.

**Geld** See *Castrate.*

**Genealogy** Recorded family descent.

**Giving tongue** *Baying* on the trail of *game.*

**Goose rump** A sharply sloping rump.

**Graioid** Belonging to the Greyhound family.

**Grizzle** Bluish-grey colour.

**Groom** To brush, comb, trim and otherwise prepare a dog's coat for show or pleasure.

**Groups** The breeds are grouped to facilitate judging.

**Guard hairs** The longer, smoother, stiffer hairs that grow through the *under-coat* and normally conceal it.

**Gundog** Dog trained to assist the hunter in the field (e.g. retrievers, setters, spaniels and pointers).

**Guns** Those who shoot at *Field trials.*

**Gun-shy** Frightened by the sound of a gun being fired.

**H**

**Hackles** Hair on the neck and back raised involuntarily in fright or anger.

**Hackney gait** A vigorous, proud, high-stepping *gait.*

**Ham** Well-developed hind leg muscles just above the knee.

**Handler** A person who handles (shows) a dog at *Dog shows, Field trials,* or obedience tests.

**Hard-mouthed** Given to biting down hard on *retrieved game;* a serious fault.

**Hare feet** Long, narrow, close-toed feet, as in the hare.

**Harlequin** A combination of colours in patches on a solid ground, as in the coat of a Great Dane; usually blue on white.

**Harness** A leather strap shaped around the shoulders and chest, with a ring at its top over the *withers.*

**Haunches** Back part of the thighs, on which the dog sits.

**Haw** A third eyelid or nictitating membrane in the inside corner of the eye.

**Heat** Seasonal period of the female, normally every six months.

**Heel** Command by *handler* to keep the dog close to his heel.

**Heel free** Command whereby the dog must walk to heel without a *lead.*

**Height** Dog's height measured from the ground to the top of the shoulder.

**Heterometropia** A condition in which the degree of refraction is different in the two eyes.

**Hie on** A command to urge the dog on; used in hunting or *Field trials.*

**High-standing** Tall and upstanding, with plenty of leg.

**Hindquarters** Rear assembly of dog (pelvis, thighs, *hocks* and paws).

**Hip dysplasia** Malformation of the ball of the hip joint; usually hereditary.

**Hocking out** Having *barrel hocks.*

**Hocks** Those joints in the hind limbs below the true knees, or *stifle* joints.

**Hocks well let down** *Hock* joints close to the ground.

**Holt** The lair of a fox or other animal in a bank, drain or other hideout.

**Honorable scars** Scars from injuries suffered as a result of work.

**Hound** A dog commonly used for hunting by scent or sight.

**Hound colours** White, tan, and black, in order of predominant colour.

**Hound jog** The usual *pace* of the *hound.*

**Hound-marked** Fox Terriers are described as hound-marked if their body patches conform to the pattern of hound markings.

**Hucklebones** The top of the hip bones.

**I**

**Inbreeding** *Mating* within the same family; a *bitch* to her sons, or a *dog* to his daughters.

**Incisors** The upper and lower front teeth, between the *canines.*

**In season** In *heat;* ready for *mating.*

**In-shoulder** Shoulders point in, not parallel with the backbone — a fault found in dogs with shoulder blades too far forward on the chest.

**Interbreeding** The breeding together of different varieties.

**Isabella** Fawn or light bay colour.

**Ischium** Hip bone.

**J**

**Jabot** A white stripe down the chest, like a shirtfront.

**Jowls** Flesh of lips and jaws.

**Judge** The adjudicator of dogs in *Dog shows,* obedience tests and *Field trials.*

**K**

**KC** Kennel Club (United Kingdom).

**Kennel** Structure where dogs are kept.

**Kink tail** A tail that is sharply bent.

**Kiss marks** Tan spots on the cheeks and over the eyes.

**Knee joint** *Stifle* joint.

**Knuckling over** Condition in which the front legs bend forward at the wrist (carpus).

**Kyphosis** An abnormal curvature of the spine, with convexity backward.

**L**

**Lack of type** Deficiency in traits that define the fundamental make-up of a *breed.*

**Landseer** A Newfoundland that is not all black, but white with black (as depicted by Sir Edward Landseer).

**Layback** The angle of the shoulder blade as compared with the vertical.

**Lead** A strap, cord or chain attached to the *collar* or *harness,* for the purpose of restraining or leading the dog; a leash.

**Leather** The flap of the ear.

**Leggy** Having legs too long for the body.

**Level back** One that makes a straight line from *withers* to tail, but is not necessarily parallel to the ground.

**Level bite** When the front teeth (*incisors*) of the upper and lower jaws meet exactly edge to edge; pincer bite.

**Level gait** Dog moves without a rise or fall of the *withers.*

**Liam** A *lead.*

**Licence** Formal permission granted by the *AKC* to a non-member club to hold a *Dog show,* or obedience test or *Field trial.* In the UK all shows in which *purebred* dogs are exhibited are held under Kennel Club licence.

**Light eyes** Yellowish eyes.

**Line breeding** The mating of related dogs of the same breed, within the line, or family, to a common ancestor e.g. a dog to his grand-dam.

**Lion colour** Tawny.

**Lippy** Having thick, hanging lips.

**Litter** The pups from one *whelping.*

**Liver** A dark reddish-brown colour.

**Loaded shoulders** Shoulders that are much too thick and heavy.

**Loin** The part of the body between the last rib and the back legs.

**Lordosis** Hollow back; *saddle back;* curvature of the spine.

**Lower thigh** See *Second thigh.*

**Lumber** Extra flesh.

**Lumbering** Awkward (*gait*).

**Lupoid** Belonging to the wolf family.

**Lurcher** A *crossbred hound.*

**Lymer** A *hound* of ancient times led on a *lead* (liam).

**M**

**Mad dog** A dog with rabies.

**Mane** Long and profuse hair on the top and sides of the neck.

**Mantle** Dark-shaded portion of the coat on the shoulders, back and sides.

**Manubrium** The portion of the malleus (hammer bone in the ear) that represents the handle.

**Mask** Dark shading on the *foreface*.

**Masseter** A powerful masticatory muscle passing from the zygomatic arch to the lower jaw.

**Match show** Usually an informal *Dog show* at which no Championship points are awarded.

**Mate** To breed a *dog* and *bitch*.

**Mealy** Covered or flecked with spots.

**Median line** See *Furrow*.

**Merle** A blue-grey mixture streaked or ticked with black, a coat colour seen in some Shetland Sheepdogs and collies.

**Milk teeth** First teeth. (Puppies lose these at 4-6 months.)

**Miscellaneous class** A competitive class at *Dog shows* for dogs of certain specified breeds for which no regular dog show classification is provided. In the UK this is usually called AV (Any Variety) not classified.

**Mismarks** Self colours with any area of white on the back between withers and tail, on the sides between elbows and back of hindquarters, or on the ears. Black with white markings and no tan present.

**Molars** Dogs have two molars on each side of the upper jaw, and three on each side of the lower jaw. Upper molars have three roots, lower have two roots.

**Molera** Incomplete, imperfect or abnormal ossification of the skull.

**Molossoid** Belonging to the Mastiff family of dogs.

**Mongrel** A dog whose parents are both of mixed breeding.

**Monorchid** A male dog, one of whose testicles has not descended into the scrotal sac; also called a unilateral *cryptorchid*.

**Mort** A flourish on the hunting-horn at the death of *game*.

**Moving close** When the *hocks* turn in and the *pasterns* drop straight to the ground and move parallel to one another, the dog is 'moving close' in the rear. Action places severe strain on ligaments and muscles.

**Moving straight** Term descriptive of balanced *gaiting* in which angle of inclination begins at the shoulder or hip joint, and the limbs remain relatively straight from these points to the pads of the feet, even as the legs flex or extend in reaching or thrusting.

**Music** The *baying* of the hounds.

**Mute** To run mute, to be silent on the trail, i.e. to trail without *baying* or barking.

**Muzzle** (1) The part of the head containing the mouth and nose. (2) A device to prevent biting.

**Muzzle band** White marking around the *muzzle*.

## N

**Neck well set on** Good neckline, merging gradually with strong *withers*, forming a pleasing transition into *topline*.

**Nick** A breeding that produces desirable puppies.

**Nictitating membrane** See *Haw*.

**Non-slip retriever** The dog that walks at heel, marks the fall, and *retrieves game* on command; not expected to find or *flush*.

**Nose** The ability to scent.

## O

**Oblique shoulders** Shoulders well laid back. The ideal shoulder should slant at 45° to the ground, forming an approximate right angle with the humerus at the shoulder joint.

**Occipital protuberance** A prominently raised *occiput* characteristic of some *gundog* breeds.

**Occiput** Upper, back point of the skull.

**Open class** For all dogs of the *breeds* or varieties for which a class is provided and eligible for entry at the show.

**Otter tail** Thick at the root, round and tapering, with the hair parted or divided on the underside.

**Out at elbows** *Elbows* turning out from the body, as opposed to being held close.

**Out at shoulder** With shoulder blades loosely attached to the body, leaving the shoulders jutting out in relief and increasing the breadth of the front.

**Out at walk** To lease or lend a puppy to someone for raising.

**Out-crossing** The mating of unrelated individuals of the same breed.

**Oval chest** Chest deeper than it is wide.

**Overhang** A heavy or pronounced brow.

**Over nose wrinkle** A fold of loose skin dropping forward from the skull onto the bridge of the nose; seen in Pugs, Pekingese and some other short-nosed breeds.

**Over-reaching** Fault in the *trot* caused by more angulation and drive from behind than in front, so that the rear feet are forced to step to one side of the forefeet to avoid interfering or *clipping*.

**Overshot** When the upper teeth project beyond the lower; also called pig jaw.

## P

**Pace** A *gait* that tends to promote a rolling motion of the body. The left foreleg and left hind leg advance together, then the right foreleg and right hind leg.

**Pack** Several *hounds* kept together in one *kennel*. A mixed pack is composed of dogs and bitches.

**Paddling** A *gaiting* fault, so named because it resembles the swing and dip of a canoeist's paddle. Pinching in at the elbows and shoulder joints causes the front legs to swing forward on a stiff outward arc. Also referred to as being tied at the elbows.

**Pads** The tough, cushioned soles of the feet.

**Paper foot** A flat foot with thin *pads*.

**Parti-colour** A term used for a dog of two colours in equal proportion, usually red and white or black and white.

**Pastern** Commonly recognized as the region of the foreleg between the carpus (wrist) and the digits.

**Patellar luxation** The knee cap or *stifle* slips or dislocates. An abnormality said to be hereditary, and found in several small breeds.

**Peak** An unusually prominent *occiput*.

**Pedigree** Written record of the names of a dog's ancestors going back at least three generations.

**Pencilling** The dark lines on the surface of the toes in some breeds, notably the English Toy Terrier [Manchester Terrier (Toy)].

**Pepper and salt** Coat colour consisting of an even mixture of grey and black hair, as in the Schnauzer.

**Pied** When two colours occur in irregular patches, one more than the other, a dog is said to be pied.

**Pigeon-breast** A chest with a short protruding *breastbone*.

**Pigeon-toed** With toes pointing in.

**Pig jaw** See *Overshot*.

**Pile** Dense *under-coat* of soft hair.

**Pily** A coat that contains both soft and coarse hair.

**Pincer bite** See *Level bite*.

**Pitching** Severe rocking of the *haunches* as the rear legs swing forward in a wide arc, rather than flexing normally at the *stifle* and *hock*.

**Plumes** Whereas the *brush* is not always bent, the term 'plumes' refers to the soft hair on the tail of the Pekingese and Pomeranian.

**Poach** When hunting, to trespass on private property.

**Point** The immovable *stance* of the hunting dog taken to indicate the presence and position of *game*.

**Points** Colour on face, ears, legs and tail when correlated — usually white, black or tan.

**Poke** To carry the neck stretched forward in an abnormally low, ungainly position, usually when moving.

**Police dog** A dog trained for police work (often the German Shepherd Dog).

**Pompon** Ball of hair left on the end of a Poodle's tail after it has been clipped.

**Pounding** *Gaiting* fault resulting when a dog's stride is shorter in front than in the rear; forefeet strike the ground hard before the rear stride is expended.

**Prick ear** Carried erect, and usually pointed at the tip.

**Professional handler** A person who shows dogs for a fee.

**Progressive Retinal Atrophy (PRA)** Sometimes incorrectly called 'night blindness': a hereditary defect of the eyes, found in several breeds, and causing early loss of sight.

**Pump handle** Long tail, carried high.

**Puppy** A dog under one year old.

**Purebred** A dog whose *sire* and *dam* belong to the same *breed*, and are themselves of unmixed descent since the recognition of the breed.

**Purling** See *Crossing over*.

**Put down** (1) To prepare a dog for the *show ring*. (2) Unplaced in competition. (3) Humanely destroy an old or terminally sick animal.

## Q

**Quality** Refinement, fineness.

## R

**Racy** Lean, long-legged, slightly built.

**Ragged** Muscles appear ragged rather than smooth (as in the English Foxhound).

**Ram's nose** See *Roman nose*.

**Rangy** Long-bodied, usually lacking depth in chest.

**Rat tail** Long pointed tail, with short thin hair.

**Reach of front** Length of forward stride taken by forelegs without wasted or excessive motion.

**Register** To record details of a dog's breeding with the respective Kennel Club.

**Retrieve** To bring back shot *game* for the huntsman.

**Ribbed up** With long ribs that angle back from the spinal column (45° is ideal); the last rib is long.

**Ringer** A substitute for another dog; a dog closely resembling another.

**Ring tail** Carried up and around almost in a circle.

**Roached** A dog's back is roached when it arches convexly, as in the Dandie Dinmont, Italian Greyhound and Whippet.

**Roan** Mixture of white with another colour, usually blue or red, in equal proportions, as in the Cocker Spaniel.

**Rocking horse** Stance with both front and rear legs extended out from the body as in an old-fashioned toy rocking horse.

**Rolling gait** Swaying, ambling *action* of the *hindquarters* when moving.

**Roman nose** A nose whose bridge is so comparatively high as to form a slightly convex line from forehead to nose tip; also called ram's nose.

**Rose-eared** When the ear, neither *pricked* nor *dropped*, folds or twists over, showing the inside, as in the Bulldog.

**Rounding** To cut or trim the end of the ear *leather* (English Foxhounds).

**Rubber hocks** See *Twisting hocks*.

**Rudder** The tail.

**Ruff** Thick, longer hair growth around the neck.

## S

**Sable** The colour of a light coat shaded with black, as in the Collie.

**Sabre tail** Carried in a semi-circle.

**Saddle** A black marking over the back, like a horse's saddle.

**Saddle back** Over-long back, with a dip behind the *withers*.

**Scapula** The shoulder blade.

**Scent** The odour left by an animal on the *trail* (ground scent), or wafted through the air (air-borne scent).

**Scissor bite** A *bite* in which the upper front teeth slightly overlap the lower front teeth.

**Screw tail** A short, twisted tail tapering to a point.

**Second thigh** That part of the *hind-quarter* from the *stifle* to the *hock*, corresponding to the human shin and calf; also called lower thigh.

**Seeing eye dog** A guide dog for the blind (in USA).

**Self colour** One colour, or whole colour, except for lighter shadings.

**Self marked** A dog is so-called when it is a whole colour, with white or pale markings on the chest, feet and tail-tip.

**Semi-prick ears** Ears carried erect with just the tips leaning forward.

**Septum** Very thin dividing wall between the nostrils.

**Set on** Insertion or attachment of tail or ears.

**Set up** Posed so as to make the most of the dog's appearance for the show ring.

**Shelly** Having a long and narrow body, like that of a Borzoi.

**Shoulder height** Height of dog's body as measured from the *withers* to the ground.

**Sickle-hocked** Unable to straighten the *hock* joint on the back reach of the hind leg.

**Sickle tail** Carried out and up in a semi-circle.

**Side-wheeling** See *Crabbing*.

**Side-winding** See *Crabbing*.

**Sighthound** A hound that hunts by sight rather than scent; also called a gazehound.

**Single tracking** All footprints falling on a single line of travel. When a dog breaks into a trot, its body is supported by only two legs at a time, which move as alternating diagonal pairs. To achieve balance, the legs angle inward toward a centre line beneath the body, and the greater the speed, the closer they come to tracking on a single line.

**Sire** The father of a *litter* of puppies.

**Skully** Thick, coarse-looking skull.

**Slab sided** Having flat ribs with too little spring from spinal column.

**Sled dogs** Dogs used in teams to pull sleds.

**Slew feet** Feet turned out.

**Slipping stifle** See *patellar luxation*.

**Sloping shoulders** Shoulders laid well back on the body.

**Smooth coat** Short, sleek hair lying close to the skin.

**Snatching hocks** A *gaiting* fault indicated by a quick outward snatching of the *hock* as it passes the supporting leg and twists the rear pastern far in beneath the body. The action causes noticeable rocking in the hindquarters.

**Snipy** Narrow, weak (in the *muzzle*).

**Soft-mouthed** Able to carry retrieved *game* in the mouth without damaging it.

**Soundness** The state of mental and physical health when all organs and faculties are complete and functioning normally, each in its rightful relation to the others.

**Spay** To perform a surgical operation (hysterectomy) on the bitch's reproductive organs to stop conception.

**Speak** To bark.

**Spectacles** Shadings or dark markings over or around the eyes or from eyes to ears.

**Spike tail** Straight short tail that tapers rapidly along its length.

**Spitz** A *breed* of dog with a tapering *muzzle*.

**Splashed** Irregularly patched, colour on white or white on colour.

**Splay feet** Feet with toes spread wide.

**Spread** Width between the forelegs, when accentuated (Bulldog).

**Spread hocks** See *Barrel hocks*.

**Spring** See *Flush*.

**Spring of ribs** Curvature of ribs for heart and lung capacity.

**Squirrel tail** Tail carried up and curving more or less forward.

**Stake** A competition held at a *Field trial*.

**Stance** Manner of standing.

**Standard** The standard of perfection for each breed.

**Stand-off coat** Rough, coarse hair that stands away from the body.

**Staring coat** Coarse hard hair, curling at the end.

**Station** Height of a dog from the ground.

**Stern** Tail of a sporting dog or *hound*.

**Sternum** See *Breastbone*.

**Stifle** That joint in the hind leg of a dog approximating to the knee in man, particularly relating to the inner side.

**Stilted** Having a stiff, awkward way of walking.

**Stop** The depression between and in front of the eyes, roughly corresponding to the bridge of the nose.

**Strabismus** Cross-eyed.

**Straight hocks** *Hocks* that are absolutely straight vertically.

**Straight in pastern** With little or no bend between joint and foot.

**Straight shoulders** Shoulder blades running almost straight up and down, without any *angulation*.

**Stud** Male used for breeding.

**Stud book** A record of the breeding particulars of dogs of recognized breeds.

**Substance** Bone.

**Superciliary arch** The ridge, projection or prominence of the frontal bone of the skull over the eye; the brow.

**Suspension trot** See *Flying trot*.

**Sway back** A sagging back.

**Symmetry** Pleasing balance between all parts of the dog.

**T**

**Tail set** How the base of the tail sets on the rump.

**Terrier** A group of dogs used originally for hunting vermin.

**Terrier front** Straight front, as found on the Fox Terrier.

**Thigh** The *hindquarter* from hip to *stifle*.

**Throaty** Having far too much skin around the throat.

**Thumb marks** Circular black marks around the ankles.

**Ticked** With small, isolated areas of black or coloured hairs on a white ground.

**Timber** Bone, especially of the legs.

**Tongue** Noise made by *hounds* when on the *trail* of *game*.

**Topknot** The longer, finer hair on the top of the head, rather like a powder-puff, as in the Dandie Dinmont.

**Topline** The dog's outline from just behind the *withers* to the tail set.

**Toy dog** One of a group of dogs characterized by very small size.

**Trace** A dark line of hair running down the back, as seen in the Pug.

**Trail** To hunt by following ground scent.

**Triangular eye** An eye set in surrounding tissue of triangular shape; a three-cornered eye.

**Tricolour** A term used when dogs have three colours more or less proportionate, usually black, tan and white, as in *hounds*.

**Trim** To groom by plucking or clipping.

**Trot** A rhythmic two-beat diagonal *gait* in which the feet at diagonally opposite ends of the body strike the ground together, i.e. right hind with left front and left hind with right front.

**Trousers** The hair on the *hindquarters*.

**Trumpet** The slight depression or hollow on either side of the skull just behind the orbit or eye socket; the region comparable with the temple.

**Truncated** Cut off. (The Old English Sheepdog standard calls for a jaw that is square and truncated.)

**Tucked-up** When the *loins* are lifted up but the chest is deep, giving a *racy* appearance, as in Borzois, Greyhounds and Whippets.

**Tulip ears** Ears carried stiff and straight, slightly open and leaning forward.

**Turn-up** An up-tilted *foreface*.

**Twisting hocks** A *gaiting* fault in which the *hock* joints twist both ways as they flex or bear weight. Also called rubber hocks.

**Type** The characteristic qualities distinguishing a *breed*; the embodiment of a *standard's* essentials.

**U**

**Under-coat** The soft, furry wool beneath the outer hair of some breeds, giving protection against cold and wet.

**Undershot** Having the lower jaw projecting; the opposite of *overshot*.

**Underslung** Low to the ground, with short legs.

**Unilateral cryptorchid** See *Cryptorchid*.

**Up-face** A *foreface* slanting upward, as in the Bulldog.

**Upper arm** The humerus or bone of the foreleg, between the shoulder blade and the *forearm*.

**V**

**Varminty** Having a bright, searching, very alert expression; usually seen in terriers.

**Vent** Both the anal opening and the small area of light hair directly beneath the tail.

**W**

**Walk** *Gaiting* pattern in which three legs are in support of the body at all times, each foot lifting from the ground one at a time in regular sequence.

**Wall eyes** Eyes *parti-coloured* white and blue, seen in *merle*-coloured collies and sheepdogs; often keenly valued.

**Weaving** See *Crossing over*.

**Weedy** Having a light, rather scrawny build.

**Well-boned** See *Bone*.

**Well let down** Having short *hocks*.

**Well-sprung ribs** Roundness or curvature of the rib cage.

**Wet neck** Loose or superfluous skin, with *dewlap*.

**Wheaten** Pale yellow colour.

**Wheel back** Another term for the *roached* back; a back that is arched or convex.

**Whelping** Giving birth to puppies.

**Whelps** Newly born puppies.

**Whip tail** A tail that is stiff and straight, as in the Pointer when the dog is *pointing*.

**Whiskers** The *beard* of a dog, as in the Miniature Schnauzer.

**Whitelies** Colour type that is white with red or dark markings (Pembroke Welsh Corgi).

**Wind** To catch the *scent* of *game*.

**Winging** A *gaiting* fault where one or both front feet twist outward as the limbs swing forward.

**Winners** Awards given at *Dog shows* to the Best Dog (Winners Dog) and Best Bitch (Winners Bitch) competing in regular classes.

**Wire-haired** Having a tough, dense, harsh coat.

**Withers** The highest point of the shoulders, just behind the neck.

**Wolf colour** Black, brown and grey distributed in equal amounts.

**Wrinkle** The loose folds of skin puckered up on the brows and sides of the face in Bloodhounds, St Bernards, Basenjis, Pugs, etc.

**Wry mouth** Mouth in which the lower jaw does not line up with the upper.

**X**

**Xiphoid** Sword-shaped.

**Y**

**Yawing** See *Crabbing*.

---

# FURTHER READING

Allcock, J. *A Dog of Your Own* Sheldon Press, London 1979

American Kennel Club Official Publication, *The Complete Dog Book* Howell Book House Inc., New York 1979 (16th Edition)

Bengtson, B. and Wintzell, A. *The Dogs of the World* David & Charles (Publishers) Ltd., Newton Abbot, England 1977

Fiorone, F. *The Encyclopedia of Dogs* Hart-Davis MacGibbon Ltd., St. Albans, England 1970

Fisher, C. *The Pan Book of Dogs* Pan Books, London 1977 (6th printing)

Fox, Dr. M.W. *Understanding Your Dog* Blond & Briggs, London 1974

Glover, H. *A Standard Guide to Pure-bred Dogs* Macmillan London Ltd., London 1977

Glyn, Sir R. *Champion Dogs of the World* George G. Harrap & Co. Ltd., London 1967

Hamilton, F. *The World Encyclopedia of Dogs* New English Library, London 1971

Johnson, N.H. *The Complete Book of Dogs* Robert Hale Ltd., London 1965

Manolson, F. *D is for Dog* Pan Books Ltd., London 1978

Mery, F. *The Dog* Cassell, London 1970

Messent, P. *Understanding Your Dog* Macdonald, London 1979

Novotny, J. and Najman, J. *A Field Guide in Colour to Dogs* Octopus Books Ltd., London 1977

Palmer, J. *Training and Caring for your Dog* Ward Lock Ltd., London 1980

Pfaffenberger, Dr. C. *New Knowledge of Dog Behaviour* Howell Book House Inc., New York

Sessions, B. *The Complete Dog Training Manual* Tab Books, Blue Ridge Summit, Pennsylvania

Stonebridge, M.A. *A Dog of Your Own* Doubleday & Co. Inc., New York 1979

Sutton, C.G. *The Observer's Book of Dogs* Frederick Warne & Co. Ltd., London 1945, 1978

Swedrup, I. *Dogs in Colour* Blandford Press Ltd., Poole, England 1975

Vine, Dr. L. *Your Dog: His Health and Happiness* Winchester Press, New York

White, K. *Dogs: Their Mating, Whelping and Weaning* K & R Books Ltd., Leicester, England 1977

Woodhouse, B. (Foreword) *Dogs* Orbis Publishing Ltd., London 1980

# INDEX OF DOG BREEDS

239

# CREDITS

### Artists
Copyright of the artwork illustrations on the pages following the artists' names is the property of Salamander Books Ltd.

### Colour artwork
John Francis (Linden Artists): Endpapers, Title page, Author's page, Contents pages, 8-9, 11, 14, 29, 59 (Bottom two) 61, 63, 66-7, 69, 73, 77-83, 87, 89, 95, 97, 100-101, 103-119, 122, 125, 127, 131-139, 143-159, 165-169
John Green (John Martin and Artists Ltd.): Half title page, Copyright page, 10, 13, 15, 17-27, 31-57, 59(TL), 65, 75, 85, 91, 93, 99, 121, 123, 129, 141, 161, 163

### Line artwork
Alan Hollingbery: 210, 212, 213, 214, 222(B)
Gordon Riley: 200, 202
Clive Spong (Linden Artists): 178, 181, 189, 190, 191, 222(T), 223, 224, 226, 228, 229
Glenn Steward (John Martin and Artists Ltd.): Size comparison symbols for the Profile Section, pages 12-169
Tyler/Camoccio Design Consul-

tants: 196, 198, 202, 203, 204
Harold White (Visualization and artwork briefs): 178, 181, 222, 223, 224, 226, 228, 229

### Photographs
The Publishers wish to thank the following photographers and agencies who have supplied photographs for this book. The photographs have been credited by page number and position on the page: (B) Bottom, (T) Top, (BL) Bottom left, etc.
Animal Graphics (Angela Sayer): 120, 140(T), 175(B), 218(B)
Animal Photography Ltd. (Sally Anne Thompson): 22(CR), 24(T,BL), 32(BR), 34(B), 36(T), 44, 46(L,R,B), 58, 62(T), 68, 70, 84, 88, 94, 98(TL,TR), 118(B), 130(Ploon de Raad), 134(T), 144, 146(Bernard Rebouleau), 148(T,BR), 150(TR, Ron Willbie), 152, 158(TR,BL), 166, 168(TR, Ron Willbie), 174(T), 176, 186(T,B), 215, 216(T), 225
Animals Unlimited (Christina Payne and Paddy Cutts): 22(CL,B), 26, 28(B), 30(TR), 36(B), 64(B), 72, 86, 96(B), 134(B), 138, 140(B), 142, 150(BL), 168(BL), 173, 180(B), 182(T), 188, 200

Anne Cumbers: 16, 20, 24(BR), 28(T), 30(B), 32(T,BL), 34(T), 52, 60, 62(B), 64(T), 96(T), 104, 106, 112, 114, 128, 160, 175(T), 177, 180(T), 181, 183, 195, 196, 207(TL), 208, 209, 212, 213, 216(B), 217, 218(T), 220, 221, 227
Michael Findlay: 204(B)
Marc Henrie: 194, 197, 201(TR), 211, 219
Roger Hyde (Copyright Salamander Books Ltd.): 170, 179, 184, 185, 189, 193, 198, 199, 201(TL), 203, 204(Top six), 205, 206, 207(TR,C), 230
Anne Roslin-Williams: 76, 82, 92, 150(BR)
Trevor Wood: 174(B)
ZEFA: 172

### Author's Acknowledgment
Joan Palmer would like to thank the Kennel Club for their kindness in granting permission for extracts from standards to be quoted; also the numerous breed club secretaries and other individuals, too numerous to list who, in many cases, went to considerable trouble to provide background information on their breeds. Addresses of breed club secretaries in the United Kingdom can be obtained from The Kennel

Club, 1-4 Clarges Street, Piccadilly, London, W1Y 8AB.
Thanks are also due to the Pedigree Petfoods Education Centre for their assistance, to The National Dog Owners' Association, and to Mrs. Joy Deacon who did so much typing.

### Publisher's Acknowledgment
The Publishers would like to thank the following individuals and organizations for their help in the preparation of this book: Elizabeth Pegg of the Royal Veterinary College, London for advice on dog parasites; Margaret Osborne for preparing text on Continental showing systems; Liz Cartledge for advice on Scandinavian showing systems; Partingdale Quarantine Kennels for location photography; Gillian Cormode and Valerie Noel-Finch for editorial help; Maureen Cartwright for copy-editing and proof-reading; David Lambert for sub-editing; Stuart Craik for preparing the index.

The recipe on page 179 is taken from the vegetarian cookbook *Laurel's Kitchen*, published by Routledge, and Keegan Paul.

St. Bernard

Newfoundland